Race

RACE

Edited by

STEVEN GREGORY and

ROGER SANJEK

Rutgers University Press
New Brunswick, New Jersey

Second paperback printing, 1996

Library of Congress Cataloging-in-Publication Data

Race / Steven Gregory and Roger Sanjek, editors.
p. cm.
Includes bibliographical references and index.
ISBN 0-8135-2108-4 (cloth) — ISBN 0-8135-2109-2 (pbk.)
1. Race—Cross-cultural studies. 2. Racism—Cross-cultural studies. 3. Ethnicity—Cross-cultural studies. 4. Social classes—Cross-cultural studies. I. Gregory, Steven, 1954– II. Sanjek, Roger, 1944–
GN269.R32 1994
305.5—dc20 94-534
CIP

British Cataloging-in-Publication information available

Manufactured in the United States of America

Contents

PERSISTING DILEMMA: SITES OF RACISM

Acknowledgments

We would like to thank the other Chicago 1991 participants whose contributions stimulated the thinking reflected in this book: Martin Bernal, George C. Bond, Marvin Harris, Walton Johnson, Charles Leslie, Leith Mullings, and Sylvia Yanagisako. And for their enthusiasm about the project, Marlie Wasserman and Kenneth Arnold of Rutgers University Press, our reader, Howard Winant, and our copy editor, Roberta Hughey.

We acknowledge permission from their publishers to reprint the essays by Gregory, Sacks, Trouillot, and Zavella, which appeared in earlier form as:

"Race, Rubbish, and Resistance: Empowering Difference in Community Politics." *Cultural Anthropology* 8 (1993):24–48 [published by the American Anthropological Association].
"On Michael Levin's 'Why Black American Anti-Semitism?' " *Jewish Currents* (June 1992).
Chapter 4 in *Haiti, State against Nation: The Origins and Legacy of Duvalierism.* New York: Monthly Review Press, 1990.
"Reflections on Diversity among Chicanas." *Frontiers* 12 (1991):73–85 [published by the Frontiers Editorial Collective].

Contributors

Robert R. Alvarez, Jr.
associate professor of anthropology, Arizona State University

John J. Attinasi
professor and director of bilingual teacher education, California State University, Long Beach

Michael L. Blakey
associate professor of anthropology, curator of the W. Montague Cobb Skeletal Collection, and director, African Burial Ground Project, Howard University

Ruth Frankenberg
assistant professor of American studies, University of California, Davis

Steven Gregory
assistant professor of anthropology and Africana studies, New York University

Susan Hautaniemi
Department of Anthropology, University of Massachusetts, Amherst

Evelyn Hu-DeHart
professor of history and director, Center for Studies of Ethnicity and Race in America, University of Colorado at Boulder

M. Annette Jaimes
instructor/lecturer in American Indian studies, Center for Studies of Ethnicity and Race in America, University of Colorado at Boulder

Soheir A. Morsy
independent scholar/consultant

Nancy Muller
Department of Anthropology, University of Massachusetts, Amherst

Robert Paynter
associate professor of anthropology, University of Massachusetts, Amherst

Clara E. Rodríguez
professor of social sciences, College at Lincoln Center, Fordham University

Renato Rosaldo
Lucie Stern Professor in the Social Sciences, Stanford University

Karen Brodkin Sacks
professor of anthropology, University of California, Los Angeles

Roger Sanjek
associate professor of anthropology, Queens College, City University of New York

Dana Y. Takagi
associate professor of sociology, University of California, Santa Cruz

Michel-Rolph Trouillot
Krieger-Eisenhower Professor of Anthropology and director, Institute for Global Studies in Culture, Power, and History, Johns Hopkins University

Brett Williams
professor of anthropology, American University

Patricia Zavella
professor of community studies, University of California, Santa Cruz

Introduction

ROGER SANJEK

The Enduring Inequalities of Race

Let's be clear from the start what this book is about. Race is the framework of ranked categories segmenting the human population that was developed by western Europeans following their global expansion beginning in the 1400s. Over the centuries during which Africa, the "New World," Asia, and the Pacific were encountered, renamed, mapped, economically penetrated and reordered, and politically dominated, the peoples of these vast areas were assigned places in what Michel-Rolph Trouillot calls "the international hierarchy of races, colors, religions, and cultures." The words of Gilbert Murray, a turn-of-the-century British imperialist, well capsulize this racialized global view: "There is in the world a hierarchy of races. . . . [T]hose nations which eat more, claim more, and get higher wages, will direct and rule the others, and the lower work of the world will tend in the long-run to be done by the lower breeds of man. This much we of the ruling colour will no doubt accept as obvious" (qtd. in Banton 1987:vii).

The labels used in race ranking—"Negro," "Indian," "white," "mulatto," "half-caste," "Oriental," "Alpine," "Aborigine"—have varied in number, currency, assumed precision, and acceptability over time. The underlying scales of imputed racial quanta of intelligence, attractiveness, cultural potential, and worth have varied hardly at all. To contemporary anthropologists, none of this scaling is "real," though it has been real enough in its effects. Race has become all too real in its social ordering of perceptions and policies, in the pervasive racism that has plagued the globe following the 1400s (cf. Balch Institute 1984; Breman 1990; Comas 1951). For worse, not better, today we all live in a racialized world.

It is essential that we historicize race and racism if we are to understand and struggle against their continuing significance in the present and the future (see Banton 1987:153–154, 164–165, 168–169). We need to understand how and why a ranked hierarchy of races has been put to such destructive uses, been affirmed "scientifically," been challenged repeatedly, and yet still dies so hard. Its toll in terms in human worth, dignity, and personhood has been enormous. It has transformed and deformed the life courses and psyches of its victims, and also of its beneficiaries. Its roots and growth lie in nothing more "real" than the conquest, dispossession, enforced transportation, and economic exploitation of human beings over five centuries that racial categorization and racist social ordering have served to expedite and justify. As part of the legacy of these centuries, millions of people today continue to accept inherited racial categories as fixed in nature, and to interpret the systemic inequalities of racist social orders as based on "real" differences among "real" races.

Racism was something new in human history when it arose following European world expansion (Cox 1948:xxx–xxxi). As anthropologist Ralph Linton put it in *The Study of Man,* a textbook published in 1936 and long in use thereafter,

> Prior to the sixteenth century the world was not race-conscious and there was no incentive for it to become so. The ancient world was a small world and, because of the gradual transition in physical types which is to be found in all continuous geographic areas, the physical differences between the classical and barbarian peoples were not very marked. . . . Even when the existence of such physical differences was recognized, they had no immediate social connotations. . . . Even the Crusades failed to make Europe race-conscious. . . . it was only with the discovery of the New World and the sea routes to Asia that race assumed a social significance. . . . Europeans have not been content merely to accept their present social and political dominance as an established fact. Almost from the first they have attempted to rationalize the situation and to prove to themselves that their subjugation of other racial groups was natural and inevitable. (46–47; see also Cox 1948:104)

Race differs from the ethnocentrism and "caste" systems that preceded it, and that persist today in certain locales (cf. Cox 1948:321–333, 477–480). Exploitation, conquest, and disfavored ranking of groups beyond one's own have certainly existed in human societies prior to and beyond the historical formation of race and racism that concerns us here. No other historical or ethnographic order, however, has been as globally inclusive in its assignment of social and cultural difference to "natural" causes as has post-1400s racism.

Ethnocentric attitudes toward neighboring societies ("we're better than them") are as widely and frequently encountered as are more tolerant live-and-let-live views ("their customs are different"). The ethnocentric ancient Greeks viewed themselves as first among civilized peoples around the Mediterranean. To the north and south they were aware of barbarian peoples whom they saw as lighter and darker. Some of these had entered into the Greek ecumene and might even assimilate its cultural attainments. Physical appearance and culture for the Greeks had apparent but changeable connections, and they were willing to grant civilized status to the Nile Valley Nubians, who were among the darkest people the Greeks knew (Snowden 1970). Culture and skin color were not tightly interlinked as they would be in post-1400s racialized ideology.

Rigid social inequality has long marked the regime of caste in South Asia. Hierarchical ordering of *varna* and *jati* assign endogamous (maritally closed) groups to ranked statuses that are associated with imputed degrees of purity or pollution, inherited occupational opportunities and limitations, and prescribed residential location. But unlike the racialized situation of white and black groups in the post-Reconstruction U.S. South—to which some have applied the term *caste* (Berreman 1960; Davis, Gardner, and Gardner 1941; Warner 1962:86–101)—observers of South Asia have long affirmed that physical appearance is no indicator of *jati* identity (see Cox 1948: 5–6, 13, 97, 108, 423; Isaacs 1964:31–32). Indians vary widely in skin color, and populations in the north tend to be lighter than those in the south, but intracaste variation in skin color overlaps with that of other local castes. Dark skin color and high-caste status is no rarity, nor is its reverse. Moreover, Hindu karma theology posits higher- or lower-caste status as a distinct possibility for all, either in previous lives or future rebirths (Cox 1948:40–42; Isaacs 1964:32). The disabilities of Harijan ("untouchable") status, which surely do compare with those of post-Reconstruction black southerners, are something a person is born into; they are not the unquestioned consequence of one's inherited racial constitution, as white southern cultural ideology long held with respect to African Americans (cf. Powdermaker 1939:23–55).

It adds little to understanding South Asian caste, or Greek and other forms of ethnocentrism, to elide them with post-1400s racism as equivalent examples of an abstract category. If the regimes of caste and race do display certain parallels in terms of exploitation and inequality, still they are historically, geographically, organizationally, and ideologically distinct sociocultural systems (Beteille 1967, 1990; Cox 1948:xii, 3–118, 423–461, 488–508, 539–544; Gould 1971; Harper 1968). Similarly, other "caste" situations like those of Japan (DeVos and Wagatsuma 1972) and Africa (Tamari 1991; Todd 1977) have their own historical and geographically limited circumstances, and, like South Asia, do not institutionalize physical appearance as social status (except, perhaps ideally, in Rwanda [Maquet 1961], where the rulers were darker than their subjects [Hiernaux 1975]).

Slavery, an important institution through much of racism's reign, is another matter. Slavery recurred extensively in post-Neolithic, preindustrial social orders (Drake 1987, 1990; Finley 1980; Goody 1980; Harris 1971; Hopkins 1978; Hurgronje 1931; Irwin 1977; Lovejoy 1983; Origo

1955; Patterson 1977; Phillips 1985; Siegel 1947; Snowden 1970; Watson 1980; Wilbur 1943). What distinguished the last slavery of the post-1400s racialized world was precisely the utilization of racial identity as its basis and its justification. The historical factors that led to the enslavement of Native Americans and Africans in the expanding western European colonies are well studied (Curtin 1971, 1990; Phillips 1985). This last slavery can be distinguished from earlier forms in that geographically noncontiguous and bounded populations constituted the slavcholding and enslaved groups (western Europeans and, by the 1600s, sub-Saharan Africans nearly exclusively). In earlier slave social orders, the same physical types, either recruited internally or from linguistically or culturally related groups, might, as fortunes changed, be either slaves or slaveholders. Slavery in ancient Egypt encompassed a wide range of skin colors, as did the Egyptian population itself, at all social levels (Drake 1987:173–174). Slavery in Europe through the 1400s had as its victims individuals whom later racial thinking would classify as Caucasoid (as well as Negroid and Mongoloid, to use one set of pseudoscientific racist labels; see Curtin 1971, 1990; Drake 1990; Finley 1980; Hopkins 1978; Origo 1955; Phillips 1985).

In addition, in earlier and non-Western slavery systems, the populations of slave descendants gradually disappeared. They blended into the dominant cultural group, frequently at low social status, but occasionally in elite circumstances (Goody 1980; Harris 1971; Hopkins 1978; Hurgronje 1931:1–20, 106–109, 221; Lovejoy 1983; Siegel 1947; Snowden 1970; Wilbur 1943). Since systemic racial ordering did not distinguish slaves and masters (if cultural differences often did), slave descendants could readily acculturate; indeed, they usually had no other choice. Slave and slaveholder populations repeatedly melded in earlier and non-Western slave regimes; they did not remain racially fixed and perpetually demarcated.

Biologically, of course, much melding has also taken place throughout the post-1400s racist global order, and its results have received varying social constructions in the United States, the Caribbean, Latin America, South Africa, and elsewhere (Banton 1983; Cohen and Greene 1972; Dominguez 1986; Fredrickson 1981; Gaikwad 1967; Gist and Dworkin 1972; Harris 1964; Hoetink 1967; Jaimes 1992; Morner 1967; Rodriguez, this volume; Sanjek 1971; van den Berghe 1967; Warner, Junker, and Adams 1941; Wertheim 1990). These diverse local cultural interpretations of racial identity, however, have all been colored by the ideological development of specieswide racial rankings, and by their political imposition through legal frameworks and racially determined limits to social interaction.

The post-1400s western European racial orders solidified from their ethnocentric beginnings over a long period (Drake 1990; Fredrickson 1981; Harris 1964). The initial racial viewpoints of the Iberians, long familiar with North and West African Muslims in their midst (Phillips 1985), were somewhat different from those of northern Europeans, who drew upon their own cultural symbolism as they began to encounter sub-Saharan Africans, but for whom they adopted the Iberian word *negro* (Jordan 1968). Still, the devaluing of both Africans (perhaps intensifying among New World Iberians) and Native Americans, and a reluctance to sanction intermarriage or to admit persons of mixed background to the full entitlements of solely European ancestry, were shared by all the western European colonial societies (including South Africa) by the later 1600s (Cohen and Greene 1972; Fredrickson 1981; Jordan 1968; Morner 1967). As the centuries of dispossession and enslavement of these peoples wore on, the ordinariness and economic utility of such treatment were accepted more and more. By the 1700s, efforts mounted within the citadels of science in western Europe to place the exploited peoples into natural schemes that fit with their current positions.

Several scholars have traced the emergence of racial classification in western Europe and the United States (Banton 1987; Barzun 1965; Bieder 1986; Gossett 1963; Gould 1981; Jordan 1968; Stanton 1960; Thomas 1989:29–31). A high point of sorts is the 1795 division of humankind by Johann Friedrich Blumenbach into Caucasian, Mongolian, Ethiopian, American, and Malayan races. Similar segmentations of the world's people into a small number of races followed, with greater and greater energy laid on anthropometric measurements to refine the categories. By the early nineteenth century, polygenist versus monogenist debate as to whether these races were separate divine creations or divergent products of natural history marked the emergence of "anthropology," as the science of races was called. Chief among the polygenists was Samuel Morton, whose meticulous studies of brain size "proving" the superiority of whites over other races (or at least that they had bigger heads) were long accepted (see Boas 1974d:329; Benedict and Weltfish [1943] 1986; Hyatt 1990:88, 93, 114). Only in 1977 did Stephen Jay Gould (1978; 1981) reanalyze Morton's data and discover that Morton's own racist bias had covered up what clearly were overlapping measurements of brain size among the "racial" samples he used. In short, there was no link at all between brain size and races of the Blumenbach-Morton sort (and big heads were no exclusive property of white people; see Comas 1951:23–24).

A radical break with the assumptions of racist categorization and ranking began with the work of anthropologist Franz Boas. Boas's famous nonequation of race, language, and culture ([1911] 1938:137–148) was derived inductively from his research among the Indians of the Northwest Coast during the 1880s and 1890s. By 1899 Boas (1974b) had discovered that mappings of biological traits, cultural similarities, and language families in this "culture area" each yielded different results. Physical types varied within one "tribe" and often were distributed across several tribes; the relatively homogeneous culture area included representatives of several language families, and these families extended beyond it into different culture areas. Boas found delight in applying his formula to a critique of European nationalism (1932:81–105), emphasizing that the flow and circulation of biological traits, cultural elements, ethnic labels, and language groupings also marked the history of that continent and tied it to similar flows and circulation beyond Europe's boundaries.

In 1908 Boas also reported that one of the favored anthropometric markers of "fixed" racial typologies, head shape, could undergo generational change among central and southern European immigrants as they moved from the Old World to the New (1974a; 1938:78–98). He publicized the results of this research to counter nativist antagonism to these new white immigrants, who were frequently identified as of inferior racial subtypes as compared to the northwest Europe–derived "old Americans" (see Barzun 1965; Comas 1951; Gossett 1963; Gould 1981; Hyatt 1990:103–122). He again took a forward position on race when he accepted an invitation from the African-American sociologist-historian and activist W.E.B. Du Bois to deliver the commencement address at Atlanta University in 1906 (Boas 1974c). There Boas hammered out an Afrocentric message that urged his black audience to feel pride in the civilizational accomplishments of Africans before the 1400s, and to understand that the present condition of black people was of historic making and could change (see also Hyatt 1990:85–88).

The Left-leaning liberal doctrine of Boas and his students held that current racial conditions and performance were environmentally determined, could change, and, on biological grounds alone, should not be expected to diverge. This was reaffirmed publically during the Nazi years (Barkan 1988; Benedict 1945; Benedict and Weltfish [1943] 1986; Boas 1945; Radin 1934). By the 1950s the message had seeped into the general liberal consciousness, where it supported the opinion that racial segregation in military service, education, and public accommodations had no objective scientific basis.

By the 1960s, physical and cultural anthropology had moved beyond even the Boasian position. No longer was ranking or the question of superiority and inferiority among races at issue. Now the target became the very idea of race itself (Alland 1971; Littlefield, Lieberman, and Reynolds 1982; Marshall 1968; Montagu 1964). The new antiracists attacked the notion that the human species was divisible into five or any other small number of races. They pointed out that racial appearance—skin color, facial physiognomy, and hair form, in essence—is determined by very few of the many genetic loci. And, like the far greater number of invisible biological traits, these few visible features vary in expression continuously across continents. Hair-form types and skin-color shades grade into each other; they do not abruptly and discretely stop and start. Simply stated, there is no line in nature between a "white" and a "black" race, or a "Caucasoid" and a "Mongoloid" race—there are no racial "continental divides." Small local populations vary slightly from each other as one proceeds east to west from East Asia to western Europe, or north to south from Scandinavia to the Congo basin. Historical movements of peoples, and intermating of populations, complicate but do not disguise the fundamentals of continuous, clinal distribution (Bowles 1977; Geipel 1969; Hiernaux 1975).

Even more destructive of categorical race thinking was the point that the many more-numerous invisible traits—blood factors and enzymes, for example—all just as real biologically as the visibles of skin color and hair form, also vary continuously across populations. But each of these invisible traits varies independently, not in parallel with visible racial markers or in concordance with each other. Marble cake, crazy quilt, and tutti-frutti are all better metaphors of human physical variability than is the x number of races of humankind. There is more "contents" than "package" in our biological makeup, and simplistic racial categories based merely upon a few "package" traits hardly constitute a scientific approach to human biovariability (see Levathes 1993).

As U.S. national consciousness over racial inequality sharpened during the 1960s, a liberal anthropology affirmed that race does not exist. But racism, the socially organized result of race ranking, clearly did, and about that anthropology had little to say. During the 1930s and 1940s, several social anthropologists, from a tradition outside the Boasian synthesis, had studied racism in southern biracial communities and in northern black ghettos (Bond 1988; Davis, Gardner, and Gardner 1941; Drake and Cayton [1945] 1962; Powdermaker 1939; Warner 1962:86–101; Warner, Junker, and Adams 1941). Their work had influenced Gunnar Myrdal's formulations in *An American Dilemma* (1944), which highlighted the contradiction between the U.S. creed of equality and the practice of racial segregation and oppression (see Drake 1987:44–46, 341; see also Cox 1948:509–538). Yet, over the years, this focus on race relations had all but evaporated in U.S. anthropology (but see Leacock

1969). As white and black ethnographers returned to Black American populations during the 1960s, they stressed their internal cultural and social dynamics (Abrahams 1964; Hannerz 1969; Keil 1966; Liebow 1967; Mitchell-Kernan 1971; Stack 1974). While this research demonstrated that poor African Americans living in a supposed culture of poverty were hardly cultureless, the points and sites of racism went largely unprobed (with the exception of Leacock and Liebow).

During the 1960s anthropologists had willingly and easily written about, or against, race and were even beginning to compare local societies within the post-1400s racist domain (Harris 1964; Hoetink 1967; van den Berghe 1967). In the 1970s, however, "ethnicity" came to center stage, and race and racism were pushed aside. Following Barth's *Ethnic Groups and Boundaries* (1969) and Cohen's *Custom and Politics in Urban Africa* (1969), the ethnicity parade began. Ethnic groups were studied everywhere, from the Australian desert to Brooklyn. (Only one of the research sites included in Barth's volume focused on an "ethnic" border produced by the post-1400s western European racist order, however—the Ladino-Maya case studied by Siverts in Chiapas, Mexico—and Cohen's volume concerned indigenous Hausa-Yoruba relations in Ibadan, Nigeria.)

This research, and much that followed in the 1970s, stressed the expressive, internal cultural processes of group formation and the symbols of inclusion. In reviewing the ethnicity wave after its crest, Michael Banton (1983) counterposed ethnicity to race, which he linked to repressive, external processes of exclusion. Banton recalled that Warner in his Yankee City studies in the 1940s had used both race, to deal with the white-black distinction, and ethnicity, to make sense of the cultural differences among Greeks, Poles, Irish, and other white American immigrant-derived groups. Banton went further and insisted that Black Americans needed to be understood from the point of view of both race (repressive exclusion) *and* ethnicity (expressive processes of cultural identification). He concluded that "good racial relations would be ethnic relations," but that the United States was not there yet (see also Kilson 1975).

A few anthropologists during the 1970s had insisted that race or "minority" legal status was *not* the same as ethnicity (Mullings 1978; Ogbu 1978; Vincent 1974; see also Cox 1948:317–320, 392–401; Drake 1987:58–60; Steinberg 1981), but most who studied the United States during that decade concentrated on ethnicity and ignored race and racism. The historic political and economic inequalities that underlie racial classification were underplayed. This, unfortunately, served a sinister agenda. A neoconservative glorification of ethnicity had been heralded in a widely read *New York Times Magazine* piece by Irving Kristol (1966), who asserted that African Americans were just another ethnic group working their way up the ladder like European immigrants. Glazer and Moynihan's *Beyond the Melting Pot* (1963) and Novak's *Rise of the Unmeltable Ethnics* (1971) also fueled this fire by portraying white ethnic groups as continuing to maintain cohesion and Old World cultural values for generations after their arrival as immigrants.

As a grandson of Croatian and Irish immigrants who has virtually no consciousness of any European cultural "roots" and cannot even correctly pronounce my last name, I found the 1970s neoconservative insistence on white ethnic-group persistence suspect at the time but felt perhaps I was the exception. I was therefore delighted with the title of Richard Alba's revisionist paper "The Twilight of Ethnicity among American Catholics of European Ancestry" (1981), and with his and others' subsequent research (discussed in Sanjek, this volume) showing how intermarriage among white ethnics increased steadily with each generation. I was no exception; white ethnic persistence was a hoax (cf. Steinberg 1981:44–74).

In fact, the masses of European immigrants over the nineteenth and twentieth centuries had paid the price of linguistic extinction and cultural loss (Portes and Rumbaut 1990:182–184; Steinberg 1981:43, 45–46) for the privilege of white racial status. The outcome of Angloconformity for non-British European immigrants has been an opportunity to share "race" with whites with whom we do not share "class." This certainly has much to do with why there is such an underdeveloped working-class or socialist tradition in the United States, and why its leadership has depended to such a great extent on spunky European immigrants with accents (Lieberson 1980:351–353; Portes and Rumbaut 1990:87–101). (Bless them for Social Security, wage and hour laws, etc.!) It also explains in part the unease and antagonism with which many white Americans view linguistic and cultural survival and resurgence among Americans of color, those for whom the Angloconformist road to white racial status has not been an option. Some degree of envy or inner turmoil perhaps accompanies the prize of race awarded upon the surrender of ethnicity.

In the 1980s, the Reagan-Bush years, a top-down "color-blind" assault on race-based claims to equality benumbed everyone, producing even a supportive crop of vocal Black conservatives, among them Justice Clarence Thomas (see Franklin 1993; Takagi 1992). Few ethnographers addressed race and racism as compared to ethnicity (see however Benson 1981; Cock 1980; Colen 1986; Cowlishaw 1988; Dominguez 1986; Fordham 1988; Merry 1981; Rollins 1985; Sheehan 1984; Williams 1988). Even worse, most of the studies of ethnicity focused on individual ethnic groups rather than the organization of ethnic diversity (Sanjek 1990). During the 1980s, the demographic impact of the post-1965 "new immigration" also registered in the academic consciousness as large Asian and Latin American populations now were evident across the national landscape. The Los Angeles disturbances in 1992 following the acquittal of Rodney King's police attackers highlighted what many saw as the "new" racial picture of an America moving "beyond black and white," or a new "gorgeous mosaic."

This picture is false, or at least distorted. The post-1400s global racial order has always extended beyond black and white in its ranked racist ordering (Balch Institute 1984; Breman 1990), but these two terms have also always defined its poles (Drake 1987:1–114; Drake and Cayton [1945] 1962:266–268; Fredrickson 1981:15; Gould 1981; Jordan 1968; Lieberson 1980:366–369). There is no decentered mosaic. Persons of African ancestry have consistently experienced extreme subjugation within the global racist order, even if its victims have never been solely black. It is a major message of this volume that we must frame our understandings of any group or struggle in the present within an analysis of racism as a system. American Indian, white, black, Puerto Rican, Chicano, Asian American, and today even Egyptian and Arab, and many other national and regional identities can only be understood within "the international hierarchy of races, colors, religions, and cultures" that encompasses us all (see also Cowlishaw 1988; Cox 1948:349–350; Nash and Ogan 1990; Wertheim 1990). This is what race *is*, and all that it is; it clarifies nothing to euphemize race with "color caste," "ethnicity," "plural society," "duality," or similar evasions (as do Bonacich [1972], Ringer [1983], Warner [1962], and many others; see Cox 1948:489–508]).

As anthropologists return to race and racism (and there are some who never turned away from it, in either their lives or their scholarship), they must also turn outside anthropology to find current and relevant ideas and writings. Anthropology's dry decades in terms of attention to race leave a relatively short shelf to which must be added work from other disciplines. (In framing the 1991 American Anthropological Association annual meeting panels from which this volume arises we invited colleagues from history, sociology, and political science.)

During the 1980s, three major works appeared that help us to understand the historical dimensions and effects of racism as a global order, the issues addressed in this essay. Historian George Fredrickson's *White Supremacy: A Comparative Study in American and South African History* (1981) charts parallels and contrasts in the development of racism in these two nations. Political scientist Martin Bernal's two-volume *Black Athena: The Afroasiatic Roots of Classical Civilization* (1987, 1991) documents the effects of the consolidation of racist thought in eighteenth-

and nineteenth-century western Europe on rewriting ancient history, and thereby erasing attested transcontinental influences and flows. Anthropologist St. Clair Drake's two-volume *Black Folk Here and There: An Essay in History and Anthropology* (1987, 1990) isolates from the standpoint of its African participants the significant features of the post-1400s racialized world in relation to its antecedents in the ancient Egyptian, Judaic, Greco-Roman, Christian, and Islamic social orders.

Race focuses on the present and future of the contemporary racial order. Its contributors explore both constructions of race and sites of struggle around persisting racism in the United States and provide comparative perspectives in essays dealing as well with Puerto Rico, Egypt, and Haiti. A second introductory essay follows this one, in which Steven Gregory treats strategically a considerable body of recent work on race, identity, and politics and situates the essays in this volume in relation to the key issues at stake therein.

We offer this book in the spirit of all that is best in the liberal Boasian heritage, particularly the gradually won realization that racial ranking has no basis in substance, and that the categories themselves are historical precipitates of a five-hundred-year world epoch that we must envision ending and that we must struggle to hasten toward its end. But we also offer this volume with awareness of the limits of liberalism—"We cannot defeat race prejudice by proving that it is wrong" (Cox 1948:462). Clear thinking may help to purge humankind of race, but political action is needed to end racism.

References

Abrahams, Roger D. 1964. *Deep Down in the Jungle: Negro Narrative Folklore from the Streets of Philadelphia.* Hatboro, Pa.: Folklore Associates.

Alba, Richard D. 1981. The Twilight of Ethnicity among American Catholics of European Ancestry. *Annals of the American Academy of Political and Social Sciences* 454:86–97.

Alland, Alexander. 1971. *Human Diversity.* New York: Columbia University Press.

Balch Institute for Ethnic Studies. 1984. *Ethnic Images in Advertising.* Philadelphia: Balch Institute for Ethnic Studies.

Banton, Michael. 1983. *Racial and Ethnic Competition.* Cambridge: Cambridge University Press.

———. 1987. *Racial Theories.* Cambridge: Cambridge University Press.

Barkan, Elazor. 1988. Mobilizing Scientists against Nazi Racism, 1933–1939. *History of Anthropology* 5:180–205.

Barth, Fredrik, ed. 1969. *Ethnic Groups and Boundaries.* Boston: Little, Brown.

Barzun, Jacques. 1965. *Race: A Study in Superstition*. New York: Harper.
Benedict, Ruth. 1945. *Race: Science and Politics*. New York: Viking.
Benedict, Ruth, and Gene Weltfish. [1943] 1986. *The Races of Mankind*. New York: Public Affairs Committee.
Benson, Susan. 1981. *Ambiguous Ethnicity: Interracial Families in London*. Cambridge: Cambridge University Press.
Bernal, Martin. 1987. *Black Athena: The Afroasiatic Roots of Classical Civilization*. Vol. 1, *The Fabrication of Ancient Greece, 1785–1985*. New Brunswick: Rutgers University Press.
———. 1991. *Black Athena: The Afroasiatic Roots of Classical Civilization*. Vol. 2, *The Archaeological and Documentary Evidence*. New Brunswick: Rutgers University Press.
Berreman, Gerald D. 1960. Caste in India and the United States. *American Journal of Sociology* 66:120–127.
Beteille, Andre. 1967. Race and Descent as Social Categories in India. *Daedalus* 96:444–463.
———. 1990. Race, Caste, and Gender. *Man* 25:489–504.
Bieder, Robert E. 1986. *Science Encounters the Indian, 1820–1880: The Early Years of American Ethnology*. Norman: University of Oklahoma Press.
Boas, Franz. [1911] 1938. *The Mind of Primitive Man*. New York: Free Press.
———. 1932. *Anthropology and Modern Life*. New York: Norton.
———. 1945. *Race and Democratic Society*. New York: Augustin.
———. 1974a. Changes in Immigrant Body Form. In *The Shaping of American Anthropology*, ed. George W. Stocking, Jr., 202–214. First published in 1908–1909.
———. 1974b. Fieldwork of the British Association, 1888–1897. In *The Shaping of American Anthropology*, ed. George W. Stocking, Jr., 88–107. First published in 1899.
———. 1974c. The Outlook for the American Negro. In *The Shaping of American Anthropology*, ed. George W. Stocking, Jr., 310–316. First published in 1906.
———. 1974d. Race Problems in America. In *The Shaping of American Anthropology*, ed. George W. Stocking, Jr., 318–330. First published in 1909.
Bonacich, Edna. 1972. A Theory of Ethnic Antagonism: The Split Labor Market. *American Sociological Review* 37:547–559.
Bond, George C. 1988. A Social Portrait of John Gibbs St. Clair Drake: An American Anthropologist. *American Ethnologist* 15:762–781.
Bowles, Gordon. 1977. *The People of Asia*. London: Weidenfeld and Nicolson.
Breman, Jan, ed. 1990. *Imperial Monkey Business: Racial Supremacy in Social Darwinist Theory and Colonial Practice*. Amsterdam: VU University Press.
Cock, Jacklyn. 1980. *Maids and Madams: A Study in the Politics of Exploitation*. Johannesburg: Ravan.
Cohen, Abner. 1969. *Custom and Politics in Urban Africa: A Study of Hausa Migrants in Yoruba Towns*. London: Routledge and Kegan Paul.
Cohen, David W., and Jack P. Greene, eds. 1972. *Neither Slave nor Free: The*

Freedmen of African Descent in the Slave Societies of the New World. Baltimore: Johns Hopkins University Press.
Colen, Shellee. 1986. "With Respect and Feelings": Voices of West Indian Child Care and Domestic Workers in New York City. In *All American Women: Lines that Divide, Ties that Bind,* ed. Johnetta B. Cole, 46–70. New York: Free Press.
Comas, Juan. 1951. *Racial Myths.* Paris: UNESCO.
Cowlishaw, Gillian. 1988. *Black, White, or Brindle: Race in Rural Australia.* Cambridge: Cambridge University Press.
Cox, Oliver C. 1948. *Caste, Class, and Race: A Study in Social Dynamics.* New York: Monthly Review Press.
Curtin, Philip D. 1971. The Atlantic Slave Trade, 1600–1800. In *History of West Africa,* vol. 1, ed. J. F. Ade Ajayi and Michael Crowder, 240–268. London: Longman.
———. 1990. *The Rise and Fall of the Plantation Complex: Essays in Atlantic History.* Cambridge: Cambridge University Press.
Davis, Allison, Burleigh B. Gardner, and Mary Gardner. 1941. *Deep South: A Social Anthropological Study of Caste and Class.* Chicago: University of Chicago Press.
DeVos, George, and Hiroshi Wagatsuma, eds. 1972. *Japan's Invisible Race: Caste in Culture and Personality.* Berkeley and Los Angeles: University of California Press.
Dominguez, Virginia. 1986. *White by Definition: Social Classification in Creole Louisiana.* New Brunswick: Rutgers University Press.
Drake, St. Clair. 1987. *Black Folk Here and There: An Essay in History and Anthropology.* Vol. 1. Los Angeles: Center for Afro-American Studies, University of California.
———. 1990. *Black Folk Here and There: An Essay in History and Anthropology.* Vol. 2. Los Angeles: Center for Afro-American Studies, University of California.
Drake, St. Clair, and Horace R. Cayton. [1945] 1962. *Black Metropolis: A Study of Negro Life in a Northern City.* Rev. and enl. ed. New York: Harper.
Finley, M. I. 1980. *Ancient Slavery and Modern Ideology.* New York: Penguin.
Fordham, Signithia. 1988. Racelessness as a Factor in Black Students' School Success: Pragmatic Strategy or Pyrrhic Victory? *Harvard Educational Review* 58:54–84.
Franklin, John Hope. 1993. *The Color Line: Legacy for the Twenty-First Century.* Columbia: University of Missouri Press.
Fredrickson, George. 1981. *White Supremacy: A Comparative Study in American and South African History.* New York: Oxford University Press.
Gaikwad, V. R. 1967. *The Anglo-Indians.* Bombay: Asia Publishing.
Geipel, John. 1969. *The Europeans.* New York: Pegasus.
Gist, Noel, and Gary Dworkin, eds. 1972. *The Blending of Races: Marginality and Identity in World Perspective.* New York: Wiley.
Glazer, Nathan, and Daniel P. Moynihan. 1963. *Beyond the Melting Pot: The*

Negroes, Puerto Ricans, Jews, Italians, and Irish of New York City. Cambridge, Mass.: MIT Press.

Goody, Jack. 1980. Slavery in Time and Space. In *Asian and African Systems of Slavery,* ed. James L. Watson, 16–42. Berkeley and Los Angeles: University of California Press.

Gossett, Thomas. 1963. *Race: The History of an Idea in America.* New York: Schocken.

Gould, Harold. 1971. *Caste and Class: A Comparative View.* McCaleb Module in Anthropology 11. Reading, Mass.: Addison-Wesley.

Gould, Stephen Jay. 1978. Morton's Ranking of Races by Cranial Capacity. *Science* 200:503–509.

———. 1981. *The Mismeasure of Man.* New York: Norton.

Hannerz, Ulf. 1969. *Soulside: Inquiries into Ghetto Culture and Community.* Stockholm: Almqvist and Wiksell.

Harper, Edward B. 1968. A Comparative Analysis of Caste: The United States and India. In *Structure and Change in Indian Society,* ed. Milton Singer and Bernard S. Cohn, 51–77. New York: Wenner-Gren Foundation for Anthropological Research.

Harris, Joseph E. 1971. *The African Presence in Asia: Consequences of the East African Slave Trade.* Evanston, Ill.: Northwestern University Press.

Harris, Marvin. 1964. *Patterns of Race in the Americas.* New York: Walker.

Hiernaux, Jean. 1975. *The People of Africa.* New York: Scribners.

Hoetink, Harry. 1967. *The Two Variants in Caribbean Race Relations: A Contribution to the Sociology of Segmented Societies.* London: Oxford University Press.

Hopkins, Keith. 1978. *Conquerors and Slaves: Sociological Studies in Roman History 1.* Cambridge: Cambridge University Press.

Hurgronje, C. Snouck. 1931. *Mekka in the Latter Part of the 19th Century.* Leiden: Brill.

Hyatt, Marshall. 1990. *Franz Boas, Social Activist.* Westport, Conn.: Greenwood.

Irwin, Graham W. 1977. *Africans Abroad: A Documentary History of the Black Diaspora in Asia, Latin America, and the Caribbean during the Age of Slavery.* New York: Columbia University Press.

Isaacs, Harold. 1964. *India's Ex-Untouchables.* New York: Harper.

Jaimes, M. Annette. 1992. Federal Indian Identification Policy: A Usurpation of Indigenous Sovereignty in North America. In *The State of Native America: Genocide, Colonization, and Resistance,* ed. M. Annette Jaimes, 123–138. Boston: South End.

Jordan, Winthrop D. 1968. *White over Black: American Attitudes towards the Negro, 1550–1812.* Baltimore: Penguin.

Keil, Charles. 1966. *Urban Blues.* Chicago: University of Chicago Press.

Kilson, Martin. 1975. Blacks and Neo-Ethnicity in American Political Life. In *Ethnicity: Theory and Experience,* ed. Nathan Glazer and Daniel P. Moynihan, 236–266. Cambridge, Mass.: Harvard University Press.

Kristol, Irving. 1966. The Negro Today Is Like the Immigrant Yesterday. *New York Times Magazine* 11:50–51, 124–142.

Leacock, Eleanor. 1969. *Teaching and Learning in City Schools: A Comparative Study*. New York: Basic.
Levathes, Louise. 1993. Scientist at Work: Luigi Luca Cavalli-Sforza; A Geneticist Maps Ancient Migrations. *New York Times,* July 27.
Lieberson, Stanley. 1980. *A Piece of the Pie: Blacks and White Immigrants since 1880*. Berkeley and Los Angeles: University of California Press.
Liebow, Elliot. 1967. *Tally's Corner: A Study of Negro Streetcorner Men*. Boston: Little, Brown.
Linton, Ralph. 1936. *The Study of Man: An Introduction*. [East Norwalk, Conn.]: Appleton-Century-Crofts.
Littlefield, Alice, Leonard Lieberman, and Larry Reynolds. 1982. Redefining Race: The Potential Demise of a Concept in Physical Anthropology. *Current Anthropology* 23:641–655.
Lovejoy, Paul. 1983. *Transformations in Slavery: A History of Slavery in Africa*. Cambridge: Cambridge University Press.
Maquet, Jacques. 1961. *The Premise of Inequality in Ruanda: A Study of Political Relations in a Central African Kingdom*. London: Oxford University Press.
Marshall, Gloria [Niara Sudarkasa]. 1968. Racial Classifications: Popular and Scientific. In *Science and the Concept of Race,* ed. Margaret Mead, Theodosius Dobzhansky, Ethel Tobach, and Robert Light, 149–164. New York: Columbia University Press.
Merry, Sally. 1981. *Urban Danger: Life in a Neighborhood of Strangers*. Philadelphia: Temple University Press.
Mitchell-Kernan, Claudia. 1971. *Language Behavior in a Black Urban Community*. Berkeley: Language-Behavior Research Laboratory, University of California.
Montagu, Ashley, ed. 1964. *The Concept of Race*. New York: Free Press.
Morner, Magnus. 1967. *Race Mixture in the History of Latin America*. Boston: Little, Brown.
Mullings, Leith. 1978. Ethnicity and Stratificaton in the Urban United States. *Annals of the New York Academy of Sciences* 218:10–22.
Myrdal, Gunnar. 1944. *An American Dilemma: The Negro Problem and Modern Democracy*. New York: Harper.
Nash, Jill, and Eugene Ogan. 1990. The Red and the Black: Bougainvillean Perceptions of Other Papua New Guineans. *Pacific Studies* 13 (2): 1–17.
Novak, Michael. 1971. *The Rise of the Unmeltable Ethnics*. New York: Macmillan.
Ogbu, John. 1978. *Minority Education and Caste: The American System in Cross-Cultural Perspective*. New York: Academic Press.
Origo, Iris. 1955. The Domestic Enemy: The Eastern Slaves in Tuscany in the fourteenth and fifteenth centuries. *Speculum* 30:321–366.
Patterson, Orlando. 1977. Slavery. *Annual Review of Sociology* 3:407–449.
Phillips, William D. 1985. *Slavery from Roman Times to the Early Transatlantic Trade*. Minneapolis: University of Minnesota Press.
Portes, Alejandro, and Ruben G. Rumbaut. 1990. *Immigrant America: A Portrait*. Berkeley and Los Angeles: University of California Press.

Powdermaker, Hortense. 1939. *After Freedom: A Cultural Study in the Deep South.* New York: Atheneum.
Radin, Paul. 1934. *The Racial Myth.* New York: McGraw-Hill.
Ringer, Benjamin. 1983. *"We the People" and Others: Duality and America's Treatment of Its Racial Minorities.* New York: Tavistock.
Rollins, Judith. 1985. *Between Women: Domestics and Their Employers.* Philadelphia: Temple University Press.
Sanjek, Roger. 1971. Brazilian Racial Terms: Some Aspects of Meaning and Learning. *American Anthropologist* 73:1126–1143.
———. 1990. Urban Anthropology in the 1980s: A World View. *Annual Review of Anthropology* 19:151–186.
Sheehan, Brian. 1984. *The Boston School Integration Dispute: Social Change and Legal Maneuvers.* New York: Columbia University Press.
Siegel, Bernard J. 1947. *Slavery during the Third Dynasty of Ur.* Memoir 66. Menasha, Wis.: American Anthropological Association.
Snowden, Frank M., Jr. 1970. *Blacks in Antiquity: Ethiopians in the Greco-Roman Experience.* Cambridge, Mass.: Harvard University Press.
Stack, Carol B. 1974. *All Our Kin: Strategies for Survival in a Black Community.* New York: Harper and Row.
Stanton, William. 1960. *The Leopard's Spots: Scientific Attitudes towards Race in America, 1815–59.* Chicago: University of Chicago Press.
Steinberg, Stephen. 1981. *The Ethnic Myth: Race, Ethnicity, and Class in America.* Boston: Beacon.
Stocking, George W., Jr., ed. 1974. *The Shaping of American Anthropology, 1883–1911: A Frank Boas Reader.* Chicago: University of Chicago Press.
Takagi, Dana Y. 1992. *The Retreat from Race: Asian Admissions and Racial Politics.* New Brunswick: Rutgers University Press.
Tamari, Tal. 1991. The Development of Caste Systems in West Africa. *Journal of African History* 32:221–250.
Thomas, Nicholas. 1989. The Force of Ethnology: Origins and Significance of the Melanesia/Polynesia Division. *Current Anthropology* 30:27–41.
Todd, D. M. 1977. Caste in Africa? *Africa* 47:398–412.
van den Berghe, Pierre. 1967. *Race and Racism: A Comparative Perspective.* New York: Wiley.
Vincent, Joan. 1974. The Structuring of Ethnicity. *Human Organization* 33: 375–379.
Warner, W. Lloyd. 1962. *American Life: Dream and Reality.* Chicago: University of Chicago Press.
Warner, W. Lloyd, Buford H. Junker, and Walter A. Adams. 1941. *Color and Human Nature: Negro Personality Development in a Northern City.* New York: Harper.
Watson, James L., ed. 1980. *Asian and African Systems of Slavery.* Berkeley and Los Angeles: University of California Press.
Wertheim, Wim F. 1990. Netherlands-Indian Colonial Racism and Dutch Home Racism. In *Imperial Monkey Business: Racial Supremacy in Social Darwinist*

Theory and Colonial Practice, ed. Jan Breman, 71–88. Amsterdam: VU University Press.

Wilbur, C. Martin. 1943. *Slavery in China during the Former Han Dynasty, 206 B.C.–A.D. 25.* Chicago: Field Museum.

Williams, Brett. 1988. *Upscaling Downtown: Stalled Gentrification in Washington, D.C.* Ithaca, N.Y.: Cornell University Press.

STEVEN GREGORY

"We've Been Down This Road Already"

In 1988 a multiethnic committee of neighborhood activists met in the basement of an African-American church in Corona, Queens, in New York City to discuss ways of improving "intergroup relations." The committee, calling itself the Cultural Awareness Council, had been formed two years earlier in the wake of the racist attack on three black men by whites in Howard Beach, Queens, resulting in the death of Michael Griffith. Most of the members of the council, which included Jews, Asians, and Latinos, were from the neighboring community of Jackson Heights and had been invited to the Corona Congregational Church by its newly appointed pastor, the Reverend Irvine Bryer.

For the five church members who attended, all well over sixty, the dimly lit and sparsely furnished church basement was steeped in community history. During the 1960s, voter registration drives, school desegregation strategies, and political campaigns had been discussed and planned there. The basement had also served as a classroom for after-school tutorial programs and, beginning in 1965, had housed the church's Head Start Program. Square wooden cupboards that once held the preschoolers' lunchboxes and book bags still lined one of the walls.

Most of the church members present that evening had participated in one way or another in those activities. John Booker, a spry retired real estate agent in his eighties, had served on the board of trustees of the Congregational Church during the 1960s and played a key role in organizing church-based employment training, a Neighborhood Youth Corps, and other Great Society programs. When the former pastor of the church ran for political office, challenging Corona's white Democratic party machine, John Booker worked to form alliances with reform Democrats in predominantly white Jackson Heights. Out of respect for his decades of activism, many in the neighborhood called him the Governor.

In fact, it was the memory of this coalition building during the 1960s that framed the opening of discussion. Judy Grubin, the Jewish founder of the Cultural Awareness Council, began the meeting by recalling the longtime relationship that activists in Jackson Heights had with African Americans in Corona. With the assembly seated in a wide circle, she recounted the long struggle twenty years before over the desegregation of the community's schools through the Princeton Plan, a controversial arrangement that paired a white elementary school in Jackson Heights with its counterpart in Corona. "We've been here," she said. "We're not just reacting to Howard Beach."

Grubin went on to describe the council's purpose. "We were formed to discuss the cultures and traditions of different groups, and to open up a dialogue." The African-American church members listened attentively, some jotting down notes on the backs of flyers announcing the meeting. "Sharing diverse ethnic backgrounds," she continued, "is just the first step towards promoting harmony among people."

Glancing at her clipboard, Grubin explained the format of the council's meetings, held monthly at various locations in the area. "Each person in the circle talks personally about their particular ethnic background and the experiences that they've had in the neighborhood." Blanche Hubbert, a church member and part-time caterer in her seventies, frowned and peered over her glasses at John Booker. "What do I want to be talkin' about my ethnic background for?" she asked him. Booker shrugged his shoulders and then focused his attention on the first speaker.

It was Zakallah Prasada, a slender man from Pakistan, who went first. Prasada described how during the Iranian hostage crisis he and his wife and children had been harassed by people because they are Muslims. "Two times they burned our mosque in Corona," he reported. "For me, religious freedom is the most important issue." Frank Weinstein, the director of a coalition of Jewish organizations in Jackson Heights, followed Prasada. He told the group that he was a child of Holocaust survivors and reported that a swastika had been painted on his synagogue during Passover.

Next in the clockwise rotation, Nayibe Nuñez Berger described her migration to the United States from Colombia in 1963 and her marriage to a Jew. "Nothing's changed in the past twenty years!" she exclaimed. "People here still misinterpret and condemn Hispanic street behavior." Yanghee Hahn, a woman from Korea, described cultural misunderstandings between Korean merchants and African Americans and emphasized the importance of good communication. An elderly Jewish man described growing up on the Lower East Side of Manhattan in the 1920s and encountering anti-Semitism when he moved to the Jewish "ghetto" in Middle Village, Queens, in the 1940s.

When Blanche Hubbert's turn came, she hesitated and fidgeted with her note pad. After an awkward silence, she spoke about food stereotypes that people have, suggesting that this was a form of prejudice. "I'm a caterer," she said, "and people always assume that I'm going to serve collard greens." Everyone smiled. John Bell, who was next, looked annoyed. Just turning seventy, Bell had been a labor organizer in the furriers union and active in Harlem politics during the 1930s and 1940s. When he moved to Corona in 1954, he worked with John Booker to establish the Frederick Douglass Democratic Club, the first black political club in the area. Youthful in appearance and debonair, Bell stood, striking a pose that betrayed decades of political speaking.

"John Booker and I are the only ones here who have been active in both communities," he began, motioning to Booker at his side. "It seems like history is repeating itself!" Pausing for effect, he described how Corona and Jackson Heights were once divided by a "Mason-Dixon line" that black children could not cross. "The Princeton Plan was a chance for Jackson Heights to get to know who we were. And we don't have that anymore." John Booker nodded in agreement. "All that you have experienced here," Bell continued, gesturing to the group from Jackson Heights, "we already experienced. We have to become a *political* force, not a social one."

Howard Cuff, an African-American resident of Corona since 1924, shook his head wearily. "This is a new world, John. People are disillusioned! We need *new* ideas, not old ideas."

Irvine Bryer, the minister, intervened. The discussion was quickly turning into a familiar debate among his congregation, pitting those advocating grass-roots political activism against those stressing "moral regeneration." Many, like Cuff, had come to feel that only a renewal of church and family values could resolve the apathy, despair, and hopelessness that some believed rested at the heart of community problems.

"The past is a teacher for the future," Bryer said. And then turning to the visitors, "Most of you benefited from the Civil Rights movement. But those of us who have been here the longest have not. We have to get angry enough to *change* the system—not just talk."

Judy Grubin nodded in agreement. "We got a lot done when we worked together in the sixties but it only lasted ten years."

After the meeting, Booker, Bell, and I accompanied the minister to his small office upstairs. He was anxious to find out what we thought about the meeting. As a newcomer to the community, Bryer relied on the Governor for political advice, and he asked Booker whether he thought the Awareness Council could be useful, and whether a second, more publicized meeting should be arranged in Corona. Booker hesitated, as if to gauge the minister's thoughts. "No, I don't think so, Reverend. We've been down this road already."

For John Booker, as for many African Americans in Corona, the end of the civil rights era marked less a political victory than a rupture with politics.[1] The sense that history is repeating itself registers not merely the awareness that the struggle for racial equality is not yet over but, more profoundly, the perception that its conditions of possibility, both political and discursive, have been weakened, if not undermined. Blanche Hubbert's choice of a story about catering and collard greens was intended neither to be humorous nor to trivialize the question of racism. Rather, it was a strained attempt to transpose the complex politics of race in the United States into the reductive logic of "cultural misunderstanding."

The Awareness Council's strategy for addressing and, indeed, speaking about the problem of "intergroup relations" captures in microcosm important changes in how many Americans have come to think, and *not* think, about issues of race, politics, and social justice in the post–civil rights era. The (re)construction of racial and other systemic inequalities as problems of individual awareness, communication, and sensitivity characterizes the manner in which a host of social issues, ranging from racially motivated violence to "multicultural" education, are framed in contemporary discussions, debates, and scholarly research.

For the appeal of John Bell and others to the past had less to do with reinventing a golden age of 1960s political activism than with recovering the field of politics and, in the process, historicizing the present. If, as Nancy Fraser suggests, we understand something to be "political" when "it is contested across a range of different discursive arenas and among a range of different publics" (1989:167), then the boundaries of the politics of race have indeed been redrawn in recent decades.[2]

In Corona, as in other communities across the United States, the civil rights era witnessed the politicization of race and the everyday facts of racial domination. Unemployment, dilapidated housing, substandard schools, police brutality, and political powerless were not only framed as issues of racial injustice and oppression but, through mass mobilizations and protests, were also projected into a heterogeneous range of social and discursive arenas.

Excluded from participation in Corona's white Democratic party clubs, African Americans "politicized" the church. For example, during the early 1960s, the Independent Citizens for Good Government, an ad hoc coalition of activists representing an assortment of diverse community groups, organized voter registration drives and political fundraisers at the Congregational church. In 1963, the Independent Citizens ran the church's pastor for city council against a conservative Republican. "The greatest domestic issue facing our country, our city, and our borough since 1860," began a letter sent to local clergy before the election, "is the moral issue of Civil Rights. We appeal to you, as a moral leader in your community, to join with us in our campaign to help rid our city of this dangerous cancer of bigotry and race hatred, with all its explosiveness. We now have the political means of doing something about this moral issue." This appeal for support defined "Civil Rights" and racism as moral issues and, equally important, constituted the church as a political and discursive space where a diverse range of social issues could be problematized, debated, and addressed.

Similarly, problems of poverty, neighborhood deterioration, and poor schools were framed as issues of racial inequality whose solutions rested in political mobilization and empowerment. "Why, one may ask, was it necessary to form such an organization?" began a pamphlet explaining the founding of a short-lived black Democratic club in Corona in 1962. "The only truthful answer could be—it grew out of the need for political representation, recognition, and consideration. That is, consideration as it pertains to patronage and other benefits which normally accrue from political participation. Plus the consideration of community problems which were brought about due to the lack of political representation."

Social service and community development needs and issues were defined and contested across a heterogeneous range of neighborhood organizations and constituencies, including school-based parents' associations, block and civic associations, as well as local chapters of the NAACP, Black Panther party, and Nation of Islam. Struggles for school desegregation, community rehabilitation, and political empowerment drew upon this complex, multiply positioned social base. When, for example, middle-class homeowners and PTA activists rallied to pressure city officials to install traffic lights at a dangerous intersection, they were joined on the picket lines by members of the Black Panther party, some of whom had once been members of Corona street gangs.

By exposing and contesting the positioning of African Americans within complex networks of power and domination, civil rights–era activism in Corona enlarged the space of the politics of race, linking diverse institutions and constituencies to shared understandings of, and ways of speaking about, the interrelation of race, identity, and power.

As Michael Omi and Howard Winant point out, the politicization of racial identity was a crucial accomplishment of 1960s activism: "This expansion of 'normal' politics to include racial issues—the 'common sense' recognition of the political elements at the heart of racial identities and meanings—made possible the movement's greatest triumphs, its most permanent successes. These did not lie in its legislative accomplishments, but rather in its ability to create new racial 'subjects.' The black movement *redefined the meaning of racial identity,* and consequently of race *itself,* in American society" (1986:93).

It is precisely this " 'common sense' recognition" of the *politics* of racial identity, won through struggles over the boundaries of the political, that has been challenged in the post–civil rights era. For diverse segments of U.S. society, race has become a tiresome topic, and one whose "polite repression," as Toni Morrison puts it, "is understood to be a graceful, even generous, liberal gesture" (1992:9–10). In debates about affirmative action, urban poverty, the criminal-justice system, and multiculturalism, the subject of race is increasingly framed as "divisive," moot, or as Shelby Steele puts it, justification for a "victim-focussed black identity" (1990:109).

This foreclosure, if not erasure, of the politics of racial identities, of the articulation of race and power in U.S. society, has complex roots and defies easy periodization. Just as a search for origins and ends of the Civil Rights and Black Power movements obscures the continuous dialectic of domination and resistance that characterizes the histories of racialized groups in the United States, locating the roots of what Dana Takagi calls the "retreat from race" (1993) in bounded concepts of "conservative backlash," or "Reagan revolution" risks simplifying the complex political, economic, and cultural forces that have rearticulated the meaning and politics of race in the post–civil rights era.

The Contested Legacy of the Civil Rights Era

One night, after an awards dinner sponsored by the Frederick Douglass Democratic Club, an officer and lifetime member of the local NAACP told me that the "Civil Rights movement was the worst thing that ever happened to Black people." He explained that civil rights–era victories "divided the Black community—destroyed our unity." Although his manner of expressing this observation was extreme by comparison, many activists in Corona–East Elmhurst convey a similar ambivalence about civil rights–era gains.

Although quick to acknowledge a reduction in overt forms of discrimination, gains in education and employment opportunities, and victories in electoral politics, many express the opinion that civil rights–era reforms have not only failed to address fundamental political and economic inequalities but have also transformed the social and institutional base of political activism in ways that weaken, if not undermine, possibilities for struggle around issues of racial inequality and domination.

Some veterans of 1960s struggles for Black political empowerment, for example, contend that electoral victories and inclusion within "mainstream" Democratic politics (made possible in part through the Voting Rights Act of 1965) not only deradicalized the community's political agenda but also restricted the sphere of *legitimate* political activism to Democratic party–sponsored political clubs, electoral tickets, and platforms. For example, when the newly appointed minister of the Corona Congregational Church and church activists attempted to organize a neighborhood coalition to, as John Booker put it, "ensure the survival of Black people," this initiative was interpreted by some residents as an attack on local black elected officials, and as an illegitimate, *political* role for the church and pastoral authority.

Similarly, some argue that the Great Society programs that led to the creation of government-funded antipoverty agencies weakened the ability of local activists to define neighborhood needs, set priorities, and participate effectively in developing and implementing problem-solving strategies. As one minister who had been active in Corona's civil rights–era struggles put it, "The loyalty of the people went to Borough Hall, rather than to the church and what it was doing." Like the NAACP officer, many believe that the proliferation of community services agencies, funded and monitored by a tangled assortment of federal, state, and local agencies, has splintered the community, channeling activists into narrow, insulated, and often competing spheres of political debate and participation. This fragmentation of political space was a result, in part, of the particular strategies pursued by the state through Great Society reforms. Demands for racial equality were met with a "politics of distribution" (Katznelson 1981), which treated intersecting political and economic oppressions tied to race as separate issues that could be addressed within the framework of "interest group pluralism" (Jackson 1993; Omi and Winant 1986; Reed 1986; Valentine 1971; Young 1990).

The case of Corona–East Elmhurst illustrates the uneven and ambiguous legacy of the civil rights era, underscoring the complex manner in which the state's response to the politicization of racial subjugation yielded limited victories, while in the process disarticulating the issues of race and racism from deeper questions concerning the intersection of race, class, and power in U.S. society.[3] From the standpoint of John Bell, Blanche Hubbert, John Booker, and many African Americans living in neighborhoods such as Corona, few public forums remained where race and racism could be raised as *political* issues, implicated in everyday conflicts and debates about the quality of the schools and municipal services, poverty, and political participation.

The containment of the politics of race in neighborhoods such as Corona, built into the strategic response of the Great Society to 1960s activism, was further consolidated, ideologically and politically, during the 1970s and 1980s. This period, symbolized by the Reagan and Bush presidencies, witnessed a pluricentered attack on both the limited gains of civil rights–era activism and its intellectual foundations. The focus of this attack was the "welfare state," which came to be viewed by many as the antithesis of the "free" market, economic prosperity, and individual liberty.

The attack on the liberal welfare state and on its real and imagined beneficiaries must be situated within a restructuring of U.S. capitalism that gathered momentum in the 1980s, stimulated in part by economic crisis the decade before. Manuel Castells summarizes this crisis in the U.S. and, indeed, the global capitalist economic order:

> Labor was steadily increasing its share of the product. Social movements outside the workplace were imposing growing constraints on the ability of capital and bureaucracies to organize production and society free from social control. The state entered a fiscal crisis brought on by the contradiction between growing expenditures (determined by social demands) and comparatively decreasing revenues (limited by the need to preserve corporate profits). The international order was disrupted by the surge of Third World nationalism (simultaneously opposed, supported, and manipulated by the strategies of the superpowers), and by the entry into the international economy of new competitive actors. (1989:22)

Declining corporate profits, federal, state, and local fiscal crises, and persistent "stagflation" stimulated a broad-based restructuring of the U.S. political economy. Businesses, hoping to reduce labor costs and increase profits, reorganized work processes and labor forces (Soja 1992). Technological innovations were employed to increase productivity, while the wages, benefits, and collective bargaining power of workers were reduced. Through corporate relocations, capital aggressively pursued low-wage, nonunion labor in sunbelt areas of the United States, as well as in locations overseas (Sassen 1988). Growing proportions of women, immigrants, and minorities were incorporated into an expanding low-skilled service sector and informal economy (Castells 1989; Mollenkopf and Castells 1992; Sassen 1989; Waldinger 1986).

This restructuring of work processes and labor markets was supported by a shift in the pattern of state intervention from an emphasis on social redistribution associated with the welfare state, to policies aggressively promoting private-sector capital accumulation. Deregulation of the private sector, regressive tax reforms, reductions in public-sector spending, fiscal austerity policies, as well as an assault on organized labor signaled the collapse of the "New Deal political order" (Fraser and Gerstle 1989).

Neoconservative politicians and public-policy analysts argued that the expansion of the welfare state during the 1960s and 1970s had obstructed "the economy's 'natural' tendencies toward recovery," absorbing tax revenues and fueling local, state, and federal deficits (Omi and Winant 1986:111). Income maintenance programs (most notably, Aid to Families with Dependent Children) became the privileged targets of neoconservative critics, who claimed that "welfare" not only was responsible in part for economic stagnation but also had undermined the work ethic, family values, and moral standards of the poor (see Block et al. 1987; Katz 1989).

Although African Americans and other racial minorities were by no means the major beneficiaries of welfare-state spending (Jackson 1993), they became the symbolic and political focus of the neoconservative offensive. War on Poverty programs had, indeed, targeted low-income minority populations in inner-city areas, creating what Castells calls a "rich and complex geography of social welfare" (1989:241; see also Katznelson 1989). Hotly contested struggles over school desegregation, black political empowerment, and housing integration—often framed by politicians, the media, and sectors of the public as pitting "welfare families" (code word: minority) against the "middle class" (code word: white)—fueled in the minds of many Americans the conflation of the welfare state with the identities, interests, and political struggles of racialized groups.

Paradoxically, although "welfare," "special interest groups" and other code words and phrases tied welfare-state expansion symbolically and politically to race, neoconservatives increasingly denied the significance of race in structuring social inequalities. George Gilder's book *Wealth and Poverty* (1981), which provided intellectual ammunition for Reagan administration attacks on social spending for the poor, argued that the expansion of the welfare state and not racial inequalities was responsible for inner-city poverty. Liberal welfare-state policies, Gilder argued, had eroded work and family values at the heart of social mobility. "The key to lowerclass life in contemporary America is that unrelated individuals, as the census calls them, are so numerous and conspicuous that they set the tone for the entire community. . . . The problem is neither race nor matriarchy in any meaningful use. It is familial anarchy among the concentrated poor of the inner-city, in which flamboyant and impulsive youths rather than responsible men provide the themes of aspiration" (qtd. in Katz 1989:145).

The claim that "familial anarchy" rather than racial inequalities lay at the core of urban poverty was enabled by the notion that the persistence of poverty in spite of Great Society reforms posed a "paradox." If race-targeted social welfare spending and institutional reforms had not eliminated inner-city poverty, some reasoned, then its origins must lie beyond race. This root syllogism, adopted by neoconservatives and "neoliberals" alike, although to contrasting ends, rested on a problematic, seldom examined, minor premise: that Great Society reforms had been an appropriate and largely successful response to the problem of *racial* inequality in the United States.

On the one hand, neoconservatives argued that civil rights–era reforms had eliminated barriers to equal opportunity, but that the expansion of the liberal welfare state had made things too easy for the poor, weakening their will to work, create stable families, and otherwise conform to mainstream values and behavioral norms (e.g., Murray 1984).[4] Some neoliberals, on the other hand, while accepting the premise that the problem of contemporary racial inequality had been resolved in the political and economic spheres, reached different conclusions concerning the impact of the welfare state. If Great Society programs did not eliminate poverty, despite the elimination of overt racial discrimination, then the causes of inner-city poverty must be tied to some variable *other* than race, such as structural unemployment. Black middle-class "progress," narrowly defined in terms of occupational and income gains, was pointed to by some as evidence that contemporary racial discrimination had ceased to be a significant factor in structuring the "life chances" of African Americans.[5]

Although neoconservatives and neoliberals differ over the effects of welfare-state intervention, as well as over the relative determinacy of "cultural" and "structural" variables in producing urban poverty, both de-emphasize, if not discount, race as a central distinction that continues to structure the U.S. political economy and the everyday experiences of racial minorities in the post–civil rights era.

Theorizing against Repetition

This collection of essays builds upon efforts to repoliticize the questions of race and racism taking place in a range of disciplines and in relation to heterogeneous political commitments. Contributors to *Race* represent an equally diverse grouping of scholars, writing from a variety of theoretical and methodological perspectives. Unifying this volume is a shared concern with exposing the ways in which race structures social hierarchies in the United States and in the global order, and with grounding questions of race and racism within nonessentialist understandings of identity. By investigating the construction of "race" and the exercise of racism(s) within the context of pluricentered power relations and along multiple axes of difference, we stress that "race matters" across the panoply of interdependent struggles for social justice and equality (West 1993).

Articles in "Shifting Lines" explore the formation of racial identities within the context of multiple constructions of difference and complex relations of power. Race never operates alone but articulates with gender, class, nation, sexuality, ethnicity, and other differences to form heterogeneous identities and crosscutting social hierarchies.

This concern with the articulation of racialized yet complex subjects contrasts with reductive approaches that treat racial meanings as ideological expressions of more "concrete" or foundational social categories (such as "class," "ethnicity," or "nation") and with perspectives, often linked to various forms of nationalism, that treat race as a privileged center from which to comprehend heterogeneous social distinctions and power relations.[6] Both tendencies dehistoricize race by *presupposing* its contingency or determinacy and obscure the processes whereby historically specific social hierarchies are constructed, legitimated, and contested along multiple axes of difference. As Etienne Balibar points out, "Racism is a social relation, not the mere ravings of racist subjects" and, as such, operates within a "system of complementary exclusions and dominations," which, in any given social formation, "are mutually interconnected" (1991b:41, 49).

Contributors to this section emphasize the historical specificity of race(s) and racism(s), mapping the multiple ways in which racial identities and social relations are constituted and articulated with other differences. This attention to context undermines static, binary constructions of "white-nonwhite," "racist-antiracist," and "colonizer-colonized," exposing not only the heterogeneity and instability of their opposing terms, but also how both can be "complicitous and resistant, victim and accomplice" (Giroux 1992:20; cf. Cooper and Stoler 1989). Attending to the reciprocal constitution of subordinate and dominant races can illuminate categories of exclusion and oppressive relations that, like gender, class, sexuality, and citizenship, crosscut and inflect racial distinctions, sometimes securing and masking them, while at other times exposing them to scrutiny and contestation.[7]

M. Annette Jaimes demonstrates how the U.S. government's policy of certifying the identities of American Indian peoples on the basis of "blood quantum" not only continues to deny them the right to self-definition but also provides legal and bureaucratic pretexts for excluding "noncertified" Indians from land, political power, and social services. When first introduced in the Allotment Act of 1887, blood quantum criteria denied land rights to Indians who were less than "half-blood," enabling federal authorities to appropriate millions of acres of "surplus" land for non-Indian settlement. Jaimes points out that the continued use of blood quantum criteria by the Bureau of Indian Affairs has not only incited conflicts among Indian peoples over benefits tied to federal recognition but has also led to the formation of intertribal alliances and identities, which base oppositional claims to power and self-determination in culturally defined constructions of a pantribal Indian nation.

Ruth Frankenburg explores the social construction of "whiteness" in white women's life narratives. "Whiteness," Frankenberg argues, is often constructed as an "empty category" tacitly understood to be normative and equivalent to "Americanness." For some of the women she interviewed, to be "white" meant to be cultureless and lacking a distinct, nameable identity. Although many linked this experience of absence to a positive valuation of "other" cultures, the failure to unpack what "whiteness" *is,* Frankenberg suggests, risks obscuring the power relations and practices that position certain subjects within its privileged space. Thus, even in antiracist discourses, Frankenberg points out, the failure to "historicize" whiteness can lead to the reaffirmation of racial dualisms that rest on ontological assessments of human difference.

Karen Sacks locates the construction of a panethnic, "white" American identity in social, political, and economic transformations after World War II. Challenging the notion that European immigrants pulled themselves up by their own bootstraps, Sacks argues that the 1944 Serviceman's Readjustment Act, or GI Bill, served as a massive affirmative action program, providing demobilized Euro-American *males*—women serving in the military were not eligible—with the wherewithal to participate in the booming postwar economy.

Job preferences, educational benefits, and low-interest home mortgages enabled Jews and other European immigrants who had been considered members of inferior races to assimilate as model white middle-class citizens. African Americans, unable to realize their GI benefits because of segregation, and women suffered a form of "reverse discrimination" through federal programs that constructed the American dream as white *and* male.

Roger Sanjek argues not only that the category "white" has expanded over time to include European groups (which, like Italians, Slavs, and Jews, were once thought to be of different races) but also that "Asian," "Hispanic" and "Native American" racial identities may be going through a similar "race-to-ethnicity conversion" whereby putatively biological differences are socially redefined as culturally based ethnic differences. Noting the high incidence of white-Asian, white-Hispanic, and white–Native American intermarriage, when compared to marriage across the white-black color line, Sanjek suggests that intermarriage may be an important social vehicle that both signals and enables the social processes through which certain racial distinctions are symbolically reworked as ethnic differences.

Jaimes, Frankenberg, Sacks, and Sanjek illuminate the unstable and contested nature of racial categories and identities in the United States. The next three authors situate processes of racial formation within global political economies, movements of population, and circuits of meaning. Transnational movements of populations, whether incited through processes of empire building, (de)colonization, or the structuring of global markets and productive relations, position populations within heterogeneous and spatially dispersed networks of power and meaning that construct and rework racial identities along multiple axes (Hall 1990; Rouse 1992).

Clara Rodríguez contrasts the binary, white-nonwhite racial order in the United States with the relatively more fluid and heterogeneous practices of racial classification in Puerto Rico. In Puerto Rico and in other areas of Latin America and the Caribbean, racial identification is closely linked to evaluations of class, social status, and appearance. Whereas in the United States race is defined at birth with reference to genealogy in accordance with the principle of "hypodescent," in Puerto Rico, social and phenotypical characteristics inflect classification such that an individual's "race" may not only change over time but also differ from that of blood relatives.[8] Rodríguez illuminates this contrast by investigating the multiple ways in which Latino immigrants in the United States negotiate and contest racial classification on the basis of skin color cum ancestry. Data from the 1980 U.S. census show that over 40 percent of Puerto Ricans and Latinos chose not to identify themselves in the racial categories provided. Instead they checked "other" and filled in "Puerto Rican," "Spanish," or other markers of ethnic and national identity. Through the life histories of Latinos living in New York, Rodríguez teases out the complex social, cultural, and political factors that contribute to this decision to be "other."

Where Rodríguez illuminates how transnational movements of population position and reposition social groups across multiple, often contrasting, racial orders, Michel Rolph-Trouillot focuses attention on changes in the significance of race that accompany political and economic transformation. Examining race or, more accurately, "color" in Haiti, Trouillot shows how the winning of independence rearticulated the colonial racial system, refracting the meaning and political significance of racial categories through postcolonial power relations and culturally inflected constructions of national and class identities.

Though years or warfare, ending with independence in 1804, rendered the white population of Haiti negligible, a color-based hierarchy persisted, differentiating *clairs,* or lighter-skinned people of mixed race, from darker-skinned *noirs.* Although this new color hierarchy linked physical features associated with "whiteness" to privileged social, political, and economic status, it was not simply a continuation of precolonial, or "Western," racial hierarchies. Since the war for independence was waged against colonialism, slavery, *and* white supremacy, ruling elites in Haiti could not ground their claims to power and legitimacy in a system of racial prejudice that explicitly denigrated "blackness." Instead, the concepts *clair* and *noir,* although tied to appearance, came to refer to a wide range of "sociocultural attributes that do not have a somatic referent." Over time, the "epidermic line" perceived to distinguish the two groups shifted to include darker-skinned people within the clair group, as some upwardly mobile noir families exchanged socioeconomic status with clair families for "epidermic capital" through cross-color marriages. Distinctions based on skin color, Trouillot argues, do not simply "reflect" class divisions in Haiti but have an "independent social value" that, in conjunction with political power, education, and other status evaluations, is factored into transgenerational strategies of social mobility and elite rule.

Like Trouillot, Soheir Morsy underscores the unstable and contingent quality of racial categories, situating the question of Egyptian identity within changing global political economics. Morsy maps the articulation of race in Egypt with shifting, multitiered constructions of national, Pan-Arab/Pan-African, Islamic, and "pharaonic" identities, patterned differently during the course of Egypt's colonial and postcolonial history. Weaving together scholarly sources and personal experience, Morsy demonstrates how the 1952 Nasserist Free Officers' coup subordinated narrow constructions of Egyptian nationalism to a concept of a transnational Pan-Arab nation, while expanding the notion of "Nile valley unity" to embrace Pan-Africanism. This state-sponsored expanded definition of identity weakened the legitimacy of European culture and racial evaluations in Egypt and promoted identification among sectors of Egyptian society with the political struggles of Africans and African Americans. Morsy shows how the articulation of race and Egyptian national identity continued to shift as Egypt's political alliances and position in the global economy changed in the post-Nasser era.

Patricia Zavella raises the key theoretical and, indeed, political question of how to conceptualize race, gender, and other *identities* without obscuring differences within these categories. Zavella suggests that, rather than derive Chicana diversity from an a priori definition of their commonality as women (that is, by "adding on" race, culture, or religion to a notion of shared women's experience), attention should focus on the specific ways in which Chicanas are located in social spaces configured by a complex set of relations that both constrain and enable the self-construction of identity. Approaches that "add on" ethnicity to gender, or gender to race, Zavella warns, can lead to an "atheoretical pluralism" that elides the ways in which identities are articulated within specific social and temporal locations.

The complexity of this social space is explored in Renato Rosaldo's reading of the Arturo Islas novel *Migrant Souls*. Static and essentialist constructions of race, Rosaldo points out, fail to capture the dynamics of racial identity and differentiation among Chicanos. Racialized categories, such as "Chicano," "Indian," and "Anglo," condense a complex and sometimes contradictory set of cultural evaluations tied to class, religion, gender, and sexuality, as well as phenotype. In Islas's novel, for example, characters aspiring to be "decent," middle-class Catholics code a range of putatively low-status and "indecent" behaviors (such as impoliteness, lateness, and homosexuality) as "Indian," as contrasted with "Spanish." Alternatively, other transgress Spanish- and Anglo-coded cultural norms, thereby embracing their "Indian blood." Rosaldo's reading of *Migrant Souls* highlights the importance not only of viewing race as a complex, shifting conjunction of social inequalities and culturally constructed differences, but also of attending to the variety of trajectories along which racial identities are inhabited, transgressed, and reworked.

Contributors to "Persisting Dilemmas" examine specific sites where knowledge about racial differences and identities is produced, empowered, and contested. From national debates about "multiculturalism" to struggles for racial justice and equality in local communities, these case studies illuminate how constructions of race shape and are shaped by complex social hierarchies, as well as recent debates concerning the meaning and scope of social justice, citizenship, and democracy.

Dana Takagi's study of the Asian-American college admissions controversy of the 1980s underscores the need to reconceptualize race relations and politics in the post–civil rights era. Takagi shows how the claims of officials at the University of California at Berkeley that increasing Asian-American enrollments threatened "racial balance" and "diversity" in the student body lent support to neoconservative arguments that affirmative action and racial preferences for *blacks* were unfair. Conflating Asian-American charges of racial discrimination with Allan Bakke's 1978 claim of "reverse discrimination," neoconservatives argued that controversies over affirmative action had moved beyond race to more "basic" issues of fairness. Takagi suggests that the controversy over Asian-American admissions registers important shifts in racial demography and politics in the post–civil rights era and underscores the need to attend theoretically to the shifting and often contradictory contours of contemporary identity politics.

Evelyn Hu-DeHart explores a second arena in which the political claims, struggles, and identities of racial minorities, women, and other oppressed groups have been recast as threatening the "fairness" of liberal democracy: the controversy over "multiculturalism." Hu-DeHart locates the political origins of multicultural education in struggles for Black, ethnic, and women's studies programs during the 1960s and 1970s and argues that the opposition to multiculturalism in recent years is tied to the impact that these "nontraditional" programs have had on the curriculum. Multicultural education, Hu-DeHart contends, exposes the contradiction between the multiracial and inegalitarian origins of U.S. society and dominant constructions of "American nationhood" as white, western European, English-speaking, and democratic. Hu-DeHart argues that neoconservative claims that multicultural education is "particularistic" and "divisive" rest on spurious assertions of a "universal" Western culture, and she demonstrates how charges of "political correctness" have been used to frame the politics of oppressed peoples as "undemocratic" and intellectually "nonobjective."

Robert Alvarez, Jr., examines strategies and practices involved in the recruitment of racial minorities and women in academia and argues that they illuminate subtle and not-so-subtle processes through which professional hierarchies and canonical boundaries are produced and maintained. Although university administrations have targeted minority scholars for recruitment, Alvarez points out, the "special" manner in which these minority searches are typically conducted releases institutions from standard procedures that ensure equity and fair treatment. Consequently, not only are "target of opportunity" searches often pursued through informal channels, but candidates for such positions are sometimes evaluated according to contrasting and vaguely defined criteria. Although universities and departments are increasingly emphasizing faculty diversity, Alvarez argues, this concern does not necessarily involve a willingness to embrace research interests, epistemological concerns, and political commitments that depart from conventional canons.

Where Takagi, Hu-DeHart, and Alvarez call attention to the interplay of race and politics in the academy, the authors of the next two essays explore how ideologies of race shape the production of knowledge within disciplines. Michael Blakey traces a "pattern of denial" of race and racism in physical anthropology, unpacking its complex origins in the belief that social differences are rooted in "nature" and the individual, rather than in political and economic inequities. Blakey argues that the presentation of a "sterilized" history of physical anthropology (one that fails to expose its intellectual foundations in scientific racism and eugenics) has not only marginalized African-American critics of racist social science in narratives of antiracist enlightenment but also mitigated against "intellectual confrontation with contemporary social inequalities."

Robert Paynter, Susan Hautaniemi, and Nancy Muller offer an archaeological perspective on race in their analysis of the boyhood home of W.E.B. Du Bois in Great Barrington, Massachusetts. The authors argue that, although the interpretive implications of race and racism have not been central themes in archaeological literature, a critical perspective on race is essential to conceptualizing not only the function, use, and social meaning of objects but also the ways material records themselves have been constituted and configured through practices of racial exclusion. Through an analysis of the homesite, archival records, and Du Bois's own writings on Great Barrington, the authors investigate important aspects of the social history of the African-American community into which Du Bois was born.

John Attinasi maps the complex ties between race, language, and power in U.S. society that give rise to a "politics of linguistic exclusion" realized in widely publicized debates over the status of English as the "official language" and in the subtle operation of a linguistic dichotomy. Attinasi argues that this dichotomy, constrasting "standard" English speakers with largely minority, non-English, and vernacular speakers, positions people of color in relations of linguistic inequality, where nonstandard speech is devalued and silenced by being interpreted as "inaccurate," "unintelligible," or otherwise indicative of cultural incompetence.

Brett Williams unpacks the race-, gender-, and class-biased assumptions about economic "independence" and the timing of life-cycle decisions that underpin images of deviant, female-headed households in discussions of the "ghetto underclass." Williams argues that racialized constructions of welfare-dependent "teen mothers" not only obscure the reasoned quality of women's life-cycle decisions but also mask the use by downwardly mobile working- and middle-class households of credit cards as a form of social welfare. Although the language of credit-card advertising stresses mobility, independence, and a "mastery" over life-style choices (the antithesis of the image of the welfare household), many Americans use their credit cards as a plastic "safety net" and express their relationship to the credit system in language that suggests dependency, lack of personal responsibility, and even addiction. Just as the construction of the "welfare mother" masks the complex intersection of poverty and race in the lives of poor women, Williams argues, the imagery of the banking credit-card system obscures the falling wages and declining life-styles of the working and middle classes.

Racialized constructions of identity that support and mask practices of domination are resisted and reworked by social groups. In an ethnographic study of a mostly black private housing complex in Queens, New York City, I show how African-American women challenged the construction of their complex as a crime-infested "welfare haven" in white activist discourse. Through the organization of events and activities for African-American youth, these women not only disrupted constructions of black identity that served to disempower African Americans in local governing institutions, but they also politicized forms of racial subjugation, like the police harassment of black teenagers, that had been excluded from the community's political agenda.

Notes

1. I use the phrase "civil rights era" here to refer to a period extending roughly from the mid-1950s to the early 1970s. Activists in Corona–East Elmhurst use this term to refer to heterogeneous local, municipal, and national political struggles around questions of racial justice, including but not reducible to the period of the Civil Rights movement.

2. Fraser refers to this sense of the political as the "discursive-political," which she distinguishes from the "institutional sense, in which a matter is deemed 'political' if it is handled directly in the institutions of the official government system, including parliaments, administrative apparatuses, and the like" (1989:166). This discursive sense underscores the social construction of the boundary separating what is deemed political from what is not in a given society, and it focuses attention on the social processes whereby issues become politicized or depoliticized. By the "politics of race," therefore, I refer to the social processes through which relations and practices of racial subjugation are contested and politicized.

3. A number of analysts of Great Society reforms and welfare state expansion underscore their effects, to some degree calculated, in containing, absorbing, or "regulating" political opposition. See, for example, Katznelson 1981; Omi and Winant 1986; Piven and Cloward 1971; Reed 1986; Valentine 1971; and Young 1990. See Gordon 1990 for a thoughtful critique of the functionalist tendencies of some applications of this social control model.

4. See Williams 1992 for an insightful critique of this and other themes in the literature on urban poverty and a discussion of alternative views developed in the anthropological literature.

5. For example, William Julius Wilson observes:

> Discrimination is the most frequently invoked explanation of social dislocations in the urban ghetto. However, proponents of the discrimination thesis often fail to make a distinction between the effects of historical discrimination, that is, discrimination before the middle of the twentieth

> century, and the effects of discrimination following that time. They therefore find it difficult to explain why the economic position of poor urban blacks actually deteriorated during the very period in which the most sweeping antidiscrimination legislation and programs were enacted and implemented. Their emphasis on discrimination becomes ever more problematic in view of the economic progress of the black middle class during the same period. (1987:30)

6. See Omi and Winant 1986 for a discussion and critique of ethnicity, class, and nation-based theories of race. See also Stuart Hall's (1980) important critique of economic reductionist approaches to race within the Marxist framework, and Etienne Balibar's (1991b) critique of approaches that view the concept of race as derivative of nationalism.

7. Research on colonial social formations, for example, highlights the link between the racialization of colonized subjects and the imagining of colonial, national, and transnational "European" identities (e.g., Balibar 1991b; Bernal 1987; Ranger 1983; Stoler 1989). Mapping these mutually determining relations across categories situates the experience of racialized groups within a wider analytic frame that problematizes the identity, agency, and political coherence of dominant racial, colonial, or imperial groups. As Cooper and Stoler (1989) point out, the "otherness" of colonized or subordinated racial populations is neither inherent nor stable but is constructed and maintained through practices of exclusion and coercion that also operate on dominant groups.

8. Etienne Balibar (1991a) points out that, although the "schema of genealogy," or the notion that the filiation of individuals transmits intergenerationally, is the kernel of the idea of race, the content of somatic, psychological, and cultural characteristics constituting this fiction of racial identity varies. Thus the relative plasticity of racial categories in Puerto Rico does not imply that genealogy is insignificant, but rather that the "substance" that is putatively inherited is, relatively speaking, less tied to aspects of phenotype.

References

Anderson, Benedict. 1983. *Imagined Communities.* London: Verso.

Balibar, Etienne. 1991a. The Nation Form. In *Race, Nation, Class,* ed. Etienne Balibar and Immanuel Wallerstein, 86–106. London: Verso.

———. 1991b. Racism and Nationalism. In *Race, Nation, Class,* ed. Etienne Balibar and Immanuel Wallerstein, 37–67. London: Verso.

Bernal, Martin. 1987. *Black Athena: The Afroasiatic Roots of Classical Civilization.* New Brunswick: Rutgers University Press.

Block, Fred, Richard A. Cloward, Barbara Ehrenreich, and Frances Fox Piven. 1987. *The Mean Season.* New York: Pantheon.

Castells, Manuel. 1989. *The Informational City.* Cambridge: Blackwell.

Cooper, Fredrick, and Ann Stoler. 1989. Tensions of Empire: Colonial Control and Visions of Rule. *American Ethnologist* 16:609–621.

Fox Piven, Frances, and Richard A. Cloward. 1971. *Regulating the Poor.* New York: Pantheon Books.
Fraser, Nancy. 1989. *Unruly Practices.* Minneapolis: University of Minnesota Press.
Fraser, Steve, and Gary Gerstle. 1989. *The Rise and Fall of the New Deal Order.* Princeton: Princeton University Press.
Gilder, George. 1981. *Wealth and Poverty.* New York: Random House.
Giroux, Henry. 1992. Post-Colonial Ruptures and Democratic Possibilities: Multiculturalism as Anti-Racist Pedagogy. *Critical Inquiry* 21:5–39.
Gordon, Linda. 1990. The New Feminist Scholarship of the Welfare State. In *Women, the State, and Welfare,* ed. Gordon, 9–35. Madison: University of Wisconsin Press.
Gregory, Steven. 1992. The Changing Significance of Race and Class in an African-American Community. *American Ethnologist* 19:255–274.
Hall, Stuart. 1980. Race, Articulation, and Societies Structured in Dominance. In *Sociological Theories: Race and Colonialism,* 305–345. Paris: UNESCO.
———. 1990. Cultural Identity and Diaspora. In *Identity: Community, Culture, Difference,* ed. Jonathan Rutherford, 222–237. London: Lawrence & Wishart.
hooks, bell. 1990. *Yearning: Race, Gender, and Cultural Politics.* Boston: South End.
Jackson, Thomas F. 1993. The State, the Movement, and the Urban Poor: The War on Poverty and Political Mobilization in the 1960s. In *The Underclass Debate,* ed. Michael B. Katz, 403–439. Princeton: Princeton University Press.
Katz, Michael B. 1989. *The Undeserving Poor.* New York: Pantheon.
Katznelson, Ira. 1981. *City Trenches.* Chicago: University of Chicago Press.
———. 1989. Was the Great Society a Lost Opportunity? In *The Rise and Fall of the New Deal Order,* ed. Fraser and Gerstle, 185–211.
Mollenkopf, John, and Manuel Castells, eds. 1992. *Dual City: Restructuring New York.* New York: Russell Sage.
Morrison, Toni. 1992. *Playing in the Dark.* Cambridge, Mass.: Harvard University Press.
Murray, Charles. 1984. *Losing Ground: American Social Policy.* New York: Basic Books.
Omi, Michael, and Howard Winant. 1986. *Racial Formation in the United States.* New York: Routledge and Kegan Paul.
Ranger, Terrence. 1983. The Invention of Tradition in Colonial Africa. In *The Invention of Tradition,* ed. Terrence Ranger and Eric Hobsbawm, 211–262. New York: Cambridge University Press.
Reed, Adolph, Jr. 1986. The "Black Revolution" and the Reconstitution of Domination. In *Race, Politics, and Culture,* ed. Adolph Reed,Jr., 61–95. Westport, Conn.: Greenwood.
Rouse, Roger. 1991. Migration and the Social Space of Postmodernism. *Diaspora* 1:8–23.

Rutherford, Jonathan, ed. 1990. *Identity: Community, Culture, Difference*. London: Lawrence and Wishart.
Sassen, Saskia. 1988. *The Mobility of Labor and Capital*. Cambridge: Cambridge University Press.
Soja, Edward. 1992. Poles Apart: Urban Restructuring in New York and Los Angeles. In *Dual City*, ed. Mollenkopf and Castells, 361–375.
Steele, Shelby. 1990. *The Content of Our Character*. New York: HarperCollins.
Stoler, Ann L. 1989. Making Empire Respectable: The Politics of Race and Sexual Morality in Twentieth-Century Colonial Cultures. *American Ethnologist* 16:634–661.
Takagi, Dana. 1993. *The Retreat from Race*. New Brunswick: Rutgers University Press.
Valentine, Charles. 1971. The "Culture of Poverty": Its Scientific Significance and Its Implications for Action. In *The Culture of Poverty: A Critique*, ed. Eleanor Burke Leacock, 193–225. New York: Simon and Schuster.
Waldinger, Roger. 1986. *Through the Eye of the Needle: Immigrants and Enterprise in New York's Garment Trades*. New York: New York University Press.
Wallace, Michele. 1990. *Black Macho and the Myth of the Superwoman*. London: Verso.
West, Cornel. 1993. *Race Matters*. Boston: Beacon Press.
Williams, Brett. 1992. Poverty among African Americans in the Urban United States. *Human Organization* 51:164–174.
Wilson, William Julius. 1978. *The Declining Significance of Race*. Chicago: University of Chicago Press.
———. 1987. *The Truly Disadvantaged*. Chicago: University of Chicago Press.
Young, Iris Marion. 1990. *Justice and the Politics of Difference*. Princeton: Princeton University Press.

Shifting Lines: Constructions of Race

M. ANNETTE JAIMES

American Racism: The Impact on American-Indian Identity and Survival

The Catch-22 is that one cannot be an American Indian unless s/he is *"federally recognized."* Conversely, one cannot be *"federally recognized"* unless one is an American Indian.

Native American Consultants, Inc.

Most discussions on U.S. racism focus on African-American subjugation by Euro-Americans, and the dominance of "whites" as a result of the historical legacy of institutionalized slavery in this country. My research takes a different approach, focusing on Euro-American conceptions and treatment of American Indians as a benchmark of racism in the United States. The impact of the mythological construct of race on American Indians was predicated on western European theology and evolved into "scientific," ecological, and bureaucratic manifestations that persist into the present.

The impact of hierarchical racist thinking on Indian people continues to be a problem today. This was evident in the violent 1974 serial murders of several Navajo men in Farmington, New Mexico. A group of white high-school boys decided to have "fun" by killing Navajos. They selected drunken victims, tortured them, and left them to die in the desert. The crimes were played down by local and national media, and two of the juvenile defendants were sent to reform school. The confessions of this murder spree explained that the boys just got a kick out of killing drunk Indians.[1] "Mixed blood" Indians, like other "hybrids," are denigrated as "mud people" by the Ku Klux Klan and other white supremacists. We are a subject of scorn and ridicule for being weak and confused inferior types, due to the abomination of the mixing of races.

Prior to the European conquest, there is no evidence that indigenous peoples of the Americas had in their societies any concept of "race" to make differentiations within the human species. Instead, cultural distinctions were made among peoples. While European colonizers would define all indigenous peoples as "a single race" among other "races," this ignored the diversity that was evident among Indian groups, both physically and culturally. Traditionally, tribal peoples organized their societies along either matrilineal or patrilineal lines and traced descent through elaborate communal kinship traditions (see Eggan 1955; Tax 1955). These cultural norms served religious as well as social needs. Clans and moieties encouraged exogamy, or intermarriage, to protect against inbreeding and to honor kin-based incest taboos. In general, there is more documentation of tribes that traced descent through the mother (matrilineal) than through the father (patrilineal). These egalitarian societies also had matrifocal and patrifocal spheres of influence and decision making. An illustration of such gender-based spheres is that adult women among southwestern tribes (Pimas, Apaches, Pueblos, etc.) had control in the education of the younger generation as well as in agrarian activity, while men appeared to wield more influence in religious rituals, although all participated in communal ceremonies.[2]

These indigenous cultures perceived diversity in physical characteristics but were more concerned with cultural differences among themselves and, following Columbus, with the European newcomers. It was not until after the conquest and the introduction of Eurocentric racist pseudoscience that the proliferation of such racialized "mixed blood" categories as mestizo, Métis, creole, half-breed, mulatto, quadroon, and so forth were imposed (Forbes 1993; Price 1953; Thornton 1987). Today, American Indians, among other peoples, have to deal with the dire consequences of the divisiveness created by Euro-American exploitation of "mixed bloods" versus "full bloods."

Traditionally, individuals could become members of an indigenous society by kinship, intermarriage, adoption, or naturalization, which included "mixed-blood identities," no matter what their "racial" or cultural background. Later, Euro-Americans as "whites" could be adopted or naturalized by Indians through intermarriage and emphasis on exogamy. After conquest and forced assimilation, some translations of Indian statements indicate that groups continued to see themselves as distinct cultural entities, with a communal concept of nationhood as "a people." Yet this is not the same as perceiving and promoting themselves as a distinct "race." This construction has been wrought by federal Indian jurisprudential and legislative constructions (Harmon 1991); as we shall see, it continues to cause problems for Indians, and to meet resistance.

While kinship, culture, and nationhood are the bedrock of Indian identity, race or ethnicity is not. As Métis Indian scholar Ward Churchill puts it,

> First, there is no given ethnicity which encompasses those who are indigenous to what is now construed as the U.S. territory. . . . Second, notions of ethnic

or racial minority status fail profoundly to convey the sense of national identity by which most or all North American indigenous populations define themselves. It is [therefore] this national identity, not the factor of ethnicity, that is most important in understanding the reality of native North America today. (1992–93:19)

Yet, we must ask ourselves if Métis nationalism is the long-term answer for our liberation from colonization.

Sowing the seeds of American racism, the Spanish Catholic invaders perceived "New World" Indians as "savages" and "heathens," justifying their imperialist aims. From that point on, European imperialist nations wiped out entire tribes and virtually destroyed the cultures of others (Churchill 1992c; Stannard 1992; Stiffarm, with Lane 1992; Thornton 1987). The western European Calvinists, who as God's "chosen" arrived in North America, believed, "If you diligently keep all [the Lord's] commandments, . . . the Lord shall out all these nations before you and you shall occupy the territory of nations greater and more powerful than you. Every place where you set the soles of your feet shall be yours" (Deut. 11:22–24). Biblical interpretation rationalized American Manifest Destiny, the ideological propaganda that justified native genocide and empire building by the United States (Acuña 1988; Drinnon 1980; Horsman 1981).[3]

Nineteenth-century Anglo-Americans were preoccupied with the pseudoscientific doctrine that assumed the superiority of the white race, with northwestern Europeans at the pinnacle of its superior Western civilization (DeMolins 1899; Peterson 1978). The "scientific" approach to race was exemplified in Samuel Morton's influential *Crania Americana,* a compendium of skull measurements of indigenous North and South American peoples, published in 1839. In his widely accepted racial hierarchy, Indians were in competition with Africans/Black Americans for the lowest place in the "great chain of being" (Benedict 1940). The criterion he established was the measurement of cranial capacity, or imputed brain size (and therefore intellect); his biased studies are now known to have been pseudoscientific and misleading (Gould 1981). What Morton proved was his own Eurocentric belief in western European superiority.

Most nineteenth-century "white" Americans believed in the mission, preordained by their God, to conquer and Christianize the native peoples, who with other people of color were of lower intellect and culture. In this endeavor, Euro-Americans often saw advantages in using their racialized categorizations to pit confused "half-breeds" against "full bloods" who were resisting western expansion. Among some non-Indian people, there even arose a preference for "mixed blood" leadership over more traditional "full blood" ranks, as it was believed the "mixed bloods" were more willing to assimilate "white men's ways."

This racist dichotomization was even seen as a solution to the Indian "problem" by a group of liberal white educators and policymakers who flourished in the late nineteenth and early twentieth centuries and called themselves "Friends of the Indians" (compared to those military and government leaders who wanted to keep on killing Indians) (Harmon 1991). They encouraged intermarriage between whites and Indians to facilitate the assimilation of native peoples. Nevertheless, there were many exceptions to the image of "mixed bloods" as being more assimilationist. Quanah Parker, a "half-breed" Comanche, and Captain Jack, a "mixed blood" leader among the Modoc and Klamath, both led resistance to European encroachment at the same time that they worked to negotiate peace.

In her well-researched work of historical literature *Mean Spirit* (1990), Linda Hogan depicts the dynamics of the racist categorizing of "mixed" and "full bloods" during the Removal and Allotment years when Indians from the southeast United States were moved to Oklahoma and other western "territories." Government agents would declare "incompetent" certain "full bloods," thereby denying them allotment payments for land taken from them. At the same time, the agents declared other Indians "disqualified" for payments due to their being "mixed blood." In these scenarios, non-Indians got both cash and land by duplicitous acts, which sometimes went as far as the murder of Indian allotees.

Ecological Racism

What I refer to as ecological racism is the outcome of the cycle of exploitation and destruction of Native Americans and their societies accomplished through the U.S. expropriation and use of their homelands. This process of conquest and colonization involved "treaty making" as well as military exploits and European settler encroachment. The process of treatying with the Indians recognized them as sovereign entities but resulted in the U.S. government violating every one of the approximately four hundred treaties made with the various tribal nations.

Vine Deloria, Jr., today's senior Indian scholar of federal Indian law, has concluded that the American colonists, as British rebels and "traitors," were concerned from the beginning with their international standing. At the same time that the colonists expected Indians to be contained and controlled, the early Republic also pursued treaties with the Indians in order to "legitimate" their conquest of this country in the eyes of other sovereign nations.

> While reciting polite phrases about the equality of man, the American revolutionaries were clearly outside the law of civilized societies in their revolt, and to gain respectability they adopted the most respectable posture towards Indians possible (in rhetoric that is), with the hope that by their ability to act in traditionally political terms they could allay the fears of other nations so as to legitimate their activities. (Deloria 1979:22–23; see also Robbins 1992)

During the nineteenth century, expansionist demands led to the wars between Indians and settlers on the Great Plains. Here theological convictions underlay a "romantic racial nationalism" (Horsman 1981), and scientific racism supported "the metaphysics of Indian-hating" (Drinnon 1990). Indian populations were decimated, only to recover their numerical growth in the twentieth century (Thornton 1987). In this process, the extermination and conquest of Indians led to the reservation system. This involved the United States in treaty making with the approximately four hundred nations, now referred to as tribes. "Reservation" originally meant to contain Indians within designated boundaries on semiarid land in order to remove them from the path of "pioneer" settlement on more valued land. As it later became apparent that the reserved Indian lands were of value to whites (for purposes including, eventually, oil and uranium exploitation), fraud and federal duplicity made them available for non-Indian settlement.

These maneuvers were accomplished in Supreme Court decisions as well as in federal Indian legislation. Churchill, building on such predecessors as Cohen (1982) and Deloria and Lytle (1983), has pointed out how a *bilateral* relationship between Indian nations and the U.S. government, originally based on the precedents of international treaty law, was reconstructed as *unilateral* subordination restricting Indian national autonomy. Two of the earliest milestone cases in federal Indian law were the Cherokee cases, *Cherokee v. Georgia* (1831) and *Worcester v. Georgia* (1832), in which Supreme Court Chief Justice John Marshall declared all Indians groups "domestic dependent nations," and therefore "wards of the government." This judgment allowed for U.S. government expropriation of their lands. Churchill cites the 1903 *Lonewolf v. Hitchcock* Supreme Court case that for the first time designated native nations as "tribes"; it held that "the U.S. enjoyed a 'right' to disregard any treaty obligation to Indians it found 'inconvenient,' but that the remaining treaty provisions continued to be binding on the Indians." This further undermined the original bilateral treaty relationship, and, violating constitutional as well as international law, left the Court "free to unilaterally 'interpret' each treaty as being a bill of sale rather than a rental agreement" (Churchill 1992–93:413 n. 26).

In another work, Churchill (1992b) expounds on how the United States wielded plenary power over the affairs of conquered indigenous nations by the use of duplicity in the guise of legal language. Treaties and other agreements were made from the time of the early Republic to insure the right of tribal nations to handle their own affairs, in short, tribal sovereignty. An extensive record of interventionist federal legislation and mandates, however, has systematically diminished this indigenous sovereignty (Churchill and Morris 1992). Among such key laws were:

- 1789, Northwest Ordinance
- 1790–1834, Trade and Intercourse Acts
- 1830, The Indian Removal Act
- 1885, The Major Crimes Act
- 1887, The General Allotment Act (Dawes Act)
- 1924, The Indian Citizenship Act
- 1934, The Indian Reorganization Act
- 1946, The Indian Claims Commission Act
- 1953, The Termination Act
- 1956, The Relocation Act
- 1968, The Indian Civil Rights Act
- 1971, The Alaska Native Claims Settlement Act (ANSCA)[4]

Today, Native American groups on the reservations experience the culmination of ecological racism. It has led to indigenous homelands becoming expendable Indian lands, and indigenous peoples becoming in effect national sacrifice peoples in a final modern-day stage of the "New World" conquest.

The Bureau of Indian Affairs (BIA), housed in the U.S. Department of Interior, has been the vehicle for implementing federal decisions, made to benefit corporate interests, which bring ecological blight upon reservation-based tribal communities. Indians today find that the U.S. government diverts their water and other resources to service the needs of mainstream populations and cities, which flagrantly violates their first claim on water rights and natural resources. Through constricting the acknowledged size of Indian populations by terminating some Indians as legal entities while relocating others off the reservations in cities, the government does not meet its obligations to reserve first rights of resource usage to Indians. This permits siphoning off artificially created "surpluses" to non-Indian agricultural, ranching, municipal, and industrial uses in the arid West (Guerrero 1992). The same principles are utilized in the assignment of fishing quotas in the Pacific Northwest, a matter related directly to the prosperity of the lucrative non-Indian fishing industry there (Institute for Natural Progress 1992).

Women of All Red Nations (WARN), a North American Indian women's organization, called attention to some of the worst scenarios of ecological racism at its 1993 conference, "Genocide of Indigenous Peoples in North America." Issues highlighted included:

- The Dann sisters' attempt to defend their right to raise cattle on their Shoshone ancestral lands, now the Nevada Test Site. Backed by tribal leadership, they have challenged the U.S. Bureau of Land Management's claim that the land is no longer theirs, countering that it was taken from them illegally. Despite threats from federal and state authorities, the family remains on their land.
- The Columbia River Project, where nuclear wastes from the Hanford Nuclear Reactor were placed in unstable containers and have leaked into Columbia River. It is believed that the project has contaminated the water table of the Yakima Nation in Washington State, and Indians are in the vanguard of protest around the project.
- The planned Canada–U.S. $60 billion hydroelectric plant in James Bay, Quebec. Just one of many dams that have flooded native lands in North America, this major facility that will bring power to forty-eight U.S. states at the expense of indigenous populations would destroy four major river systems and deforest 356,000 square miles. Already, the first phase has brought mercury soil poisoning and caribou drownings on surrounding Cree and Inuit lands.

Earlier, WARN (1992) pointed to Indian grievances motivated by the 1978 American Indian Religious Freedom Act. One is against the Columbus Project, a $200 million observatory to be built on Mount Graham, near Tucson, by the University of Arizona in collaboration with the Roman Catholic church. This site is sacred to the San Carlos Apache, who are protesting in the area. Another is the Dickson Mounds conflict in which, after pressure from a large Indian demonstration, the governor of Illinois has ordered that the doors to exhibit an Indian ancestral burial at the mounds be closed to tourists and school groups. As in struggles around other archaeological digs and repatriation protests, Indians fear the governor's action is only temporary, and that the site will be reopened when the furor dies down.

Winona LaDuke, in collaboration with Churchill (1992) have coined the term "radioactive colonization" for the ecological racism that targets reservation lands and their peoples *first* for uranium and other toxic development projects. They note the scenario of duplicity in federal "trusteeship" over Indian peoples and their rights. Among the most notorious cases have been the Four Corners area on Navajo land, Black

Mesa in Hopi territory, and Laguna Pueblo (also known as Acoma Sky City) in New Mexico, which the Nixon administration officially but not publicly designated "national sacrifice areas" (Churchill and LaDuke 1992:253). This example of ecological racism was rationalized, like earlier instances of Manifest Destiny, as for the common good and in the nation's best interest, which benefits non-Indians at the expense of native peoples on reservation lands.

Bureaucratic Racism

A bureaucratic maze of federal and state obfuscation and duplicity not only deals with Native land but operates to define who may or may not be recognized as Indian. Hence, one aftermath of the five-hundred-year heritage of colonialist ideological and legal constructions of American Indians is the continuing struggle against federal policies that determine who we are. It remains true not only that the U.S. government continues to control all Indian land and natural resources, but also that we are the most regulated and controlled people in the country, both on and off the reservations.

The policing of "American Indian blood," propelled by nineteenth century scientific racism and implemented by bureaucrats, is at odds with the still-surviving kinship and cultural traditions of native peoples (see Jaimes 1992a). It is an example of *institutionalized racism,* those "processes which, intentionally or not, result in the continued exclusion of a subordinate group [and] . . . activities and practices which are intended to protect the advantages of the dominant group and/or maintain or widen the unequal position of a subordinate group" (Miles 1989:50). The intricate system of bureaucratic racism has been wrought as a result of the U.S. government treatment of indigenous populations as a colonized people in their own homelands.

This is blatantly manifest in how the government determines American Indian identification. Against a diversity of internal tribal membership criteria, the government imposes its external identification processes, implemented and regulated by several agencies of the bureaucracy. In addition, more recently the government has allowed an individual of intertribal descent to claim recognition as Indian through only one parent's tribal affiliations, and that tribe must have "federal recognition" (Jaimes 1990a).

The development of recorded tribal rolls is a result of conquest and the historical transformation of bilateral Indian nation–U.S. government relations into unilateral subordination. The BIA was originally established in 1820 in the Office of War and was later transferred to the

Department of Interior. Most tribes have had to succumb to the formal enrollment process in order to insure federal recognition via the BIA. Today, some tribes require birth on the reservation, and others have grandfather clauses that extend membership to all descendants of a person identified as Indian before a certain date, regardless of other personal circumstances. Certain tribal roll policies, distinct from traditional customs of kinship and culture, have been influenced by and formed in reaction to federal "blood quantum" rules implemented by the BIA. Indian quasi-national entities may designate varying requirements of blood compared to the BIA quarter-blood criterion. Some, such as the Oklahoma Cherokee, do not have a blood quantum threshold, but new applicants for enrollment still have to meet BIA standards; and the stipulated proportion varies from quarter-blood to none at all among the Sioux (Lakota, Dakota, Oglala, Hunkpapa, Santee, etc.) (see Jaimes 1990a:159–238). Traditional approaches to determine indigenous nationhood also persist, officially and unofficially, in contrast to the racist blood quantum criteria that have resulted from colonization.

The blood quantum formulation was first introduced in the General Allotment (or Dawes) Act of 1887, which mandated all persons eligible for individual land allotments must be of "one half or more Indian blood" (see Jaimes 1992a:123–138; McDonnell 1991). This legislation was designed to break up the communal land base by dividing land among individual tribe members so as to coerce them into "white man's civilization." The hidden agenda, soon apparent, was to co-opt land for non-Indian usage. Indians who failed as farmers either sold or leased their allotments to whites. Some white males married Indian women in order to inherit their allotments legally as the head of a patriarchal family, and a few Indian wives even died under suspicious circumstances (Weatherford 1991:19–36). As a result of trusteeship by their federal guardian, Indian land lost through the Dawes Act is estimated at some 100 million acres, or two-thirds of the 1887 land base. In addition, once "blooded" Indians were allotted, the BIA opened up remaining "surplus" lands to non-Indian settlement. Finally, in the 1928 Merriam Report to the U.S. Congress, it came to light that many non-Indians had been placed on the 1887 Dawes rolls by the chicanery of BIA commissioners; the Cherokees are chided more than most for the Dawes rolls rise.

As a result of all these practices, today Indian communities such as the Oklahoma Cherokees are checkerboarded, with non-Indian holdings dispersed among those of descendants of Indian allotees. There are many contemporary cases of divisive conflict arising out of the dispossession and bureaucratic racism of the Dawes Act legacy. Holly Youngbear-Tibbetts (1991) discusses the "perplexing issue of blood quantum as a legal doctrine" in the Minnesota White Earth land claims case where "full bloods" have been pitted against "mixed bloods" as a result of federal intervention in traditional communal considerations about rights of tribal members. In addition, following a 1978 BIA research contract that led to validation of some thirteen hundred Chippewa land title claims, "interracial tensions' with the surrounding non-Indian community have also flared. "While institutional racism and mutual suspicion have long marked relations between the Anishanaabeg and their Anglo neighbors, current levels have reached unprecedented heights. The impetus lies, predictably enough, in conflicting claims to reservation lands that were brought to community attention" after 1978 (Youngbear-Tibbetts 1991:93).

The BIA implements regulations set by the secretary of interior, the top federal authority on Indian affairs (none of whom, incidentally, has been an Indian). BIA policy has held, for the most part, to reservation-based, federally recognized, and one-quarter blood quantum criteria for determination of group and individual designation as "real" Indians. BIA bureaucrats have focused narrowly on blood quantum in administering the Johnson-O'Malley programs for public schools with Indian student populations, developed since the Snyder Act of 1921. As mandated American citizens since the Indian Citizenship Act of 1924, which was promoted by the Friends of the Indians to foster "Americanization," all Indians are subject to the provisions of the U.S. Constitution and to other laws that protect minority populations. This narrow interpretation of who is Indian, and therefore a minority-group member, has provoked heated response from many Indian spokespersons. Some even call blood-quantum criteria a "racist policy" utilized to manipulate eligibility in order to deny services to Indian children of less than one-quarter blood, as well as a kind of genocide of native peoples and their cultures.[5]

The pseudoscientific BIA blood quantum formula today is still viewed as racist by many Indians, as well as by many non-Indians who are even aware of it. It is causing ludicrous but serious problems for the younger Indian generations. Under federal regulations, the offspring of intertribal marriages can claim only one-half of their Indian parentage on only one of their parents' tribal rolls. To illustrate, a child of "one-half blood" Navajo (Dine) and "one-half blood" Sioux (Lakota) parents can be federally recognized on only one tribal roll, making him or her officially a "one-quarter blood quantum Indian." There are many other cases equally as absurd, especially in the "less than quarter blood" categories.[6] The result is that many Indians have to submit to the social and psychological oppression of the query "What kind of Indian are you?"—

that is, if we are not prepared to challenge the ahistorical and racist nature of U.S. determination that controls Indian identity.

In the legal arena, the 1985 *Zarr v. Barlow, et al.* decision involved a California Indian woman who sued the BIA for denying her federal Indian benefits because she was "less than quarter-blood." Recognized by her own Sherwood Valley Pomo tribe as a member on its roll, Diana Zarr won her case on the grounds of racial discrimination and the right of Pomo sovereignty in such internal affairs (Native American Rights Fund 1985). This case should have set a precedent for similar grievances, but during the Reagan-Bush years an ultraconservative trend went in the other direction. It appears that many similar cases are now settled out of court. Recently, it seems that the higher up in the judicial system a case goes, the more likely a pro-Indian position is to lose. This is borne out by Supreme Court decisions on American Indian religious freedom violations, in the 1988 *Lyng v. Northwest Indian Cemetery Protective Association* and the 1990 *Employment Division, Department of Human Resources v. Smith* cases, where Indian positions have been overruled (Deloria 1992).

Federal recognition also leads to racist implementation of bureaucratic procedure at the individual level when an Indian is from a nonrecognized tribe. This applies to several California groups, where eighteen treaties were "lost." Other groups, such as the Lumbee (Blu 1980), have state recognition but have been refused federal recognition. Still others did not ratify treaties, often for political reasons, or were terminated or declared extinct (among others, some California mission bands in 1971). Federal recognition has also been affected by decisions of the 1946–1979 Indian Land Claims Commission; this body was created in response to negative international publicity on U.S. treatment of its native populations, but it has a bad reputation among many Indians because of charges of fraud in its decisions (see Churchill 1992–93:197–215; Deloria and Lytle 1983; Jaimes 1987).

In northern California, the Hoopa-Yurok multitribe and mixed-blood settlement of 1876 resulted in a joint tribal government, with membership originally based on geography, not blood. For political reasons, the Yurok did not join the congressionally approved "tribe" under the 1934 Indian Reorganization Act. A Hoopa faction was awarded federal recognition, with a greater share of land than the "mixedbloods," who lost the best land and resources. Under the Reagan administration, the Hoopa were able to renounce their "non-Indian" Yurok relations, although a legal challenge to this is still pending (Davis 1992).

All persons claiming American Indian descent as eligibility for federal Indian entitlements have to produce a "Certificate with Degree of

Indian Blood" issued by a BIA regional agency; this suffices, regardless of whether or not they are recognized by their tribal communities according to traditional kinship or have been excluded as a result of tribal partisan politics (see Jaimes 1990a). The situation was exacerbated politically during the Bush years by implementation of the Indian Arts and Crafts Act of 1990, which makes it a crime to publically identify oneself as American Indian when selling artwork, or for a gallery to exhibit art as "Indian" if the artist cannot provide federal certification. Supposedly an expansion of 1930s legislation protecting Indian artisans, this bill was solicited by David Bradley, a certified Indian himself and a little-known artist residing in Santa Fe before 1990. It was introduced by white Arizona congressman John Kyl and supported by the recently BIA-certified Indian (and jewelry designer) Colorado congressman (now senator) Ben Nighthorse Campbell.[7]

Since passage of the bill, mediocre but certified "Indian" artists have become a self-serving Indian identity police, traveling around the country to denounce non–federally certified Indian artists whom they perceive as competitors. Bradley criticizes anyone who disagrees with his myopic politics and stereotypes of Native art and culture; his hit list includes famed Cherokee artist and activist Jimmie Durham, who for reasons of political principle refused to be processed as a certified Indian by the BIA (Churchill 1991). The new law led in December 1992 to the closing of the Muskogee Museum in Oklahoma because it was named in honor of a noncertified Cherokee. BIA Indian certification also works the other way, when instant Indians are created, as was the case with the Bush-appointed BIA commissioner Ed Brown, who was certified a Pascua Yaqui *after* his Department of Interior designation.

The implications of the arts and crafts bill go far beyond the Indian art market. The self-ordained Indian identity police have begun to spread rumors and spurious allegations on university campuses and in other institutions about persons whom they claim are imposters "masquerading as real Indians." Those on their hit lists are accused of "ethnic fraud" (see Cook-Lynn 1993), often behind closed doors, in private phone calls, and in secret meetings that include those of hiring committees in U.S. institutions.[8] The motivations for such actions appear to include jealousy, envy, mean-spiritedness, and self-interested careerism. The targets face the loss of job opportunities, professional credibility, and their integrity as they become suspect of what is interpreted as "ethnic fraud." They are forced to prove themselves "real Indians" by producing the documents called for by their accusers. In some cases, even BIA certification may not suffice, as the Indian identity agents, motivated by tribal and male-dominated partisan politics, demand federally recognized tribal affiliation.

As a result of federal initiatives, twentieth-century interstate migration patterns have produced an American Indian diaspora in which it is estimated that most of the native population now lives in urban areas, with the highest concentration in the megametropolitan dystopia called Los Angeles (Churchill 1992a; Jaimes 1990b). From the 1940s to the 1960s, America's Indians were out of public sight for the most part; they remained contained on reservations or became visible only as alcoholics is urban ghettos. The Relocation policy, begun in the 1940s and implemented through the BIA, moved individual Indians and families off reservations to major cities. Indians were portrayed as recipients of a benevolent federal effort to depart from high unemployment and Third World-like conditions on the reservation, and to improve their lot by mainstream assimilation. But the real motive was for the government to reduce its monetary obligations to reservation-based Indians, who remained wards of the federal system (Jaimes 1990a:100–158; 1990b). With the legal termination of tribes during the 1950s, Relocation resulted in a high concentration of Indians, most now non–federally recognized, in the urban anonymity of megacities.

In recognition of this situation, the "Kennedy Report" (U.S. Senate 1969; cf. Jaimes 1990b) led to a definition broader than the BIA criteria for Indian eligibility under the new Indian Education Act (IEA) programs passed during the 1970s, administered by the Office of Indian Education (OIE) in the Department of Education. The IEA does not include a blood quantum requirement, but it too is in the business of federal certification of who is a real Indian. It builds upon BIA and U.S. census procedures, thus restricting an individual who claims Indian identity from any other minority racial category, often at the expense of "mixed bloods" and children of intermarriages who fall between the socioracial cracks (Forbes 1990).[9] The federal government's ahistorical bureaucratic racism comes full circle here—in treaties during the 1700s and 1800s Indian nations recognized "mixed blood" members, and some agreements even included stipulations for them, supported by tribal leaders, in order to protect them from dispossession by their U.S. treaty partner (Cohen 1982; Deloria and Lytle 1983).

Toward Indigenous Liberation

It has been ironic that the increasing number of Indian individuals, usually male, who find themselves in one of this nation's many prisons seem to have more freedom to proclaim themselves Indian behind bars than do those walking the streets of this supposed free society (Hilligoss 1987).[10] Recently, however, the federal prison system began to require

Indian inmates of both genders to show BIA certification of tribal enrollment in a "federally recognized" tribe.

Periodically the federal government has threatened to dismantle the BIA, the OIE, and other federal Indian programs. During the Bush years, the case for BIA termination was led by Senator Daniel Inouye, who holds an influential position that impacts American Indians and other indigenous peopes as chair of the Senate Select Committee on Indian Affairs.[11] Anti-Indian congressional campaigns are particularly evident in times of economic recession. The Reagan-Bush years actually contributed to Indian unrest by ruthless budget cuts of Indian services and programs. Such threats and moves are often followed by Indian protests, especially because they violate federal obligations due Native groups under U.S. treaties (Jaimes 1990a).

Still, many Indians believe it is to their benefit to be controlled and regulated under the bestowal of federal recognition. Terminated and nontreaty tribes continue to seek the immediate, if short-term, gains of federal education, health, and housing programs that this status is meant to bring (Jaimes 1990a). But tribal groups and Native individuals are also discovering that federal recognition brings federal dependency and federal intervention in internal tribal affairs, and that the effort to achieve federal recognition involves onerous legal expenses and the building of partisan political support and is a time-consuming bureaucratic process with no guarantee of success.

Cases in point include the Pascua Yaquis, on the margin of Tucson, who enlisted non-Indian Arizona politicians in a ten-year struggle for their 1978 federal recognition. They have taken almost as long to have their tribal constitution endorsed by the federal government, which has held up federal funds for community services and development. Other Yaqui communities remain non–federally recognized, and several, such as Vista del Sol in Scottsdale, Arizona, in the 1970s have been bulldozed over as eyesores to the elite suburbs adjacent to them. On the other hand, the North Carolina Lumbees were denied federal recognition partly because of political pressure from a coalition of federally recognized tribes, mostly in the Northeast, who have yet to explain their motives for opposing clearly overdue Lumbee recognition (see Blu 1980). The California mission band Juaneños (of which I am a BIA-certified member) has also been pursuing this strenuous quest. In these times of shrinking budgets, however, it is not likely that the government will be adding to its list of federally recognized tribal groups.

There is a long-held myth that all Indians receive annual or monthly tax-exempt government payments. This is fueled by Indian hate groups pushing for anti-Indian federal legislation, and for state control of Indian lands and resources. The cost of federal dependency may be greater in the long run, with escalating federal and state controls over internal Indian affairs, and for non–federally recognized groups, with the depletion of community resources in the attempt to achieve it. Many have already learned the hard way that what Congress gives to the Indian it can, and does, just as easily take away, even when legally obligated not to by treaty (Churchill 1983; Deloria and Lytle 1983, 1984).

Recently, certain Indian tribal leaders have been supporting new narrowly defined and restrictive federal Indian identification legislation. They appear to be motivated by self-interest, and group ethnocentrism, as well as by a realistic perception of a shrinking federal beneficence. Such Indian representatives are apparently willing to deny other Indians their heritage and ancestry, as well as federal services, based on a narrow construction of Indian identity. And several of these "Indian" spokespersons have only attained federal certification or tribal affiliation very recently themselves—and so can be called instant Indians—for political expediency in both federal and tribal partisan politics. It seems to be the case that such self-designated Indian spokespersons are actually the brokers for concessions to the federal authorities who in turn cast them as champions of Indian peoples. There are also U.S. court cases on the books under which Native women are more likely than men to lose their tribal status if they marry outside the tribe, either to a member of another tribe or a non-Indian, regardless of matrilineal tradition (e.g., *Santa Clara Pueblo v. Martinez;* see Jaimes, with Halsey 1992).

On the other hand, there has always been a significant voice among Indian peoples that is against any abuse by the non-Indian apparatus in identification procedures which lead to the denial of rights. In both reservation and other rural and urban communities, kinship traditions are still in practice to determine group membership. On this basis, there is Indian opposition to the new identification legislation; it is seen as another strategy in the long record of colonial intervention among Indian peoples, and especially in its dire consequences for the younger generation who marry and move outside the tribal community (Gonzales 1992).

In times when reservation-based leadership, federal and regional politics, and national deficits generate exclusion of "ineligible" Indians, it is important that the mass of urban Indians, the most disenfranchised and dispossessed among us, be recognized for their contribution to Indian resistance and survival. This is most apparent in the so-called Pan-Indian movement, which actually is composed of intertribal political alliances that have demanded Indian civil rights and been in the forefront of grassroots struggles for Indian sovereignty (Thomas 1972). Since the 1960s, these movements have drawn membership from ghettoized urban Indians, many of whom have been lost in anonymity and apathy, resulting in their invisibility to mainstream society (Szaz 1977; U.S. Senate 1969).

With the rise of "Pan-Indian" nationalist agendas, major events have taken place under the coordination of such urban-centered organizations as the American Indian Movement (AIM). They have drawn attention to the plight of Indians on the reservation, often with local grass-roots alliances and support, as in the Wounded Knee Siege of 1973 (Churchill and Vander Wall 1988). The 1972 "On the Trail of Broken Treaties" AIM campaign resulted in the occupation of the Washington, D.C., BIA headquarters. Its "Twenty Points" declaration, among other grievances and demands, condemned the federal blood quantum criteria as cultural "genocide" and called on all Indians to oppose it (Akwesasne Notes 1973).

As new strategems are designed to dispossess us of what is left of being Indian, we are told to give up the last vestiges of our "Indianness" and compete like everyone else for what we have never been allowed since the European invasion—our own liberation. But liberation from colonization requires self-sufficiency and self-determination—subsistance economies instead of the cash economy that has eroded our agricultural sustainability, and self-governance in our internal affairs (Jaimes 1992b). In resisting the racist oppression of BIA certification that undermines our sense of self, it may come to pass that we need to seek "political asylum" on reservations, among our own relations, to redress this society's negation of who we are, and for our genuine ontology of being.

At the same time, American Eurocentrism is becoming globalized through economic domination and political hegemony. This especially impacts on Third World countries with their concentration of indigenous peoples, even within native homelands, and foments counterresistances internationally. There is a need for alliances with organizations of Native peoples and other disenfranchised and dispossessed groups, in order to fight high-tech, even computer-assisted, racism and other forms of oppression. We need alternative movements that envision our cultural and historical diversity as mutually respectful, and that seek to dismantle Eurocentric power and "white" supremacy.

These liberation struggles require recovery of indigenous land and resources, reassertion of genuine self-determination, and reconstitution of Native cultural lifeways, worldviews, and kinship traditions. Hence, within this settler-state legacy and the present state of Native America, indigenous peoples must resist being relegated as relics of the past, our cultures becoming fossilized artifacts, and our ancestors viewed as mythological creatures. Because we are indigenous to the Americas, our cultural identity is rooted in the land, in the environment, in our nationhood, and, when all else seems lost, in preservation of the ethos and integrity of our indigenism. As we enter the twenty-first century in these divisive but challenging times for Native peoples throughout the Americas, a liberation movement of indigenism must take pride in our traditional Native ancestry and heritage. It must also work toward dismantling U.S. colonialism and racism, not at the expense of one for another, but for the liberation of humanity at large.

Notes

I would like to acknowledge the Society for the Humanities at Cornell University for a research fellowship (academic year 1991–92) and the Rockefeller Foundation for an international scholar's residency (summer of 1993 in Bellagio, Italy), which provided support for completion of my work on this issue. I am preparing an anthology on the subject, entitled *American Indians, American Justice,* to be published in 1996.

1. These little-known events could have easily been forgotten if it was not for a recent book about the case by Rodney Barker, *The Broken Circle* (1992), which includes details of the aftermath of the incident for Navajos and other Indians, the local townspeople, and the murderers.

2. There is no empirical evidence, as even some Indian feminists attempt to claim, that traditional precontact indigenous societies were "matriarchies" (see Jaimes, with Halsey 1992).

3. Churchill (1992–93) correlates Manifest Destiny doctrine with the later German Nazi ideological concept of *Lebensraum,* the need for "living space," used to justify World War II and the Holocaust. Indeed, Hitler expressed interest in the earlier U.S. genocide of Indian peoples and their cultures as a model to be emulated in his extermination of the Jews and other "undesirables." Churchill (1986) carries this "Western" saga one step further in examining how the concentration of tribal groups into "homelands" by South Africa's white racist leaders under apartheid was influenced by the U.S. system of Indian reservations.

4. For details, and for additional laws and significant court cases with jurisdictional decisions systematically eroding tribal sovereignty from 1810 to the present, see Churchill and Morris 1992.

5. See Jaimes 1990a, which refers to Frank A. Ryan's 1979 position paper for the BIA and the Department of Education Indian Education Program, "A Working Paper Prepared for the National Advisory Council on Indian Education"; on Reagan-era restrictions, see also Chief Charles Dawes, "Tribal Leaders See Danger in Use to Blood Quantum as Eligibility Standards," *Uset Calumet* (bulletin of southern and eastern tribes), February–March 1986, 7–8, later reprinted in *National Indian Health Board Health Report;* and Ron Martz, "Indians Decry

Verification Plan for Federally-funded Health Care," *Cox News Service,* October 7, 1986.

6. A Mohawk graduate student who wants to remain anonymous told me how difficult it is in today's tribal councils to hold to rigid restrictions on tribal membership, based even on "quarter blood" criteria, since when one begins tracing descent by biological kinship there are very few members who can meet the federal standard. He was hired by his tribe in Canada to record these lineages, among other things.

7. Known as Ben "Nightmare" Campbell to his Indian critics, this legislator had shown no interest and accumulated no record in Indian affairs before his 1992 senatorial race. Since then he gained notoriety with his appearance on horseback and in full Plains Indian regalia in a recent Columbus Day parade, arousing the animosity of Native peoples across the country who see Columbus as an imperialist invader and slave trader.

8. Cook-Lynn does not take a position for or against the statement on "ethnic fraud" that she reports.

9. According to Gonzales (1992), approximately 50 percent of American Indians marry outside their tribe, either intertribally or with non-Indians with male exogamy rates slightly higher than those of females. Native women tend to marry intertribally, while Native men usually marry non-Indians.

10. D. G. Hilligoss is a spokesperson for native people's prison rights. This point was also emphasized by George Tinker, a political prisoner–activist and Lutheran minister of Living Waters Church, Denver, as a guest speaker for a law school seminar at the University of Colorado, Boulder, April 8, 1993.

11. See "Hawaiian Sovereignty: Decision Time," *Honolulu Advertiser,* January 6, 1992. Senator Inouye, of Japanese-American ethnicity, is seen as a collaborator with whites by Native Hawaiians who support traditional issues and agendas, including scholar-activist Haunani-Kay Trask. Since he works against their concerns, Inouye is termed "oho'o haole" (honorary white man). Native Hawaiians have to meet a 50 percent blood quantum standard in the islands (see Trask 1993).

References

Acuña, Rudolfo. 1988. *Occupied America: The History of Chicanos* 3d ed. New York: HarperCollins.

Akwesasne Notes. 1973. *BIA, I'm Not Your Indian Anymore.* Roosevelt, N.Y.: Akwesasne Notes.

Barker, Rodney. 1992. *The Broken Circle.* New York: Simon and Schuster.

Benedict, Ruth. 1940. *Race: Science and Politics.* New York: Modern Age.

Blu, Karen. 1980. *The Lumbee Problem: The Making of an American Indian People.* New York: Cambridge University Press.

Churchill, Ward. 1983. Implications of Treaty Relationships between the United States of America and Various American Indian Nations. Briefing paper for Colorado Commission on Indian Affairs, July.

———. 1986. Genocide: Towards a Functional Definition. *Alternative Press: Social Transformations and Humane Governance* 2: 403–430.

———. 1992a. Like Sand in the Wind: The Making of an American Indian Diaspora in the (U.S.). Paper presented at "Colors of the Diaspora: International Conference on Race and Ethnicity in Comparative Perspective," April 23–25, University of Colorado, Boulder.

———. 1992b. Naming Our Destiny: Towards a Language of Liberation. *Global Justice* 3(2/3): 22–33.

———. 1992c. Since Predator Came: A Survey of Native North America since 1492. *Current Wisdom* 1(1): 5–7, 24–28.

———. 1992–1993. *Struggle for the Land: Indigenous Resistance to Genocide, Ecocide, and Expropriation.* Monroe, Maine.: Common Courage.

———. 1993. Nobody's Pet Poodle: Jimmie Durham, an Artist for Native North America. In *Indians Are Us?* Monroe, Maine: Common Courage.

Churchill, Ward, and Glenn Morris. 1992. Key Indian Laws and Cases. In *The State of Native America,* ed. M. Annette Jaimes, 13–21.

Churchill, Ward, and Jim Vander Wall. 1988. *Agents of Repression: The FBI's Secret Wars on the Black Panther Party and the American Indian Movement.* Boston: South End.

Churchill, Ward, and Winona LaDuke. 1992. Native America: The Political Economy of Radioactive Colonization. In *The State of Native America,* ed. M. Annette Jaimes, 241–266.

Cohen, Felix S. 1982. *Handbook of Federal Indian Law.* Albuquerque: University of New Mexico Press, 1942. Reprint.

Cook-Lynn, Elizabeth. 1993. Meeting of Indian Professors Takes Up Issues of "Ethnic Fraud," Sovereignty, and Research Needs. *Wicazo Sa Review* 9(1): 57–59.

Davis, Susan E. 1992. Tribal Rights, Tribal Wrongs: Hoopa, Yurok, and Congress. *Nation,* March 23, 376–380.

Deloria, Vine, Jr. 1979. *A Brief History of the Federal Responsibility to the American Indians.* Washington, D.C.: Office of Education, Department of Health, Education and Welfare.

———. 1992. Trouble in High Places: Erosion of American Indian Rights to Religious Freedom in the United States. In *The State of Native America,* ed. M. Annette Jaimes, 267–290.

Deloria, Vine, Jr., and C. M. Lytle. 1983. *American Indians, American Justice.* Austin: University of Texas Press.

———. 1984. *The Nations Within: The Past and Future of American Indian Sovereignty.* New York: Pantheon.

DeMolins, Edmond. 1899. *Anglo-Saxon Superiority: To What It Is Due.* Trans. Louis Bert-Lavigne. New York: Leadenhall.

Drinnon, Richard. 1990. *Facing West: The Metaphysics of Indian-Hating and Empire Building.* New York: Schocken.

Eggan, Fred, ed. 1955. *Social Anthropology of North American Tribes.* Enl. ed. Chicago: University of Chicago Press.

Forbes, Jack D. 1990. Undercounting Native Americans: The 1980 Census and the Manipulation of Racial Identity in the United States. *Wicazo Sa Review* 6(1): 2–26.

———. 1993. *Africans and Native Americans: The Language of Race and the Evolution of Red-Black Peoples.* 2d ed. Urbana: University of Illinois Press.

Gonzales, Sandy. 1992. Intermarriage and Assimilation: The Beginning or the End? *Wicazo Sa Review* 8(2): 48–52.

Gould, Stephen Jay. 1981. *The Mismeasure of Man.* New York: Norton.

Guerrero, Marianna. 1992. American Indian Water Rights: The Blood of Life in Native North America. In *The State of Native America,* ed. M. Annette Jaimes, 189–215.

Harmon, Alexandra. 1991. When Is an Indian Not an Indian? "Friends of the Indian" and the Problem of Indian Identity. *Journal of Ethnic Studies* 18 (2): 95–123.

Hilligoss, D. G. 1987. Racism, Cultural Genocide, and the Case of Native Americans' Religious Freedom. Oklahoma State Penitentiary. Files of author.

Hogan, Linda. 1990. *Mean Spirit.* New York: Atheneum.

Horsman, Reginald. 1981. *Race and Manifest Destiny: The Origins of American Racial Anglo-Saxonism.* Cambridge, Mass.: Harvard University Press.

Institute for Natural Progress. 1992. In Usual and Accustomed Places: Contemporary American Indian Fishing Rights Struggles. In *The State of Native America,* ed. M. Annette Jaimes, 217–239.

Jaimes, M. Annette. 1987. The Pit River Indian Land Claim Disputes in Northern California. *Journal of Ethnic Studies* 4(4): 47–64.

———. 1990a. *Federal Indian Identification Policy.* Ph.D. diss., Arizona State University.

———. 1990b. The Hollow Icon: An American Indian Analysis of the Kennedy Myth and Federal Indian Policy. *Wicazo Sa Review* 7(1): 34–44.

———. 1992a. Federal Indian Indentification Policy: A Usurpation of Indigenous Sovereignty in North America. In *The State of Native America,* ed. Jaimes, 123–138.

———. 1992b. Revisioning Native America: An Indigenist View of Primitivism and Industrialism. *Social Justice* 19 (2): 5–34.

———, ed. 1992c. *The State of Native America: Genocide, Colonization, and Resistance.* Boston: South End.

Jaimes, M. Annette, with Theresa Halsey. 1992. American Indian Women: At the Center of Indigenous Resistance in North America. In *The State of Native America,* ed. Jaimes, 311–344.

McDonnell, Janet. 1991. *The Dispossession of the American Indian, 1887–1934.* Bloomington: University of Indiana Press.

Miles, Robert. 1989. *Racism.* New York: Tavistock.

Native American Rights Fund. 1985. *NARF National Indian Law Library,* December 30.

Peterson, Thomas V. 1978. *Ham and Japeth: The Mythic World of Whites in the Antebellum South.* Metuchen, N.J.: Scarecrow.

Price, Edward. 1953. A Geographic Analysis of White-Negro-Indian Racial Mixtures in the Eastern United States. *Annals of the Association of American Geographers* 43:138–155.

Robbins, Rebecca L. 1992. Self-Determination and Subordination: The Past, Present, and Future of American Indian Governance. In *The State of Native America,* ed. M. Annette Jaimes, 87–121.

Stannard, David E. 1992. *American Holocaust: Columbus and the Conquest of the New World.* New York: Oxford University Press.

Stanton, William. 1960. *The Leopard's Spots: Scientific Attitudes toward Race in America, 1815–59.* Chicago: University of Chicago press.

Stiffarm, Lenore A., with Phil Lane, Jr. 1992. The Demography of Native North America: A Question of American Indian Survival. In *The State of Native America,* ed. M. Annette Jaimes, 23–53.

Szaz, Margaret. 1977. *Education of the American Indian: The Road to Self-Determination.* Albuquerque: University of New Mexico Press.

Tax, Sol. 1955. Some Problems of Social Organization. In *Social Anthropology of North American Tribes,* ed. Fred Eggan, 1–32.

Thomas, Robert K. 1972. Pan-Indianism. In *The Emergent Native Americans: A Reader in Culture Contact,* ed. Deward Walker, 741–746. Boston: Little, Brown.

Thornton, Russell. 1987. *American Indian Holocaust and Survival: A Population History since 1492.* Norman: University of Oklahoma Press.

Trask, Haunani-Kay. 1993. *From a Native Daughter: Colonialism and Sovereignty in Hawai'i.* Monroe, Maine: Common Courage.

U.S. Senate. 1969. *American Indian Education: A National Tragedy—An National Challenge.* Report of the Special Committee on Indian Education of the Committee on Labor and Public Welfare, Senator Edward Kennedy, chair, November 3.

WARN [Women of All Red Nations]. 1992. *WARN April News Bulletin.*

Weatherford, Jack. 1991. *Native Roots: How the Indians Enriched America.* New York: Crown.

Youngbear-Tibbetts, Holly. 1991. Without Due Process: The Alienation of Individual Trust Allotments of the White Earth Ashinaabeg. *American Indian Culture and Research Journal* 15(2): 93–138.

RUTH FRANKENBERG

Whiteness and Americanness: Examining Constructions of Race, Culture, and Nation in White Women's Life Narratives

The project designated in the title of this essay would, I think, be meaningless outside the broad context in which communities and intellectuals of color continue to analyze, redefine, and rearticulate aspects of the racial order. Conversely, the tasks of redefining and rehistoricizing "whiteness" are, it seems to me, vital concomitants of politicocultural struggles around race, from curriculum and canon transformation to the defense and extension of civil rights and racial equality. In other words, I would argue that critical engagements with the racial order must deconstruct and rearticulate whiteness at the same time as recentering the "others" upon whose existence the notion of whiteness depends. From the subject positions of white progressive, or potentially progressive, persons, collective failure to engage both sides of this dialectic can, I think, defuse and confuse participation in critique of racism. In this essay I explore white, U.S. American women's constructions of race, culture, nation, and belonging, drawing on life history interviews undertaken for a study of the social construction of whiteness (Frankenberg 1993). I focus in particular on nine white women, each of whom declared themselves sympathetic to, or involved in, antiracist or promulticultural activity.

It should also be noted that in looking at white women's life narratives I am, of course, engaging specifically *white* constructions of whiteness. These, as bell hooks (1991) among others has pointed out, must be distinguished from, for example, Black constructions of whiteness. I must emphasize too that my argument here about the mutual constitution of whiteness and its discursive others should not be taken as claiming to exhaustively describe the content of the cultural practice of any group—if such were the case, my analysis would be reductive in the extreme. Rather, I intend here to elucidate the structures and contents of a set of (white) discursive constructions of self and other. What is being examined, then, is a particular and delimitable discursive constellation—but one that, like all dominant fictions, is actually more than fiction because of its association with ruling apparatuses.

There was, in these women's narratives, a continual discursive traffic between three sites: "whiteness" as a location of racial dominance; "Americanness" as a location of cultural dominance or normativity within the United States; and "Americanness" as a location of political domination on a global scale. Given this, I focus on the construction of a dominant whiteness in relation to what one might call nondominant whitenesses as much as on whiteness in relation to, so to speak, racial others.

If the women I interviewed are at all representative, white racial subjects (including myself) are in fact repositories of key moments in the last five hundred years of "race-thinking" in North America and beyond, interwoven and entangled in complex ways. Here, I examine three discursive repertoires that shaped these women's words, beginning by schematizing them and then revisiting each repertoire through readings of white women's words.[1]

It is striking that the discursive repertoire most powerful in structuring these women's senses of racial and cultural selfhood and otherness was also the oldest one: that which I will refer to as colonial discourse. The term *colonial discourse* is a broad one, designating the range of conceptual schemata emergent alongside—and enabling—processes of European colonial exploration, expansion, and rule beginning in the late 1400s. (The 1980s saw an outpouring of critical work on the cultural and discursive dimensions of colonialism. As points of entry into the critical study of colonial discourse, Barker et al. 1985, volumes 1 and 2, demonstrate the scope and power of work in the field. Ahmad 1992: 159–219; Parry 1987; and Young 1990 offer critical discussions of key thinkers in the area. It should be noted, however, that a brief referential note such as this one is inevitably selective and limited.) Colonial discourse (like racist discourse) is in many ways heterogeneous rather than univocal, not surprising given the extent and geographical dispersion of European colonizing projects. However, if a common thread runs through the whole range of instances of colonial discourse, it is the construction of alterity along racial and/or cultural lines—the construction of others conceived as fundamentally different from, and inferior to, white European, metropolitan selves (Said 1979). It must also be noted—and this is a point perhaps more difficult to grasp upon first encounter with it—that it is precisely by means of the construction of a range of others that the self or dominant center constitutes itself. White/European self-constitution is, in other words, fundamentally tied to the process of discursive production of others, rather than preexisting that process. (For a discussion of this point in relation to colonial expansion, see Mohanty 1988; for a compelling analysis of the production of white racial identity in the United States, see Roediger 1992.)

In the present discussion of whiteness and Americanness it was, I suggest, the legacy of colonial discourse that generated a sense of whiteness as an "empty" but simultaneously normative space, contrasted with a range of ontologically other cultures, possible to name precisely as a result of their exclusion from normativity—as a result of what Trinh T. Min-ha (1986–1987) has referred to as the "boundedness" of the latter. Colonial discourse also shaped the construction of Americanness in the narratives, as similarly normative/empty, and as excluding of communities of color and so-called white ethnic groups. Processes of reification and at times also exoticization of nondominant cultures, both key to colonial discourse, were thus in play. In parallel, nondominant forms of whiteness and Americanness were conceptualized as bounded, marked spaces of belonging in contrast with a generic, normative notion of whiteness. Here one might argue that pastoralism (Williams 1978)—the romanticization of earlier moments in European history—at times shaped valorizations of white ethnic identities.

Second and, one might imagine, in contrast with colonial discourse, these women also drew on discursive repertoires associated with twentieth-century struggles for decolonization and antiracism. In this context, they viewed white culture and Americanness as "bad" because both were seen as definitively linked to domination. However, I will suggest that women's deployments of antiracist and anti-imperialist discursive repertoires as critiques were blunted and disempowered, in part because they remained entangled with elements of colonial discourse.

These women's impulse toward antiracism was also disempowered by its entanglement with the third repertoire in play: what I call a color- and power-evasive discursive repertoire-more commonly referred to as "color blindness."[2] Color blindness, assimilationism, and limited forms of pluralism emerged in the first half of the twentieth century in the United States as critique, both of longstanding essentialist racisms, and of political, economic, and institutional racial inequalities. However, a color- and power-evasive repertoire has also been readily harnessed to conservative political agendas in the Reagan-Bush years, because it sidesteps recognition of the historical and structural dimensions of racism (for an excellent discussion of this history see Omi and Winant 1986: 9–24). As such, this discursive repertoire throws culpability for racial inequality, when it *is* recognized, onto the individual subject, usually the subject of color (victim blaming). When, as was the case in the narratives I am examining here, a color- and power-evasive repertoire is refracted through antiracist sentiment, it could place culpability onto the *white* subject—in principle, one might imagine, not such a bad idea. However, for these white women, it did so in ways that, I will suggest, were individualistic, totalizing, and ahistorical and thus helped generate backlash from within antiracist discourses themselves.

I have begun here by conceptually separating the three repertoires just named—a move that is possible and productive given the specifiably separate moments of emergence of each. However, I have already noted the close interweaving of discursive repertoires in white women's narratives. In fact, one of the most striking theoretical findings here is precisely the temporal and conceptual disorder of discourses on whiteness in shaping white racial subjectivity. This will become clearer in concrete terms as I trace the deployment of the three discursive repertoires through the narratives.

As noted earlier, the white women discussed here are unusual in the extent of their professed commitments to multiculturalism and antiracism. Some women's antiracism was demonstrated at work. Thus Sandy Alvarez and Clare Traverso, both bilingual education teachers in a multiethnic high school, saw part of their jobs as empowering their students of color; Margaret Phillips had worked for several years at a project whose goal was to eliminate sexist, racist, and disablist images from school textbooks; and Marjorie Hoffman, now retired, had spent a good part of her working life as the only white employee at a pathbreaking race relations institute in the southern United States.[3] Some of the women more than others had been or continued to be political activists. Marjorie had been a fund-raiser for the Student Nonviolent Coordinating Committee during the Civil Rights movement. Louise Glebocki was still politically active in a Left political party, multiracial in its leadership and antiracist in its goals. Three women—Cathy Thomas, Chris Patterson, and Pat Bowen—had become involved in debates over racism in the feminist movement and in women's studies classrooms. For all three, antiracist activity had been mostly confined to discussion and self-questioning. Four women—Helen Standish, Louise Glebocki, Sandy Alvarez, and Cathy Thomas—described primary partnerships with men or women of color of at least four years' duration (Louise's and Sandy's were ongoing). In short, by comparison with most U.S. white women, these women were unusually race conscious. This, of course, makes even more troubling their continued deployments of colonial and color- or power-evasive languages of race.

A key feature of these narratives was the sense of whiteness as unmarked marker, very often viewed as substantively empty and yet taken as normative. The same characteristics marked Americanness, so that the two place markers "white" and "American" at times operated interchangeably, though not always through the production of the same others. Thus for many, being white felt like being cultureless. Cathy Thomas spoke despairingly of

> the formlessness of being white. Now if I was a middle western girl, or a New Yorker, if I had a fixed regional identity that was something palpable, then I'd be a white New Yorker, no doubt, but I'd still be a New Yorker. . . . Being a Californian, I'm sure it has its hallmarks, but to me they were invisible. . . . If I had an ethnic base to identify from, if I was even Irish American, that would have been something formed, if I was a working-class woman, that would have been something formed. But to be a Heinz 57 American, a white, class-confused American, Land-of-the-Kleenex-type American, is so formless in and of itself. It only takes shape in relation to other people.

Here one sees very explicitly the operation of a dualism—white or normative versus other. This generates a process of naming identities by means of their exclusion from a white norm that is at the same time a residue: the discursive bifurcation of an apparently generic location and a range of other identities marked by race, ethnicity, region, and class. It is crucial to note that the extent to which identities can be named is patterned by an inverse relationship to power in the U.S. social structure. Thus Irishness and working-class positioning—both in different ways signaling nondominant white identity—appear to Cathy to have content and "form," in contrast with her own perceived identity.

Chris Patterson actually provided a key dimension of the analysis of Cathy Thomas's description: "I'm probably at the stage where I'm beginning to see that you can come up with a definition of white. Before, I didn't know that you could turn it around and say, 'Well, what *does* white mean?' One thing is, it's taken for granted. . . . [To be white means to] have some sort of advantage or privilege, even if it's something as simple as not having a definition." The phrase "turning it around" indicates Chris's crucial realization that, most often, whiteness stands as an unmarked or neutral category, in relation to which others are named or marked other.

Already, one sees here the complex formation of white women's constructions of racialized selves and others. First, as just suggested, one sees the effects of a colonial notion of culture in the contrasts made between generic and nameable identities. Second, and in partial contrast with this first point, one may note Cathy's and Chris's criticism of whiteness and thereby see the impact of later anti-imperialist and antiracist discursive moments alongside the traces of colonial discourse. Thus Chris explicitly links whiteness to domination and in fact notes and challenges the naming system itself. In Cathy's identification of whiteness with the brand names of commodities, we see a linkage of whiteness to capitalism that simultaneously implies a linkage to domination. It should be noted, though, that Cathy ultimately holds onto the dualistic construction of self and other, wherein whiteness remains seemingly formless if it is not modulated by any kind of nondominance based on class or ethnicity.

Clare Traverso further underscores the complex linkage between whiteness, capitalism, and "badness" when she says, "The good things about whites are to do with folk arts, music. Because other things have power associated with them." Underpinning Clare's comment, and in fact immanent in Cathy's description also, are the processes of industrialization and white assimilation (one might even say, accession to the status of whiteness on the part of European immigrants) ongoing through the nineteenth and early twentieth centuries in the United States. For these processes have indeed been coextensive *both* with the increasing incorporation of mass-produced commodities and mass culture into white cultural practice, *and* with the enfranchisement of increasing numbers of "non-white" citizens in a racially hierarchical society (Kasaba 1991; Roediger 1992; for examples of early-twentieth-century depictions of "white ethnic groups" as either "nonwhite" or difficult to assimilate, see Dillingham 1911; Talbot 1917, esp. 251–258).[4]

The habit of turning to white culture as reference point was tenacious. Even Sandy Alvarez and Loiuse Glebocki, who had elsewhere expressed acute awareness of racial inequality and who were both, through marriage, members of ethnically mixed, Chicano-white families, referred to "Mexican" music versus "regular" music, where regular meant "white." Thus for example, Louise described her aunt and uncle's (bicultural) household in the following way: "I remember, like, with these relatives, the Chicanos, they would always joke around, you know, around us being Polish, and white . . . you know, 'You honkies gotta learn more . . .' and stuff. And in terms of their house? They'd play a lot of Mexican music and a lot of regular music, and have stuff on the Indians up on the walls, and from Mexico." Here, Louise speaks in terms that name the specificity of her own racial location and then almost immediately repositions whiteness as normative.

Americanness was, in these narratives, constructed in much the same way as whiteness, simultaneously formless or empty, and normative. Helen Standish's description of the differences she perceived between white communities in her growing-up years in a small New England town captures this situation well. Asked about her own cultural identity, Helen explained that "it didn't seem like a culture because everyone else was the same." However, she had previously mentioned the presence of Italian Americans in the town. Asked about their status, she responded as follows, adopting at first the voice of childhood: "They are different, but I'm the same as everybody else. They speak Italian, but everybody else in the U.S. speaks English. They eat strange, different food, but I eat the same kind of food as everybody else in the U.S. . . . The way I was brought up was to think that everybody who was the same as me were Americans, and the other people were of such-and-such descent." Viewing the Italian Americans as different and oneself as "same" serves, first, to marginalize the former group. At the same time, claiming to be the same as *everyone* else actually makes invisible or eclipses other cultural groups. The category of "American" represents simultaneously the normative and the residual, the dominant culture and a nonculture.

Although Helen's discussion here is about types of white people, it is also fairly clear that people of color would not have counted among the "same" group but among the communities of "such-and-such descent." Whites, within this universe of discourse, become conceptually the real Americans, and only certain kinds of whites actually qualify. Thus even for these politically conscious women, whiteness and Americanness both come to stand as normative and exclusive categories, in relation to which other cultures are identified and marginalized. And this clarifies that there are two kinds of whites, just as there are two kinds of Americans: those who are truly or only white, and those who are white but also something more—or is it something less?

Conceptualizations of white cultural markers, practices, and identities were contradictory in their effects. On one hand, as long as whiteness seemed unspecifiable, it remained normative. At the same time, for many, whiteness was on the surface of things unappealing. As Helen Standish put it, "[We had] Wonder Bread, white bread. I'm more interested in, you know, what's a bagel?—in other people's cultures rather than my own."

In addition to identifying whiteness by reference to brand names such as Kleenex and Wonder Bread, another set of signifiers constructed whiteness as embodying (and tainted by) the modern condition—white neighborhoods as privatized or alienated, for example. The linking of white culture with white objects, viewing whiteness as "bland," "blah," the clichéd "white bread and mayonnaise," suggests either paleness or neutrality. These images connoted several things—color itself (although exaggerated), lack of vitality (Wonder Bread is highly processed), and homogeneity.

However, such characterizations are at all times perched on a slippery slope, suggesting "white" identified at once as a color but an unappealing one, and as an *absence* of color, that is, white as the unmarked marker. Thus, albeit in context of a negative valorization, the dualistic structure of colonial discourse remains intact: white versus nonwhite; modern versus traditional; active versus passive; mobile versus static; normative versus different; and, moreover, whiteness and nonwhiteness as profoundly different from one another.

Discussions of race and culture at times revealed a view of people of color as themselves actually embodying difference while whites, by implications, stood for neutrality or normalcy. Hence, Margaret Phillips, an upper-middle-class white woman in her forties raised in Chicago, said of her Jamaican, Rastafarian daughter-in-law: "She *really* comes with diversity." This mode of thinking about "difference" expresses clearly the double-edged sword of a "power-evasive" discourse on race: it apparently valorizes cultural difference but does so in a way that leaves racial and cultural hierarchies intact (Frankenberg 1993). In a later comment, Margaret said of racial inequality in the United States: "It's true, we're still a culture that's uncomfortable with differences. . . . It's just that much tougher if you are not white. . . . [P]eople don't know how it feels . . . when you need your start, not to get it." Here, Margaret in a sense acknowledges the racism of the dominant society, albeit in a way that reduces structural issues to questions of individual attitude. But clearly the "we" of her statement and the "people" she invokes are, although she does not say so, white Americans. "White," here, is implicitly equivalent to self, norm, and nation. Nonwhites are marginal, the differers. Their inclusion in the nation, although it might well be an act of compassion, is construed here as optional: the nation does not require their presence in order to be fully formed.

I was reminded of Margaret Phillips when, in 1990, the institution in which I worked responded to demographic shifts in the Seattle population, and a concomitant increase in numbers of students of color at the university, by hosting a one-day workshop for teaching assistants and their trainers, in which "we" were asked the question, "How is your department manifesting diversity?"

The assumption here is of a homogeneous entity, which at a certain point somehow magically sprouts "difference" and which is in fact apparently ruptured by "difference," viewed as extraneous rather than intrinsic. Notions of normativity and otherness are retained. The historical conditions for the construction of a white, dominant self or center are not, in other words, called into question. Further, as with anything extraneous, the attitude of those who are "same" to those who are "different" is optional and in the hands of the former rather than the latter group. And to take the argument a step further, it is in this context that white-dominated institutions quickly find themselves asking, "What more do 'they' want?"

Within the conceptual universe under discussion here, whiteness and Americanness on the one side, and nonwhiteness/non-Americanness on the other, are mutually constitutive, discursively dependent on one another. On one hand, whiteness and Americanness emerge as normative markers in relation to which others are constructed. But on the other hand, if others are constructed in relation to whiteness, whiteness is simultaneously in part a residual category, constructed out of the process of positioning others at its borders (Mohanty 1988). To be white within this universe of discourse is thus to *not* be a number of other things: *not* Jamaican, *not* a person of color. Similarly, to be American is to be *not* Italian descended, *not* Irish descended, and also *not* a person of color.

The inadvertent interplay in the women's speech of elements of images and ideas drawn from racist and antiracist discourses was frequently complex. Thus, for example, Louise Glebocki referred to the working-class Chicanos with whom she had grown up as less "pretentious," "closer to the truth," more "down-to-earth." In a similar vein Marjorie Hoffman spoke of the "earthy humor" of Black people whom she met in the context of her work as a volunteer in the New York settlement houses of the 1920s. On the one hand, as has been pointed out by a long line of scholars and activists from Karl Marx on, the positioning of a group (here, people of color) at the bottom of a social and economic hierarchy creates the potential for a critique of the system as a whole, and for a consciousness of the need to resist. Indeed, from the standpoint of race privilege, the system of racism (and thereby, one could well argue, the "truth" about U.S. society) is made structurally invisible (Frankenberg 1993). However, on the other hand, descriptions of this kind leave in place a troubling dichotomy, which can be appropriated as easily by racist as antiracist forces. For example, there is an affinity between the image of Black people as "earthy" and the conservative racist view that African-American culture leaves African-American people ill-equipped for advancement in the modern age. Here, both Chicanos and African Americans are placed conceptually on the borders of nature and culture, in fact echoing with older racist discourses. For often, the traits white women envied in other cultures were in fact the product of economic hardship or methods of production and consumption linked to such hardship. Thus for example, one interviewee warmly described Chicanas' relationship to the kitchen, viewing that space as "the hearth of the home." However it seems to me that this space, and women's relationships to it, might also be linked as much to intensive domestic work as to a cultural value per se. Again, other interviewees' image of the neighborhoods of people of color as more lively and characterized by an active street life might, one could argue, have more than a little to do with conditions of overcrowding and inadequate private space.

By the same token, often that which the women criticized as "white" reflected middle-class status as much as whiteness per se. Thus, for example, Louise Glebocki's image of her fate had she married a white man entailed a class-coded description of a white-collar, nuclear family: "Him saying, 'I'm home dear,' and me with an apron on—ugh!"

There were other ways in which the women's words obscured the intersections of class, race, and culture in the shaping of daily life. In this regard, Pat Bowen, a white working-class woman, was angry with some of her middle-class white feminist friends who, she felt, embrace as "cultural" some aspects of African-American, Chicano, and Native-American cultures, such as artwork or dance performances, but would reject as "tacky" (her term), those aspects of daily experience that communities of color shared with working-class whites, such as buying from the stores and supermarkets of poor neighborhoods. This, she felt, was tantamount to a selective expansion of middle-class aesthetic horizons, but not to true antiracism or to true comprehension of the cultures of people of color. Pat also felt that middle-class white feminists were able to use such selective engagement to avoid addressing their class privilege.

As Pat's comment begins to suggest, the tie between economics and culture, or between daily practices and values, was potentially more evident to women in relation to their own experiences of oppression or hardship. Clare Traverso, for example, remarked that her natal family's emphasis on "traditional" values, such as not eating in restaurants and making and mending clothes at home, had as much to do with poverty as with cultural values per se. However, precisely because of their material dimension, Clare rejected the idea that such values and practices might be part of a distinctive cultural heritage.

Part of what one sees in many of these narratives might be called a discursive draining process being applied both to whiteness and to Americanness. In it, any practice engaged in by a white person that is not identical to the dominant culture is automatically counted as either "not really white" and equally "not really American" (but rather of "such-and-such descent"), or as "not really cultural" (but rather "economic"). In this process, both whiteness and nonwhiteness are reified, made into objects rather than processes, and robbed of historical context and human agency. As long as the discussion remains couched in these terms, a critique of whiteness remains a double-edged sword. For one thing, whiteness remains normative because there is no way to name the cultural practices associated with it *as* cultural. Moreover, whether whiteness is viewed as more civilized (and therefore *better*) or, as for most of the women I have quoted here, more artificial and dominating (and therefore, *worse*), whiteness and all varieties of nonwhiteness continue to be viewed as ontologically different from one another.

So far, I have examined the ways white women's words about whiteness and Americanness, self and other, are marked by two discursive repertoires: colonial and antiracist. Of the third, color- and power-evasive repertoire, one effect is of particular relevance.[5] One feature that a color- and power-evasive repertoire on race shares with colonial constructions of culture is the repression or evasion of the historical context for the production of racial and cultural categories and of racial and cultural inequality. This repression of historical context enables the maintenance of reified and dualistic constructions of "culture" and "norm/residue." Linked to the evasion of structure and history, women's participation in a color- and power-evasive repertoire led them at times to conceive white selves, including their own, as identified with dominance in a totalizing manner. This in turn often generated further, equally totalizing rejections of any notion of white enlistment into racism and thus threatened to create backlash from within the terms of the discourse itself.

In this context, some of the women I interviewed, while at one moment articulating angry denunciations of whiteness and Americanness, almost immediately took them back. Cathy Thomas, for example, posed a rhetorical question that powerfully encapsulated the impact of imperial expansion on culture and material life: "What is there to us? Besides the largest colonial legacy anyone has ever seen in history, and the complete rewriting of everything anyone else knows himself by?" But, in contrast, here is Cathy Thomas again, reflecting on her involvement in discussions of racism in the feminist movement: "I took on the whole ridiculous, sordid, murderous past of white people. . . . It's a dead end . . . that generates backlash, because people don't know why they have to hate themselves, they don't remember doing anything horrendous in their lives. They never lynched anybody . . . when do you stop paying? is a big question. It was for me." Clare Traverso said, in response to a question from me about what the term *white* meant to her: "I think of people like the Ku Klux Klanners when I think of 'white.' And *I'm* not Ku Klux Klan. But my subconscious says, 'Yes, you are,' because that's what we learn about what white is, 'White did this, white did that, to this people, to that people,'—that's not all that we are! You know, there's something good in us, what is it? And where is it? And can't we articulate that too? And maybe people think it's already articulated: 'We're wonderful, we have the right to take from you.' But there's something else, isn't there?"

Cathy's and Clare's words here draw on the terms of reference of the antiracist and anti-imperialist movements of the latter half of the twentieth century. However, their deployment of them owes as much to color and power evasion as it does to movements for racial equality. For on the one hand, characterizing white people by reference to U.S. imperialism, European colonialism, the Klan, presents an explicit challenge and contrast to the desire embedded in a color-and power-evasive repertoire not to name oppressive systems or structures. But on the other hand, the Klan and imperialism are invoked here in rhetorical ways that expose but do not undo the dualism of the dominant discourse itself. These descriptions of complicity are thus constructed as dualisms: either an individual is fully complicit with racism and imperialism, or not complicit at all.

Using the Klan and colonialism to characterize white individuals' complicity with racism is a powerful rhetorical move if the goal is to disrupt the complacency of a dominant culture that refuses to acknowledge structural racial inequality. Equally important, Cathy's and Clare's conceptualizations insist on raising rather than evading the question of individual white people's relationships with racism. However, like most rhetorical strategies, the Klan and colonialism are simultaneously reductive and excessive as reference points if used literally as tools for analyzing the status of white, non-Klan-supporting persons in relation to racial domination. (By contrast, more complex and materially based analyses of the Klan, colonialism, and neoimperialism are important elements of antiracist strategy.)

Thus, Cathy and Clare spoke of and then rejected an undifferentiated "we" of domination, Cathy suggesting that there is *nothing* to "us" except for active participation in colonialism, and Clare expressing her fear that, in fact, she *is* like a Ku Klux Klan member, both because she is white and because she, as a white person, is linked to colonialism in a generalized sense. Some of the potential effects of these simple inversions of color and power evasion were evident in Clare's back-and-forth movement between two poles: I am like the Klan/U.S. imperialism, and I am *not* like the Klan/U.S. imperialism. Clare was clear, it seemed, that while neither statement was fully correct, neither statement was in fact fully *incorrect,* either. But at the same time she was puzzled about how to escape this dualism.

Each of these positions is, I suggest, an effect of the other, and each is equally inadequate. In the end, Cathy and Clare move rapidly through three stages: first, a sense of an undifferentiated white/American "we" or "I" that is entirely responsible as active agent for both racism and imperialism; second, a total rejection of any first-person relationship to domination (I'm not the KKK; when do I stop paying for something I never did?); and third, a return to questions and confusion about how to conceptualize the relationships between whiteness, Americanness, and domination.

Both these women end up with genuine anxiety about their complicity with racial domination. However, it is worth noting that, in fact, the rhetoric of racist backlash movements like the National Association for the Advancement of White People and the White Aryan Resistance works in part by taking people through the first two stages of Cathy's and Clare's process, beginning with a hostile backward glance at the Civil Rights movement and ending with the question, When do I stop paying? These movements capitalize, in short, on resentment. Clearly, neither Cathy nor Clare shares the hostility expressed in far right rhetoric. But neither is sure where to move past the moment of dualistic ambivalence just described. The next step for women like Cathy and Clare might be to enter into more complex, dynamic, and historically situated analyses of their positionings as white subjects in a racially hierarchical society.

I do not want to end this essay simply by criticizing as conceptually inadequate these women's descriptions of whiteness. For, especially in their comments about the links of whiteness and Americanness to domination, we see sadness and frustration about the meaning of whiteness at this moment in history. It becomes important, then, to engage in an analysis of contradictions rather than in a unilateral critique—to acknowledge the intent and the anger of these women, and to use the lessons that come out of a close reading of their words to move toward a critical analysis of white Americanness that is freer of colonial and power-evasive legacies.

Key, here, is the task of rehistoricizing the categories of race and culture: insisting on antiessentialist conceptions of race, ethnicity, and culture, while at the same time emphasizing that these categories are made materially "real" within matrices of power relations. For white women and men, attention to the histories of cultural practice, belonging, and identity should lead to the recognition that, when one yearns to belong to a culture that is bounded, nameable, or, in Cathy Thomas's words, "formed," one risks the twin errors of romanticizing oppression and erasing the labor of those movements that struggle against racial and cultural domination. For one thing, as noted here, "boundedness" is most often an effect of subordination; the non-normativity of particular sets of cultural practices (and the seeming noncontamination of those practices by relationships to dominance) most often goes along with political and economic disenfranchisement. Moreover, for the greater part of U.S. history, racial and ethnic nondominance has been anything but fashionable, even selectively. The partial and still incomplete recognition and value accorded some nondominant cultural practices is, in fact, the result of hard-fought and still ongoing battles not only for recognition and respect from the dominant society but also and equally important for the *self*-respect of groups and individuals. There is thus a way in which this kind of yearning may be premised on the reification of communities, of identities, and of the notion of culture.

Rehistoricizing whiteness and Americanness as locations of cultural practice entails learning more about the the multiple histories of assimilation, appropriation, and exclusion that shape the cultural field(s) that white Americans now inhabit. Rehistoricization also requires engagement with whiteness and Americanness as culturally specific spaces rather than as cultureless, culturally neutral, or culturally generic terrain. To adapt Paul Gilroy's phrase, whiteness and Americanness are, like other cultural assemblages, "field[s] articulating the life world of subjects . . . and the structures created by human activity" (1987:17), fields that generate norms, ways of understanding history, ways of thinking about self and other, and, in fact, ways of thinking about race, culture, and nation as categories.

Finally, white subjects (and again I include myself) must continue to examine whiteness and Americanness as sites of dominance. But as we do this, we must note that not all white American people, and not all forms of whiteness, have the same access to power. It is critical to think clearly and carefully about the parts white people play in the maintenance of the racial order, and to ask how our locations in it—and our complicity with it—are marked by other dimensions of our privilege and oppression, including class, gender, and sexuality. The point of work of this kind would not, however, be that of constructing hierarchies either of oppression or of blame. Rather, its purpose would be to sharpen our analysis of how systems of domination coconstruct one another, and how we are "enlisted," materially and ideologically, in their continued operation.

Notes

My thanks to Brackette Williams, Steven Gregory, and Roger Sanjek for their work in organizing the American Ethnological Society and American Anthropological Association panels that enabled presentation of the papers upon which this essay draws. I am also grateful to Lata Mani, Eleanor Soto, Ted Swedenburg, and Yvonne Yarbro-Bejarano for their comments on its various versions.

1. The notion of a discursive "repertoire" is employed here in the effort to name the simultaneous flexibility, individuality, and yet clearly sociohistorically limited and constrained relationship to conceptualizations of race and culture that were evident in the narratives. I am indebted to Chetan Bhatt for the concept of discursive repertoire.

2. I am intentionally avoiding as far as possible any use of the term *colorblind,* in part because it deploys and judges negatively a physical disability, and in part because it is in any case misleading given that, for the most part, this discursive repertoire is organized around evading difference or acknowledging it selectively, rather than literally not "seeing" differences of race, culture, and color.

3. All interviewees are referred to by pseudonyms.

4. I am indebted to Kathie Friedman Kasaba for these early references and for her discussions with me about working-class, female European immigrants to the United States at the turn of the twentieth century.

5. The historical context, deployment, and effects of color and power evasion in white women's discourse are discussed in detail in Frankenberg 1993, esp. chap. 6.

References

Ahmad, Aijaz. 1992. *In Theory: Classes, Nations, Literatures.* London: Verso.

Barker, Francis et al., eds. 1985. *Europe and Its Others. Proceedings of the Essex Conference on the Sociology of Literature.* 2 vols. Colchester, Eng.: University of Essex.

Dillingham, Mr. 1911. *Dictionary of Races or Peoples.* Report of the Immigration Commission, Committee on Immigration. Washington, D.C.: U.S. Government Printing Office.

Frankenberg, Ruth. 1993. *White Women, Race Matters: The Social Construction of Whiteness.* Minneapolis: University of Minnesota Press.

Gilroy, Paul. 1987. *There Ain't No Black in the Union Jack.* London: Hutchinson.

hooks, bell. 1991. Representing Whiteness in the Black Imagination. In *Cultural Studies,* ed. Larry Grossberg, Cary Nelson, and Paula Treichler, pp. 338–346. New York: Routledge.

Kasaba, Kathie Friedman. 1991. "To Become a Person": The Experience of Gender, Ethnicity, and Work in the Lives of Immigrant Women, New York City, 1870–1940. Ph.D. diss., State University of New York, Binghamton.

Mohanty, Chandra Talpade. 1988. Under Western Eyes: Feminist Scholarship and Colonial Discourses. *Feminist Review* (Autumn): 60–88.

Omi, Michael, and Howard Winant. 1986. *Racial Formation in the United States: From the 1960s to the 1980s.* New York: Routledge.

Parry, Benita. 1987. Problems in Current Theories of Colonial Discourse. *Oxford Literary Review* 9(1–2): 27–58.

Roediger, David. 1992. *The Wages of Whiteness: Race and the Making of the American Working Class.* London: Verso.

Said, Edward. 1979. *Orientalism.* New York: Random House.

Talbot, Winthrop, ed. 1917. *Americanization.* New York: Wilson.

Trinh T. Minh-ha. 1986–1987. Difference: A Special Third World Women Issue. *Discourse* (special issue, *She, the Inappropriate/d Other*) 8 (Fall–Winter): 11–37.

Williams, Raymond. 1978. *The Country and the City.* New York: Oxford University Press.

Young, Robert. 1990. *White Mythologies: Writing History and the West.* London: Routledge.

KAREN BRODKIN SACKS

How Did Jews Become White Folks?

The American nation was founded and developed by the Nordic race, but if a few more million members of the Alpine, Mediterranean and Semitic races are poured among us, the result must inevitably be a hybrid race of people as worthless and futile as the good-for-nothing mongrels of Central America and Southeastern Europe.
(Kenneth Roberts, qtd. in Carlson and Colburn 1972:312)

It is clear that Kenneth Roberts did not think of my ancestors as white like him. The late nineteenth and early decades of the twentieth centuries saw a steady stream of warnings by scientists, policymakers, and the popular press that "mongrelization" of the Nordic or Anglo-Saxon race—the real Americans—by inferior European races (as well as inferior non-European ones) was destroying the fabric of the nation. I continue to be surprised to read that America did not always regard its immigrant European workers as white, that they thought people from different nations were biologically different. My parents, who are first-generation U.S.-born Eastern European Jews, are not surprised. They expect anti-Semitism to be part of the fabric of daily life, much as I expect racism to be part of it. They came of age in a Jewish world in the 1920s and 1930s at the peak of anti-Semitism in the United States (Gerber 1986a). They are proud of their upward mobility and think of themselves as pulling themselves up by their own bootstraps. I grew up during the 1950s in the Euroethnic New York suburb of Valley Stream where Jews were simply one kind of white folks and where ethnicity meant little more to my generation than food and family heritage. Part of my familized ethnic heritage was the belief that Jews were smart and that our success was the result of our own efforts and abilities, reinforced by a culture that valued sticking together, hard work, education, and deferred gratification. Today, this belief in a Jewish version of Horatio Alger has become an entry point for racism by some mainstream Jewish organizations against African Americans especially, and for their opposition to affirmative action for people of color (Gordon 1964; Sowell 1983; Steinberg 1989: chap. 3).

It is certainly true that the United States has a history of anti-Semitism and of beliefs that Jews were members of an inferior race. But Jews were hardly alone. American anti-Semitism was part of a broader pattern of late-nineteenth-century racism against all southern and eastern European immigrants, as well as against Asian immigrants. These views justified all sorts of discriminatory treatment including closing the doors to immigration from Europe and Asia in the 1920s.[1] This picture changed radically after World War II. Suddenly the same folks who promoted nativism and xenophobia were eager to believe that the Euro-origin people whom they had deported, reviled as members of inferior races, and prevented from immigrating only a few years earlier were now model middle-class white suburban citizens.

It was not an educational epiphany that made those in power change their hearts, their minds, and our race. Instead, it was the biggest and best affirmative action program in the history of our nation, and it was for Euromales. There are similarities and differences in the ways each of the European immigrant groups became "whitened." I want to tell the story in a way that links anti-Semitism to other varieties of anti-European racism, because this foregrounds what Jews shared with other Euroimmigrants and shows changing notions of whiteness to be part of America's larger system of institutional racism.

Euroraces

The U.S. "discovery" that Europe had inferior and superior races came in response to the great waves of immigration from southern and eastern Europe in the late nineteenth century. Before that time, European immigrants—including Jews—had been largely assimilated into the white population. The twenty-three million European immigrants who came to work in U.S. cities after 1880 were too many and too concentrated to disperse and blend. Instead, they piled up in the country's most dilapidated urban areas, where they built new kinds of working-class ethnic communities. Since immigrants and their children made up more than 70 percent of the population of most of the country's largest cities, urban America came to take on a distinctly immigrant flavor. The golden age of industrialization in the United States was also the golden age of class struggle between the captains of the new industrial empires and the masses of manual workers whose labor made them rich. As the majority of mining and manufacturing workers, immigrants were visibly major players in these struggles (Higham 1955:226; Steinberg 1989:36).[2]

The Red Scare of 1919 clearly linked anti-immigrant to anti-working-class sentiment—to the extent that the Seattle general strike of native-born workers was blamed on foreign agitators. The Red Scare was fueled by economic depression, a massive postwar strike wave, the Russian revolution, and a new wave of postwar immigration. Strikers in steel, and the garment and textile workers in New York and New England, were mainly new immigrants. "As part of a fierce counteroffensive, employers inflamed the historic identification of class conflict with immigrant radicalism." Anticommunism and anti-immigrant sentiment came together in the Palmer raids and deportation of immigrant working-class activists. There was real fear of revolution. One of President Wilson's aides feared it was "the first appearance of the soviet in this country" (Higham 1955:226).

Not surprisingly, the belief in European races took root most deeply among the wealthy U.S.-born Protestant elite, who feared a hostile and seemingly unassimilable working class. By the end of the nineteenth century, Senator Henry Cabot Lodge pressed Congress to cut off immigration to the United States; Teddy Roosevelt raised the alarm of "race suicide" and took Anglo-Saxon women to task for allowing "native" stock to be outbred by inferior immigrants. In the twentieth century, these fears gained a great deal of social legitimacy thanks to the efforts of an influential network of aristocrats and scientists who developed theories of eugenics—breeding for a "better" humanity—and scientific racism. Key to these efforts was Madison Grant's influential *Passing of the Great Race*, in which he shared his discovery that there were three or four major European races ranging from the superior Nordics of northwestern Europe to the inferior southern and eastern races of Alpines, Mediterraneans, and, worst of all, Jews, who seemed to be everywhere in his native New York City. Grant's nightmare was race mixing among Europeans. For him, "the cross between any of the three European races and a Jew is a Jew" (qtd. in Higham 1955:156). He didn't have good things to say about Alpine or Mediterranean "races" either. For Grant, race and class were interwoven: the upper class was racially pure Nordic, and the lower classes came from the lower races.

Far from being on the fringe, Grant's views resonated with those of the nonimmigrant middle class. A *New York Times* reporter wrote of his visit to the Lower East Side:

> This neighborhood, peopled almost entirely by the people who claim to have been driven from Poland and Russia, is the eyesore of New York and perhaps the filthiest place on the western continent. It is impossible for a Christian to live there because he will be driven out, either by blows or the dirt and stench. Cleanliness is an unknown quantity to these people. They cannot be lifted up to a higher plane because they do not want to be. If the cholera should ever

> get among these people, they would scatter its germs as a sower does grain. (qtd. in Schoener 1967:58)[3]

Such views were well within the mainstream of the early-twentieth-century scientific community. Grant and eugenicist Charles B. Davenport organized the Galton Society in 1918 in order to foster research and to otherwise promote eugenics and immigration restriction.[4] Lewis Terman, Henry Goddard, and Robert Yerkes, developers of the so-called intelligence test, believed firmly that southeastern European immigrants, African Americans, American Indians, and Mexicans were "feebleminded." And indeed, more than 80 percent of the immigrants whom Goddard tested at Ellis Island in 1912 turned out to be just that. Racism fused with eugenics in scientific circles, and the eugenics circles overlapped with the nativism of WASP aristocrats. During World War I, racism shaped the army's development of a mass intelligence test. Psychologist Robert Yerkes, who developed the test, became an even stronger advocate of eugenics after the war. Writing in the *Atlantic Monthly* in 1923, he noted:

> If we may safely judge by the army measurements of intelligence, races are quite as significantly different as individuals. . . . [and] almost as great as the intellectual difference between negro and white in the army are the differences between white racial groups. . . .
>
> For the past ten years or so the intellectual status of immigrants has been disquietingly low. Perhaps this is because of the dominance of the Mediterranean races, as contrasted with the Nordic and Alpine. (qtd. in Carlson and Colburn 1972:333–334)

By the 1920s, scientific racism sanctified the notion that real Americans were white and real whites came from northwest Europe. Racism animated laws excluding and expelling Chinese in 1882, and then closing the door to immigration by virtually all Asians and most Europeans in 1924 (Saxton 1971, 1990). Northwestern European ancestry as a requisite for whiteness was set in legal concrete when the Supreme Court denied Bhagat Singh Thind the right to become a naturalized citizen under a 1790 federal law that allowed whites the right to become naturalized citizens. Thind argued that Asian Indians were the real Aryans and Caucasians, and therefore white. The Court countered that the United States only wanted blond Aryans and Caucasians, "that the blond Scandinavian and the brown Hindu have a common ancestor in the dim reaches of antiquity, but the average man knows perfectly well that there are unmistakable and profound differencess between them today" (Takaki 1989:298–299). A narrowly defined white, Christian race was also built into the 1705 Virginia "Act concerning servants and slaves." This statute stated "that no negroes, mulattos and Indians or other infidels or jews, Moors, Mahometans or other infidels shall, at any time, purchase any christian servant, nor any other except of their own complexion" (Martyn 1979:111).[5]

The 1930 census added its voice, distinguishing not only immigrant from "native" whites, but also native whites of native white parentage, and native whites of immigrant (or mixed) parentage. In distinguishing immigrant (southern and eastern Europeans) from "native" (northwestern Europeans), the census reflected the racial distinctions of the eugenicist-inspired intelligence tests.[6]

Racism and anti-immigrant sentiment in general and anti-Semitism in particular flourished in higher education. Jews were the first of the Euroimmigrant groups to enter colleges in significant numbers, so it wasn't surprising that they faced the brunt of discrimination there.[7] The Protestant elite complained that Jews were unwashed, uncouth, unrefined, loud, and pushy. Harvard University President A. Lawrence Lowell, who was also a vice president of the Immigration Restriction League, was openly opposed to Jews at Harvard. The Seven Sisters schools had a reputation for "flagrant discrimination." M. Carey Thomas, Bryn Mawr president, may have been a feminist of a kind, but she also was an admirer of scientific racism and an advocate of immigration restriction. She "blocked both the admission of black students and the promotion of Jewish instructors" (Synott 1986:233, 238–239, 249–250).

Anti-Semitic patterns set by these elite schools influenced standards of other schools, made anti-Semitism acceptable, and "made the aura of exclusivity a desirable commodity for the college-seeking clientele" (Synott 1986:250; and see Karabel 1984; Silberman 1985; Steinberg 1989: chaps. 5, 9). Fear that colleges "might soon be overrun by Jews" were publicly expressed at a 1918 meeting of the Association of New England Deans. In 1919 Columbia University took steps to decrease the number of entering Jews by a set of practices that soon came to be widely adopted. The school developed a psychological test based on the World War I army intelligence tests to measure "innate ability—and middle-class home environment" and redesigned the admission application to ask for religion, father's name and birthplace, a photo, and a personal interview (Synott 1986:239–240). Other techniques for excluding Jews, like a fixed class size, a chapel requirement, and preference for children of alumni were less obvious. Sociologist Jerome Karabel (1984) has argued that these exclusionary efforts provided the basis for contemporary criteria for college admission that mix grades and test scores with criteria for well-roundedness and character, as well as affirmative action for athletes and children of alumni, which allowed schools to select more affluent Protestants. Their proliferation in the 1920s caused the intended drop in the number of Jewish students in law, dental, and medical schools and also saw the imposition of quotas in engineering, pharmacy, and veterinary schools.[8]

Columbia's quota against Jews was well known in my parents' community. My father is very proud of having beaten it and of being admitted to Columbia Dental School on the basis of his sculpting skill. In addition to demonstrating academic qualifications, he was asked to carve a soap ball, which he did so well and fast that his Protestant interviewer was willing to accept him. Although he became a teacher instead because the dental school tuition was too high, he took me to the dentist every week of my childhood and prolonged the agony by discussing the finer points of tooth filling and dental care. My father also almost failed the speech test required for his teaching license because he didn't speak "standard"—that is, nonimmigrant, nonaccented—English. For my parents and most of their friends, English was a second language learned when they went to school, since their home language was Yiddish. They saw the speech test as designed to keep all ethnics, not just Jews, out of teaching. There is an ironic twist to this story. My mother was always urging me to speak well and correctly, like her friend Ruth Saronson, who was a speech teacher. Ruth remained my model for perfect diction until I went away to college. When I talked to her on one of my visits home, I heard just how New York–accented my version of "standard" English was now that I had met the Boston academic version.

My parents' conclusion is that Jewish success, like their own, was the result of hard work and of placing a high value on education. They went to Brooklyn College during the depression. My mother worked days and started school at night, and my father went during the day. Both their families encouraged them. More accurately, their families expected this effort from them. Everyone they knew was in the same boat, and their world was made up of Jews who advanced as they did. The picture of New York—where most Jews lived—seems to back them up. In 1920, Jews made up 80 percent of the students at New York's City College, 90 percent of Hunter College, and before World War I, 40 percent of private Columbia University. By 1934, Jews made up almost 24 percent of all law students nationally, and 56 percent of those in New York City. Still, more Jews became public school teachers, like my parents and their friends, than doctors or lawyers (Steinberg 1989:137, 227). Steinberg has debunked the myth that Jews advanced because of the cultural value placed on education. This is not to say that Jews did not advance. They did. "Jewish success in America was a matter of historical timing. . . . [T]here was a fortuitous match between the experience and skills of Jewish immigrants, on the one hand, and the manpower needs and opportunity structures, on the other" (1989:103). Jews were the only ones among the southern and eastern European immigrants who came from urban, commercial, craft, and manufacturing backgrounds, not least of which was garment manufacturing They entered the United States in New York, center of the nation's booming garment industry, soon came to dominate its skilled (male) and "unskilled" (female) jobs, and found it an industry amenable to low-capital entrepreneurship. As a result, Jews were the first of the new European immigrants to create a middle class of small businesspersons early in the twentieth century. Jewish educational advances followed this business success and depended upon it, rather than creating it (see also Bodnar 1985 for a similar argument about mobility).

In the early twentieth century, Jewish college students entered a contested terrain in which the elite social mission was under challenge by a newer professional training mission. Pressure for change had begun to transform the curriculum and reorient college from a gentleman's bastion to a training ground for the middle-class professionals needed by an industrial economy. "The curriculum was overhauled to prepare students for careers in business, engineering, scientific farming, and the arts, and a variety of new professions such as accounting and pharmacy that were making their appearance in American colleges for the first time" (Steinberg 1989:229). Occupational training was precisely what drew Jews to college. In a setting where disparagement of intellectual pursuits and the gentleman's C were badges of distinction, it was not hard for Jews to excel.

How we interpret Jewish social mobility in this milieu depends on whom we compare Jews to. Compared with other immigrants, Jews were upwardly mobile. But compared with that of nonimmigrant whites, their mobility was very limited and circumscribed. Anti-immigrant racist and anti-Semitic barriers kept the Jewish middle class confined to a small number of occupations. Jews were excluded from mainstream corporate management and corporately employed professions, except in the garment and movie industries, which they built. Jews were almost totally excluded from university faculties (and the few that made it had powerful patrons). Jews were concentrated in small businesses, and in professions where they served a largely Jewish clientele (Davis 1990:146 n. 25; Silberman 1985:88–117; Sklare 1971:63–67).

We shouldn't forget Jews' success in organized crime in the 1920s and 1930s as an aspect of upward mobility. Arnold Rothstein "transformed crime from a haphazard, small-scale activity into a well-organized and well-financed business operation." There was also Detroit's Purple Gang, Murder Incorporated in New York, and a host of other big-city Jewish gangs in organized crime, and of course Meyer Lansky (Silberman 1985:127–130).

Although Jews were the Euroethnic vanguard in college and became well established in public school teaching, as well as being visible in law, medicine, pharmacy, and librarianship before the postwar boom, these professions should be understood in the context of their times (Gerber 1986a:26). In the 1930s they lacked the corporate context they have today, and Jews in these professions were certainly not corporation based. Most lawyers, doctors, dentists, and pharmacists were solo practitioners and were considerably less affluent than their postwar counterparts.

Compared to Jewish progress after the war, Jews' prewar mobility was also very limited. It was the children of Jewish businessmen, not those of Jewish workers, who flocked to college. Indeed, in 1905 New York, the children of Jewish workers had as little schooling as children of other immigrant workers.[9] My family was quite modal in this respect. My grandparents did not go to college, but they did have a modicum of small-business success. My father's family owned a pharmacy. Although my mother's father was a skilled garment worker, her mother's family was large and always had one or another grocery or deli in which my grandmother participated. It was the relatively privileged children of upwardly mobile Jewish immigrants like my grandparents who began to push on the doors to higher education even before my parents were born. Especially in New York City—which had almost 1.25 million Jews by 1910 and remained the biggest concentration of the nation's 4 million Jews in 1924 (Steinberg 1989:225)—Jews built a small-business-based middle class and began to develop a second-generation professional class in the interwar years.[10] Still, despite the high percentages of Jews in eastern colleges, most Jews were not middle class, and fewer than 3 percent were professionals, compared to somewhere between 20 and 32 percent in the 1960s (Sklare 1971:63).

My parents' generation believed that Jews overcame anti-Semitic barriers because Jews are special. My belief is that the Jews who were upwardly mobile were special among Jews (and were also well placed to write the story). My generation might well counter our parents' story of pulling themselves up by their own bootstraps with, "But think what you might have been without the racism and with some affirmative action!" And that is precisely what the postwar boom, the decline of systematic, public anti-immigrant racism and anti-Semitism, and governmental affirmative action extended to white males.

Euroethnics into Whites

By the time I was an adolescent, Jews were just as white as the next white person. Until I was eight, I was a Jew in a world of Jews. Everyone on Avenue Z in Sheepshead Bay was Jewish. I spent my days playing and going to school on three blocks of Avenue Z, and visiting my grandparents in the nearby Jewish neighborhoods of Brighton Beach and Coney Island. There were plenty of Italians in my neighborhood, but they lived around the corner. They were a kind of Jew, but on the margins of my social horizons. Portugese were even more distant, at the end of the bus ride, at Sheepshead Bay. The schul, or temple, was on Avenue Z, and I begged my father to take me like all the other fathers took their kids, but religion wasn't part of my family's Judaism. Just how Jewish my neighborhood was hit me in first grade when I was one of two kids in my class to go to school on Rosh Hashanah. My teacher was shocked—she was Jewish too—and I was embarrassed to tears when she sent me home. I was never again sent to school on Jewish holidays. We left that world in 1949 when we moved to Valley Stream, Long Island, which was Protestant, Republican, and even had farms until Irish, Italian, and Jewish exurbanites like us gave it a more suburban and Democratic flavor. Neither religion nor ethnicity separated us at school or in the neighborhood. Except temporarily. In elementary school years, I remember a fair number of dirt-bomb (a good suburban weapon) wars on the block. Periodically one of the Catholic boys would accuse me or my brother of killing his God, to which we would reply, "Did not" and start lobbing dirt-bombs. Sometimes he would get his friends from Catholic school, and I would get mine from public school kids on the block, some of whom were Catholic. Hostilities lasted no more than a couple of hours and punctuated an otherwise friendly relationship. They ended by junior high years, when other things became more important. Jews, Catholics, and Protestants, Italians, Irish, Poles, and "English" (I don't remember hearing WASP as a kid) were mixed up on the block and in school. We thought of ourselves as middle class and very enlightened because our ethnic backgrounds seemed so irrelevant to high school culture. We didn't see race (we thought), and racism was not part of our peer consciousness, nor were the immigrant or working-class histories of our families.

Like most chicken and egg problems, it's hard to know which came first. Did Jews and other Euroethnics become white because they became middle class? That is, did money whiten? Or did being incorporated in an expanded version of whiteness open up the economic doors to a middle-class status? Clearly, both tendencies were at work. Some of the changes set in motion during the war against fascism led to a more inclusive version of whiteness. Anti-Semitism and anti-European racism lost respectability. The 1940 census no longer distinguished native whites of native parentage from those, like my parents, of immigrant parentage, so that Euroimmigrants and their children were more securely white by submersion in an expanded notion of whiteness. (This census also changed the race of Mexicans to white [U.S. Bureau of the Census, 1940: 4].) Theories of nurture and culture replaced theories of nature and biology. Instead of dirty and dangerous races who would destroy U.S. democracy, immigrants became ethnic groups whose children had successfully assimilated into the mainstream and risen to the middle class. In this new myth, Euroethnic suburbs like mine became the measure of U.S. democracy's victory over racism. Jewish mobility became a new Horatio Alger story. In time and with hard work, every ethnic group would get a piece of the pie, and the United States would be a nation with equal opportunity for all its people to become part of a prosperous middle-class majority. And it seemed that Euroethnic immigrants and their children were delighted to join middle America.[11]

This is not to say that anti-Semitism disappeared after World War II, only that it fell from fashion and was driven underground. Micah Sifry's (1993) revelations of Richard Nixon's and George Bush's personal anti-Semitism and its prevalence in both their administrations indicate its persistence in the Protestant elite. There has also been an alarming rise of anti-Semitic and anti–African American hate groups and hate crimes in recent years. While elites do not have a monopoly on anti-Semitism, they do have the ability to restrict Jews' access to the top echelons of corporate America. Since the war, the remaining glass ceilings on Jewish mobility have gotten fewer and higher. Although they may still keep down the number of Jews and other Euroethnics in the upper class, it has been a long time since they could keep them out of the middle class. However, a 1987 Supreme Court ruling that Jews and Arabs could use civil rights laws to gain redress for discrimination against them did so on the grounds that they are not racial whites. As historian Barbara Jeanne Fields (1990:97) notes, "[T]he court knew no better way to rectify injustice at the end of the twentieth century than to re-enthrone the superstitious racial dogma of the nineteenth century."[12]

Although changing views on who was white made it easier for Euroethnics to become middle class, it was also the case that economic prosperity played a very powerful role in the whitening process. Economic mobility of Jews and other Euroethnics rested ultimately on U.S. post war economic prosperity with its enormously expanded need for professional, technical, and managerial labor, and on government assistance in providing it. The United States emerged from the war with the strongest economy in the world. Real wages rose between 1946 and 1960, increasing buying power a hefty 22 percent and giving most Americans some discretionary income (Nash et al. 1986:885–886). U.S. manufacturing, banking, and business services became increasingly dominated by large corporations, and these grew into multinational corporations. Their organizational centers lay in big, new urban headquarters that demanded growing numbers of technical and managerial workers. The postwar period was a historic moment for real class mobility and for the affluence we have erroneously come to believe was the U.S. norm. It was a time when the old white and the newly white masses became middle class.

The GI Bill of Rights, as the 1944 Serviceman's Readjustment Act was known, was arguably the most massive affirmative action program in U.S. history. It was created to develop needed labor-force skills, and to provide those who had them with a life-style that reflected their value to the economy. The GI benefits ultimately extended to sixteen million GIs (veterans of the Korean War as well) included priority in jobs—that is, preferential hiring, but no one objected to it then—financial support during the job search; small loans for starting up businesses; and, most important, low-interest home loans and educational benefits, which included tuition and living expenses (Brown 1946; Hurd 1946; Mosch 1975; *Postwar Jobs for Veterans* 1945; Willenz 1983). This legislation was rightly regarded as one of the most revolutionary postwar programs. I call it affirmative action because it was aimed at and disproportionately helped male, Euro-origin GIs.

GI benefits, like the New Deal affirmative action programs before them and the 1960s affirmative action programs after them, were responses to protest. Business executives and the general public believed that the war economy had only temporarily halted the Great Depression. Many feared its return and a return to the labor strife and radicalism of the 1930s (Eichler 1982:4; Nash et al. 1986:885). "[M]emories of the Depression remained vivid and many people suffered from what Davis Ross has aptly called 'depression psychosis'—the fear that the war would inevitably be followed by layoffs and mass unemployment" (Wynn 1976:15).

It was a reasonable fear. The eleven million military personnel who were demobilized in the 1940s represented a quarter of the U.S. labor force (Mosch 1975:1, 20). In addition, ending war production brought a huge number of layoffs, growing unemployment, and a high rate of inflation. To recoup wartime losses in real wages caused by inflation as well as by the unions' no-strike pledge in support of the war effort, workers staged a massive wave of strikes in 1946. More workers went out on strike that year than ever before, and there were strikes in all the heavy industries: railroads, coal mining, auto, steel, and electrical. For a brief moment, it looked like class struggle all over again. But government and business leaders had learned from the experience of bitter labor struggles after World War I just how important it was to assist demobilized soldiers. The GI Bill resulted from their determination to avoid those mistakes this time. The biggest benefits of this legislation were for college and technical school education, and for very cheap home mortgages.

Education and Occupation

It is important to remember that prior to the war, a college degree was still very much a "mark of the upper class" (Willenz 1983:165). Colleges were largely finishing schools for Protestant elites. Before the postwar boom, schools could not begin to accommodate the American masses. Even in New York City before the 1930s, neither the public schools nor City College had room for more than a tiny fraction of potential immigrant students.

Not so after the war. The almost eight million GIs who took advantage of their educational benefits under the GI bill caused "the greatest wave of college building in American history" (Nash et al. 1986:885). White male GIs were able to take advantage of their educational benefits for college and technical training, so they were particularly well positioned to seize the opportunities provided by the new demands for professional, managerial, and technical labor. "It has been well documented that the GI educational benefits transformed American higher education and raised the educational level of that generation and generations to come. With many provisions for assistance in upgrading their educational attainments veterans pulled ahead of nonveterans in earning capacity. In the long run it was the nonveterans who had fewer opportunities" (Willenz 1983:165).[13]

Just how valuable a college education was for white men's occupational mobility can be seen in John Keller's study of who benefited from the metamorphosis of California's Santa Clara Valley into Silicon Valley. Formerly an agricultural region, in the 1950s the area became the scene of explosive growth in the semiconductor electronics industry. This industry epitomized the postwar economy and occupational structure. It owed its existence directly to the military and to the National Aeronautics and Space Administration (NASA), who were its major funders and its major markets. It had an increasingly white-collar work force. White men, who were the initial production workers in the 1950s, quickly transformed themselves into a technical and professional work force thanks largely to GI benefits and the new junior college training programs designed to meet the industry's growing work-force needs. Keller notes that "62 percent of enrollees at San Jose Junior College (later renamed San Jose City College) came from blue-collar families, and 55 percent of all job placements were as electronics technicians in the industrial and service sectors of the county economy" (1983:363). As white men left assembly work and the industry expanded between 1950 and 1960, they were replaced initially by Latinas and African-American women, who were joined after 1970 by new immigrant women. Inmigrating men tended to work in the better-paid unionized industries that grew up in the area (Keller 1983:346–373).

Postwar expansion made college accessible to the mass of Euromales in general and to Jews in particular. My generation's "Think what you could have been!" answer to our parents became our reality as quotas and old occupational barriers fell and new fields opened up to Jews. The most striking result was a sharp decline in Jewish small businesses and a skyrocketing of Jewish professionals. For example, as quotas in medical schools fell the numbers of Jewish doctors mushroomed. If Boston is an indication, just over 1 percent of all Jewish men before the war were doctors compared to 16 percent of the postwar generation (Silberman 1985:124, and see 118–126). A similar Jewish mass movement took place into college and university faculties, especially in "new and expanding fields in the social and natural sciences" (Steinberg 1989:137).[14] Although these Jewish college professors tended to be sons of businesspersons and professionals, the postwar boom saw the first large-scale class mobility among Jewish men. Sons of working-class Jews now went to college and became professionals themselves, according to the Boston survey, almost two-thirds of them. This compared favorably with three-quarters of the sons of professional fathers (Silberman 1985: 121–122).[15]

Even more significantly, the postwar boom transformed the U.S. class structure—or at least its status structure—so that the middle class expanded to encompass most of the population. Before the war, most Jews, like most other Americans, were working class. Already upwardly mobile before the war relative to other immigrants, Jews floated high on this rising economic tide, and most of them entered the middle class. Still, even the high tide missed some Jews. As late as 1973, some 15 percent of New York's Jews were poor or near-poor, and in the 1960s, almost 25 percent of employed Jewish men remained manual workers (Steinberg 1989:89–90).

Educational and occupational GI benefits really constituted affirmative action programs for white males because they were decidedly not extended to African Americans or to women of any race. White male privilege was shaped against the backdrop of wartime racism and post-war sexism. During and after the war, there was an upsurge in white racist violence against black servicemen in public schools, and in the KKK, which spread to California and New York (Dalfiume 1969:133–134). The number of lynchings rose during the war, and in 1943 there were antiblack race riots in several large northern cities. Although there was a wartime labor shortage, black people were discriminated against in access to well-paid defense industry jobs and in housing. In 1946 there were white riots against African Americans across the South, and in Chicago and Philadelphia as well. Gains made as a result of the wartime Civil Rights movement, especially employment in defense-related industries, were lost with peacetime conversion as black workers were the first fired, often in violation of seniority (Wynn 1976:114, 116). White women were also laid off, ostensibly to make jobs for demobilized servicemen, and in the long run women lost most of the gains they had made in wartime (Kessler-Harris 1982). We now know that women did not leave the labor force in any significant numbers but instead were forced to find inferior jobs, largely nonunion, parttime, and clerical.

Theoretically available to all veterans, in practice women and black veterans did not get anywhere near their share of GI benefits. Because women's units were not treated as part of the military, women in them were not considered veterans and were ineligible for Veterans' Administration (VA) benefits (Willenz 1983:168). The barriers that almost completely shut African-American GIs out of their benefits were more complex. In Wynn's portrait (1976:115), black GIs anticipated starting new lives, just like their white counterparts. Over 43 percent hoped to return to school and most expected to relocate, to find better jobs in new lines of work. The exodus from the South toward the North and far West was particularly large. So it wasn't a question of any lack of ambition on the part of African-American GIs.

Rather, the military, the Veterans' Administration, the U.S. Employment Service, and the Federal Housing Administration (FHA) effectively denied African-American GIs access to their benefits and to the new educational, occupational, and residential opportunities. Black GIs who served in the thoroughly segregated armed forces during World War II served under white officers, usually southerners (Binkin and Eitelberg 1982; Dalfiume 1969; Foner 1974; Johnson 1967; Nalty and MacGregor 1981). African-American soldiers were disproportionately given dishonorable discharges, which denied them veterans' rights under the GI Bill. Thus between August and November 1946, 21 percent of white soldiers and 39 percent of black soldiers were dishonorably discharged. Those who did get an honorable discharge then faced the Veterans' Administration and the U.S. Employment Service. The latter, which was responsible for job placements, employed very few African Americans, especially in the South. This meant that black veterans did not receive much employment information, and that the offers they did receive were for low-paid and menial jobs. "In one survey of 50 cities, the movement of blacks into peacetime employment was found to be lagging far behind that of white veterans: in Arkansas 95 percent of the placements made by the USES for Afro-Americans were in service or unskilled jobs" (Nalty and MacGregor 1981:218, and see 60–61). African Americans were also less likely than whites, regardless of GI status, to gain new jobs commensurate with their wartime jobs, and they suffered more heavily. For example, in San Francisco by 1948, Black Americans "had dropped back halfway to their pre-war employment status" (Wynn 1976:114, 116).[16]

Black GIs faced discrimination in the educational system as well. Despite the end of restrictions on Jews and other Euroethnics, African Americans were not welcome in white colleges. Black colleges were overcrowded, and the combination of segregation and prejudice made for few alternatives. About twenty thousand black veterans attended college by 1947, most in black colleges, but almost as many, fifteen thousand could not gain entry. Predictably, the disproportionately few African Americans who did gain access to their educational benefits were able, like their white counterparts, to become doctors and engineers, and to enter the black middle class (Walker 1970).

Suburbanization

In 1949, ensconced at Valley Stream, I watched potato farms turn into Levittown and into Idlewild (later Kennedy) Airport. This was a major spectator sport in our first years on suburban Long Island. A typical weekend would bring various aunts, uncles, and cousins out from the city. After a huge meal we would pile in the car—itself a novelty—to look at the bulldozed acres and comment on the matchbox construction. During the week, my mother and I would look at the houses going up within walking distance.

Bill Levitt built a basic 900–1,000-square-foot, somewhat expandable house for a lower-middle-class and working-class market on Long Island, and later in Pennsylvania and New Jersey (Gans 1967). Levittown started out as two thousand units of rental housing at sixty dollars a month, designed to meet the low-income housing needs of returning war vets, many of whom, like my Aunt Evie and Uncle Julie, were living in quonset huts. By May 1947, Levitt and Sons had acquired enough land in Hempstead Township on Long Island to build four thousand houses, and by the next February, he'd built six thousand units and named the development after himself. After 1948, federal financing for the construction of rental housing tightened, and Levitt switched to building houses for sale. By 1951 Levittown was a development of some fifteen thousand families.

Hartman (1975:141–142) cites massive abuses in the 1940s and 1950s by builders under Section 608, a program in which "the FHA granted extraordinarily liberal concessions to lackadaisically supervised private developers to induce them to produce rental housing rapidly in the postwar period." Eichler (1982) indicates that things were not that different in the subsequent FHA-funded home-building industry.

At the beginning of World War II, about 33 percent of all U.S. families owned their houses. That percentage doubled in twenty years. Most Levittowners looked just like my family. They came from New York City or Long Island; about 17 percent were military, from nearby Mitchell Field; Levittown was their first house; and almost everyone was married. The 1947 inhabitants were over 75 percent white collar, but by 1950 more blue-collar families moved in, so that by 1951, "barely half" of the new residents were white collar, and by 1960 their occupational profile was somewhat more working class than for Nassau County as a whole. By this time too, almost one-third of Levittown's people were either foreign-born or, like my parents, first-generation U.S. born (Dobriner 1963:91, 100).

The FHA was key to buyers and builders alike. Thanks to it, suburbia was open to more than GIs. People like us would never have been in the market for houses without FHA and VA low-down-payment, low-interest, long-term loans to young buyers.[17] Most suburbs were built by "merchant builders," large-scale entrepreneurs like Levitt, who obtained their own direct FHA and VA loans (Jackson 1985:215). In the view of one major builder, "Without FHA and VA loans merchant building would not have happened" (Eichler 1982:9). A great deal was at stake. The FHA and VA had to approve subdivision plans and make the appraisals upon which house buyers' loans were calculated. FHA appraisals effectively set the price a house could sell for, since the FHA established the amount of the mortgage it would insure. The VA was created after the war, and it followed FHA policies. Most of the benefits in both programs went to suburbs, and half of all suburban housing in the 1950s and 1960s was financed by FHA/VA loans. Federal highway funding was also important to suburbanization. The National Defense Highway Act of 1941 put the government in the business of funding 90 percent of a national highway system (the other 10 percent came from states), which developed a network of freeways between and around the nation's metropolitan areas, making suburbs and automobile commuting a way of life. State zoning laws and services were also key. "A significant and often crucial portion of the required infrastructure—typically water, sewer, roads, parks, schools—was provided by the existing community, which was in effect subsidizing the builder and indirectly the new buyer or renter" (Eichler 1982:13).[18]

In residential life as in jobs and education, federal programs and GI benefits were crucial for mass entry into a middle-class homeowning suburban life-style. Indeed, they raised the U.S. standard of living to a middle-class one.

It was here that the federal government's racism reached its high point. Begun in 1934, the FHA was a New Deal program whose original intent was to stimulate the construction industry by insuring private loans to buy or build houses. Even before the war, it had stimulated a building boom. The FHA was "largely run by representatives of the real estate and banking industries" (Jackson 1985:203–205; Weiss 1987:146). It is fair to say that the "FHA exhorted segregation and enshrined it as public policy" (Jackson 1985:213). As early as 1955, Charles Abrams blasted it:

> A government offering such bounty to builders and lenders could have required compliance with a nondiscrimination policy. Or the agency could at least have pursued a course of evasion, or hidden behind the screen of local autonomy. Instead, FHA adopted a racial policy that could well have been culled from the Nuremberg laws. From its inception FHA set itself up as the protector of the all white neighborhood. It sent its agents into the field to keep Negroes and other minorities from buying houses in white neighborhood. (1955:229; see also Gelfand 1975; Lief and Goering 1987)

The FHA believed in racial segregation. Throughout its history, it publicly and actively promoted restrictive covenants. Before the war, these forbade sale to Jews and Catholics as well as to African Americans. The deed to my house in Detroit had such a covenant, which theoretically prevented it from being sold to Jews or African Americans. Even after the Supreme Court ended legal enforcement of restrictive covenants in 1948, the FHA continued to encourage builders to write them against African Americans. FHA underwriting manuals openly insisted on racially homogeneous neighborhoods, and their loans were made only in white neighborhoods. I bought my Detroit house in 1972 from Jews who were leaving a largely African-American neighborhood. By that time, after the 1968

Fair Housing Act, restrictive covenants were a dead letter (although blockbusting by realtors was rapidly replacing it).

With the federal government behind them, virtually all developers refused to sell to African Americans. Palo Alto and Levittown, like most suburbs as late as 1960, were virtually all white. Out of 15,741 houses and 65,276 people, averaging 4.2 people per house, only 220 Levittowners, or 52 households, were "nonwhite." In 1958 Levitt announced publicly at a press conference to open his New Jersey development that he would not sell to black buyers. This caused a furor, since the state of New Jersey (but not the U.S. government) prohibited discrimination in federally subsidized housing. Levitt was sued and fought it, although he was ultimately persuaded by township ministers to integrate. There had been a white riot in his Pennsylvania development when a black family moved in a few years earlier. West Coast builder Joe Eichler had a policy of selling to any African Americans who could afford to buy. But his son pointed out that his father's clientele in more affluent Palo Alto was less likely to feel threatened. Eichler's clients tended to think of themselves as liberal, which was relatively easy to do because there were few African Americans in the Bay area, and fewer still could afford homes in Palo Alto (Eichler 1982; see also Center for the Study of Democratic Institutions 1964).

The result of these policies was that African Americans were totally shut out of the suburban boom. An article in *Harper's* described the housing available to black GIs. "On his way to the base each morning, Sergeant Smith passes an attractive air-conditioned, FHA-financed housing project. It was built for service families. Its rents are little more than the Smiths pay for their shack. And there are half-a-dozen vacancies, but none for Negroes" (qtd. in Foner 1974:195).

Where my family felt the seductive pull of suburbia, Marshall Berman's experienced the brutal push of urban renewal. In the Bronx in the 1950s, Robert Moses's Cross-Bronx Expressway erased "a dozen solid, settled, densely populated neighborhoods like our own; . . . something like 60,000 working- and lower-middle-class people, mostly Jews, but with many Italians, Irish and Blacks thrown in, would be thrown out of their homes. . . . For ten years, through the late 1950s and early 1960s, the center of the Bronx was pounded and blasted and smashed" (1982:292).

Urban renewal made postwar cities into bad places to live. At a physical level, urban renewal reshaped them, and federal programs brought private developers and public officials together to create downtown central business districts where there had formerly been a mix of manufacturing, commerce, and working-class neighborhoods. Manufacturing was scattered to the peripheries of the city, which were ringed and bisected by a national system of highways. Some working-class neighborhoods were bulldozed, but others remained (Greer 1965; Hartman 1975; Squires 1989). In Los Angeles, as in New York's Bronx, the postwar period saw massive freeway construction right through the heart of old working-class neighborhoods. In East Los Angeles and Santa Monica, Chicano and African-American communities were divided in half or blasted to smithereens by the highways bringing Angelenos to the new white suburbs, or to make way for civic monuments like Dodger Stadium (Pardo 1990; Social and Public Arts Resource Center 1990:80, 1983:12–13).

Urban renewal was the other side of the process by which Jewish and other working-class Euroimmigrants became middle class. It was the push to suburbia's seductive pull. The fortunate white survivors of urban renewal headed disproportionately for suburbia, where they could partake of prosperity and the good life. There was a reason for its attraction. It was often cheaper to buy in the suburbs than to rent in the city (Jackson 1985:206). Even Euroethnics and families who would be considered working class based on their occupations were able to buy into the emerging white suburban life style. And as Levittown indicates, they did so in increasing numbers, so that by 1966 50 percent of all workers and 75 percent of those under age forty nationwide lived in suburbs (Brody 1980:192). They too were considered middle class.

If the federal stick of urban renewal joined the FHA carrot of cheap mortgages to send masses of Euros to the suburbs, the FHA had a different kind of one-two punch for African-Americans. Segregation kept them out of the suburbs, and redlining made sure they could not buy or repair their homes in the neighborhoods where they were allowed to live. The FHA practiced systematic redlining. This was a system developed by its predecessor, the Home Owners Loan Corporation (HOLC), which in the 1930s developed an elaborate neighborhood rating system that placed the highest (green) value on all-white, middle-class neighborhoods, and the lowest (red) on racially nonwhite or mixed and working-class neighborhoods. High ratings meant high property values. The idea was that low property values in redlined neighborhoods made them bad investments. The FHA was, after all, created by and for banks and the housing industry. Redlining warned banks not to lend there, and the FHA would not insure mortgages in such neighborhoods. Redlining created a self-fulfilling prophecy. "With the assistance of local realtors and banks, it assigned one of the four ratings to every block in every city. The resulting information was then translated into the appropriate color [green, blue, yellow, and red] and duly recorded on secret 'Residential Security Maps' in local HOLC offices. The maps themselves were placed in elaborate 'City Survey Files,' which consisted of reports, questionnaires, and workpapers relating to current and future values of real estate" (Jackson 1985:199).[19]

FHA's and VA's refusal to guarantee loans in redlined neighborhoods made it virtually impossible for African Americans to borrow money for home improvement or purchase. Because these maps and surveys were quite secret, it took the 1960s Civil Rights movement to make these practices and their devastating consequences public. As a result, those who fought urban renewal or who sought to make a home in the urban ruins found themselves locked out of the middle class. They also faced an ideological assault that labeled their neighborhoods slums and called those who lived in them slum dwellers (Gans 1962).

The record is very clear that instead of seizing the opportunity to end institutionalized racism, the federal government did its best to shut and double seal the postwar window of opportunity in African Americans' faces. It consistently refused to combat segregation in the social institutions that were key for upward mobility: education, housing, and employment. Moreover, federal programs that were themselves designed to assist demobilized GIs and young families systematically discriminated against African Americans. Such programs reinforced white/nonwhite racial distinctions even as intrawhite racialization was falling out of fashion. This other side of the coin, that white men of northwestern and southeastern European ancestry were treated equally in theory and in practice with regard to the benefits they received, was part of the larger postwar whitening of Jews and other eastern and southern Europeans.

The myth that Jews pulled themselves up by their own bootstraps ignores the fact that it took federal programs to create the conditions whereby the abilities of Jews and other European immigrants could be recognized and rewarded rather than denigrated and denied. The GI Bill and FHA and VA mortgages were forms of affirmative action that allowed male Jews and other Euro-American men to become suburban homeowners and to get the training that allowed them—but not women vets or war workers—to become professionals, technicians, salesmen, and managers in a growing economy. Jews' and other white ethnics' upward mobility was the result of programs that allowed us to float on a rising economic tide. To African Americans, the government offered the cement boots of segregation, redlining, urban renewal, and discrimination.

Those racially skewed gains have been passed across the generations, so that racial inequality seems to maintain itself "naturally," even after legal segregation ended. Today, in a shrinking economy where downward mobility is the norm, the children and grandchildren of the postwar beneficiaries of the economic boom have some precious advantages. For example, having parents who own their own homes or who have decent retirement benefits can make a real difference in young people's ability to take on huge college loans or to come up with a down payment for a house. Even this simple inheritance helps perpetuate the gap between whites and nonwhites. Sure Jews needed ability, but ability was not enough to make it. The same applies even more in today's long recession.

Notes

This is a revised and expanded version of a paper published in *Jewish Currents* in June 1992 and delivered at the 1992 meetings of the American Anthropological Association in the session *Blacks and Jews, 1992: Reaching across the Cultural Boundaries* organized by Angela Gilliam. I would like to thank Emily Abel, Katya Gibel Azoulay, Edna Bonacich, Angela Gilliam, Isabelle Gunning, Valerie Matsumoto, Regina Morantz-Sanchez, Roger Sanjek, Rabbi Chaim Seidler-Feller, Janet Silverstein, and Eloise Klein Healy's writing group for uncovering wonderful sources and for critical readings along the way.

1. Indeed, Boasian and Du Boisian anthropology developed in active political opposition to this nativism; on Du Bois, see Harrison and Nonini 1992.
2. On immigrants as part of the industrial work force, see Steinberg 1989: 36.
3. I thank Roger Sanjek for providing me with this source.
4. It was intended, as Davenport wrote to the president of the American Museum of Natural History, Henry Fairfield Osborne, as "an anthropological society . . . with a central governing body, self-elected and self-perpetuating, and very limited in members, and also confined to native Americans who are anthropologically, socially and politically sound, no Bolsheviki need apply" (Barkan 1991:67–68).
5. I thank Valerie Matsumoto for telling me about the Thind case and Katya Gibel Azoulay for providing this information to me on the Virginia statute.
6. "The distinction between white and colored" has been "the only racial classification which has been carried through all the 15 censuses." "Colored" consisted of "Negroes" and "other races": Mexican, Indian, Chinese, Japanese, Filipino, Hindu, Korean, Hawaiian, Malay, Siamese, and Samoan. (U.S. Bureau of the Census, 1930:25, 26).
7. For why Jews entered colleges earlier than other immigrants, and for a challenge to views that attribute it to Jewish culture, see Steinberg 1989.
8. Although quotas on Jews persisted into the 1950s in some of the elite

schools, they were much attenuated, as the postwar college-building boom gave the coup-de-grace to the gentleman's finishing school.

9. Steinberg (1989: chap. 5), challenging the belief that education was the source of Jewish mobility, cites Gutman's comparison of a working-class Jewish neighborhood on Cherry Street and a business and professional one on East Broadway in 1905, showing that children of Jewish workers did not go to college.

10. Between 1900 and 1930 New York City's population grew from 3.4 million to 6.9 million, and at both times immigrants and the children of immigrants were 80 percent of all white household heads (Moore 1992:270, n. 28).

11. Indeed, Jewish social scientists were prominent in creating this ideology of the United States as a meritocracy. Most prominent of course was Nathan Glazer, but among them also were Charles Silberman and Marshall Sklare.

12. I am indebted to Katya Gibel Azoulay for bringing this to my attention.

13. The belief was widespread that "the GI Bill . . . helped millions of families move into the middle class" (Nash et al. 1986:885). A study that compares mobility among veterans and nonveterans provides a kind of confirmation. In an unnamed small city in Illinois, Havighurst and his colleagues (1951) found no significant difference between veterans and nonveterans, but this was because apparently very few veterans used any of their GI benefits.

14. Interestingly, Steinberg (1989:149) shows that Jewish professionals tended to be children of small-business owners, but their Catholic counterparts tended to be children of workers.

15. None of the Jewish surveys seem to have asked what women were doing. Silberman (1985) claims that Jewish women stayed out of the labor force prior to the 1970s, but if my parents' circle is any indication, there were plenty of working professional women.

16. African Americans and Japanese Americans were the main target of wartime racism (see Murray 1992). By contrast, there were virtually no anti-German American or anti-Italian American policies in World War II (see Takaki 1989:357–406).

17. See Eichler 1982:5 for homeowning percentages; Jackson (1985:205) found an increase in families living in owner-occupied buildings, rising from 44 percent in 1934 to 63 percent in 1972; see Monkkonen 1988 on scarcity of mortgages; and Gelfand 1975, esp. chap. 6, on federal programs.

18. In the location of highway interchanges, as in the appraisal and inspection process, Eichler (1982) claims that large-scale builders often bribed and otherwise influenced the outcomes in their favor.

19. These ideas from the real estate industry were "codified and legitimated in 1930s work by University of Chicago sociologist Robert Park and real estate professor Homer Hoyt" (Jackson 1985:198–199).

References

Abrams, Charles. 1955. *Forbidden Neighbors: A Study of Prejudice in Housing.* New York: Harper.

Barkan, Elazar. 1991. *The Retreat of Scientific Racism: Changing Concepts of Race in Britain and the United States between the World Wars.* Cambridge: Cambridge University Press.
Berman, Marshall. 1982. *All That Is Solid Melts into Air: The Experience of Modernity.* New York: Simon and Schuster.
Binkin, Martin, and Mark J. Eitelberg. 1982. *Blacks and the Military.* Washington, D.C.: Brookings.
Bodnar, John. 1985. *The Transplanted: A History of Immigrants in Urban America.* Bloomington: Indiana University Press.
Brody, David. 1980. *Workers in Industrial America: Essays of the Twentieth Century Struggle.* New York: Oxford University Press.
Brown, Francis J. 1946. *Educational Opportunities for Veterans.* Washington, D.C.: Public Affairs Press, American Council on Public Affairs.
Carlson, Lewis H., and George A. Colburn. 1972. *In Their Place: White America Defines Her Minorities, 1850–1950.* New York: Wiley.
Center for the Study of Democratic Institutions. *Race and Housing: An Interview with Edward P. Eichler, President, Eichler Homes, Inc.* 1964. Santa Barbara: Center for the Study of Democratic Institutions.
Dalfiume, Richard M. 1969. *Desegregation of the U.S. Armed Forces: Fighting on Two Fronts, 1939–1953.* Columbia: University of Missouri Press.
Davis, Mike. 1990. *City of Quartz.* London: Verso.
Dobriner, William M. 1963. *Class in Suburbia.* Englewood Cliffs, N.J.: Prentice-Hall.
Eichler, Ned. 1982. *The Merchant Builders.* Cambridge, Mass.: MIT Press.
Fields, Barbara Jeanne. 1990. Slavery, Race, and Ideology in the United States of America. *New Left Review* 181:95–118.
Foner, Jack. 1974. *Blacks and the Military in American History: A New Perspective.* New York: Praeger.
Gans, Herbert. 1962. *The Urban Villagers.* New York: Free Press.
———. 1967. *The Levittowners.* New York: Pantheon.
Gelfand, Mark. 1975. *A Nation of Cities: The Federal Government and Urban America, 1933–1965.* New York: Oxford University Press.
Gerber, David. 1986a. Introduction. In *Anti-Semitism in American History,* ed. Gerber, 3–56.
———, ed. 1986b. *Anti-Semitism in American History.* Urbana: University of Illinois Press.
Glazer, Nathan, and Patrick Moynihan. 1963. *Beyond the Melting Pot: The Negroes, Puerto Ricans, Jews, Italians, and Irish of New York City.* Cambridge, Mass.: MIT Press.
Gordon, Milton. 1964. *Assimilation in American Life.* New York: Oxford University Press.
Greer, Scott. 1965. *Urban Renewal and American Cities.* Indianapolis: Bobbs-Merrill.
Harrison, Faye V., and Donald Nonini, eds. 1992 *Critique of Anthropology* (special issue on W.E.B. Du Bois and anthropology) 12(3).

Hartman, Chester. 1975. *Housing and Social Policy.* Englewood Cliffs, N.J.: Prentice-Hall.

Havighurst, Robert J., John W. Baughman, Walter H. Eaton, and Ernest W. Burgess. 1951. *The American Veteran Back Home: A Study of Veteran Readjustment.* New York: Longmans, Green.

Higham, John. 1955. *Strangers in the Land.* New Brunswick: Rutgers University Press.

Hurd, Charles. 1946. *The Veterans' Program: A Complete Guide to Its Benefits, Rights, and Options.* New York: McGraw-Hill.

Jackson, Kenneth T. 1985. *Crabgrass Frontier: The Suburbanization of the United States.* New York: Oxford University Press.

Johnson, Jesse J. 1967. *Ebony Brass: An Autobiography of Negro Frustration amid Aspiration.* New York: Frederick.

Karabel, Jerome. 1984. Status-Group Struggle, Organizational Interests, and the Limits of Institutional Autonomy. *Theory and Society* 13:1–40.

Kessler-Harris, Alice. 1982. *Out to Work: A History of Wage-Earning Women in the United States.* New York: Oxford University Press.

Lief, Beth J., and Susan Goering. 1987. The Implementation of the Federal Mandate for Fair Housing. In *Divided Neighborhoods,* ed. Gary A. Tobin, 227–267.

Martyn, Byron Curti. 1979. Racism in the U.S.: A History of Anti-Miscegenation Legislation and Litigation. Ph.D. diss., University of Southern California.

Monkkonen, Eric H. 1988. *America Becomes Urban.* Berkeley and Los Angeles: University of California Press.

Moore, Deborah Dash. 1992. On the Fringes of the City: Jewish Neighborhoods in Three Boroughs. In *The Landscape of Modernity: Essays on New York City, 1900–1940,* ed. David Ward and Olivier Zunz, 252–272. New York: Russell Sage.

Mosch, Theodore R. 1975. *The GI Bill: A Breakthrough in Educational and Social Policy in the United States.* Hicksville, N.Y.: Exposition.

Murray, Alice Yang. 1992. Japanese Americans, Redress, and Reparations: A Study of Community, Family, and Gender, 1940–1990. Ph.D. diss., Stanford University.

Nalty, Bernard C., and Morris J. MacGregor, eds. 1981. *Blacks in the Military: Essential Documents.* Wilmington, Del.: Scholarly Resources.

Nash, Gary B., Julie Roy Jeffrey, John R. Howe, Allen F. Davis, Peter J. Frederick, and Allen M. Winkler. 1986. *The American People: Creating a Nation and a Society.* New York: Harper and Row.

Pardo, Mary. 1990. Mexican-American Women Grassroots Community Activists: "Mothers of East Los Angeles." *Frontiers* 11:1–7.

Postwar Jobs for Veterans. 1945. *Annals of the American Academy of Political and Social Science* 238 (March).

Saxton, Alexander. 1971. *The Indispensible Enemy.* Berkeley and Los Angeles: University of California Press.

———. 1990. *The Rise and Fall of the White Republic*. London: Verso.
Schoener, Allon. 1967. *Portal to America: The Lower East Side, 1870–1925*. New York: Holt, Rinehart and Winston.
Sifry, Micah. 1993. Anti-Semitism in America. *Nation*, January 25, 92–99.
Silberman, Charles. 1985. *A Certain People: American Jews and Their Lives Today*. New York: Summit.
Sklare, Marshall. 1971. *America's Jews*. New York: Random House.
Social and Public Arts Resource Center. 1990. *Signs from the Heart: California Chicano Murals*. Venice, Calif.: Social and Public Art Resource Center.
———. 1983. *Walking Tour and Guide to the Great Wall of Los Angeles*. Venice, Calif.: Social and Public Arts Resource Center.
Sowell, Thomas. 1981. *Ethnic America: A History*. New York: Basic.
Squires, Gregory D., ed. 1989. *Unequal Partnerships: The Political Economy of Urban Redevelopment in Postwar America*. New Brunswick: Rutgers University Press.
Steinberg, Stephen. 1989. *The Ethnic Myth: Race, Ethnicity, and Class in America*. 2d ed. Boston: Beacon.
Synott, Marcia Graham. 1986. Anti-Semitism and American Universities: Did Quotas Follow the Jews? In *Anti-Semitism in American History*, ed. David A. Gerber, 233–274.
Takaki, Ronald. 1989. *Strangers from a Different Shore*. Boston: Little, Brown.
Tobin, Gary A., ed. 1987. *Divided Neighborhoods: Changing Patterns of Racial Segregation*. Beverly Hills: Sage.
U.S. Bureau of the Census. 1930. *Fifteenth Census of the United States*. Vol. 2. Washington, D.C.: U.S. Government Printing Office.
———. 1940. *Sixteenth Census of the United States*, vol. 2. Washington, D.C.: U.S. Government Printing Office.
Walker, Olive. 1970. The Windsor Hills School Story. *Integrated Education: Race and Schools* 8(3): 4–9.
Weiss, Marc A. 1987. *The Rise of the Community Builders: The American Real Estate Industry and Urban Land Planning*. New York: Columbia University Press.
Willenz, June A. 1983. *Women Veterans: America's Forgotten Heroines*. New York: Continuum.
Wynn, Neil A. 1976. *The Afro-American and the Second World War*. London: Elek.

ROGER SANJEK

Intermarriage and the Future of Races in the United States

Race, sex, and power remain the essential ingredients of the continuing 'American dilemma' of the United States. Race, sex, and power head the agenda of the country's social and political unfinished business. Within this biracially divided social order where, until recently, all but a few at its margins were either white or black, the power of race has long been expressed and mediated through sex. Rape, forced disruption of black conjugal ties and kinship networks, sexual mythology and fear, legal bars to interracial marriage, and the overriding of kinship by race are historic features of the race-sex-power equation (Jordan 1968; Spickard 1989:235–342; Washington 1970; Williamson 1980).

Through nearly four centuries, from the early 1600s, white and black Americans have lived together in this land. They did so in closer propinquity through the twenty-five decades during which this was a slave society than in the thirteen decades since, decades marked by a still deeply entrenched pattern of black-white residential segregration (Lieberson 1980:253–291; Massey and Denton 1993; O'Hare et al. 1991:9).[1] St. Clair Drake and Horace Cayton characterized the racial segregation of Chicago in the early 1940s as "a pattern of relations which reduces to a minimum any neighborly contacts, school contacts, or chance meetings in stores, taverns, and movie houses between Negroes and whites" ([1945] 1962:195). In view of this history, it is hardly surprising that the prevalence of white-black intermarriage remains exceedingly low, at 3 percent for married blacks by 1990 (2 percent in 1980), and far less than 1 percent for whites (Alba 1990:12–13; Collins 1985; O'Hare and Felt 1991:12; Spickard 1989:280; Spigner 1990).

Despite the low rate of white-black intermarriage throughout U.S. history, great numbers of white males have been ready to "bed but not wed" black women (Davis et al. 1941:24–38; Drake and Cayton [1945] 1962:116–136, 556–557, 638; Powdermaker 1939; Washington 1970; Williamson 1980). This history of sexual abuse and exploitation has never inspired any mass enthusiasm by African Americans in favor of marriage with whites. And a negative attitude to interracial marriage has been held by whites, for whom the rhetorical question "Would you want your daughter to marry a Negro?" long required no answer. But black and white opinion frequently divided on the question of laws forbidding interracial marriage, of which a new round were proposed in many states in the Jim Crow decades of the late nineteenth and early twentieth centuries. In 1921, the black scholar and activist W.E.B. Du Bois reiterated a widely held African-American position opposing such laws:

> We have not asked amalgamation; we have resisted it. It has been forced upon us by brute strength, ignorance, poverty, degradation and fraud. It is the white race . . . that has left its trail of bastards and outraged women and then raised holy hands to heaven and deplored "race mixture." No, we are not demanding and do not want amalgamation, but the reasons are ours and not yours. It is not because we are unworthy of intermarriage—either physically or mentally or morally. . . . It is because no real men accept any alliance except on terms of absolute equal regard and because we are abundantly satisfied with our own race and blood. And at the same time we . . . as free men must say that whenever two human beings of any nation or race desire each other in marriage, the denial of their legal right to marry is . . . simply wrong (qtd. in Spickard 1989:299).[2]

African-American opposition to laws barring interracial marriage, led by Du Bois and the NAACP, was aimed at the overtly racist presumption of black inferiority that these laws contained (Washington 1970:69–97). At the same time, black opinion has also resisted the more subtle but still racist viewpoint of white liberals who have favored interracial marriage as a "solution" to America's race problem. This position, according to which African Americans would melt into the white population and eventually disappear, was advocated by anthropologists Franz Boas and Ralph Linton (Washington 1970:4–7, 114, 131–139, 153–155, 173–179, 187). As Boas wrote in 1921,

> [T]he greatest hope for the immediate future lies in a lessening of the contrast between negroes and whites. . . . Intermixture will decrease the contrast between extreme racial forms. . . . In a race of octoroons, living among whites, the color question would probably disappear. . . . It would seem, therefore, to be in the interest of society to permit rather than to restrain marriages between white men and negro women. It would be futile to expect that our people would tolerate intermarriages in the opposite direction. (qtd. in Washington 1970:5)

Boas had even calculated in an article published in 1909 that with unrestricted mating in a population where 90 percent was of one type and 10 percent of another, the minority type would effectively disappear in one hundred years (Boas 1974:327–328). Boas and Linton certainly did oppose the more grossly racist position that "miscegenation" was biologically objectionable. Still, as Washington (1970:154, 177) aptly remarks, their recommended "paling out of blacks as the ultimate solution" denied "equality for the black male" and ruled out cultural "acceptance of blackness as a firm and rich experience"; it remained "unconsciously bent on genocide" (see also Hyatt 1990:89–91).

Sexual contact between interacting populations may be a universal feature of human history, but its behavioral specifics—whether coerced or chosen, in or out of marriage, at high or low rates—are historical, political, and cultural issues that require analysis and explanation. In recent decades, white-black intermarriage rates have been increasing. There were 51,000 such couples in the United States in 1960; 65,000 in 1970; 167,000 in 1980; and 211,000 in 1990 (Spigner 1990; Wilkerson 1991; Williamson 1980:189). Black-white intermarriage rates are higher in the North than the South, in the West than the East, and in locales of small black percentages than large (Collins 1985; Heer 1980; Spickard 1989:306). Still, the 3 percent rate of intermarriage for African Americans remains small in comparison with other patterns of interracial marriage in the contemporary United States. "Data from the 1990 Current Population Survey indicate that 17 percent of married Asian Americans have a non-Asian spouse. About the same level of intermarriage is seen among Latinos" (O'Hare and Felt 1991:12). This entire set of social facts is what I will address in this essay.

Race and Ethnicity

Let us turn now to those others, neither white nor black, who until recently were at the margins of the social order. American Indians are still at the margins. The experience of native peoples over the past four centuries has been more that of enemy aliens and prisoners of war than first- or second-class, or even naturalized, citizens (see Baca 1988; Jaimes 1992; McNickle 1973). The point I wish to raise in this regard, however, is one that should challenge us to reconsider whatever defining features we assign to the concepts of race and ethnicity.

In the 1980 U.S. census, 1.4 million persons identified themselves as American Indian by race, yet 5.3 million whites (by race) claimed some American Indian ancestry on the separate ethnic-origin question (Lieberson and Waters 1988:18). There is probably some puffery in this second figure, yet evidently 5.3 million persons attest to a nonwhite

American Indian ancestor alongside European forbears but simultaneously consider themselves white (Johnson 1991; for instances, see Alba 1990:32–34, 47–48, 138, 340, 342; Waters 1990:14, 61, 92). For many of these persons the Indian ancestry is remote, but for others it is not. More than half of American Indians today are married to non-Indian spouses, most of whom are white (Collins 1985; Gonzalez 1992; cf. Alba and Golden 1986).

It is this high rate of intermarriage, I contend, that destablizes an ethnicity versus race distinction in this case. By race, some 1.4 million Native Americans see themselves as Indian in distinction to white (see Lieberson and Waters 1988:169), yet millions more whites view their own Indian ancestry as ethnicity. Cultural and political identifications are also involved, as some former "whites" changed their race to Indian in the 1990 census (Johnson 1991).

It is intermarriage, I believe, that has transformed American Indian racial difference (see Jordan 1968:89–91, 162–163, 217–228, 239–242, 477–481) into ethnicity for some whites. Such a transformation historically has also accorded ambiguously defined European "others" an unambiguous white racial status in the United States. The boundaries of "white" in the nation's history have expanded continuously with this "naturalization" of non-British Europeans. In 1751, Benjamin Franklin railed against German "*aliens*" whose presence interfered with the dominance of "purely White People" (see Jordan 1968:102, 143, 254). Later nativist and white supremacist groups would choose other targets, like Italians, Greeks, Slavs, and Jews, all today safely considered white and marriageable by the majority of white Americans (Colford, 1987; Omi and Winant 1986:64–65; Waters 1990:2–3, 76).

In eighteenth-century New York, intermarriage solidified first its English, Dutch, and French residents (Goodfriend 1992) and accorded each an ethnicity. Over time ethnicity came to stand for little more than an ancestral-origin claim as differences of language, diet, worship, and popular culture attenuated (see Gans 1979; Waters 1990). Nineteenth-century intermarriage accorded Irish, Germans, and other Europeans ethnicity within the white racial fold; and a third wave of intermarriage beginning around the turn of the twentieth century resulted in the extension of ethnicity to southern and eastern European "new immigrants" (Alba 1990; Draschler 1921; Waters 1990). Among whites who intermarried, ethnicity supplied *contrast* at symbolic cultural points (surnames, cuisines, festivities, language), even if these contrasts would become progressively vitiated in substance with each U.S.-born generation. Children inherited the ethnic identities of *both* their parents.

Historically, intermarriage among Europeans began soon after immigration and frequently occurred across language boundaries. Let me give some examples from New York. In the late 1600s, English settler Richard Alsop married his Dutch wife, Hannah, "whom he courted through an interpreter" according to Newtown tradition (Riker 1852:335). This match initiated more extensive eighteenth-century Dutch-English intermarriage in this Queens County township first settled in 1652. Later, during the period of heavy European immigration to New York City in the 1840s and 1850s, although statistical information is lacking, Ernst notes cases of "Irish-German, Irish-Chinese, Irish-French, German-French, [and] French-English [intermarriage], and numerous instances of immigrants marrying native [white] Americans" (1949:295).

Draschler's comprehensive study of intermarriage in the city during 1908–1912, the peak "new immigration" years, found first-generation intermarriage rates of 6 percent for southern Italian immigrants, 8 percent for Hungarians, 15 percent for Irish, 22 percent for Greeks, 27 percent for Swedes, 38 percent for Norwegians, 40 percent for French, 50 percent for Scots, 52 percent for north Germans, and 55 percent for south Germans. (All immigrant Jewish groups had intermarriage rates of 5 percent or less.) Marriages occured in virtually every ethnic combination; among Norwegian female immigrants, for example, foreign-born husbands include thirty-six Swedes, sixteen Danes, nine English, nine Germans, nine Irish, six Italians, three Scots, three Swiss, two Austrians, two Russians (one Jewish), and one each from Canada, Finland, Greece, Portugal, and Turkey. In addition, Norwegian immigrant women married four non-European husbands—British West Indian, Chinese, Japanese, and Peruvian (Draschler 1921:91, 175).

My interpretation of the historical significance of intermarriage in relation to ethnicity differs totally from that of Gordon (1964), who sees intermarriage as the *final* step in a series of cultural and structural assimilations. As just noted, intermarriages began *immediately* upon each new wave of European immigration. I suggest that these marriages became the social vehicle through which cultural contrasts with "people we marry" were construed as ethnic on the part of the existing white American population. Over time, as intermarriage rates increased with each generation, there was less and less cultural stuff requiring any assimilation. Gordon's intermarriage caboose is my engine of cultural change among white Americans.

Race, where the possibility of intermarriage ended or was shunned by whites, stood for biologically defined *difference*, and for the denial of any conceivable or discussable cultural contrast within a white kinship network. Offspring of any white-black marriages were considered black. They did *not* inherit the ethnic identity of their white parent in any socially recognized manner and were not incorporated into their white parent's kinship network. Today's substantial white-Asian and white-Hispanic intermarriage rates, however, raise the questions of whether, and why, a contemporary round of race-to-ethnicity conversion may be in motion. Will some white Americans, at least, accord ethnicity through intermarriage across what have been racial lines and admit to Polish-Mexican, or Jewish-Chinese, or French-German-Puerto Rican, or WASP-Korean kinspersons?

The grounds for a parallel conversion of race to ethnicity barely exist across the white-black line, however, where the intermarriage rate is not high but very low. There are undoubtedly more than 5.3 million whites (the number who acknowledge some American Indian ancestry) who are unaware of their African ancestry, or who are aware of but do not admit it (Stuckert 1964). (Stuckert estimated that by 1960 some 23 million white Americans had some degree of African genetic ancestry.) The cultural calculus of race in the United States still does not permit any black ethnicity among the multiple ethnic strands a white person may claim (Harris 1964:56–57; Lieberson and Waters 1988:169; Omi and Winant 1986:57; Spickard 1989:331). A white person may be Croatian-Irish, but not Croatian–Irish–African American. In the eyes of white Americans, at least up to now, such a person is black, and race overrides ethnicity (see Waters 1990:18–19, 167).[3]

But today there are other eyes, other ways of seeing, and others in addition to American Indians now no longer at the margins. Increasingly, these others appear in central institutional locations—city neighborhoods, universities, public and corporate bureaucracies—alongside white and black Americans. Predictions abound as to the "majority minority" future of the United States, when Americans other than those of European ancestry will form more than half of the population. Bouvier and Gardner (1986:27) estimate that in 2080 the U.S. population will be 50 percent white, 23 percent Hispanic, 15 percent black, and 12 percent Asian; O'Hare (1992:18) calculates that by 2035 only 49 percent of children under eighteen will be white. A "majority minority" already exists in many cities, and New York is an example. In 1990, the census figures described a city 43 percent white, 25 percent black, 24 percent Hispanic, and 7 percent Asian. Predictions envisage the city in the year 2030 as 41 percent Hispanic, 30 percent black, 15 percent white, and 14 percent Asian (Bouvier and Briggs 1988:35).

This white-black-Hispanic-Asian formula constitutes a new four-races framework, with American Indians the fifth race (although they are not often mentioned as such in New York City). Native-American anthropologist Jack Forbes (1990) has carefully described the bureaucratic formulation of this five-race framework, which began in the Nixon administration in 1973. As policy discussion moved through federal interagency committees and received input from Republican officials who favored a new "Hispanic" label, five "mutually exclusive categories" were finally promulgated for official government use in a 1977 Office of Management and Budget (OMB) circular titled "Race and Ethnic Standards for Federal Statistics and Administrative Reporting." They were: (1) "American Indian and Alaskan Native," which applied only to North America; (2) "Asian and Pacific Islander," with a westward beginning point in Pakistan; (3) "Black," which included persons of African origin but did not specify where "white" North Africa begins; (4) "Hispanic," which included Spaniards and all inhabitants of Western Hemisphere Spanish-speaking nations, and their descendants; and (5) "White," including persons who trace their origins to the "original peoples" of Europe, North Africa, and the Middle East to the Pakistan border (cf. O'Hare 1992:6–7).[4]

This state-defined view of five races is increasingly common in political and street-level discourse (see Murguia and Martinelli 1991; Nakashima 1992:162; Omi and Winant 1986; Waters 1990:99, 101, 108–110, 156–168). If we accept that race has always been a concept of state-level social ordering, a process that easily disregards linguistic, cultural, and immigrant or creole ethnic difference, there should be no objection to considering white, black, Hispanic, Asian, and American Indian as races according to how the current U.S. social order defines race. When people in the contemporary United States talk about racial politics, racial discrimination, or racial violence, it is this white-black-Hispanic-Asian (plus American Indian in some localities) framework that they speak within, and I will do the same.

Sociologist Ivan Light (1981) would prefer "continental ethnicity" instead of "race," but I do not (see also Alba's ethnic versus racial use of "European American" instead of "white" [1990:3, 36, 292–293, 312–319]). Sociologists regularly subordinate "race" to "ethnicity," using ethnicity as the master concept (see Alba 1990:311; Bonacich 1972:548; Light 1981; Spickard 1989:9–10). Putting ethnicity at the center of analysis, however, regularly leads to treating African Americans as merely an exception to general processes that affect everyone else (see Glazer, cited in Omi and Winant 1986:166; Spickard 1989:235), and to underplaying the historic legal and popular denial of equality accorded to Native, Asian, and Hispanic Americans (see Ringer 1983).[5]

Omi and Winant (1986) supply a valuable critique of this "all-is-ethnicity-except-blacks" position, pointing to the irreducible and fundamental constitution of the U.S. social order in racial terms. The ahistorical, neoconservative construction of African Americans as a late-arriving urban ethnic group, downplaying the significance of race, was first articulated in the 1950s and 1960s by Handlin (1959), Glazer and Moynihan (1963), and Kristol (1966). An alternative position, that we need both race and ethnicity as concepts, was maintained through the ethnicity-gripped decades of the 1970s and 1980s by several anthropologists among others (see Banton 1983; Kilson 1975; Sanjek, introduction, this volume). Both repressive processes of exclusion (race) and expressive processes of inclusion (ethnicity) must be accounted for on our analytic ledgers.

Historical Perspectives on Interracial Marriage

From my New York standpoint, the historical emergence of Hispanic and Asian populations in substantial numbers, and the subsequent addition of these terms to the biracial black-white framework, is recent. Although the first person other than the native Munsee to live in what became New York City was Juan Rodriguez, described as "a mulatto from San Domingo" at the time of his arrival in 1612 (Bachman 1969:6–7, 11; Rink 1986:33–36, 42), only with the growing numbers of Puerto Ricans from the 1930s on did a separate racial category of persons not white and not black begin to take hold. And even through the 1950s individual Puerto Ricans experienced social pressures to identify as white or black (Padilla 1958; Rivera 1982; Thomas 1967; see also Rios 1991). With the large post-1965 Latin American immigration to the city, the Hispanic or Latino (in Spanish, *Hispano* or *Latinoamericano;* and in street English, "Spanish" [see Dominguez 1973]) population has become a familiar element of the city's humanscape to all its inhabitants, whatever national (or Latin American ethnic) identities they may recognize among this collectivity of immigrants and U.S. citizens.

A few Chinese resided in New York during the 1830s, but their numbers, with those of other Asians, long remained tiny (Draschler 1921; Ernst 1949; Tchen 1990). By the 1870s (McCabe 1872:734–737), Chinese were widely recognized in the city as an exotic group, not white and not black, but the political significance of Asians on the citywide scene, parallel to whites, blacks, and Hispanics, dates only since the large influx of Asian immigrants to New York after 1965. Today, political language and calculation regularly includes the racial category Asian.

This Big Apple–centric racial history differs considerably from that of the Southwest and Pacific regions, where a mid-nineteenth-century implanted U.S. social order included Hispanics and Asians from its start or soon thereafter. Mexicans in the Southwest, and Chinese and then Japanese in the Pacific and mountain states, were subjected to second-class citizenship, racial mythology, targeted violence, labor exploitation, and legal and social bars to marriage with whites, all similar to what blacks continued to experience after Emancipation in the East and South (Daniels 1962; Galarza 1972; Gamio 1930, 1931; Ichioka 1988; Montejano 1987; Ringer 1983; Spickard 1989:36; Tchen 1984; Zavella, this volume).

Blacks in substantial numbers arrived in the Southwest and Pacific regions later than whites, and mainly after 1940. When they did, their position in these regions was consistent with that back east and down south—residential segregation, job restriction, and low black-white intermarriage rates. By the 1960s, the white-black-Hispanic-Asian racial formula could be applied nationwide, and it was reinforced by continuous Latin American and Asian immigration during the 1970s and 1980s, with substantial immigrant settlement, despite particular local ethnic representation, in all regions of the United States.

In the 1960s, the intermarriage rates (both incidence and prevalence) rose sharply for Asians and Latinos, and these reflected mainly marriages to whites. For Japanese Americans, the well-studied Seattle case is typical of the picture elsewhere; from racial exogamy rates of less than 10 percent before 1950, intermarriage climbed from 17 percent in the early 1960s, to 30 percent later in the decade, and to over 50 percent by 1975 (Leonetti and Newell-Morris 1982:25; cf. Kikumura and Kitano 1973 on Los Angeles, and California State; Spickard 1989:25–120; Tinker 1973 on Fresno). Among Chinese Americans nationally, during the 1960s some 11.5 percent of males and 12.8 percent of females married white spouses (Yuan 1980:185). A study of Los Angeles County marriage licenses for 1979 showed a 50 percent interracial marriage rate for Japanese, 30 percent for Chinese, and 19 percent for Koreans (Kitano et al. 1984:181). In New York City, Chinese intermarried, again mainly with whites, at a 27 percent incidence in both 1972 and 1982 (Sung 1990:11–12). According to 1980 U.S. census data, the national prevalence of intermarriage with whites in that year was 27 percent among Japanese Americans, 25 percent among Koreans, 22 percent among Filipinos, 17 percent among Vietnamese, 13 percent among Indians, and 10 percent among Chinese (calculated from Lee and Yamanaka 1990:291).

Mexican-American intermarriage, also mainly with whites, occurred before 1960 at prevalences of 10 percent or less in Los Angeles, Albuquerque, and San Antonio. By 1963 the incidence of such marriages in Los Angeles had climbed to 25 percent (Mittelback and Moore 1968:51–53, 58). Statewide data for Spanish-surnamed California residents showed even higher intermarriage rates for the 1960s and 1970s, ranging from 38 percent in 1962, to 34 percent in 1974 (Schoen, Nelson, and Collins

1978:362–363). In eight Arizona counties, the incidence of Chicano-Anglo marriage was 16 percent in 1960, 24 percent in 1970, and 28 percent in 1980 (Fernandez and Holscher 1983:299–300). The figure for Albuquerque was similar, with an incidence of intermarriage of 24 percent in 1971; the rate in San Antonio, a predominantly Mexican-American city, was lower, at 16 percent in 1973 (Murguia and Frisbie 1979:384). In heavily Mexican-American rural south Texas, rates remained at less than 10 percent through the 1970s (Cazares et al. 1984; Murguia and Frisbie 1979:384–385). Overall, the prevalence of Mexican-American intermarriage nationally was 17 percent in both 1980 and 1990 (Falcon 1993:12; Sung 1990:18).

Puerto Rican intermarriage in 1980 was 26 percent nationally (Sung 1990:18), a figure that includes marriages to blacks and other Hispanics as well as to whites. An analysis of marriage licenses issued in 1975 in New York City, where the largest concentration of mainland Puerto Ricans resides, found that 12 percent of males and 15 percent of females married non-Hispanic spouses that year (Fitzpatrick and Gurak 1979:34). Data on the race of these spouses are missing (Gurak and Fitzpatrick 1982:992), but nearly half the grooms and more than a fourth of the brides were probably white (of non-Hispanic foreign stock), as were an additional but unknown proportion of the remainder. In 1990, the national intermarriage rate for Puerto Ricans was 19 percent, with a 40 percent intermarriage rate with non-Latinos among the mainland-born (Falcon 1993:12).

The 1975 marriage license study in New York also tallied the incidence of intermarriage to non-Hispanic spouses for other Latin Americans. The rates for Cubans were 23 percent (males) and 32 percent (females); Central Americans, 24 percent (males) and 23 percent (females); South Americans, 16 percent (males) and 22 percent (females); and Dominicans, 6 percent (males) and 8 percent (females) (Fitzpatrick and Gurak 1979:34). An unknown but substantial proportion of these intermarriages was with white spouses. In 1980, 13 percent of all Hispanic Americans were intermarried, most of them to whites (Lee and Yamanaka 1990:291). In 1990, some 14 percent of Cubans nationwide were married to non-Hispanics (Falcon 1993:12).

In interpreting these figures on Asian and Hispanic intermarriage, we may note the Supreme Court decision striking down existing anti-miscegenation laws in 1967. We may also note, but need not limit ourselves to, other "factors" (group size, gender ratios, gender of spouse, generation since immigration, socioeconomic status) that sociologists have proposed to "explain" intermarriage rates (Alba and Golden 1986; Fitzpatrick and Gurak 1979:1–12; Heer 1980; Merton 1941; Spickard 1989:6–9, 361–369). I contend, however, that any appraisal of the meaning of intermarriage statistics must first acknowledge that during the same decades in which Asian-white and Hispanic-white intermarriages rates rose sharply, black-white intermarriage rates remained flat in comparison (Heer 1980; Hirschman 1983).

It is also worthy of closer historical probing to note that Asian and Mexican intermarriage rates with whites appear to have increased only after blacks became part of the West Coast social order in substantial numbers. African Americans form the historic racially defined reserve labor pool in the United States, and they still have not been displaced from this role. In this regard, their low intermarriage rate indexes a persisting identification of Black Americans by race rather than ethnicity on the part of whites. It thus appears that Asians and Mexicans, who undeniably played this same reserve labor pool role before blacks arrived, became marriageable—and ethnic—to whites only after the U.S. black-white racial regime was numerically and institutionally established in the western states.

In New York City, where blacks were long and firmly fixed in the basement of the labor market, Asian and Hispanic intermarriage with whites had already achieved high rates (although in tiny numbers) by the first decade of the twentieth century. The marriage registry data for 1908–1912 compiled by Draschler (1921) show intermarriage rates to white spouses (both U.S.-born and European immigrant) of 53 percent for Chinese (among the $N = 34$ Chinese individuals who married in New York during those years), 60 percent for Japanese ($N = 42$), 44 percent for Cubans ($N = 155$), 37 percent for Puerto Ricans ($N = 79$), 63 percent for Mexicans ($N = 35$), and 78 percent for Central and South Americans ($N = 40$). During these same years, the rate of intermarriage with white spouses for African Americans was 1 percent ($N = 4{,}784$). Overall, only 63 blacks (51 U.S.-born plus 12 black immigrants) married whites during 1908–1912, as compared to 82 Asians and 309 Latin Americans.[6]

By 1980, nationwide 13 percent of Hispanics and 25 percent of Asians were married outside their group, mainly to white spouses (at rates varying among specific Latino and Asian ethnic groups); black-white rates remained at 2 percent (Lee and Yamanaka 1990:291). By 1990, after a decade of heavy Latin American and Asian immigration (which depressed rising intermarriage rates among earlier arrivals and the U.S.-born), one in six of all Asians and Hispanics were interracially married, compared to one in thirty-three blacks (O'Hare 1992:14; O'Hare et al. 1991:19).

It is well documented that Hispanics and Asians become more likely to marry whites with each generation of residence in the United States, and as income and education levels increase. The same factors apply historically to white ethnic intermarriage, a phenomenon now well studied (Alba 1990; Alba and Golden 1986; Draschler 1921; Goodfriend 1992; Lieberson 1985; Lieberson and Waters 1988; Waters 1990). Today, the great majority of white Americans is of multiple European ancestry and admits to such. It is thus more typical to be Croatian-Irish, or some other mix, than simply Croatian American or Irish American. Yet at the same time, small but increasing numbers of "unhyphenated whites," as sociologist Stanley Lieberson (1985) terms them, answer only "American," or give no response, when queried as to their ethnicity. Two-thirds of this ethnicless segment of the white population consists of southern whites and is more rural and less well educated than the white population overall; the other component is well-off, northern, and likely to be Roman Catholic (Lieberson and Waters 1988:264–267).

Intermarriage, Kinship, and Community

In 1987, some 99 percent of white Americans were married to other whites. Of those who were not, 77 percent were married to Hispanics and Asians (or others), and only 23 percent to blacks (calculated from Spigner 1990:215). The interracially married white percentage is growing, certainly with the increase in Latin American and Asian numbers, and perhaps absolutely as well. If we were to grant each intermarried white spouse sixteen relatives and assume these kin do not reject the intermarried couple, potentially one-sixth of white Americans now have a nonwhite affinal relative and are likely to have a racially mixed kinsperson, the offspring of the interracial marriage. Looking at things from the other side, many more than this proportion of Hispanic and Asian Americans have white and half-white relatives, since one-sixth themselves are interracially married. The logic of the numbers suggests that *most* Asians and Hispanics now have white relatives. Such existing, potential, and growing kinship links are far fewer between black and white Americans, or between blacks and Hispanics or Asians, for that matter.

My numerical suggestions are hardly precise. There are sociologists better skilled than I at number crunching, but as an anthropologist I am compelled to consider intermarriage in relation to kinship networks (see Benson 1981), and then to connect these social facts to politics. There is a host of theoretical and cultural questions we need to formulate about race, kinship, and identity, questions that may be provoked by examination of quantitative census and marriage registration data, but that cannot be answered with them. Interracial trends are identifiable, but they need to be clarified with ethnography.

Since 1983 I have been studying a large New York City community district that has shifted from majority white (98 percent) in 1960, to "majority minority" in 1990 (45 percent Hispanic, 26 percent Asian, 10 percent black, and 18 percent white) (Sanjek 1989, 1992, N.d.). Asian and Latin American immigrants first appeared in small numbers in the 1960s and were widely dispersed throughout the area, living scattered among white residents on homeowner blocks and in rental apartments. Blacks, who arrived in substantial numbers in the 1970s, settled in just a few census tracts. In 1990, the black population was still concentrated in these same tracts, now mainly black, but the immigrants remained widely dispersed, now in far greater numbers. In effect, Latin American and Asian immigrants arrived everywhere, and their populations grew in place. Black residents (including some Caribbean and African immigrants) appeared in circumscribed areas and largely remain there.

Turning to civic politics, African Americans have formed mainly black civic organizations in the area where most of them reside (Gregory, this volume). Elsewhere in the district, whites remain well organized, and some of their neighborhood and block associations now include Latin American and Asian members. Fewer ongoing local political ties exist between blacks and whites, or between blacks and Asian and Latin American immigrants, than between whites and these immigrants, though key leaders in each group, most often women, see the need to work with persons of other races.

Churches present a similar picture. Blacks attend black churches, while the historically white churches that survive today now serve substantial majorities of Asian and Latin American worshippers, some in services in their own languages, and others in racially mixed English-language services (Sanjek 1989). There are also separate churches organized by these immigrants, as there are also many ethnic civic and service organizations, but again, there is far more white-immigrant interaction in churches than there is black-white or black-immigrant interaction. When whites (and Latin American and Asian immigrants) interact with blacks at church, these are predominantly Haitian, English-speaking Caribbean, or African immigrants, and not African Americans.

While my data on white American kinship networks are not extensive, nor a random sample, they are consistent with the national picture detailed in quantitative studies. In sixteen intensive interviews with white residents, I found widespread intermarriage among white ethnic groups—WASP-Italian, Italian-Irish, Polish-Russian, German-Scotch-English, and so on. Five of the sixteen kinship networks included an interracial marriage, with two Hispanic (Mexican, Puerto Rican) and two Asian (Chinese, Korean) spouses. Three of these marriages were warmly received by other white relatives, and the fourth had just taken place. The fifth marriage was to a black spouse in Hawaii and apparently received little acceptance from the white kinship group.[7]

Political Scenarios

Political readings of various projections of future racial composition—the percentages of whites, blacks, Hispanics, and Asians in given cities, states, or the nation—do not take into account the trends of intermarriage, the nature of racial identification of mixed persons, or the significance of intermarriage within kinship networks. These cultural and social themes offer incredibly fertile ground for ethnography, for answers to research questions about the unfolding race-sex-power configuration of the United States. I approach this issue through a presentation of six alternative scenarios now under public and academic scrutiny. They are not mutually exclusive, in my opinion, and each may portend a glimpse of one aspect of our future. There are good reasons to expect that each of these alternatives simultaneously will find advocates and supporters as the nation passes into the twenty-first century.

Scenario one—a social order in which racial groups compete and contend for relative political advantage. Activists and analysts who consider racially based politics to be fundamental in the United States range considerably in political orientation (see Flynn and Gerhardt 1989; Glazer and Moynihan 1963; Kilson 1975; Omi and Winant 1986:38–51, 89–135). Interpreting recent politics in New York City, economist Robert Fitch (1989, 1991) argues that an apartheidlike, divide-and-rule elite strategy underpinned the move to define a large number (fifty-one) of small racial and ethnic districts in the 1991 city council redistricting. Struggles over boundaries were phrased in racial terms, with demands for more black and Hispanic seats (including specific Caribbean and Dominican districts) and for the creation of an Asian district. As the reality set in that blacks are more residentially concentrated than Hispanics and Asians (so, by the way, are whites), and that black electoral districts were far easier to draw than Latino ones, black-Hispanic conflicts surfaced between political activists. Fitch sees this division as serving the entrenched white political interests of the city's "permanent government."

Intermarriage patterns might tend to mitigate racial separateness and promote alliance along the lines where they are strongest. In this regard, it is significant to note that the *New York Times* in recent years has printed notices of interracial marriages in the higher circles, often with photographs. I counted eighteen such notices in 1991, twelve of them of white-Asian intermarriages, four white-Hispanic, one white-black, and one black-Asian.

Factors other than intermarriage may reinforce racial categorization and mobilization. The most important of these is continuing immigration, bringing new Latin American, Asian, Caribbean, and African arrivals who will likely be counted and appealed to in racial terms. Another element is the continuing exhortations by political leaders who advocate ethnic or racial voting, or forms of racial separatism, often with as great an effect upon persons beyond their assumed constituency as within it. (Political candidate David Duke of Louisiana and Afrocentric spokesman Professor Leonard Jeffries of New York are examples; see also di Leonardo 1984:28–29).

Scenario two—People-of-color unity among black, Hispanic, and Asian groups. Political analyst Manning Marable (1990) has spotlighted several issues that confront all nonwhite U.S. residents in a widely read article calling for a rethinking of African-American political strategy. People-of-color ideology has many spokespersons among political activists, but in New York City, where action on common issues of housing, education, and health-care services would benefit from it, this ideology has little reality in either community or citywide politics (see Falcon 1988). My own prediction is that it will encounter greater support in glass-ceiling workplace situations where qualified professionals of color find opportunities and promotions blocked by racial discrimination from whites.

Current intermarriage patterns are in line with a relative underdevelopment of people-of-color political unity. Most intermarriages involving Asians, Latin Americans, and blacks are with whites, and not with other persons of color. Nationally in 1987, some 93 percent of interracial marriages involving Asians, Hispanics, or American Indians were with whites, and 7 percent with blacks; and 83 percent of black interracial marriages were with whites, and 17 percent with other people of color (calculated from Spigner 1990:215). Nonetheless, incidents of racial harassment in public settings, housing discrimination in white neighborhoods, and racial violence continue to provide a potential common platform for a people-of-color alliance.

Scenario three—transition from a white-black racial order to a light-dark order in which Asians and some Hispanics align with whites. In this scenario, Asians, whose intermarriage rates with whites are already quite high, will blend into the white population, as will lighter Hispanics.

Hispanics of visible African ancestry and family background will be pushed off the Anglo-conformist immigrant track and join Black Americans and black Caribbean and African immigrants in continuing racial subordination (see Alba 1990:9–10, 312; Bouvier and Briggs 1988:82–83; Heer 1980:521; Hirschman 1983).

The intermarriage numbers might be evidence for supporters of this scenario, but the racial identification of half-white and half-Asian, or half-Hispanic, persons is not predictable merely from the numbers. While some children of such interracial marriages do identify as "white," or as racially neutral "Americans," others choose to identify with their Asian or Hispanic parent. For some this is determined in part by their physical appearance and place of residence, but for others it is a political or ethnic affirmation (see Bradshaw 1992; Mass 1992; Nakashima 1992; Posadas 1981; Salgado de Snyder and Padilla 1982; Spickard 1989:109–17, 149–151, 367, 408; Sung 1990:100–115; Valle 1991:79).

No one knows what proportions now, or in the future, will assimilate to white or identify as Asian or Hispanic or claim, for example, Chinese or Mexican ethnic strands along with their European ethnicities, as 5.3 million whites claim an American Indian strand. There is no research as yet concerning the degree to which white Americans in kinship networks with no interracial marriages, or even those with them, will admit that intermarriage and multiracial kinship transmutes race into ethnicity. It does appear that mixed persons have a degree of choice in self-identification depending upon class, closeness to each parent, region of residence, or phenotypic appearance. But we simply cannot state firmly at this point that a widening of "white" will occur to include Asian and Hispanic ethnic strands (as has occurred with American Indian roots), or that an unmarked "American" identity open to light part-whites will emerge in contrast with a marked "African-American" one. This may occur, for some persons and in some places, but it is certain to be contested by others, of all colors, as well.

The locales for ethnographic work on such questions extend far beyond the racially diverse Queens neighborhood I have studied, but where I have not probed this issue. We all need to remember President George Bush's remark about "Jebby's kids, the little brown ones," his grandfatherly reference to Jeb, Jr., Noelle, and George Prescott Bush III, the children of his son Jeb and his Mexican wife, Columba. Are these children Hispanic, or white, or both, or just "American," or something else?

Scenario four—increasing use of racially mixed identification, even to the point of a "mixed" U.S. census racial category, as some already urge.

College campuses, where racial identity today is clearly at issue, are cauldrons in which formation of organizations of racially mixed persons is under way. Many such groups have emerged, with some consisting of "hapa," or half Asian-half white, persons; some of "biracial" persons of black and white parentage; and others of more complex racially mixed constituency (Atkins 1991; Campos Rajs 1991; Daniel 1992; Fernandez 1992:141; Spickard 1989:338–339, 376). Persons in these groups may both affirm their dual or multiple origins and reject membership in organizations addressing only black or only Asian racial interests. The self-identifications that persons of racially mixed parentage use also need to be studied in workplace and community settings, beyond the arenas of campus identity politics. Ideological commitments in college years may shift when the white-black-Hispanic-Asian formula is imposed by employers or by politics. On the other hand, these campus commitments to emerging identities may also begin to change today's hegemonic racial formula.

Racially mixed spokespersons have raised the call for revision of the U.S. census race categories to provide a more affirmative choice than "other" (Daniel 1992; Hall 1992b; Root 1992a; Thornton 1992; cf. O'Hare 1992:14). The choice of a "mixed" category, supported by some, is resisted in particular by African-American leaders who fear that growing numbers of "biracial" offspring of black-white marriages will reduce "black" numbers. African Americans may also resist the ideological message that seeks to expand mixed-race numbers by calling attention to varying racial strands in their own history, as well as those of Hispanics and American Indians. For Black Americans, racial mixing in the past either was unwelcomed or, when chosen, was denied any ethnic acceptability by whites and thus differs from the current situation of black-white marriage, which may in some instances now be approaching the "equal regard" demanded by Du Bois (and Washington 1970; but see Wilkerson 1991).

Perhaps a more negotiable position from the mixed-race advocates will be to allow a person more than one racial choice on the U.S. census (as the Canadian census does; Campos Rajs 1991), just as whites are permitted multiple ethnic listings. This would preserve a full count of people of African ancestry. Along this line, Root suggests that "[t]he census to be taken in the year 2000 will provide an opportunity . . . to count in a way that will allow a more accurate understanding of who lives in the United States. Rather than perpetuating the forced-choice nature of most forms . . . the census might reveal a very different-looking population if people are allowed to choose more than one category under race" (1992a:346). The issue is not going away. Today scholars who are the children of interracial marriages are proclaiming a "sense of wholeness that is more than the sum of the parts of a person's heritages . . . of being 'both' and 'neither' throughout life" (Kich 1992:317). As Hall puts it, "We are everywhere, and the United States will have to adjust to our presence in many ways" (1992a:326).

Scenario five—Latin American–styled views of race as appearance, not ancestry, may gain ascendance. Great masses of Latin American peoples who are now U.S. residents acknowledge their racially mixed background, not in the immediate parental generation but in the formative periods of their ancestral national histories (see Fernandez 1992). In Latin America, certain elites and regional subpopulations maintain they are of unmixed European descent, but millions of Mexicans, Puerto Ricans, Dominicans, Colombians, and others acknowledge varying combinations of European, African, and American Indian ancestry.

Centuries of white racial dominance are reflected in continuing notions that light skin, straight hair, and European facial features are prestigious, but families and kinship networks include persons who vary widely in racial physiognomy. Racial terms translatable as "white," "black," or "Indian" refer to appearance, not beliefs about absence or presence of African or American Indian ancestry. In addition, other terms exist to identify persons of intermediate combinations of skin color, hair form, and facial features, much as white Americans distinguish blonds, brunets, or redheads, and pale to olive-skinned complexions (see Padilla 1958; Rios 1991; Rodriguez 1989; Sanjek 1971; Zavella, this volume).

As Clara Rodríguez (1989) has pointed out, in recent decades increasing numbers of Hispanics are answering "other" to the U.S. census race question, rejecting white or black. Some, she adds, read this as a cultural question as well, viewing themselves culturally as other than white American or African American. When I mentioned this choice of "other" in one of my classes, two Egyptian sisters who grew up in Queens joined a Colombian friend in saying, "That's what we do."

Increasing numbers of persons like these may choose "other" when the choice is white or black, but they are likely to use more specific and affirmative self-identifications in everyday life. What are they? How do persons from world regions or of mixed ancestries not conforming to stereotypic white, black, or East Asian racial images describe themselves? Will new concepts of race as appearance, not ancestry, and a new vocabulary gain greater currency?[8] In this regard, the future

United States might be better served by a Spanish Only movement than English Only.

Scenario six—a people-of-all-colors ideology promoting unity among working- and lower-middle-class persons, and identifying their class enemies. Marable (1991) argues for this strategy, as well as for people-of-color unity (see also Omi and Winant 1986:142–143), though he does not discuss the relationship between these two political scenarios. In the Queens community district I have studied, a quality-of-life politics that underplays race and stresses common needs for improved city services and local programs has established itself amidst the racial change of the 1970s and 1980s. Its chief obstacles to success remain the control of information, organization, and procedure by nonlocal, upper-middle-class bureaucrats, and the continuing force of racially defined political competition.

I repeat that all six scenarios may simultaneously find supporters and advocates and may affect thinking about race in the future. In the year 2030, or 2100, it may be less easy than today to assign persons a place within the white-black-Hispanic-Asian-American Indian framework. Growing numbers of racially mixed persons, and complex kinship networks that cross these racial lines, will be more apparent. Another factor moving kinship ties in this direction is the adoption of children across racial and international lines by white Americans as their own birthrate declines (Wheeler 1993). In 1986 some 10,000 foreign-born children were adopted, the largest number from South Korea, with the previously rising number of adoptees from Latin America then in decline as a result of tightened home-country restrictions (Welt 1988). And in 1988 Congress approved funding to bring up to 30,000 Amerasian children and their accompanying family members from Vietnam to the United States (Teltsch 1988; Valverde 1992).

The white population increasingly may divide into two groups. The first will be those "Americans" who admit to no ethnicity, continue to practice racial exclusion, and define fewer and fewer U.S. residents as white. The second will consist of those whites who, along with persons of other and mixed racial identities, maintain social ties and practice politics that increasingly discount race, and that accord ethnicity across today's racial boundaries.[9] This second grouping will have its conservative and progressive elements, dividing on issues we may now not easily predict. A foretaste, however, may be evident in the following instance.

In 1985 Federal District Court Judge Leonard B. Sand ruled that the city of Yonkers, just north of New York City, must erect new low-income housing units in its white neighborhoods to remedy forty years of housing segregation aimed at black residents. Among the politicians who fought the order was a white city council member, Peter Chema, who continued his resistance as an unsuccessful mayoral candidate in 1991. Chema, however, objected to being called a racist, protesting, "I live in an integrated building in an integrated neighborhood. My wife is a minority. My brother-in-law is a minority." His wife is Filipino, and his brother-in-law is Peruvian. Chema also teaches martial arts at the Yonkers Chinese Community Center and has appeared in a Kung-fu movie (Feron 1991; Foderaro 1991; Rimer 1988). He exemplifies racism with a multicultural face.

In the end, then, the critical racial issue will continue to be the place that persons of African descent occupy within the U.S. social order. As Banton (1983:397) puts it, "Good race relations would be ethnic relations" (see also Kilson 1975:236–237; Waters 1990:167), but black and white Americans are not there yet. If even a partial transformation into ethnicity of Asian and Hispanic racial identity is effected through intermarriage, will the denial of ethnicity to African Americans continue to endure, reinforced and symbolized by continuing low rates of intermarriage (see Washington 1970)?[10] Will today's patterns of housing, educational, and employment discrimination for large numbers of Black Americans (Alba 1990:268–270; Farley and Allen 1987; Massey and Denton 1993; O'Hare et al. 1991; Stafford 1985) be dismantled, or persist? We do have unfinished business, for, however it is drawn, the problem of the twenty-first century will remain the problem of the color line.

Notes

For comments and advice on earlier versions of this paper, I thank Parminder Bhachu, Jennifer Brown, Ulf Hannerz, Karen Ito, James Ito-Adler, Max Manes, Sally McBeth, Leith Mullings, Ellen Rosenberg, Lillian Rubin, Lani Sanjek, Judith Stacey, Jack Tchen, Howard Winant, Helena Wulff, and Sylvia Yanagisako.

1. According to 1990 census data, about 30 percent of black Americans lived in neighborhoods at least 90 percent black; in 1980 the figure was 34 percent. In 1990 some 68 percent of whites lived in nearly all-white neighborhoods, down from 76 percent in 1980 (see "Racial Segregation," *Newsday,* April 10, 1991).

2. In a 1991 National Opinion Research Center poll, nearly two-thirds of African-American respondents said that they would neither favor nor oppose the marriage of a relative to someone of a different race (Wilkerson 1991).

3. After I presented an earlier version of this paper at the American Studies

Association in 1988, however, an African-American audience member related that his wife, the daughter of black and Italian parents, considers herself black, but her sister, he added, identifies herself as both black and Italian. Several contributors to Maria P. P. Root's volume *Racially Mixed People in America* (1992) discuss "biracial," "black-Japanese," "interracial," and "mixed" self-identifications by persons with one black and one white or Japanese-American parent (Daniel 1992; Gibbs and Hines 1992; Hall 1992b).

4. Forbes provides a valuable critique of the OMB race circular, particularly as it concerns the classification of native peoples of the entire Western Hemisphere. He also interprets "Hispanic" as a Republican effort to diminish the impact of affirmative action policies on peoples of color by defining as "minority" white Cubans and South Americans who were never victims of racial discrimination in their homelands or in the United States.

5. Spickard thus can make much of the fact that Japanese intermarriage patterns mirror the first-, second-, and third-generational experience of European immigrant groups. Yet he devotes only one paragraph (1989:33) in ninety-five pages on Japanese Americans to the racist and wrenching imprisonment of this entire population in U.S. concentration camps during World War II, hardly a "part of the orderly progression of generations among American immigrant groups" (60). If Japanese Americans have been treated more in ethnic than racial terms by white Americans since the 1960s, as I think they have been, the race-to-ethnicity question becomes one to explain, not avoid.

6. I have calculated these rates from Draschler's tables, combining figures for men and women, and lumping together separate counts for "Spanish" and "Colored" Cubans and Puerto Ricans. The Central and South Americans who married included persons from Argentina (one), Bolivia (one), Brazil (eight), Chile (six), Colombia (four), Ecuador (three), Guatemala (three), Honduras (one), Peru (two), and Venezuela (eleven). In addition to Japanese and Chinese who intermarried in New York City during 1908–1912, other Asians marrying white spouses included two of four Indians who married, two of three Koreans, and two of three Filipinos. Schwartz (1951) traces the declining interracial marriage rate for New York Chinese men from 55 percent early in this century and into the 1920s, to 20 percent by the late 1930s (see also Posadas 1981 on high intermarriage rates among Filipino men in Chicago during the 1920s).

7. On kin-group acceptance, a subject neglected in the post-1960s sociological literature on intermarriage, see Susan Benson's 1981 ethnographic study of black-white marriages in London (see also Gibbs and Hines 1992; Hall 1992b; Mass 1992; Nakashima 1992).

8. Nomenclature for shades and hues in cosmetics marketing might be an interesting place to probe this issue. With 25 percent of the U.S. population now of non-European ancestry, cosmetics firms are marketing new lines to a broader spectrum of customers, with such names as Color Deeps, Sheer Intensities, Shades of You, Shade Extensions, and All Skins (Kerr 1991).

9. According to a 1991 National Opinion Research Center poll, 66 percent of white Americans opposed interracial marriage with blacks, and one in five

believed it should be barred by law. Some 34 percent did not object to black-white marriage. As to intermarriage with Asians or Hispanics, 45 percent of white Americans opposed it, and 55 percent did not (Wilkerson 1991).

10. While interracial marriage still involves a much smaller proportion of black Americans than of Asians or Hispanics, the actual number of such marriages has increased geometrically in recent years. Some 9,600 babies were born to black-white couples in 1968, compared to 51,000 babies in 1988 (Atkins 1991). Black-white romance and marriage also has become a theme of many contemporary television programs and movies, including "The Days and Nights of Molly Dodd" and "Jungle Fever" (see Buckley 1991; Gates 1991). And the interracial marriages (and divorces) of such African-American show-business celebrities as Diana Ross to Robert Silberstein and Arne Naess, and Diahann Carroll to Vic Damone, receive coverage no more sensational than the monochromatic romantic affairs of white celebrities.

References

Alba, Richard D. 1990. *Ethnic Identity: The Transformation of White America.* New Haven, Conn.: Yale University Press.

Alba, Richard D., and Reid M. Golden. 1986. Patterns of Ethnic Marriage in the United States. *Social Forces* 65:202–223.

Atkins, Elizabeth. 1991. When Life Simply Isn't Black or White. *New York Times,* June 5.

Baca, Lawrence. 1988. The Legal Status of American Indians. In *History of Indian-White Relations,* ed. Wilcomb E. Washburn, 230–237. Handbook of North American Indians 4. Washington, D.C.: Smithsonian.

Bachman, Van Cleaf. 1969. *Peltries or Plantations: The Economic Policies of the Dutch West India Company in New Netherland, 1623–1639.* Baltimore: Johns Hopkins University Press.

Banton, Michael. 1983. *Racial and Ethnic Competition.* Cambridge: Cambridge University Press.

Benson, Susan. 1981. *Ambiguous Ethnicity: Interracial Families in London.* Cambridge: Cambridge University Press.

Boas, Franz. 1974. Race Problems in America. In *The Shaping of American Anthropology, 1883–1911: A Franz Boas Reader,* ed. George W. Stocking, Jr., 318–330. Chicago: University of Chicago Press. First published in 1909.

———. 1945. The Problem of the American Negro. In *Race and Democratic Society,* 70–81. New York: Augustin. First published in 1921, *Yale Quarterly Review* 10:384–395.

Bonacich, Edna. 1972. A Theory of Ethnic Antagonism: The Split Labor Market. *American Sociological Review* 37:547–559.

Bouvier, Leon F., and Robert W. Gardner. 1986. *Immigration to the U.S.: The Unfinished Story.* Washington, D.C.: Population Reference Bureau.

Bouvier, Leon F., and Vernon M. Briggs, Jr. 1988. *The Population and Labor*

Force of New York: 1990–2050. Washington, D.C.: Population Reference Bureau.

Bradshaw, Karla. 1992. Beauty and the Beast: On Racial Ambiguity. In *Racially Mixed People in America,* ed. Maria P. P. Root, 77–88.

Buckley, Gail Lumet. 1991. When a Kiss Is Not Just a Kiss. *New York Times,* March 31.

Campos Rajs, Elizabeth. 1991. Pros, Cons of Ethnic Labels: Standard Categories Don't Fit Multiethnic Population. *UC Focus,* May/June.

Cazares, Ralph B., Edward Murguia, and W. Parker Frisbie. 1984. Mexican American Intermarriage in a Nonmetropolitan Context. *Social Science Quarterly* 65:626–634.

Colford, Paul. 1987. An Inside Look at the Klan. *Newsday,* February 18.

Collins, Glenn. 1985. A New Look at Intermarriage in the U.S. *New York Times,* February 11.

Daniel, G. Reginald. 1992. Beyond Black and White: The New Multiracial Consciousness. In *Racially Mixed People in America,* ed. Maria P. P. Root, 333–341.

Daniels, Roger. 1962. *The Politics of Prejudice: The Anti-Japanese Movement in California and the Struggle for Japanese Exclusion.* New York: Atheneum.

Davis, Allison, Burleigh B. Gardner, and Mary Gardner. 1941. *Deep South: A Social Anthropological Study of Caste and Class.* Chicago: University of Chicago Press.

di Leonardo, Micaela. 1984. *The Varieties of Ethnic Experience: Kinship, Class, and Gender among California Italian-Americans.* Ithaca, N.Y.: Cornell University Press.

Dominguez, Virginia. 1973. Spanish-Speaking Caribbeans in New York: "The Middle Race." *Interamerican Review* 3(2): 135–143.

Drake, St. Clair, and Horace R. Cayton. [1945] 1962. *Black Metropolis: A Study of Negro Life in a Northern City.* Rev. and enl. ed. New York: Harper.

Draschler, Julius. 1921. *Intermarriage in New York City: A Statistical Study of the Amalgamation of European Peoples.* New York: AMS.

Ernst, Robert. 1949. *Immigrant Life in New York City, 1825–1863.* Port Washington, N.Y.: Friedman.

Falcon, Angelo. 1988. Black and Latino Politics in New York City: Race and Ethnicity in a Changing Urban Context. In *Latinos and the Political System,* ed. F. Chris Garcia, 171–194. Notre Dame, Ind.: Notre Dame University Press.

———. 1993. The Puerto Rican Community: A Status Report. *Dialogo: Newsletter of the National Puerto Rican Policy Network* 7:1, 5, 10–13.

Farley, Reynolds, and Walter R. Allen. 1987. *The Color Line and the Quality of Life in America.* New York: Russell Sage.

Fernandez, Carlos. 1992. La Raza and the Melting Pot: A Comparative Look at Multiethnicity. In *Racially Mixed People in America,* ed. Maria P. P. Root, 126–143.

Fernandez, Celestino, and Louis M. Holscher. 1983. Chicano-Anglo Intermarriage in Arizona. *Hispanic Journal of Behavioral Sciences* 5:291–304.

Feron, James. 1991. The Next Battle in Yonkers Will Be over Power. *New York Times,* January 27.

Fitch, Robert. 1989. Foundations and the Charter: Making New York Safe for Plutocracy. *Nation,* December 11, 709–714.

———. 1991. Mauling the Mosaic: Redistricting Was Meant to Boost Minorities; It Ended Up Preserving White Power. *Village Voice,* June 18, 11–15.

Fitzpatrick, Joseph P., and Douglas T. Gurak. 1979. *Hispanic Intermarriage in New York City: 1975.* New York: Hispanic Research Center, Fordham University.

Flynn, Kevin, and Gary Gerhardt. 1989. *The Silent Brotherhood: Inside America's Racist Underground.* New York: Free Press.

Foderaro, Lisa. 1991. Yonkers Public Housing Is Now a Cooler Issue. *New York Times,* October 21.

Forbes, Jack D. 1990. Undercounting Native Americans: The 1980 Census and the Manipulation of Racial Identity in the United States. *Wicazo Sa Review* 6(1): 2–26.

Galarza, Ernesto. 1972. Mexicans in the Southwest: A Culture in Process. In *Plural Society in the Southwest,* ed. Edward H. Spicer and Raymond H. Thompson, 261–297. Albuquerque: University of New Mexico Press.

Gamio, Manuel. 1930. *Mexican Immigration to the United States: A Study of Human Migration and Adjustment.* New York: Dover.

———. 1931. *The Mexican Immigrant: His Life-Story.* New York: Dover.

Gans, Herbert J. 1979. Symbolic Ethnicity: The Future of Ethnic Groups and Cultures in America. *Ethnic and Racial Studies* 2:1–20.

Gates, Henry Louis, Jr. 1991. "Jungle Fever" Charts Black Middle-Class Angst. *New York Times,* June 23.

Gibbs, Jewelle Taylor, and Alice Hines. 1992. Negotiating Ethnic Identity: Issues for Black-White Biracial Adolescents. In *Racially Mixed People in America,* ed. Maria P. P. Root, 223–238.

Glazer, Nathan, and Daniel P. Moynihan. 1963. *Beyond the Melting Pot: The Negroes, Puerto Ricans, Jews, Italians, and Irish of New York City.* Cambridge, Mass.: MIT Press.

Gonzalez, Sandy. 1992. Intermarriage and Assimilation: The Beginning or the End? *Wicazo Sa Review* 8(2): 48–52.

Goodfriend, Joyce D. 1992. *Before the Melting Pot: Society and Culture in Colonial New York, 1664–1730.* Princeton: Princeton University Press.

Gordon, Milton. 1964. *Assimilation in American Life: The Role of Race, Religion, and National Origins.* New York: Oxford University Press.

Gurak, Douglas T., and Joseph P. Fitzpatrick. 1982. Intermarriage among Hispanic Ethnic Groups in New York City. *American Journal of Sociology* 87:921–934.

Hall, Christine Iijima. 1992a. Coloring outside the Lines. In *Racially Mixed People in America,* ed. Maria P. P. Root, 326–329.

———. 1992b. Please Choose One: Ethnic Identity Choices for Biracial Individuals. In *Racially Mixed People in America,* ed. Maria P. P. Root, 250–264.

Handlin, Oscar. 1959. *The Newcomers: Negroes and Puerto Ricans in a Changing Metropolis*. New York: Anchor.

Harris, Marvin. 1964. *Patterns of Race in the Americas*. New York: Walker.

Heer, David M. 1980. Intermarriage. In *The Harvard Encyclopedia of American Ethnic Groups*, ed. Stephen Thernstrom, 513–521. Cambridge, Mass.: Harvard University Press.

Hirschman, Charles. 1983. America's Melting Pot Reconsidered. *Annual Review of Sociology* 9:397–423.

Hyatt, Marshall. 1990. *Franz Boas, Social Activist*. Westport, Conn.: Greenwood.

Ichioka, Yuji. 1988. *The Issei: The World of the First Generation Japanese Immigrants, 1885–1924*. New York: Free Press.

Jaimes, M. Annette, ed. 1992. *The State of Native America: Genocide, Colonization, and Resistance*. Boston: South End.

Johnson, Dirk. 1991. Census Finds Many Claiming New Identity: Indian. *New York Times*, March 5.

Jordan, Winthrop D. 1968. *White over Black: American Attitudes toward the Negro, 1550–1812*. Baltimore: Penguin.

Kerr, Peter. 1991. Cosmetics Makers Read the Census. *New York Times*, August 29.

Kich, George Kitahara. 1992. The Developmental Process of Asserting a Biracial, Bicultural Identity. In *Racially Mixed People in America*, ed. Maria P. P. Root, 304–317.

Kikumura, Akemi, and Harry Kitano. 1973. Interracial Marriage: A Picture of the Japanese Americans. *Journal of Social Issues* 29:67–81.

Kilson, Martin. 1975. Blacks and Neo-Ethnicity in American Political Life. In *Ethnicity: Theory and Experience*, ed. Nathan Glazer and Daniel P. Moynihan, 236–266. Cambridge, Mass.: Harvard University Press.

Kitano, Harry, Wai-tsang Yeung, Lynn Chai, and Herbert Hatanaka. 1984. Asian-American Interracial Marriage. *Journal of Marriage and the Family* 46:179–190.

Kristol, Irving. 1966. The Negro Today Is Like the Immigrant Yesterday. *New York Times Magazines*, September 11, 50–51, 124–142.

Lee, Sharon, and Keiko Yamanaka. 1990. Patterns of Asian American Intermarriage and Marital Assimilation. *Journal of Comparative Family Studies* 21:287–305.

Leonetti, Donna, and Laura Newell-Morris. 1982. Exogamy and Change in the Biosocial Structure of a Modern Urban Population. *American Anthropologist* 84:19–36.

Lieberson, Stanley. 1980. *A Piece of the Pie: Blacks and White Immigrants since 1880*. Berkeley and Los Angeles: University of California Press.

———. 1985. Unhyphenated Whites in the United States. *Ethnic and Racial Studies* 8:159–180.

Lieberson, Stanley, and Mary C. Waters. 1988. *From Many Strands: Ethnic and Racial Groups in Contemporary America*. New York: Russell Sage.

Light, Ivan. 1981. Ethnic Succession. In *Ethnic Change,* ed. Charles F. Keyes, 53–86. Seattle: University of Washington Press.
Marable, Manning. 1990. A New Black Politics. *Progressive,* August, 18–23.
Mass, Amy Iwasaki. 1992. Interracial Japanese Americans: The Best of Both Worlds or the End of the Japanese American Community? In *Racially Mixed People in America,* ed. Maria P. P. Root, 265–279.
Massey, Douglas, and Nancy Denton. 1993. *American Apartheid: Segregation and the Making of the Underclass.* Cambridge, Mass.: Harvard University Press.
McCabe, James D., Jr. 1872. *Lights and Shadows of New York Life: Or, the Sights and Sensations of the Great City.* New York: Farrar, Straus and Giroux.
McNickle, D'Arcy. 1973. *Native American Tribalism: Indian Survivals and Renewals.* New York: Oxford University Press.
Merton, Robert K. 1941 [1976]. Intermarriage and the Social Structure. In *Sociological Ambivalence and Other Essays.* New York: Free Press.
Mittelback, F. G., and Joan W. Moore. 1968. Ethnic Endogamy—The Case of Mexican Americans. *American Journal of Sociology* 74:50–62.
Montejano, David. 1987. *Anglos and Mexicans in the Making of Texas, 1836–1986.* Austin: University of Texas Press.
Murguia, Edward, and Phylis Cancilla Martinelli, eds. 1991. *Latino Studies Journal* (special issue on Latino/Hispanic ethnic identity) 2(3): 5–83.
Murguia, Edward, and W. Parker Frisbie. 1979. Trends in Mexican American Intermarriage. *Social Science Quarterly* 58:374–389.
Nakashima, Cynthia. 1992. An Invisible Monster: The Creation and Denial of Mixed-Race People in America. In *Racially Mixed People in America,* ed. Maria P. P. Root, 162–178.
O'Hare, William P. 1992. *America's Minorities—The Demographics of Diversity.* Washington, D.C.: Population Reference Bureau.
O'Hare, William P., and Judy C. Felt. 1991. *Asian Americans: America's Fastest Growing Minority Group.* Washington, D.C.: Population Reference Bureau.
O'Hare, William P., Kelvin M. Pollard, Taynia L. Mann, and Mary M. Kent. 1991. *African Americans in the 1990s.* Washington, D.C.: Population Reference Bureau.
Omi, Michael, and Howard Winant. 1986. *Racial Formation in the United States: From the 1960s to the 1980s.* New York: Routledge and Kegan Paul.
Padilla, Elena. 1958. *Up from Puerto Rico.* New York: Columbia University Press.
Posadas, Barbara M. 1981. Crossed Boundaries in Interracial Chicago: Filipino American Families since 1925. *Amerasia Journal* 8(2): 31–52.
Powdermaker, Hortense. 1939. *After Freedom: A Cultural Study in the Deep South.* New York: Atheneum.
Riker, James, Jr. 1852. *The Annals of Newtown in Queens County, New-York.* New York: Fanshaw.
Rimer, Sara. 1988. Defiant 4: The Councilmen Who Are Blocking the Yonkers Housing Plan. *New York Times,* August 31.

Ringer, Benjamin. 1983. *"We the People" and Others: Duality and America's Treatment of Its Racial Minorities.* New York: Tavistock.

Rink, Oliver A. 1986. *Holland on the Hudson: An Economic and Social History of Dutch New York.* Ithaca, N.Y.: Cornell University Press.

Rios, Palmira N. 1991. Black Latinos' Double Jeopardy. *Newsday,* October 25.

Rivera, Edward. 1982. *Family Installments: Memories of Growing Up Hispanic.* New York: Penguin.

Rodríguez, Clara E. 1989. *Puerto Ricans: Born in the U.S.A.* Boston: Unwin Hyman.

Root, Maria P. P. 1992a. From Shortcuts to Solutions. In *Racially Mixed People in America,* ed. Root, 342–347.

———, ed. 1992b. *Racially Mixed People in America.* Newbury Park, Calif.: Sage.

Salgado de Snyder, Nelly, and Amado M. Padilla. 1982. Cultural and Ethnic Maintenance of Interethnically Married Mexican Americans. *Human Organization* 41:359–362.

Sanjek, Roger. 1971. Brazilian Racial Terms: Some Aspects of Meaning and Learning. *American Anthropologist* 73:1126–1143.

———. 1992. The Organization of Festivals and Ceremonies among Americans and Immigrants in Queens, New York. In *To Make the World Safe for Diversity: Towards an Understanding of Multi-Cultural Societies,* ed. Ake Daun, Billy Ehn, and Barbro Klein, 123–143. Stockholm: Swedish Immigration Institute and Museum and Ethnology Institute, Stockholm University.

———. N.d. *Indigenous New York: Race, Immigration, Neighborhood Politics, and the Future of Us All.* In preparation.

———, ed. 1989. *Worship and Community: Christianity and Hinduism in Contemporary Queens.* Flushing, N.Y.: Asian/American Center, Queens College.

Schoen, Robert, Verne E. Nelson, and Marion Collins. 1978. Intermarriage among Spanish Surnamed Californians, 1962–1974. *International Migration Review* 12:359–369.

Schwartz, Shepard. 1951. Mate Selection among New York City's Chinese Males, 1931–38. *American Journal of Sociology* 56:562–568.

Spickard, Paul R. 1989. *Mixed Blood: Intermarriage and Ethnic Identity in Twentieth-Century America.* Madison: University of Wisconsin Press.

Spigner, Clarence. 1990. Black/White Interracial Marriages: A Brief Overview of U.S. Census Data, 1980–1987. *Western Journal of Black Studies* 14:214–216.

Stafford, Walter W. 1985. *Closed Labor Markets: Underrepresentation of Blacks, Hispanics, and Women in New York City's Core Industries and Jobs.* New York: Community Service Society.

Stuckert, Robert P. 1964. Race Mixture: The African Ancestry of White Americans. In *Physical Anthropology and Archaeology: Selected Readings,* ed. Peter B. Hammond, 192–197. New York: Macmillan.

Sung, Betty Lee. 1990. *Chinese American Intermarriage.* New York: Center for Migration Studies.

Tchen, John Kuo Wei. 1984. Text for *Genthe's Photographs of San Francisco's Old Chinatown.* New York: Dover.

———. 1990. New York Chinese: The Nineteenth-Century Pre-Chinatown Settlement. In *Chinese America: History and Perspectives, 1990,* Chinese Historical Society of America annual series, 157–192. San Francisco: Chinese Historical Society of America.

Teltsch, Kathleen. 1988. Amerasian Influx Expected by U.S. *New York Times,* October 9.

Thomas, Piri. 1967. *Down These Mean Streets.* New York: Vintage.

Thornton, Michael. 1992. Is Multiracial Status Unique? The Personal and Social Experience. In *Racially Mixed People in America,* ed. Maria P. P. Root, 321–325.

Tinker, John. 1973. Intermarriage and Ethnic Boundaries: The Japanese American Case. *Journal of Social Issues* 29:49–65.

Valle, Maria Eva. 1991. The Quest for Ethnic Solidarity and a New Public Identity among Chicanos and Latinos. *Latino Studies Journal* 2(3): 72–83.

Valverde, Kieu-Linh Caroline. 1992. From Dust to Gold: The Vietnamese Amerasian Experience. In *Racially Mixed People in America,* ed. Maria P. P. Root, 144–161.

Washington, Joseph R., Jr. 1970. *Marriage in Black and White.* Boston: Beacon.

Waters, Mary. 1990. *Ethnic Options: Choosing Identities in America.* Berkeley and Los Angeles: University of California Press.

Welt, Vivienne. 1988. Foreign Adoptions Open New World of Love. *Newsday,* November 6.

Wheeler, David. 1993. Black Children, White Parents: The Difficult Issue of Transracial Adoption. *Chronicle of Higher Education,* September 15, 8–9, 16.

Wilkerson, Isabel. 1991. Black-White Marriages Rise, But Couples Still Face Scorn. *New York Times,* December 2.

Williamson, Joel. 1980. *New People: Miscegenation and Mulattoes in the United States.* New York: New York University Press.

Yuan, D. Y. 1980. Significant Demographic Characteristics of Chinese Who Intermarry in the United States. *California Sociologist* 3:184–196.

CLARA E. RODRÍGUEZ

Challenging Racial Hegemony: Puerto Ricans in the United States

Puerto Ricans came to the United States with racial perceptions and experiences that differed from those on the North American mainland. Like the conceptions of race of other Latin Americans, those of Puerto Ricans are as much cultural and social as folk-biological (see Ginorio 1979, 1986; Harris 1970; Padilla 1958:75; Petrullo 1947:16; Pitt-Rivers 1975; Wade 1985; Wagley 1965). These concepts of race have been a strong theme in Latin American literature and political thought (Muñoz 1982; Vasconcelos 1966). With antecedents in Spain, New World Hispanic views of race were redefined in the colonial context of extensive mixing among Europeans, Africans, and Indians. They may now again be in the process of redefinition by Latinos in the United States.[1]

Although each country in Latin America has evolved its own unique racial context, a number of authors argue that Latinos, as a whole, have a different conception of race than that commonly held in the United States (Ginorio 1986; Wade 1985; Wagley 1965). First, in Latin America, race is often conceived of as a continuum with no fixed demarcation between categories. This is in contrast to the United States, where race is seen as a dichotomous variable of white or black, and differences in appearance among whites and among blacks are subordinate to the biracial dividing line. Second, in the United States, racial distinctions are limited to a very small number of categories—three or perhaps five, if, in addition to white, black, and yellow, red and brown are used as racial categories. In Latin America there are usually many more categories. In Brazil, for example, over a hundred racial terms and their variations may be used in a single community (Sanjek 1971). Finally, the basis for racial distinctions in the United States is strictly genealogical, while in Latin America other social variables may be calculated in racial identification, for example, class and education (Ginorio 1986).

That race may be perceived differently in Latin America, or that it may be less discussed there, does not mean that all tensions or sensitivity about race have been effectively resolved (Betances 1972; Rodríguez

1991: chap. 3; Wade 1985). Race has always been an important, but not always commendable, part of the evolution and development of Latin America. The enslavement of both Africans and indigenous peoples was widespread, and it was often accompanied by cruelty and harsh treatment. Neither Puerto Rico nor other parts of Latin America have been racial paradises. The emphasis on the racial superiority of white Europeans during Spain's colonization period became part of Spain's legacy to Latin America. This emphasis can be seen among some elites and others who maintain their "pure" European ancestry as a way of distinguishing themselves from the masses.

As Latin Americans, Puerto Ricans thus came to the U.S. mainland with perceptions of race that differed from the perceptions of those they met here. After 1917, they arrived as an ethnically different but homogenous group of multiracial U.S. citizens. They entered a U.S. society that had a biologically based biracial structure that assumed a white-nonwhite division of the world. Euro-American whites were at one pole, and African-American blacks were at the other.

Groups who had also been in the United States since its earliest beginnings, such as Native Americans and Asians, occupied ambiguous gray positions vis-à-vis this dichotomy. They were not white; they were not black. The geographic distribution or enforced isolation of these groups, plus historical events, tended to make their racial position more ambiguous in the white American public mind. What was most salient was the basic white-black racial dichotomy.

Puerto Ricans also entered a society where the racial status of other Latinos had been similarly ambiguous. This ambiguity is reflected in the changing racial classifications that Hispanics have had in the U.S. census over time.[2] In 1930, Mexican and Mexican-origin persons who were *not* "definitely White, Negro, Indian, Chinese, or Japanese" were counted as "Mexican." By 1960, all Mexicans, Puerto Ricans, and other persons of "Latin descent" were counted as "White" unless they were "definitely Negro, Indian, or some other race (as determined by observation)." In 1980, Hispanics were free to identify themselves as they chose, and those who indicated they were "other" than black or white were left in this category (Martin et al. 1990:4).

Thus, some Hispanics have been variously counted as Mexicans who were not any other race; as "white," unless they were definitely one of the other races; and finally as they chose to identify themselves by race. Given the different racial perceptions that Puerto Ricans bring, and the ambiguity in the United States over the racial status of Hispanics (or other multiracial groups), the racial experience of Puerto Ricans in the United States has not been an easy one.

Racial Themes in the Literature on Puerto Ricans

The difficulties of this experience and the clash of race orders can be clearly seen in the social science literature on Puerto Ricans published between 1938 and 1973. During that period, Puerto Ricans were relative newcomers, and issues of race were not yet affected by the subsequent and substantial changes introduced by the Black Power movement. The Black Power movement affected Puerto Ricans and other groups by increasing pride in African ancestry and by increasing ethnic pride.

In my review of nearly a score of works of the period, most by North Americans, I found that all authors agreed that race in Puerto Rico was different from race in the United States.[3] Running across this literature were three major themes: (1) Puerto Rico had a continuum of racial types, with a corresponding nomenclature for this variation; (2) Puerto Rico had a more "benign" quality of race relations than did the mainland United States; and (3) darker Puerto Ricans experienced negative social and economic consequences upon migrating to the United States. There was as well some discussion of what I term "mistaken identity," that is, being identified in the United States racially, as black or white, instead of culturally, as Puerto Rican.[4] This theme is found more emphatically in biographical or fictional writing by Puerto Ricans themselves.

The continuum of racial types referred to in several of the studies carries with it such terms as *blanco* (white), *indio* (dark skinned and straight haired), *moreno* (dark skinned but with a variety of Negroid or Caucasian features and hair forms), *negro* (black or African-American in appearance), and *trigueño* (wheat-colored), a term that can be applied broadly to each of the foregoing types except for very blond blancos (Fitzpatrick 1971; Glazer and Moynihan 1970; Gosnell 1945; Landy 1959; La Ruffa 1971; Mills et al. 1950; Mintz 1960; Padilla 1958; Steward 1956). (The term *negro* is also commonly used in Puerto Rico as a term of endearment, without regard to racial appearance.)

Where each of these categories ends and another begins is vague, and there is not always agreement on their use or range of application (Ginorio and Berry 1972). A more analytic conception of this continuum was advanced by Padilla (1958:74). She argued that in Puerto Rico there was a biracial continuum, with the two poles being white and black. Within this overarching biracial structure, however, she maintained that, contrary to the situation in the United States, the categories in the middle of the continuum were not castelike social groups and that one could experience mobility within one's lifetime from one racial designation to another.

In contrast to this spectrum of racial categories, found in similar forms elsewhere in the Caribbean and other parts of Latin America, racial discourse in the United States had evolved around how to best conceptualize the "other" or nonwhite group. In the United States, racial terms for African Americans have changed over time, from *African* to *colored* to *Negro* to *black* to *African American*. The U.S. census has even used mixed-race categories, like mulatto or octoroon, at various points in its history (Martin et al. 1990). However, the underlying referent remained the same—they were members of an "other," nonwhite group. In comparison, in Puerto Rico the terms *moreno, trigueño,* and even *negro* have multiple connotations and do not refer to socially and politically bounded groups (Rodríguez and Cordero-Guzmán 1992). In Puerto Rico, members of the same kin groups can be identified with varying racial terms, and an individual might change racial status with changes in class or education. On the contrary, in the United States no individual of any degree of African descent can leave the "black race" group, regardless of changes in social and economic status.

The majority of North American social scientists who studied the island found race relations within its body politic to be "benign," as they often phrased it, and relatively unimportant (Chenault [1938] 1970; Glazer and Moynihan 1970; Mintz 1960; Petrullo 1947; Steward 1956; see also Giles et al. 1979). Overall there was general agreement that the quality of race relations in Puerto Rico made for a less divided and unequal society than that in the United States. Despite this consensus on the relative insignificance of race in institutional treatment, there was some disagreement on how salient or significant race was on other more personal levels. Some authors concluded that color was also less important to Puerto Ricans in their primary interpersonal social and family relations than was the case in the United States (Chenault [1938] 1970; Glazer and Moynihan 1970:142). Others (Landy 1959; G. Lewis 1963:424; Steward 1956:291; Tumin and Feldman 1971:228) argued that Puerto Ricans in Puerto Rico were very conscious of race, especially skin color. La Ruffa (1971) went further and asserted there was covert racism on the island toward African ancestry and heritage, while Padilla (1958:74) stated that it was to one's advantage to look white in Puerto Rico.

An interesting perspective was presented by Gordon Lewis, who saw racial mixture in Puerto Rico as having produced a massive psychological color complex "with serious results both for the quality of self-esteem and of social life" (1963:225). Lewis agreed there was little overt racism but said there was a very real sense of color snobbishness based on the awareness of "shades." The whitening or bleaching phenomenon that exists in Latin America is to some degree rooted in the idea that one should *adelantar la raza* (improve the race) by always attempting to marry individuals who are lighter than one is. Thus, upwardly mobile, darker males, for example, would marry lighter or white women, and darker women would marry lighter men, even those who might be lower in socioeconomic status or of lower "moral" quality, for example, womanizers. Lewis viewed this type of racial transformation as a problem, for it implied that self-worth revolved around whether or not individuals were able to garner the resources and recognition necessary to become so "whitened." (Lewis did not discuss the increasing economic and political influence of the United States on racial perceptions in Puerto Rico and Latin America.)

If Lewis is correct, then migrants to New York may have brought a sensitivity to color and race that became all the more acute with the sharp, biologically based segregation existent in the United States, and with the significant changes wrought by the Black Power movement. Fitzpatrick (1971) alluded to this when he said that the Puerto Rican's problem with color in New York was a concern already present in a much different context in Puerto Rico.

In this literature from 1938 to 1973, there is an awareness of the harshness of the U.S. race order, particularly on darker Puerto Ricans. The influence this system had on economic status and migration patterns was noted by a number of authors (Chenault [1938] 1970:24, 60–61; Katzman 1968; Mills et al. 1950:48, 72–74; Petrullo 1947:23; Senior 1965:28). Chenault ([1938] 1970), speaking of the pre–World War II New York community, noted that instances of difficulty on account of color were so frequent that numerous examples could be given. Rand stated, "An outsider cannot easily tell how the color line works in Puerto Rico but there seems no doubt that dark skin is a worse handicap in New York than there, and that realization of this can shock the dark-skinned migrant" (1958: 27).

In the housing area, there were many mentions made of difficulties experienced because of race (Chenault [1938] 1970:127; Gosnell 1945:313; Senior 1965:28). Also noted were the less visible but nonetheless significant social and psychological racial reassessments experienced by Puerto Ricans as a result of the new race order in the United States (Gosnell 1945:310–311; López 1973; Mills et al. 1950:7; Padilla 1958:75ff). There was even speculation about the negative impact of race on mental health (Berle 1958; Longres 1974:67; Malzberg 1967; Teichner and Berry 1981:281).

Being classified according to U.S. racial standards meant being identified racially instead of culturally. For many Puerto Ricans this meant being reclassified into a different culture. This reclassification and its consequences have affected Puerto Ricans of all colors and have been persistent themes in the autobiographical literature, found in the *Memorias de Bernardo Vega* (Iglesias 1977), Jesus Colon's *Puerto Rican in New York* (1961), Piri Thomas's *Down These Mean Streets* (1967), and Edward Rivera's *Family Installments* (1983). The most-cited experience was that of the darker Puerto Rican who is taken to be "Negro," "colored," or "Black."

However, the perplexing situation of the Puerto Rican who is viewed as a white American is a complementary experience that similarly yields confusion, anger, and a clear awareness of group divisions. In the stories retold by Colon (1961), a white-looking daughter cannot meet her darker mother at her workplace because her employers do not like colored people; or *only* the white Puerto Ricans in an extended family are served at a segregated restaurant in the pre-1960s period. Vega notes how an apartment was rented to a white-looking member of a family, but when the others arrived, they all became the object of discrimination (see Iglesias 1977).

If such reclassifications did not have real-life consequences, they might be seen as trivial aberrations in the stream of life. However, this has not been the case. Identification by white Americans as Black, or even as a racially mixed or white-appearing Puerto Rican, has had economic, residential, social, and even political results. The real-life consequences of such classifications in the United States—*regardless of appearance*—were made explicit by one respondent in Oscar Lewis's *La Vida:* "I'm so white that they've even taken me for a Jew, but when they see my Spanish name, they back right off" (1966:180–181). Although the political consequences of race for Latinos have been less well documented in the literature reviewed here, it is clear that gerrymandering made possible by housing discrimination has been used to suppress the Puerto Rican "minority" in the U.S. mainland.

Some Puerto Ricans were faced with the historical choice that many white ethnic Americans met, whether to Anglicize their name and pass for nonethnic, or whether to keep their ethnic name and pay the consequences. But for Puerto Ricans the process was more complicated. Another choice had to be made, whether to be of the "white" race, or of a "not white" race. It appears that when Puerto Ricans first arrived on the mainland they perceived that there were two paths, one to the white world and one to the not-white world. Two realities seemed to be evident, and the choice of paths was dependent on racial classification according to U.S. standards. Race influenced the rewards to be gained from the system—housing, jobs, income. It seemed, however, that use of these standards would divide the group, split families, negate the cultural existence of Puerto Ricans, and ignore their expectation that they be treated as one group, irrespective of race (Rodriguez 1989).

This was the situation into which the earliest Puerto Ricans in the United States stepped. The assumption or conclusion of many scholars was that, with greater time on the mainland, Puerto Rican racial attitudes would become more like those in the United States (Chenault [1938] 1970:151; Fitzpatrick 1971; Handlin 1959:60ff.). Thus, it was anticipated that Puerto Ricans would become white or black over time. Alternatively, if Puerto Ricans were to retain a "coherent," integrated, cultural community, their success would ultimately depend on the reactions of the larger community and on a decline in biracial consciousness.

That the prediction of racial assimilation to U.S. standards has *not* occurred is evidenced by the 1980 and 1990 U.S. census results. While most non-Latinos responded they were "white" or "black" on the census race question, the responses of Puerto Ricans and other Latinos were quite different.[5] Over 40 percent of Puerto Ricans and Latinos in the country did not check off "white," "black," or any of the Asian or indigenous categories provided in this question (Denton and Massey 1989; Rodríguez 1991).[6] Instead, they checked off the last category, "other." In the blank space adjacent to the "other" category, many further specified that they were Puerto Rican, Spanish, Boricua (referring to the Amerindian name for the island), and so on.

Between 1980 and 1990, the proportion of Hispanics indicating they were "other" in response to the census race item increased by 2.7 percent. This occurred despite changes in the format of the census that were intended to discourage this "other" response (Rodríguez 1992). These results suggest that the racial self-identification of many Puerto Ricans and other Latinos in the United States continues to defy assimilation to either Euro-American or African-American groups.[7]

Case Studies

The experience of Puerto Ricans in the United States illustrates a clash of race orders. This clash has been experienced by other Latino groups to greater and lesser degrees. By examining the life histories of individuals within the Puerto Rican community we see the choices people are forced to make under these conditions and the resistance they display. The following case studies are extracted from a larger, ongoing research project on racial identity.[8] The major question probed in these life histories is how Latinos identify racially in the United States. The first case study illustrates a Puerto Rican adaptation to the traditional mode of

European immigrant racial assimilation; the second, resistance to the U.S. biracial requirement; and the third, an encounter with the U.S. racial system and its pressures on dark Latinos to identify as Black.

The first subject, José Peterson, is single, twenty-five, and a college graduate who works as an administrator in the arts field. Peterson's parents migrated from Puerto Rico to New York when they were in their early twenties. They settled in a section of the city with a high incidence of violent crime. Peterson lived in this area for the first eight years of his life, until his parents moved to a more stable working-class area, where he continues to reside. Both Spanish and English are spoken in the home, but Peterson says his Spanish is not good. He indicated his background was working class and said he felt this way because his father did manual labor. He is the fourth child in a family of five siblings and the first to receive a college education.

Peterson was viewed by the interviewer as being "white." When asked questions about his race, Peterson answered consistently and unequivocally that he was "white." However, when asked questions that he interpreted as relevant to his ethnic identity, he answered Puerto Rican American. For example, on the census race question, he had checked "other" and specified he was "Puerto Rican-American." He explained that he attributed his Puerto Rican heritage to his parents, but that he identified as American because he was born in the States. He also added that he was bicultural because he was influenced by "various aspects of both the American and Puerto Rican cultures." When asked the general question of how he identified himself, he again said, "Puerto Rican American."

When asked how he would racially identify himself—white, black, or other—he said "white" because of his European (Spanish) background. He also made reference to being "white" when asked about his color, how North Americans viewed him, or how he would describe himself over the phone. He classified everyone in his family as white—except for two grandmothers who, he said, had "Indian blood."

Thus, Peterson consistently answered that he was white when he understood the questions to be about his physical appearance, but he said he was a hyphenated American (Puerto Rican–American) when he perceived the question to be about his cultural identity. He has thus adapted to the U.S. racial system in the same way that previous European immigrants have. His responses are similar to those we might expect of Italian, Greek, or Irish Americans—the only difference being that they would not say they have grandmothers with Indian blood.

More resistant to the U.S. biracial scheme is the second subject, Arco Iris, a sixty-two-year-old professional in the criminal justice system.

Arco Iris also represents a unique resolution to the clash of race orders, but one that is more innovation than adaptation. He, and others like him, identify strongly with color and express a preference for racial diversity and mixture. Such individuals acknowledge a bi- or triracial heritage with pride. They see themselves as combinations of African, European, and indigenous Indian and are proud of these racial components. The consolidation or crystallization of these rainbow identities represents a unique form of resistance to the dichotomized racial structure of the United States.

Arco Iris was born and raised in East Harlem and the South Bronx, in predominantly Black American and Hispanic neighborhoods. Both of his parents were born and raised in Puerto Rico and migrated to New York before World War II. He describes the household in which he was raised as a Spanish-speaking, lower-middle-class home. He feels his roots are in Harlem; he has spent little time living in Puerto Rico. He is fluent in Spanish but is more comfortable in English. He is married to a West Indian woman and has three children.

He was described by the interviewer as "not white/not black." In response to the census race question, he had checked "other" and had written "Puerto Rican" in the blank space. Responding to the question "How would you describe yourself racially?" and "What do you consider yourself to be?" he stated in both instances: "I am a mixture of black, white, and possibly Indian." He described his color as brown and stated that North Americans tend to see him as a "brown-skinned Puerto Rican or a light-skinned black."

On a five-point color scale, he described his mother as a one (light) and his father as a five (dark), and he identified himself as a four. This was darker than the interviewer's view of Arco Iris as a three (intermediate in color). When asked why he characterized himself as darker than North Americans might perceive him, he stated that "four is more biologically accurate" and further explained that he identified himself as dark out of respect and loyalty for his brown-skinned father.

Arco Iris's race varies with the eye of the beholder. He noted that since childhood he has been taken to be white, black, Greek, Arab, and Asian. These many instances of "mistaken identity" have prompted him to think about his identity more than others might. That he is able to crystallize his identity in the way that he has is a result of this self-reflection.

Arco Iris's racial identity is also of interest because he noted that it has changed over time. "As a child, I perceived myself as a Puerto Rican and distinctly apart from black and white. But as I grew, I understood Puerto Rican as a mixture, and I could identify with both blacks and whites." The way he viewed his ancestral background has also changed:

"I would have considered myself more white up to the age of nine. As I got older, I developed a broader definition of race and acknowledged greater mixture."

The third subject, José Ali, who is not Puerto Rican but Dominican, illustrates that the dynamics described for Puerto Ricans are also at work among other Latino groups. Ali presents the conflict depicted in the literature on the Puerto Rican migration since earliest times (Colon 1961; Iglesias 1977), perhaps most vividly in Piri Thomas's *Down These Mean Streets* (1967). It is the imposition of the black-white racial order on Latinos, thereby separating them into whites and blacks, and in the process attempting to create new African Americans and new hyphenated Americans—"Puerto Rican–Americans," "Dominican-Americans," "Colombian-Americans," and so on.

This phenomenon is understood by Latinos as one wherein they are perceived racially but not culturally, for Latinos today are subject to the pressure to be black, white, or perhaps now brown in the United States as opposed to being identified by national heritage and culture. At the same time, members of Hispanic groups whose continuing arrival in the United States accentuates their national identity focus on cultural differences between their own and other groups, both Latino and non-Latino.

José Ali's case represents the pressure to be Black. Ali is a twenty-four-year-old single Dominican male, and a full-time student at a public university. He has a part-time job in an advertising firm, where the majority of his co-workers are white. He was born and raised in New York of Dominican immigrant parents. He has visited the Dominican Republic only once, when he was five. He was raised in a predominantly Hispanic neighborhood until he was eight years old, and Spanish was the only language spoken at home until he was twelve. Subsequently he moved to another area of New York that had a large African-American population. He describes his family as working class; his father worked in the metal goods industry, and his mother was an office worker. He does not have a Hispanic surname.

His appearance is described by the interviewer as "a stereotypically dark-skinned Latino or a light skinned Afro-American." He answered "other, Hispanic" to the census race question. He commented, "By inheritance I am Hispanic. However, I identify more with Blacks due to the fact that to white America, if you are my color you are a nigger. I can't change my color, and I do not wish to." He consistently alluded to his identification as Black when responding to other racial items in the interview, responding, for example, "Hispanic, yet I identify as black," or "I describe myself as black." When asked what the word *black* meant to him, he said, "As other people see me." Finally, when asked. "Why do you see yourself as black?" his answer was: "Because, when I was jumped by whites I was not called a 'spic,' but I was called a 'nigger.' "

During the interview, José Ali explained that he feels everybody at his job assumes that he is Black, and he does not "want to burst their bubble." He said he goes along with their assumption as long as he is treated well. He admitted that he accepts the identity attributed to him because it would take him more time to explain why he is not, culturally, an African American. He pointed out that "when you are seen as a certain race, you are also seen culturally the same." But when people assume that he is Black American, they are "disregarding my own feelings. They don't ask, they simply assume."

Asked if his identity had changed over time, Ali said yes. "I realized that although I feel Hispanic, I was not seen as Hispanic or Latino, but as Black. Now, I agree with whomever thinks I'm Black. There is no point in trying to prove that I'm not Black . . . after being practically attacked by whites because of the way I look. I decided to accept the fact that no matter who I feel to be, I am categorized as Black."

Many other respondents in the sample also described how non-Hispanics assumed they were black or white Americans, and therefore not Hispanic. For many Latinos in the United States, their world was inverted; their racial appearance became more important than their culture. These intense pressures led, in many cases, to the development of both an internal cultural identity as a Latino or Dominican, for example, and an external identity as black or white in U.S. terms. It resulted in some cases in their adopting or affecting more than one racial or ethnic identity, and in hiding their background or exhibiting chameleonlike behavior in differing social contexts (see Rodríguez 1991).

The three cases presented illustrate paradigmatic reactions to the U.S. race order. The first case, José Peterson, depicts the familiar immigrant model of white racial-identity formation, although in this Latino case, the acknowledgment of "Indian" ancestry was offered unproblematically. The second case, Arco Iris, illustrates defiance of the dichotomized racial classification system in the United States. Arco Iris does not place himself in any of the accepted U.S. racial categories. Rather he presents a "mixed" racial identity that acknowledges racial mixture positively. The last case, José Ali, illustrates the clash of racial structures at work. His case represents the conflict that occurs when society racially classifies individuals in a way that differs from the way in which the individuals see themselves. These three case studies illustrate the range of choices people are forced to make, and the resistances multiracial Latinos display, in a biracial United States.

Notes

1. The terms *Latino* and *Hispanic* are used interchangeably throughout this essay.

2. When the 1990 census was being planned, the issue of how Latinos should be counted was again raised, and the suggestion was made that perhaps they should be counted as a separate racial group. This suggestion was defeated through strenuous community opposition, "the most aggressive campaign ever seen by the bureau" (Nampeo McKenney, a Bureau of the Census official, qtd. in *Hispanic Link Weekly Report,* May 26, 1986). Census agency officials decided to abandon the proposal, fearing it would cause a withdrawal of needed community support. In essence, Latinos rejected the conception that they should be counted as a separate race group. From the perspective of some, this left Latinos again straddling the white–not white race order.

3. These works were: Berle 1958; Chenault [1938] 1970; Fitzpatrick 1971; Glazer and Moynihan 1971; Gosnell 1945; Handlin 1959; Katzman 1968; Landy 1959; La Ruffa 1971; G. Lewis 1963; O. Lewis 1966; Longres 1974; López 1973; Malzberg 1967; Mills et al. 1950; Mintz 1960; Padilla 1958; Petrullo 1947; Rand 1958; Senior 1965; Steward 1956; Teichner and Berry 1981; Tumin and Feldman 1971. With the exception of community studies by Gosnell, López, and Padilla, all are by North American social scientists using a variety of descriptive, ethnographic, and survey-research methods.

4. Over other themes in this literature there was disagreement. One was the question of whether Puerto Ricans are a race or a multiracial society. Although this has been a constant question, it has not yielded a definitive answer.

5. According to the 1980 census, the overwhelming majority of non-Hispanic Americans chose racial categories traditional in the U.S., i.e., white or black; the percentage who identified as "other" was less than 3 percent in all states, including Hawaii (Rodríguez 1991).

6. The other categories indicated on the census form were: Japanese, Chinese, Filipino, Korean, Vietnamese, Indian (Amer.), Asian Indian, Hawaiian, Guamanian, Samoan, Eskimo, and Aleut.

7. The various Hispanic groups differed in the extent to which they checked off "other," but they all used this category to a considerable degree. Tienda and Ortiz (1986) had suggested that the format of the race item may have made for some misinterpretation of the question. The item included as possible answers to the race question various Asian groups; it was argued this may have induced some Latinos to respond culturally, seeing "white" and "black" as two North American cultural populations to which they do not belong. However, the work of Martin et al. (1990), which explored the format and order of the race and Hispanic identifier, suggests that the tendency to select "other" persisted, especially for the foreign-born.

8. See Rodríguez et al. 1991 for a description of the racial identity project.

References

Berle, Beatrice. 1958. *80 Puerto Rican Families in New York City.* New York: Columbia University Press.

Betances, Samuel. 1972. The Prejudice of Having No Prejudice. *Rican* 1:41–54.

Chenault, Lawrence. [1938] 1970. *The Puerto Rican Migrant in New York City.* New York: Columbia University Press.

Colon, Jesus. 1961. *A Puerto Rican in New York and Other Sketches.* New York: International Publishers.

Denton, Nancy A., and Douglas S. Massey. 1989. Racial Identity among Caribbean Hispanics: The Effect of Double Minority Status on Residential Segregation. *American Sociological Review* 54:790–808.

Fitzpatrick, Joseph. 1971. *Puerto Rican Americans.* Englewood Cliffs, N.J.: Prentice-Hall.

Giles, H., N. Llado, D. J. McKirnan, and D. M. Taylor. 1979. Social Identity in Puerto Rico. *International Journal of Psychology* 14:185–201.

Ginorio, Angela. 1979. A Comparison of Puerto Ricans in New York with Native Puerto Ricans and Native Americans on Two Measures of Acculturation: Gender Role and Racial Identification. Ph.D. diss., Fordham University.

———. 1986. Puerto Ricans and Interethnic Conflict. In *International Perspectives on Ethnic Conflict: Antecedents and Dynamics,* ed. Jerry O. Boucher, Dan Landis, and Karen Arnold. Newbury Park, Calif.: Sage.

Ginorio, Angela, and Paul C. Berry. 1972. Summary of Measuring Puerto Ricans' Perceptions of Racial Characteristics. *Proceedings of the 80th Annual Convention of the American Psychological Association* 7:287–288.

Glazer, Nathan, and Daniel P. Moynihan. 1970. *Beyond the Melting Pot.* 2d ed. Cambridge, Mass.: MIT Press.

Gosnell Aran, Patria. 1945. The Puerto Ricans in New York City. Ph.D. diss., New York University.

Handlin, Oscar. 1959. *The Newcomers: Negroes and Puerto Ricans in a Changing Metropolis.* Cambridge, Mass.: Harvard University Press.

Harris, Marvin. 1970. Referential Ambiguity in the Calculus of Brazilian Racial Identity. In *Afro-American Anthropology,* ed. Norman Whitten, Jr., and John F. Szwed, 75–85. New York: Free Press.

Iglesias, César Andreu. 1977. *Memorias de Bernardo Vega: Una Contribución a la Historia de la Comunidad Puertorriquena en Nueva York.* Río Piedras, P.R.: Ediciones Huracán. Available in English, Monthly Review Press, 1984.

Katzman, Martin. 1968. Discrimination, Subculture, and the Economic Performance of Negroes, Puerto Ricans, and Mexican-Americans. *American Journal of Economics and Society* 27:371–375.

Landy, David. 1965. *Tropical Childhood.* Chapel Hill: University of North Carolina Press.

La Ruffa, Anthony. 1971. *San Cipriano: Life in a Puerto Rican Community.* New York: Gordon and Breach.

Lewis, Gordon K. 1966. *Puerto Rico: Freedom and Power in the Caribbean.* New York: Monthly Review Press.

Lewis, Oscar. 1966. *La Vida: A Puerto Rican Family in the Culture of Poverty—San Juan and New York.* New York: Random House.

Longres, John F. 1974. Racism and Its Effects on Puerto Rican Continentals. *Social Casework* 55:67–99.

López, Alfredo. 1973. *The Puerto Rican Papers.* New York: Bobbs-Merrill.

Malzberg, Benjamin. 1967. Internal Migration and Mental Disease among the White Population of New York State, 1960–61. *International Journal of Social Psychiatry* 13:184–191.

Martin, Elizabeth, Theresa J. DeMaio, and Pamela C. Campanelli. 1990. Context Effects for Census Measures of Race and Hispanic Origin. *Public Opinion Quarterly* 54:551–566.

Mills, C. Wright, Clarence Senior, and Rose Goldsen. 1950. *The Puerto Rican Journey: New York's Newest Migrants.* New York: Harper.

Mintz, Sidney W. 1960. *Worker in the Cane.* New Haven, Conn.: Yale University Press.

Muñoz, Braulio. 1982. *Sons of the Wind: The Search for Identity in Spanish American Indian Literature.* New Brunswick: Rutgers University Press.

Padilla, Elena. 1958. *Up from Puerto Rico.* New York: Columbia University Press.

Petrullo, Vincenzo. 1947. *Puerto Rican Paradox.* Philadelphia: University of Pennsylvania Press.

Pitt-Rivers, Julian. 1975. Race, Color, and Class in Central America and the Andes. In *Majority and Minority,* ed. Norman R. Yetman and C. Hoy Steele, 90–97. Boston: Allyn and Bacon.

Rand, Christopher. 1958. *The Puerto Ricans.* New York: Oxford University Press.

Rivera, Edward. 1983. *Family Installments: Memories of Growing Up Hispanic.* New York: Penguin.

Rodríguez, Clara. 1990. Racial Identification among Puerto Ricans in New York. *Hispanic Journal of Behavioral Sciences* 12:366–379.

———. 1991. *Puerto Ricans: Born in the USA.* Boston: Unwin Hyman, 1989. Reprint, Boulder, Colo.: Westview.

———. 1992. Race, Culture, and Latino "Otherness" in the 1980 Census. *Social Science Quarterly* 73:930–937.

Rodríguez, Clara, Aida Castro, Oscar García, and Analisa Torres. 1991. Latino Racial Identity: In the Eye of the Beholder? *Latino Studies Journal* 2(3): 33–48.

Rodríguez, Clara, and Héctor Cordero-Guzmán. 1992. Placing Race in Context. *Ethnic and Racial Studies* 15:523–542.

Sanjek, Roger. 1971. Brazilian Racial Terms: Some Aspects of Meaning and Learning. *American Anthropologist* 73:1126–1143.

Senior, Clarence. 1965. *Strangers, Then Neighbors: From Pilgrims to Puerto Ricans.* Chicago: Quadrangle.

Steward, Julian. 1965. *The People of Puerto Rico.* Urbana: University of Illinois Press.

Teichner, Victor J., and Gail W. Berry. 1981. The Puerto Rican Patient: Some Historical and Psychological Aspects. *Journal of the American Academy of Psychoanalysis* 9:277–289.

Thomas, Piri. 1967. *Down These Mean Streets.* New York: Knopf.

Tienda, Marta, and Vilma Ortiz. 1986. "Hispanicity" and the 1980 Census. *Social Science Quarterly* 67:3–20.

Tumin, Melvin, and Arnold Feldman. 1971. *Social Class and Social Change in Puerto Rico.* 2d ed. Princeton: Princeton University Press.

Vasconcelos, José. 1966. *La Raza Cosmica.* 3d ed. Mexico: Espasa-Calpe.

Wade, Peter. 1985. Race and Class: The Case of South American Blacks. *Ethnic and Racial Studies* 8:233–249.

Wagley, Charles. 1965. On the Concept of Social Race in the Americas. In *Contemporary Cultures and Societies of Latin America: A Reader in the Social Anthropology of Middle and South America and the Caribbean,* ed. Dwight B. Health and Richard N. Adams, 531–545. New York: Random House.

MICHEL-ROLPH TROUILLOT

Culture, Color, and Politics in Haiti

The first difficulty in dealing with color and politics in Haiti is that the Haitian "color question" cannot be separated from Western cultural influence and a worldwide hierarchy of races, religions, and cultures, yet cannot be reduced either to a mere avatar of Western prejudices. Indeed, few Haitian practices and beliefs can be considered derivatively Western. In the social perception and use of somatic differences, as in most domains, the cultural influence of the West is constantly being challenged, even if only partially, by local practices, beliefs, and values.

A second difficulty stems from the fact that in Haiti conflict between color-cum-social categories does not simply reflect an opposition between social classes, however defined: the dominant classes are not composed exclusively of light-skinned individuals, nor do all such individuals belong to those classes. A third difficulty is the widespread disapproval of discourses and practices that hint at institutional discrimination on the basis of color—or "race"—alone. Models of discrimination on the basis of appearance, drawn from the experiences of South Africa or the United States, lose their meaning in Haiti because the social postulates on which they are based (and which are, in turn, maintained by discrimination) simply do not apply. Neither do traditional models of racial conflict. There are no bomb threats for moving into the "wrong" neighborhood, no graffiti slurs on school walls, no lynchings, no street wars. Haiti never had a "color riot," let alone a "race riot."

An underlying proposition of this essay is that the beliefs and practices that Haitian urbanites refer to as the "color question" do not operate in a social vacuum. Instead, color-cum-social categories operate in various spheres of urban life as part of different strategies of competition and struggle. They materialize most vividly in the familial alliances typical of certain urban classes, and they are often a favored idiom of politics. But they also function as referents for sociocultural oppositions outside the immediate political arena. It is this complexity that explains the fact that references to the "color question" could bestow upon twentieth-century politicians, such as François "Papa Doc" Duvalier, the legitimacy they then claimed for themselves. To discover the roots of this legitimacy we must first turn to the international hierarchy of races, colors, religions, and cultures, and to the ambivalent response of the Haitian elites to the cultural domination of the West.

The "Color" Complex

Those who persist in claiming that the West is *merely* capitalist will have difficulty acknowledging that the international division of labor is paired with a hierarchy of races, colors, religions, and cultures whose complexity cannot be reduced to labor-market segmentation. Ethnocentrism preceded the creation of a European proletariat, let alone an international one. It is fair to say that para-ethnic identity even foreshadowed the advent of class-based societies. The comparison between "us" and "them" implies, among other evaluative criteria, the existence of what Harry Hoetink (1967) called a somatic norm-image, a physical ideal of beauty. All things being equal, "we" are always more attractive than "they."[1] At the very least, "we" are closer to what human beings really should look like.

But things are not always equal. Because of the differential accumulation of technology, as well as the institutionalization of a combative posture that marked the evolution of Mediterranean peoples well before the rise of capitalism, what came to be called the West gave itself a distinct identity. The West defined itself, so to speak, in the course of a history punctuated by internal and external conquests, a history engaged almost from the start in a legitimizing discourse. These conquests and this discourse preceded the north-south social fissure of the Mediterranean from which Europe, as we now know it, was born. Aristotle had already formulated the hypothesis, echoed in fifteenth-century Spain, that some humans were inferior and therefore fated to be slaves. Diodorus Siculus found the Ethiopians "primitive," and from Pliny the Elder's imagination sprang monstrous subhumans in the heart of black Africa—beings without mouths, noses, voices, or eyes, unspeakably ugly monsters.

No doubt other cultures developed similar themes of exclusion of the Other. But as I said earlier, all things were not equal, for the accounts that have come down to us are those of Diodorus and Pliny, along with those of myriads of Westerners, from the Renaissance to the present. When Christendom became the West, it also gave itself a European past and a global future. I would thus hesitate to argue that capitalism alone allowed Europe to spread and systematize an unflattering image of others. At any rate, that spread and that systematization brought qualitative changes in the European social perception of somatic differences. If ethnocentrism was ever naive, it certainly stopped being so after the systematic demeaning of the cultures of the Other used to justify colonial conquests and plantation slavery. This new threshold required in turn the European vision to be just as systematically imposed on the dominated peoples themselves. By the 1620s, Africans and Amerindians of the Antilles and the Atlantic coast of the American mainland had to be aware of their differential status on the European-imposed scale, just as Asian immigrants were to find out in the 1850s that European preconceptions of their failures and worth had accompanied them to the New World (Du Tertre 1667; Gage [1648] 1958; Trollope [1859] 1985).

All this is to say—and it is of extreme importance—that the phenomenon described in Haiti in rather sibylline terms as the "color question" is etched within the framework of an international hierarchy that was formalized well before Haitian independence in 1804. A female member of the Haitian bourgeoisie conveniently reaffirmed this age-old context when she told anthropologist Micheline Labelle, "If they marry a *noir,* people will say that the children are horrible, and since color prejudice is international, if they are sent abroad to study they will have problems" (Labelle 1976:35).

The French colony of Saint-Domingue, and later independent Haiti, thus inherited a differential evaluation of races, colors, religions, and cultures. This evaluation included an aesthetic in which blackness was found at the bottom of the scale. To pretend that this aesthetic has disappeared is ludicrous: photos of recent beauty contests or the sight of advertising posters confirm its continued existence. Admittedly, aesthetic evaluations vary according to the socioeconomic class and phenotype of those who judge, and the results are sometimes surprising to foreigners (Labelle 1976, 1978). Generally speaking "white," for example, is *not* considered to be the most pleasing color. Social evaluations of phenotypes in Haiti are nonetheless generally *Western dominated* and, other things being equal, beyond a certain degree of increased melanin, these evaluations imply a denigration of blackness.

But here again, other things are rarely equal. Thus the reader who is unfamiliar with Haiti must be immediately cautioned lest he or she take the preceding to imply that Haitian color prejudice is simply a toned-down version of Western racism. As Sidney Mintz has lucidly written, "North American ideas about what 'color' someone is are far more hindrance than help in understanding Haiti" (1984:299). Nor am I certain that a European perception would be more useful.[2] To start with, Haitian "color" categories refer to many more aspects of phenotype than skin color alone, even when their etymology seems to indicate an exclusively epidermic referent. Epidermic shade remains crucial, but skin texture and depth of skin tone, hair color and appearance, and facial features also figure in any categorization. Thus two individuals who seem to be the same "color" can be classed in different categories because of other somatic criteria. Color thus functions as a dividing line, negatively delimiting a field of possible categories. In other words, it would be much easier for two Haitians to agree that X could *not* be considered noir because he is too "light," or that Y could *not* be considered *mulâtre* because he is too "dark," than to agree on the category (which is not always intermediate) in which to place X or Y. The color line that separates *clairs* (including subgroups such as mulâtres, *griffes, grimauds,* and *mulâtres bruns*) from noirs (including the more-or-less dark epidermic shades and various types of hair) is the most important among a number of somatic boundaries that operate together. Color never operates alone, even in the perception of physical difference.

More importantly, color categories embrace characteristics that go far beyond the perceived phenotype into the field of social relations. These can include income, social origin, level of formal education, customary behavior, ties of kinship or marriage, and other characteristics. And different combinations of these social traits can move a person from one category to a more or less proximate one. Thus terms such as *mulâtre* and *noir* do not simply mean—and sometimes do not mean at all—"mulatto" or "black" in the U.S. sense. The kind of social discrimination that operates in Haiti is not exclusively based on physical features, even when phenotype plays a role in the application and description of this discrimination. For example, up until very recently some people were discouraged from frequenting certain clubs because they were "too noir," although others, visibly darker, could enter. In short, Haitian color categories refer not only to skin color and other somatic features, but to a large range of sociocultural attributes that do not have a somatic referent.

The reshaping of these categories—a process that has been going on at least since independence—has been facilitated by the growth of beliefs and practices in which Western influence figures but does not go uncontested. If it is important to note that Haitian color prejudice relates to a Western-dominated hierarchy of races, colors, religions, and cultures, it is equally crucial to note that very few Haitians, even among the elites, ever accepted that hierarchy as a "true" depiction of their reality. In any case, the urban elites, the most Westernized part of the population, never gained such full control of the cultural terrain that they could impose a prepackaged Western view on the rest of the population.

The Cultural Guerrilla War

Various observers of Haiti endorse a dualist view that treats Haitian society as if it consisted of two separate parts (Denis and Duvalier 1938).

I have shown elsewhere the limits of this dualist view; at the very least, the physical to-and-fro of the peasantry from the hinterland to the urban trenches meant that it has come to occupy part of the urban social and cultural terrain (Trouillot 1990:80–82). That terrain does not simply mirror the political scene. Nor is it a mere reflection of economic structures: while the economic and political divisions may be reminiscent of trench warfare, the cultural relations between the classes are more reminiscent of a guerrilla war. The peasantry is not the master of this space—or never for long—but it penetrates it deeply and harasses the enemy, while remaining ready to retreat at any point. It does not dictate the dominant cultural codes, but those who impose them must take its values into account. The history of urban arts, of painting and music—as well as of religion, language, and the organization of kinship networks—all indicate the existence within civil society of another order of relationships alongside the dominant one. The peasantry cannot be said to be victorious in the cultural sphere, but it has an implicitly acknowledged presence there, to a degree as yet unmatched in the political and economic arenas.

Of course, even in this cultural domain the peasantry does not have the last word. Just as peasant practices filter into the city, the dominant culture's hostility to many of these practices filters back to the peasantry, subtly adding to its isolation by repeatedly stressing its inferiority.[3] Thus the cultural distance between town and countryside lies as much in the social assessment of practices and beliefs as in their actual distribution. A significant number of peasant practices that are publicly spurned by the elites are still nurtured privately among all urban classes. More importantly, even when practices vary—as of course they do—they often spring from the same underlying values. The crux of the matter is that these underlying values are differently acknowledged and carry a different symbolic weight in different class presentations.

Religion provides a good example of these similarities and differences. In the half-century of incubation that followed independence, what is commonly referred to as Vodoun by nonpractitioners emerged as the religion of the majority, a distinctly Haitian complex of philosophical tenets, religious beliefs, and ritual practices. But while the masses publicly cherished these practices and beliefs, which they never considered antithetic to Catholicism, the urbanites always professed an exclusive adherence to orthodox Christianity, even though, to different degrees, they shared religious beliefs rooted in the same African-dominated cosmology and took part in similar rituals. Elite distortion of Catholic (and today Protestant) theology and liturgy ended only when and where the influence of Vodoun on their "Christian" practice was publicly identifiable. Short of that, substantial tenets of the same philosophy and a number of the same basic beliefs are held by most Haitians.

Language offers another example. Most linguists have stopped calling Haiti bilingual. They speak instead of a diglossic situation, in which a bilingual minority imposes one language as the language of power. This analysis is a positive intellectual development but may still fall short of the truth. Two languages do indeed coexist in Haiti: French and Haitian. The Haitian (Creole) language probably arose during slavery and solidified during the first half-century of independence. All Haitians speak Haitian as their native language: only a few of the most educated urbanites are native bilingual. The majority of French speakers (less than 8 percent of the total population) reach varying degrees of competence through the school system. Thus the linguistic dichotomy does not appear at the level of communication, or even in an unqualified preference for French: any Haitian is capable of communicating anything to any other Haitian in Haitian, and the most francophile urbanites often prefer to use Haitian in situations where everyone is competent in French.[4] Rather, the dichotomy resides in the power attached to certain forms of communication, most of which include the use of French; in the fact that mere knowledge of French gives differential access to power; in the prestige attached to that language; and in the fact that this prestige is nationwide—even the peasantry believes in it to some extent. The political consequence is that the exclusive use of French in the nation's official discourse appears "natural." In point of fact, the elites have never bothered to make that exclusivity official: French became Haiti's official language during the U.S. occupation through a constitution that Franklin D. Roosevelt later claimed to have written personally. By then, French exclusivity in the spheres of power was threatened by English rather than by the Haitian language, and legitimization was seen by many as reinforcing not just French, but the entire French/Creole complex, set in contradistinction to English.

In its own way, the example of language hints at the complexity of Haitian cultural traditions and struggles, and at the cultural ambivalence of the Haitian elites. Because these elites inherited some of the ambiguities of the French colonists' sense of identity, and because the peasantry consistently preserved its claim to the cultural arena, the dominant classes never succeeded in imposing Western cultural domination on the people (Trouillot 1990:35–40). It is even more startling that they may never have entirely wished to do so. Haitian writers have rarely presented the West as a sociocultural ideal in toto, even though they clearly saw France, Germany, Holland, and the United States—more or less in that order—as imitable superiors in specific domains. But even those specific achievements did not imply the innate superiority of the "whites," inasmuch as many Haitian literati genuinely believed in the perfectibility of all human groups—the ultimate primacy of culture over nature. Within that framework, the recognition of Western achievements did not carry with it the need to reject all indigenous practices. Thus while the Haitian elites placed French literature on a pedestal, they reserved for themselves the right to speak the native language, to sing Creole songs, to write of the beauty of the peasant woman in verses patterned after what they perceived as the latest Parisian literary style. While they held foreign—especially French—diplomas in high esteem, they continually decried the lack of natural and human warmth in the Western countries they visited. While they proudly adopted European manners, they also engaged proudly in many indigenous practices that they judged worthy of their time and attention. This in turn meant that the peasantry—and many customs or features than the elites' imagination associated with that peasantry, including "blackness"—were often ennobled in words, even if kept at safe distance in practice. It also meant that the Western-dominated hierarchy of races, colors, religions, and cultures was never swallowed whole, never accepted without modification.

Understandably, then, *mulâtrisme* as an ideology of mulâtre power, has always been on the defensive in Haiti, in part because it could always be accused of being a version of Western racism. Its most die-hard proponents—who often looked, sounded, or acted more "Western" than other Haitians—rarely dared to claim exclusive social and political rights for any group of Haitians identified on the basis of "color," however defined. Light-skinned politicians and intellectuals consistently denied any trace of color prejudice. Even an immigrant like Joseph Saint-Rémy could write: "I belong to no caste, to no sect" (Nicholls 1979:94). In public, at least, they professed varying degrees of paternalistic "respect" for the black peasantry and many of its cultural traditions—Vodoun being for a long time the major exception. Early mulâtre claims to political control were therefore not based on assertions of inherited superiority but on the allegedly greater contribution made by their light-skinned ancestors in the forging of the Haitian nation.

The impossibility of publicly advocating color prejudice in Haiti in face-to-face debates was furthered by the history of Haiti itself—or by the elites' perception of that history. More for them perhaps than for the common folk, the Haitian revolution was and remains the final symbol of the regeneration of the entire "black race" from the abyss imposed by slavery (Nicholls 1979; Trouillot, N.d.). The revolutionary war was a war against the "whites," and independence in 1804 a victory over colonialism, slavery, *and* white supremacy. Further, the relentless ostracism imposed on the black republic during the nineteenth century reinforced, among Haitian urbanites, a sense of racial identity that included all blacks. Thus, after the murder of Jean Jacques Dessalines, Haiti's first chief of state (1804–1806), the country split into two states, with mulatto president Alexandre Pétion running the southern part and dark-skinned president and, later, king Henry Christophe (1807–1820) the northern one. Interestingly, neither Pétion (1807–1818) nor his successor, president Jean-Pierre Boyer, abrogated Dessalines's law that gave automatic citizenship to any black person landing on Haitian soil. Similarly, both Pétion and Boyer tried to help antislavery forces throughout the Americas as much as they could. Disagreements about the state notwithstanding, from the war of independence to the present the nation has always conceived of itself as a "black" community. This racial sense imposed severe limits on the expression of mulâtre ideology.

Demographics reinforced these limits, especially after 1843, when it became clear that power would have to be shared with a minority of dark-skinned individuals. The use of color rhetoric by black politicians since Toussaint Louverture had taught light-skinned leaders that it was politically dangerous to be either prowhite or antiblack in Haiti. If some light-skinned individuals did claim a privileged right to govern, they made it clear that this right proceeded in part from the blackness they shared with the rest of the population. Whether or not they were sincere is hard to tell, and probably beside the point. The important fact is that a combination of historical, cultural, and demographic factors made it impossible for them to claim political legitimacy if they excluded all positive references to blackness.

Given that there has never been a public discourse denigrating blackness in independent Haiti, some authors have concluded that color prejudice as such does not exist and that the "color question" is nothing more than "metaphysical sophistry" (e.g., Lamartinière 1976). I have already suggested that, contrary to such assertions, color is indeed salient in Haiti, if only because of the Western influence on sociocultural ratings, including aesthetic evaluations. The next three sections will show how color materializes in the play of familial and class alliances among the urban population.

Reproduction of Color and Class

Consider the demographic data for Saint-Domingue at the start of the slave uprising in 1791. How does it happen that there are so many people in Haiti who are still light enough to be considered clairs or mulâtres? The answer to this question unequivocally proves that color is salient when there are social choices.[5] For however much one plays with the figures, they do not agree with the statistical probabilities of demography or physical anthropology. The conclusion is obvious: it is just as impossible to explain the survival of light-skinned people in Haiti by genetic coincidence as it is to explain the survival of a black minority in the United States without reference to the (social) segregation of biological reproduction.

In 1789, the French colony of Saint-Domingue had around 500,000 blacks, 27,500 free *gens de couleur,* and about 31,000 whites. Although in absolute terms the war of independence killed a greater number of blacks, it affected the other two groups to a proportionately greater degree because they were so much smaller (Auguste and Auguste 1985). The slaves' victory reduced the white presence to a negligible number and also sharply reduced the number of individuals of mixed descent, many of whom left the country for other islands or for the United States (particularly Louisiana, Maryland, and Pennsylvania). Thus Haiti became independent with a tiny white population (probably less than 1 percent) and a small mulatto minority (5 percent at most). Under these conditions, the laws of biological reproduction cannot explain the survival of this minority, which should have collapsed under the weight of a darker majority.

And that weight was substantial. Indeed, the epidermic line separating clairs and noirs itself shifted because of the preponderance of the darker tones: darker and darker people began to be included within the group of clairs almost by default, so that a large number of individuals who are considered mulâtres today would have flunked the exam, on somatic grounds, at the end of the last century. But the clair/noir divide does not disappear under the weight of genetics; instead the main somatic boundary continues to shift. It is the elasticity and resilience of this boundary—the fact that it always allows for the isolation of a category of people called clairs—that bears witness to the social reality of color. It is the very survival of such categories and subcategories, all with increasingly fluid somatic referents, that shows the preeminence of social over biological reproduction.

One cannot make reference to the continued immigration of whites and mulâtres to explain the survival of persons considered "clairs." White and mulâtre immigration certainly played a role, but it was more social than biological. Candler, during his visit of 1838–1840, noted that "a large number among the class of *mulâtre* citizens residing in the capital were immigrants from the United States" (1842:165). Later, white and light-skinned newcomers had different points of origin: Cuba, the Dominican Republic, France, the British West Indies, Austria, Corsica, Sicily, Syria, Lebanon, Germany, and especially Martinique and Guadeloupe. Many adapted quickly and formed prominent "Haitian" families (Aubin 1910). But the inflow was too slow for this immigration alone to maintain the biological reproduction of a clair group. In addition, the migratory flow was not in one direction. The long regimes of Soulouque (1847–1859) and of Salomon (1879–1888), for instance, which were dominated by noirs, forced numerous mulâtres to leave the country.

The clairs of Haiti reproduced themselves essentially "from the inside" (that is, with no significant alliances with white outsiders), with the most mulâtre families (those that best combined light skin, valued facial and hair characteristics, *and* economic and social success) leading the way. In addition, the mulâtre sector of the Haitian elites has practiced an endogamous policy, marrying its sons to its daughters whenever possible. This choice can only be explained in terms of color prejudice, because class relations do not lend themselves to the same divisions. This is, moreover, the dilemma that (traditional) Marxist analysis of the noirisme/mulâtrisme duo refuses to confront. Either the color question is an immediate reflection of class relations—and then it would have no autonomy, for *the entire dominant class would be clair and all the clairs would be of the dominant class* (which is obviously false, and very close to the Denis-Duvalier 1938 thesis)—or color prejudice is relatively autonomous with regard to economic structures, and this autonomy must be taken into account.

Color divisions do not simply replicate socioeconomic classes, or even income groups. In fact, the "color line" (the key boundary between noirs and clairs) and the boundary between poor and rich have both been moving since independence, each in its own direction. As mentioned before, somatic boundaries have moved to include darker and darker epidermic shades among the clairs. At the same time, fewer and fewer clairs are found among the underprivileged classes. Jean-Jacques Acau, the nineteenth-century leader of a private rural army that once controlled parts of the South and repeatedly challenged Port-au-Prince's central power, is credited with the famous saying "Nèg rich se milat; milat pov se nèg" (The rich black is a mulatto; the poor mulatto is a black).[6] But we must face the facts. Today there are many black-skinned individuals among the rich—or at least many more than before—but few light-skinned individuals among the very poor. We are far from the time when Candler (1842:55) met, among the peasantry, a poor mulatto woman whose prejudice seemed to him more virulent than that of her urban counterparts.[7] Let me suggest that the movement of those two lines, color and income, is connected—and that it is through this dual movement that the reproduction of a social stratum perceived as clair fits within the reproduction of the dominant urban strata.

Jean Price-Mars, the dean of Haitian ethnology, provides the example that I shall use as a point of departure. Around 1870 in Cap-Haïtien, on the same street where Anténor Firmin, a young black-skinned intellectual, lived with his aunt, there also lived "a pretty young girl, a *mulâtresse brune,* Mlle. Marie Louise Salnave, also known as Rosa. [She was the daughter of Sylvain Salnave, the president who was executed in January 1870.] She lived with her mother, brothers, and sisters. . . . The two young people, Anténor and Rosa, fell in love and promised to marry. But on both sides of the two families, the parents, it seems, opposed the marriage" (Price-Mars [1979?]: 119). The reasons were unclear, but wags hinted that the heart of the matter was that the Salnave family, which was light skinned, believed that the union was a mismatch. At any rate, in 1876 Rosa Salnave married a clair. In 1878 Rosa's husband died. Three years later, she took Anténor Firmin as her second husband.

Price-Mars refers to numerous alliances between noir and mulâtre families of Cap-Haïtien and to the imposing number of prominent noirs of the North in order to suggest that color prejudice was not at work in the region and therefore cannot explain Anténor's first rejection ([1979?]: 119–127). I accept Price-Mars's description of these alliances, but I would like to suggest that they prove the opposite thesis. What these alliances suggest, and what Anténor's and Rosa's marriage indicates, is that even in Cap-Haïtien, not just any noir could marry a mulâtre.

Price-Mars's analysis falls short in the secondary role that it attributes to what I call "social direction," that is, the path that an individual is perceived to be taking up or down the social ladder. Assuming that social positions are never fully guaranteed in complex societies, that they must be gained or maintained and can always be lost, I would suggest that individuals are always in motion on that ladder, however minimally. Society judges this continuous movement positively or negatively, and "social direction" is the result of that judgment. It is a measure of the social distance between what is thought to be known of an individual's origin and what is thought to be known of his or her future. It is a value-laden perception of a projected distance. Individual time matters a great deal in that light.

In the case of Salnave and Firmin, we can see how individual time mattered. To be sure, between 1870 and 1881 the actors' phenotypes had not changed: the individuals were the same, only older. But it is surprising that an ethnologist makes so little of the fact that this was a second marriage for Salnave. Her social direction was no longer on the ascent. On the other side of the somatic boundary—that is, on the Firmin side—there had been a rise in social standing and, more importantly, the promise of a future that might even end in the presidency. Price-Mars admits that between the young intellectual of 1870 and the man who married the claire daughter of a former president lay the difference of time and social promotion. In other words, by 1881 Firmin was one of the very few noirs who could enter what Price-Mars calls the clique "of patricians, who, because of their position of wealth, or what so appeared, occupied the summit of the social hierarchy" ([1972?]:126).

Price-Mars's references to cross-color marriages among the northern elites take on their full meaning once couched in these terms. It was not that the North did not know color prejudice but that the aristocracy that had sprung from Henry Christophe's secessionist kingdom had produced an extraordinary number of noirs who could marry mulâtres if their hearts so desired (Trouillot 1990:47–48). I am prepared to concede that if this aristocracy had reproduced itself across the entire country, and if the promotion of urban blacks like Firmin had been more widespread, color prejudice would perhaps have disappeared. Socioeconomic status would have achieved the upper hand in what Lévi-Straussian anthropology pompously calls "wife exchange." But Christophe's kingdom did not extend across the entire country, and the alliance it produced between the noir and mulâtre landed aristocracies did not operate on the national level, where the prejudice itself was regenerated. Moreover, the original northern alliance across the epidermic line was based on the accumulation of land. Yet mulâtre leaders squeezed by the peasantry, abandoned land accumulation in favor of an exploitative system centered around the customhouses. The feudal dream in which a noir aristocracy would have equal footing with its mulâtre counterparts crumbled with this choice.

In other words, even though color has never functioned alone, it has had an independent social value, even in the North. It is a commodity in the game of inter- and intraclass alliances. It has an exchange value that can be and is calculated, even if that value is much lower in the North than in the West (e.g., Jacmel) or the South (e.g., Jérémie). Color is always part of what Price-Mars delicately refers to as the "particularities of the social condition" in Haiti ([1979?]:126). And as a particularity of an individual's social condition, color plays a role in the reproduction of the social groups to which the individual belongs.

The historian Jean Fouchard (1983) reminds us that a number of families in the Haitian elites have a noir branch and a mulâtre branch, while other families move from the noir to the mulâtre pole of intellectual and political factions, and vice versa. This is true, even though it is difficult to find noir branches among the families who have traditionally been at the very top of the economic ladder. But what no one has ever emphasized is the socioeconomic exchange governing these passages or alternations. Here, I would submit—as a working hypothesis that must be further developed—that the passage from the noir side to the mulâtre side is often coupled with socioeconomic promotion. Conversely, the passage from the clair side to the noir side is often an indication of demotion. Demotions and promotions crosscut one another, because the respective social directions of bride and groom usually cancel each other out, with the darker partner being, most often, the one on the rise. Thus the couple as such neither rises nor falls—it becomes. The results of the exchange are confirmed only one or two generations later.

I will take a classic case. A young woman who can be placed in the clair category works as a salesgirl in a store or as a secretary in public administration. Her limited education betrays her lower-middle-class origins, but she spends much more money on clothes than her darker colleagues. What she guarantees by her dress, her discretion, and the places she frequents is in the end a social investment—her color. She will probably not marry into the top layer of the mulâtre elite, because the mulâtre aristocracy is endogamous. But she will try to marry "up," to marry a businessman, a professional, a well-placed public servant, preferably also a clair. Chances, are, however, that the desired clairs will tend to think twice about a legal union with her, since they are playing the same game. Hence it is most likely that the young lady will marry within the noir group. But not any noir will do. First, the groom will probably have one of the few phenotypes somatically valued in spite of dark complexion (e.g., *bon noir, noir fin, mârabout*). More important, his social direction will be unambiguously upward.

In short, the light-skinned bride contributes epidermic capital while her darker husband brings a diploma, savings, or the promise of a successful future, together with a reasonably acceptable somatic package. Social direction being a projection into the future, the promise may never materialize. Further, even if the projection is correct, the results will not be immediately apparent. Once more, the couple as such does not rise, or barely. It will not be admitted into the crême de la crême; people will "forget" to invite them to certain birthday or tennis parties. But their children, already lighter than their father, will freely associate with those who match their status, family income, and perceived phenotype. Increasingly, they will gravitate toward individuals a shade lighter than themselves. The children are the ones who will enter smaller and smaller circles inaccessible to both parents: they are the ones who have a chance of becoming mulâtres of a kind. And their own children—if they marry a clair—will become part of an endogamous circle, pushing the somatic boundaries a little further in the direction of darker shades, but in doing so continuing to guarantee the domination of color.

Race and color are always gendered. However, for the purposes of this exercise, we may reverse the genders and place a male on the clair side of the exchange. We need make only small modifications to our scenario—he would need a higher level of formal education than his female counterpart, a professional diploma, a successful military career, or the label of "intellectual."[8] Numerous *p'tits mulâtres de province* have bartered their skin color for security. Not for their own security, perhaps (because they do not enter ipso facto into the most exclusive circles), but for the security of their children—or, to be more exact, for the security of their names.

For color prejudice weighed on the progeny very early. Jonathan Brown ([1837]1971:284) reports the case of a mulâtresse who rejected one of the best catches of Boyer's republic on the basis of his color. The young lady insisted, with arrogant frankness, that she herself cared little about the pigmentation of her suitor. "But to have children blacker than herself, *petits enfants griffes,* how horrible!" And as the main somatic divide moved to include darker skins among the clairs, this emphasis on the progeny increased.

And here is where the exchange is deceptive: it does not operate immediately but over the span of generations. In the to-and-fro of the exchange, many are the clair families that have a noir skeleton in the closet. And while these families have made it their duty to exhibit this skeleton if necessary to prove their blackness, in the meantime the reproduction of prejudice continues along on its merry way. Mothers know this—they who so strictly control those whom their sons and (especially) their daughters associate with. It is a matter of reducing the field in such a way that the exchange can involve only the trade-off between social promotion and phenotype, the other possibilities having been eliminated by restricted association. Numerous common expressions jovially but discreetly exchanged among close friends and relatives register the trade-off. The darker partner is said to be "putting some milk into his or her coffee," or simply "improving the race." The lighter one is said to be aware of his or her own game (in Haitian, "Se li ki konnen zafè li"). Yet the returns are not necessarily collected during the time span of the marriage, but later on, even generations later. Thus the display of wealth and influence, or the schema of economic structures, never reflect color cleavages in the short run. At any given moment the exchange guarantees a discrepancy between the economic and political domains and socioepidermic classifications. But the very fact that the exchange continues, and that most urbanites participate in it—within their own restricted pool—maintains the pernicious impression of "an aristocracy of the skin" that all the involved parties believe in. The phrase attributed to Acau can now be modified: a rich black *becomes* a mulatto, a poor mulatto *becomes* black.

Color and Politics

The ambiguity inherent in the practices described here have made color prejudice a choice subject for dark politicians. While they could not easily point in Haiti to such institutionalized discriminatory practices as those of the United States or South Africa, they had no need to prove the existence of an epidermal elite because everyone believed it existed. Predominantly mulâtre clubs, schools, neighborhoods, and political cliques existed, even though legally everyone had access to them and even though a small number of noirs were found there. Over time, this perception of an epidermal elite whose income, education, and social status remained inaccessible to the majority and who treated that majority with arrogant indifference created extraordinary resentment among urban noirs, particularly those of the middle classes. This resentment, which reached its height in 1946, reinforced the twentieth-century version of *noirisme.*

Ironically, the *noiriste* theory of power finds its direct origins in the political ideology espoused by many mulattoes from the 1780s to the 1830s. It boils down to an epidermic quota: the representatives of the largest color group should have "natural" access to power. This is an argument whose origins can be traced to certain preindependence mulattoes, such as Vincent Ogé, but slavery and colonial rule limited its impact. After independence, Beaubrun Ardouin, writer, politician, and mulâtre ideologue, took up with renewed enthusiasm Ogé's argument that the mulattoes and their descendants had a natural right to rule Haiti by virtue of their origins—because the blacks came from Africa and the whites from Europe.

The noiriste theory of power is one more version of this argument of "natural" legitimacy. The crucial difference is that in the mouths of politicians perceived as darker than their opponents, in a context where color matters—even if in the rather labyrinthine manner described here—the argument could both refer and appeal to much larger segments of the citizenry. As such, noirisme has always been an extremely potent discourse in Haiti, and it is likely to remain so as long as the perception of an "aristocracy of the skin" remains. An embryonic noirisme was already visible in Louverture's polemical use of the "color question" against Rigaud in the late 1790s. Noiriste arguments appeared in 1843 in the fight against Boyer, then less subtly in the 1860s with the Parti National, whose slogan was, significantly, "The greatest good for the greatest number." There was no doubt in this context to whom the "greatest number" referred.

Whereas noirisme tends to make explicit references to skin color, mulâtrisme avoids them at all cost. After independence, light-skinned politicians systematically denied the existence of color prejudice. Once they had established the mulâtre-controlled form of "government by understudy," they removed most references to color from their political discourse. To be sure, they first tried, in vain, to associate Saint-Domingue mulattoes with the leadership of the Haitian revolution; but once that strategy failed, mulâtrisme capitalized on the illusion of competence. The theory was encapsulated by the middle of the nineteenth century in the slogan of Edmond Paul, a dark-skinned theoretician of the Parti Libéral: "Le pouvoir aux plus capables" (Power to the most competent). One can trace the roots of that slogan in the writings of many mulâtres in the immediate aftermath of independence.

The reference to competence gave a distinct advantage to the clairs especially in the nineteenth century. Just as everyone knew to whom the "greatest number" referred, so they knew who claimed to be "most capable." As a group, the clairs had clear economic and educational advantages since before independence: they could indeed define what it meant to be "capable." But the reference to competence allowed them to claim power for themselves while deflecting accusations of discrimination. Competence was a commodity supposedly available to everyone, an objective toward which the noirs themselves aimed. In contradistinction, phenotypical resemblance to the majority was not an ideal, even for noir leaders. Indeed, a majority of the noiriste ideologues had light-skinned wives, light-skinned progeny, or at the very least progeny lighter than themselves. So did the vast majority of political leaders and chiefs of state who have consistently or temporarily utilized noiriste rhetoric. Salomon married a Frenchwoman, Estimé and François Duvalier married women less dark than themselves; Jean-Claude Duvalier had a child with a mulâtresse before he married Michèle Bennett, a *clair* though not, as often claimed in the international press, a wealthy mulâtresse.

The competition between noir and mulâtre factions for control of the state apparatus never took on the appearance of an all-out color war. The "most capable," like the "greatest number" or other expressions of this type, functioned as a polite code behind which everyone recognized the "color question," without it being explicitly formulated and detailed. In fact, noiriste political factions never got rid of their own mulattoes. The most recent example of this is François Duvalier, but President Salomon also put the presence of "his" mulâtres in the state apparatus to good use. Mulâtre political factions in turn almost always included black intellectuals and military men. Edmond Paul and Anténor Firmin, the most coherent theoreticians of the Parti Libéral (the mulâtre party par excellence) had black skins. Nord Alexis, a powerful general who sold his support to the highest-bidding mulâtristes, was also black. Even in 1946, when the electoral battle clearly took on the aspect of a color struggle, the rivals of the noiriste candidate, Dumarsais Estimé, were all black skinned (Bonhomme 1957).

Contrary, therefore, to the interplay of family alliances, the appeal to color in the field of politics did not need a concrete somatic referent. Anténor Firmin asserted that, in the electoral campaign of 1879, mulâtres of Cap-Haïtien campaigned against him, a dark-skinned liberal allied to a mulâtre party, by arguing that he was "a *mulâtre* as light-skinned as a white" (cited in Price-Mars [1979?]: 117). Price-Mars doubted the veracity of this report, which reflects negatively on his native province, but one cannot doubt that similar tactics were used in the North, both in the nineteenth century and at other times, as well as in other places.[9] Light-skinned Sylvain Salnave sent his nephew into areas of the northern countryside, where he himself was not known, to campaign against the "yellow people." Early supporters of François Duvalier report that in 1957, Duvalier's opponent, Louis Déjoie, was described as being "very light-skinned," "almost white," in several areas of the Artibonite Valley, about a hundred miles north of Port-au-Prince, where the masses of voters had never seen him. The game went on intermittently, the mulâtres making reference to their competence, which was more apparent than real, the noirs to their "natural" representativeness, which was just as much a matter of appearance.

But appearances mattered, if only because of the conflicting associations they engendered. The mulâtres' praise of the virtues of "competence" and "civilization," as well as their palpable somatic preference, linked them vaguely with a more sympathetic view of the West. Yet that linkage was denied by the mulâtres themselves whenever it seemed to displace the association between Haiti and blackness, or the fundamental values that permeated the cultural terrain. That, more than the personal shame of being taken for blatant racists, was what had kept the mulâtres on the defensive after independence. The U.S. occupation (1915–1934) and the presidency of Elie Lescot (1941–1946) removed this defensive attitude, sharpening the conflict and putting it in terms that convinced a majority of urbanites that Haiti's political and cultural future was at stake.

The Color of the Occupation

The U.S. desire to create an American-style middle class in urban Haiti during the occupation remained unfulfilled. But the harassment of small landowners, the building of new roads, and the administrative and political centralization carried out by the U.S. Marines swelled the ranks of the peasants, artisans, students, and professionals who found their way to the coastal cities, and especially to Port-au-Prince. Between 1915 and 1945, an ever increasing number of newcomers rushed into the already limited space within which the ultimate battle for power was traditionally fought.

The noirs who surged into this urban arena did not always believe themselves destined to occupy its lowest rungs. Dark-skinned residents of Port-au-Prince were becoming increasingly qualified for public service although their qualifications did not—as they had not for numerous mulâtres before them—go beyond the secondary school *baccalauréat.* Since 1804, if not before, a minority of black business people, intellectuals, professionals, and politicians had carved for themselves a niche in the structure of urban life. In the latter part of the century they were joined by the inheritors of the more open system of public education developed under Salomon (1879–1888). In the 1880s, Salomon, whose grandfather had been one of the few black magistrates of the Louverture regime, explicitly tried to give to a significant number of blacks what public education under Pétion had given to many light-skinned families—the hereditary privilege of academic competence. Competence doubtless varied from Grandpapa's primary school education to the prodigy grandson's European diploma, but its genealogical transmission occurred among a large segment of the population. Together, the descendants of the pre-1804 black professionals, the relatively recent elites created by Salomon, and the newcomers fleeing the decline of the provincial pyramids formed a new intellectual majority in the capital. The time was gone when economist Edmond Paul, himself a member of a dark elite family, could exclaim in all sincerity, "Le pouvoir aux plus capables," with the conviction that the "most capable" were also the lightest. Sometime before the end of the occupation, the reference to competence ceased to be to the exclusive advantage of the mulâtre minority.

But now that the "greatest number" also had their own "most capable," the mulâtres, who had been the previous winners in the war of rhetoric, suddenly changed the rules of the game. They abruptly revealed themselves to be less than conciliatory. They denied most of the newcomers the intellectual and political recognition they had been hoping for, the "elite" membership traditionally allowed to successful noirs. Naked color prejudice now supplanted the rule of the most capable, behind which it had been conveniently hidden.

Infractions of the law of the most capable preceded the occupation. The very existence of color prejudice and its mode of operation implied that, given equal levels of competence, the perception of "color," if not the exact degree of pigmentation, worked to the disadvantage of the noir. But U.S. racism added its institutional systematism to Haitian colorist favoritism. The U.S. Marines witnessed the successive installation of five clair presidents, three of whom were undeniably mulâtres. The U.S. "advisers," who in fact ran many government services, openly showed their preference for light-skinned officials, without considering the elaborate etiquette that the Haitian "aristocrats of the skin" had patiently refined for a century. The visibility of the mulâtres grew—as did their arrogance. These political precedents portended a battle of new dimensions, particularly since the occupation had affected the ideological landscape at least as profoundly as it had changed the rules of political competition.

I have already mentioned that in spite of color prejudice, Haitian national identity implied a positive identification with the black race. Martinquan writer Aimé Césaire put it quite simply: it was in Haiti that *négritude* first appeared. However, this nationalist posture was always circumscribed by the intellectual and emotional attachment of the elites to the West, and to France in particular. These elites preferred Latin cultures and ways to Anglo-Saxon technocentrism and lack of polish: it was French literature that supplied them with their thematic and formal models. But they also valued what they saw as the achievements of northern Europe and the United States. In their view, there were no superior races, but there were superior cultures (Lewis 1983:317). And since those cultures were European (or European derivatives), whiteness evoked a certain savoir-faire as well as a certain *savoir-vivre.*

The U.S. occupation, in different degrees and for different reasons called each of these propositions into question. Savoir-vivre was the first to go. North Americans were not *sans-manières* (without manners) in the sense that the elites would say this of the peasants, implying perfectibility. Instead they had crude manners, being by choice *de grossiers personnages.* Savoir-faire was more tenacious, but the occupation did not bring the spectacular changes in technology and material life for which many in the elites had been secretly hoping.

As the occupation forced a redefinition of whiteness, it also questioned its nemesis, blackness. The strong identification with blackness and the nationalist posture that cemented the ideological world of the elites could only be seen in the light of the slave revolution and independence. The nation stood for blackness because its black forefathers had fought for freedom *and* won over the best European army of the time. Indeed, this victory had been the sole empirical reference point of Haitian nationalist discourse. By the 1920s, however, the daily presence of the U.S. Marines had brought into question contemporary Haitians' claims that they shared their ancestors' courage and nobility (Danache 1950).

The pre-1915 Haitian elites had never held to any ideological proposition with fanatical conviction—except perhaps the association of the 1804 revolution with the regeneration of the black race. Ambiguity was their forte. But by undermining many tenets of the elites' vision of themselves and others, the occupation revealed inconsistencies inherent in that vision that they had conveniently ignored. More important, in questioning political independence—the proof of 1804—the occupation undermined the basis of the delicate edifice that these contradictory propositions constituted. The times called for a redefinition, or at least for a reshaping, of the old categories within a more coherent whole (Mintz 1984:263–288). It is this reformulation that various intellectuals, loosely referred to by later writers as the *mouvement indigéniste,* tried to supply.

In the late 1920s, the publication of *La Revue Indigène,* quickly followed by that of Jean Price-Mars's book *Ainsi parla l'oncle* in 1928 (1983), launched the Haitian indigéniste movement (Trouillot 1993). A series of attempts by noir and clair intellectuals to mount a wide-ranging reevaluation of the national culture followed. These writers criticized the elites' tendency to imitate the West and to ignore peasant culture. They emphasized the need to study the peasantry, to make an inventory of its practices, and to take into account the African roots of Haitian culture. The indigénistes' critique suggested that the elites' political failure stemmed in part from their contempt of Haitian popular culture, an argument at times quite explicit in Price-Mars's other writings (Antoine 1981; Trouillot 1986). But *indigénisme* as such had no political program and regrouped intellectuals of different political persuasions, including a few socialists (Trouillot 1993).[10]

This cultural nationalism can be distinguished therefore from noirisme, a strictly political ideology rooted in claims of "natural" legitimacy and calling for a color quota within the state apparatus. Indigénisme overlaps with négritude, but the scope of négritude is much wider. Whereas the range of noirisme is limited to relations of state power (and thus essentially to the urban arena), and indigénisme aims for the national arena, négritude theoretically aims for the world space in which the unequal evaluation of peoples, religions, and cultures originates.

These distinctions are important inasmuch as they continuously influenced political alignments among the elites. Since the nineteenth century, numerous clairs and other supporters of mulâtre political factions forcefully argued for the equality of all human races in the international arena while maintaining the colorist status quo in their own country (Firmin 1885; Nicholls 1979; Price 1900). By the same token, Jean Price-Mars, the founder of indigénisme, never endorsed noiriste politics; more, he publically disassociated himself from noirisme during François Duvalier's regime, no small sign of intellectual integrity and personal courage (Antoine 1981; Trouillot 1993).

Mass political symbolism, however, proceeds by association rather than by an intellectual exercise in classification. Haitian mulâtrisme had always been susceptible to the charge of duplicating white racism, even though, as we have seen, it was no mere derivative of Western values. It had survived the association with the West, in part because of another association equally potent among the elites: that of whiteness and savoir-faire. I have suggested that the practices of the U.S. occupiers raised questions about the Haitians' views of whiteness. The indigéniste movement provided new answers: no culture was superior, either in savoir-faire or savoir-vivre. Thus the most Westernized Haitians were not necessarily the best Haitians, nor the most useful to the country. These answers were not immediately "political." But in challenging the superiority of "white cultures" in the midst of the occupation, the indigéniste movement dealt a major blow to the rationale behind the claims to "competence."

The indigéniste reevaluation of the cultural roots and tendencies of the nation opened the political field for the proponents of "legitimacy," the self-proclaimed advocates of the "greatest number." They could now insist on the associations implicit in the nineteenth-century worldview conveniently ignored by previous generations. And those associations themselves had become more powerful once négritude and indigénisme gave noirisme a new critical mass. If most of the indigéniste writers were not noiristes, most noiristes were indigénistes with an eye on the worldwide négritude movement. Thus, although noirisme itself was not in fact as popular in the political field as it now appears in retrospect, it had all the right cultural associations. By 1938, some noiriste intellectuals associated with the Griots group (which included a number of self-trained ethnologists and historians, among whom was Francois Duvalier) started to think of political strategies based upon these associations (Denis and

Duvalier 1938). By 1945, President Lescot's growing unpopularity made it possible for most noiriste factions to call on such associations.

Lescot (1941–1946) not only pursued the U.S. practice of systematically placing light-skinned individuals in the top echelons of the public service, but he also extended color favoritism to all levels of the administration without the slightest bow to the rule of perceived competence. In so doing, he repeatedly violated tradition. By 1945, for the first time in Haitian history, the distribution of power had become explicitly colorist. By then also—and again for the first time in Haitian history—a mulâtre regime was being accused of incompetence and judged guilty by a majority of urbanites. To add insult to injury, Lescot took many stands against the national culture, notably by facilitating an "antisuperstition campaign" that the Catholic church organized against Vodoun in the years 1941–1942.

By 1945 these flagrant violations of political tradition and cultural tolerance, carried out in the midst of the intellectual reaction to the effects of the occupation, allowed a group of politicians to intermix noirisme, indigénisme, and négritude in the perception of most urbanites. Antimulâtre resentment was at its height among the noir intellectuals and politicians, among students, and among the urban masses. At the same time, a majority of the population in the cities and towns was supportive of any atttempt to restore national and cultural dignity, especially since the Marines had displayed to the Haitians, in their own country, the crassest dimensions of international racism. The most vocal among the noiriste intellectuals and politicians found themselves at the intersection of the three movements. Being from the masses, they said, they were its most "authentic" representatives, alone capable of ushering in the "new order" (Bonhomme 1946, 1957). Hadn't Lescot's government shown that a class of men born with silver spoons in their mouths would do anything to maintain its privileges? For the *authentiques,* the most vocal of the 1946 noiristes, cultural reevaluation and the regaining of national dignity, like the end of arbitrariness, required a change of "class" within the state apparatus.

Naïveté or Machiavellianism? Probably a little of both. The various associations put forward by the authentiques had been made implicitly by many urbanites since the nineteenth century, and it is possible that some of the 1946 leaders saw them as irrevocably intertwined. The fact remains that people who might not have supported the authentiques in other circumstances took their side in the battle against Lescot. The fusion of noirisme, indigénisme, and négritude—facilitated by the general indignation over Lescot's practices and the reevaluation of the nation in the light of the occupation—created an ideological tidal wave unprecedented in Haitian history, which imposed the presidency of Dumarsais Estimé.

Today it is easy to see that the noiriste retaliation against mulâtre power also hid a trap. But in rereading contemporary accounts (e.g., Collectif Paroles 1976; Dorsinville 1972; Pierre 1987), we realize that in 1946, as would also be true in 1957, noirisme was perceived as the only viable political alternative by the vast majority of the middle classes. The very terms of urban political debate would not allow the question of color to be set aside. As a privileged witness, Roger Dorsinville, confirms:

> I told you: I was a "*noiriste.*" And I will add that whoever in my social class in Haiti, after Lescot, under Lescot, whoever was not a *noiriste* would have been scum. . . . They forced upon us a culture of contempt. To this culture of contempt, we opposed our resistance and our hate. (1985:21)

> All the ministers, all the important administrative posts, all the embassies were in the hands of *mulâtres,* the administrative offices of subcontracting companies were full of light-skinned girls. (1972:130–131)

> They ran the country as they would have run a plantation. And me, living there, the fruit of a certain culture, of a certain education, being conscious of my identity, I would not have been *noiriste? Merde!* (1985:21)

It must be understood how much this merde was shared among the middle classes, how it had profound repercussions for the thousands of intellectuals, artisans, small shopowners, well-to-do peasants, commodity *spéculateurs,* and vast segments of the lumpen masses. Moreover this bitterness still resonates, because Duvalierism could not resolve either the color question or the more or less subtle forms of cultural and social domination. Nevertheless, in 1946 this general resentment against the mulâtre faction of the elites gave Estimé a political mandate of rare dimensions in Haitian history—as it would also give Duvalier, in 1957, the benefit of the doubt.

Estimé did little with his mandate. He enjoyed unlimited support in the first years of his presidency, but his popularity declined precipitously. His attempt to get reelected facilitated the army's takeover. The same three-man junta that had ensured the transition from Lescot to Estimé announced new elections. Colonel Paul Magloire, once more the junta strongman, quickly became a presidential candidate. He won the 1950 elections—the first in which all adult males could vote directly for president—almost without electoral opposition.

The authentiques experienced Magloire's presidency (1950–1956) as a frustrating interim. And, in many respects, this period was indeed a parenthesis, a reprieve in the denouement of the crisis. But for those who had lived through 1946, the frustration could be traced back to Estimé himself. The president had not been the "mulâtre-eater" his enemies had feared and his supporters had hoped. He had, of course, applied "color mathematics," giving an extraordinary number of noirs access to government positions. But he did not have a program that distinguished him from his predecessors, and the authentiques found his reforms limited (Bonhomme 1957:13; Collectif Paroles 1976). Their frustration increased with Magloire, whom they saw as the very negation of the 1946 revolution, a reign of "*noirs* without color" at the service of the mulâtre bourgeoisie (Bonhomme 1957:40). When the bourgeoisie itself seemed ready to abandon Magloire, when the church and commercial interests opposed his attempts to illegally prolong his term, it became necessary for the authentiques to find themselves a crown prince, an heir who would close the parentheses and carry on the uncompleted work of Estimé, who had since died in exile.

Only now have we begun to learn the appalling details of the maneuvering that permitted François Duvalier to surface as the Estimist representative in the 1957 elections.[11] The fact remains that this was Duvalier's most difficult campaign. Once he had won the backing—or silence—of the most prominent Estimists, he inherited a political mantle and an apparatus that had solid support among lower-level army officers and intellectuals. Above all, he inherited a vision of Haitian society that, vague and poorly defined as it was, presupposed continuity in change, the desire to complete an unfinished "revolution." If the reevaluation of the black race was legitimate, if the reevaluation of national culture and the restoration of national dignity was legitimate, then noirisme was legitimate. And if noirisme was legitimate, then Duvalier was legitimate. We now know that those syllogisms were profoundly incorrect; but once more, political symbolism proceeds by association; it feeds on analogies rather than on logic.

Victory was not easy, however. Duvalier's arguments were not remarkable, his personal image was rather dull. But though his campaign took time to get off the ground, by February 1957 he was considered a serious contender by those who had dismissed him a few months earlier. From then on, he campaigned seriously (Célestin 1958a, b, 1959; Duvalier 1966). By April he had mastered all the right analogies and had begun to take full advantage of his opponents' symbolic and tactical mistakes. More important, with the help of noiriste army officers, he virtually forced all the other dark-skinned candidates out of the race—a process of elimination that left him in a head-to-head contest with mulâtre Louis

Déjoie on election day. Finally, the election itself was fraudulent: Duvalier won some districts with more votes than the actual number of residents.

Thus Duvalier ultimately owed his power to the army, which supervised the voting process and exercised a veto over the presidency. In fact, the army dominated the long transition from Magloire to Duvalier, shaped the climate for the presidential campaign, and paved the way for totalitarianism (Trouillot 1990:139–162). Yet in spite of the fraud and the superficial character of the campaign, there is no evidence to indicate that Duvalier would not have won in regular elections. The dream of 1946 carried him, and it was a dream that embodied a century and a half of urban and rural frustration—frustration that the new middle classes that had arisen from the occupation, the self-proclaimed representatives of the masses in the state apparatus, decided to end once and for all.

If race matters, color often matters within race. Social categories premised on physical appearance are not restricted to the major racial divisions imposed on humankind by European technology and conquest. Phenotype can be salient within societies or communities that see themselves as racially homogeneous and take pride in that homogeneity. Even the absence of clearly defined ethnic groups and boundaries does not guarantee the irrelevance of phenotypic features such as hair type and skin color.

The value added to these phenotypes often includes an aesthetics of gender obliquely influenced by a North Atlantic *imaginaire,* complex and contradictory images of beauty, maleness, civilization, and otherness shaped by the experience of western Europe and North America. The social value of phenotypes, even among nonwhites, is thus best understood against the background of a worldwide hierarchy of races, religions, and cultures imposed by the West since the Renaissance.

If this hierarchy is now inescapable, the local categories that it makes possible are given life and enacted upon by specific populations with their own stakes and rules in the interplay of power and phenotype. In Haiti, as in Brazil or Thailand or, for that matter, among U.S. blacks, internal categories bear the imprint of the West but are not localized versions of an abstract North Atlantic vision brought, as it were, one level down. Local history influences both the creation and reproduction of such categories with its contradictory bundle of aesthetic judgments, class and state struggles, gender roles, and demographic trends. To state perhaps the obvious: The way in which race and color matter at the local level is always the product of complex processes.

What is less obvious is that at any point in time we see only the aggregate results of these processes and that the interpretation of such aggregates is often deceptive. In the Haitian case, observers have reached with equal conviction two incompatible conclusions. Based on the distribution of economic and political power among the elites, some have argued that color does not matter in Haiti. Looking at national aggregates, others have condemned color prejudice for the uneven distribution of power across phenotypes. But in the absence of formal practices of discrimination, social scientists have not been able to make the causal links between phenotypes and sociological attributes so easily (perhaps too easily) made in societies such as the United States. At the same time, the Duvalierists effectively used the identity politics based on these aggregates to secure and consolidate power with disastrous consequences for the very majority they claimed to defend.

This essay suggests that we need to focus less on these sociological aggregates and more on the processes of which they are a temporary reflection. Attention to such processes requires a sensitivity to history and ethnography. The complexity of the Haitian case arises from Haitian specifics, but it also hints at the complexities of race and color elsewhere.

Notes

1. In any given society, the somatic norm-image is likely to vary according to class and ethnic origins. In the extreme case of societies with multiple ethnic mixtures, such as Venezuela, Colombia, or Brazil, the category as defined by Hoetink could even turn out to be inoperative. But this is not the case in Haiti.

2. Indeed, foreign observers tend to make major mistakes in specifying the "color" of specific Haitians. One counts among the most important gaffes Leyburn's (1941:316) classification of President Salnave as "dark" and, more recently, Ferguson's (1987:72) branding of Simone Duvalier (François's wife) as a "mulatto"!

3. The Haitian school of ethnology, oriented toward folklore, has not touched on the complex relationship between culture and power. Only recently have a few works of cultural anthropology, published abroad, begun to sketch out paths of inquiry in this area (Amer and Coulanges 1974; Bebel-Gisler and Hurbon 1975; Hurbon 1979).

4. The preferred use of Haitian varies with age, gender, and the context of communication among the elites, but there are social penalties for using French at the "wrong" time, just as there are penalties for the improper use of Haitian by French-competent speakers.

5. I thank Czerny Brasuell and Michel Acacia, who forced me to deal with this question.

6. Maxime Raybaud, who lived in Haiti during Acau's lifetime, gives a

detailed version of the origin of this saying. It seems that during a demonstration Acau demanded that *all* the mulattoes be expropriated. A disapproving murmur came from the crowd, in which there were mulattoes in rags. Acau replied, "Oh! *These* are blacks!" Then, says Raybaud, "a black of about thirty years of age, who worked as a laborer in a rum plant, stepped forth and said to the crowd: 'Acau is right, because the Virgin said, "*Nèque rich qui connait lit et écri, cila mulâtre, mulâtre pauve qui pas connait li ni écri, cila nèque.*" ' [The rich black who knows how to read and write is a mulatto, the poor mulatto who does not know how to read or write is a black.] This black was named Joseph, and from that day on he called himself *Brother Joseph.* With a white kerchief on his head, dressed in a white shirt which gripped a pair of white pants, he walked, candle in hand, among Acau's troops [repeating]: '*The rich black who knows how to read and write is a mulatto, etc.*' " (d'Alaux 1856:112–113). Note the association of "reading" and "writing" to wealth and skin color in this early version of the saying.

7. The disappearance of poor mulattoes might also explain the double semantic twist in the term *mulâtre,* which has come to include darker and darker people but also to increasingly exclude individuals at the bottom of the social ladder. Today in the countryside there is a tendency to call a very light-skinned peasant *ti rouj, ti blan,* or simply *blan* (literally, little red one, little white one, white) rather than *milat.* The same is done in the city for an artisan, a laborer, or a member of the *Lumpenproletariat.*

8. Jacqueline Gautier and Evelyne Trouillot have both suggested to me that the assimilation of the Western-dominated aesthetic is stronger among Haitian men than among Haitian women, at least in the petite bourgeoisie. In other words, my example reversing the genders might not be completely justified. It is possible that the interiorization of the mulâtre aesthetic is more common among men, and that the emphasis on social promotion through the offspring is more systematic among women. Cultural anthropologists have yet to systematically study relations of alliance and kinship in urban Haiti and their influence on class reproduction.

9. Price-Mars knew well that color prejudice could decide a candidate's lot. As a noir, he did not use it, and this speaks well of him (Antoine 1981:190–191), but the maneuver was possible and it usually worked.

10. The most comprehensive treatment of the indigéniste movement to date is a two-volume special issue of *Conjonction,* No. 197 (January-March 1993), the journal of the Institut Français d'Haïti.

11. There were others who seemed much more qualified to be Estimé's heir, either because of their greater ideological allegiance to noiriste dogma, their greater partisan loyalty to Estimé, or their political preparation. According to Col. Pressoir Pierre, a personal friend of Duvalier, his success was due mainly to a palace coup, as it were, that took place within the ranks of the ex-president's supporters after Estimé's death in exile. Some young officers (among them Pierre), profiting from support given by Estimé's widow, tipped the balance in favor of Papa Doc (Pierre 1987). It has also been said that Duvalier made a pact

with several Estimist leaders, promising them that he would pass power on to them after his term was over.

References

Amer, Michel, and J. Coulanges. 1974. Mini-Jazz: sens et significations. *Lakansièl* 2:8–20.

Antoine, Jacques Carmeleau. 1981. *Jean Price-Mars and Haiti.* Washington, D.C.: Three Continents.

Aubin, Eugène. 1910. *En Haïti: Planteurs d'autrefois, nègres d'aujourd'hui.* Paris: Colin.

Auguste, Claude B., and Marcel B. Auguste. 1985. *L'expédition Leclerc, 1801–1803.* Port-au-Prince: Deschamps.

Bebel-Gisler, Dany, and L. Hurbon. 1975. *Cultures et pouvoir dans la Caraïbe.* Paris: L'Harmattan.

Bonhomme, Colbert. 1946. *Les Origines et les leçons d'une révolution profonde et pacifique.* Port-au-Prince: Imprimerie de l'Etat.

———. 1957. *Révolution et contre-révolution en Haïti, de 1946 à 1957.* Port-au-Prince: Imprimerie de l'Etat.

Brown, Jonathan. [1837] 1971. *The History and Present Condition of St. Domingo.* Reprint. London: Cass.

Candler, John. 1842. *Brief Notices of Hayti: With Its Conditions, Resources, and Prospects.* London: Ward.

Célestin, Clément. 1958a. *Compilations pour l'histoire.* Vol 1. Port-au-Prince: Théodore.

———. 1958b. *Compilations pour l'histoire.* Vol. 2. Port-au-Prince: Théodore.

———. 1959. *Compilations pour l'histoire.* Vol. 3. Port-au-Prince: Théodore.

Collectif Paroles. 1976. *1946–1976, Trente ans de pouvoir noir en Haïti.* La Salle, Can.: Collectif Paroles.

d'Alaux, Gustave [Maxime Raybaud]. 1856. *L'Empereur Soulouque et son empire.* Paris: Lévy Frères.

Danache, B[ertomieux]. 1950. *Le Président Dartiguenave et les américains.* Port-au-Prince: Imprimerie de l'Etat.

Denis, Lorimer, and François Duvalier. 1938. *Le Problème des classes à travers l'histoire d'Haïti.* Port-au-Prince: N.p.

Dorsinville, Roger. 1972. 1946 ou le délire opportuniste. *Nouvelle Optique* 6:117–140.

———. 1985. Dans le fauteuil de l'histoire. Propos recueillis par Michel Adam et Edgard Th. Gousse. *Etincelles* 1(10): 18–21.

Du Tertre, Jean-Baptsiste. 1667. *Histoire générale des Antilles habitées par les français.* Paris: Jolly.

Duvalier, François. 1966. *Oeuvres essentielles.* Vol. 2, *La Marche à la présidence.* Port-au-Prince: Presses Nationales d'Haiti.

Ferguson, James. 1987. *Papa Doc, Baby Doc: Haiti and the Duvaliers.* Oxford: Blackwell.

Firmin, Anténor. 1885. *De l'Egalité des races humaines*. Paris: Pichon.
Fouchard, Jean. [1972] 1981. *The Haitian Maroons: Liberty or Death*. New York: Blyden.
Gage, Thomas. [1648] 1958. *Thomas Gage's Travels in the New World*. Intro. and ed. J. Eric Thompson. Norman: University of Oklahoma Press.
Gaillard, Roger. 1974–1984. *Les Blancs débarquent*. 5 vols. Port-au-Prince: Presses Nationales, Natal.
Hoetink, Harry. 1967. *The Two Variants in Caribbean Race Relations: A Contribution to the Sociology of Segmented Societies*. London: Oxford University Press.
Hurbon, Laennec. 1979. *Culture et dictature en Haïti: L'Imaginaire sous contrôle*. Paris: L'Harmattan.
Labelle, Micheline. 1976. Témoignages sur la question de couleur. *Lankasièl* 5:25–43.
———. 1978. *Idéologie de couleur et classes sociales en Haïti*. Montreal: Les Presses de l'Université de Montréal.
Lamartinière, Jacqueline. 1976. *Noirisme*. Paris: MHL.
Lewis, Gordon. 1983. *Main Currents in Caribbean Thought*. Baltimore: Johns Hopkins University Press.
Leyburn, James G. 1941. *The Haitian People*. New Haven, Conn.: Yale University Press.
Mintz, Sidney. [1974] 1984. *Caribbean Transformations*. Baltimore: Johns Hopkins University Press. Reprint.
Nicholls, David. 1979. *From Dessalines to Duvalier: Race, Colour, and National Independence in Haiti*. Cambridge: Cambridge University Press.
Pierre, Pressoir. 1987. *Témoignages: 1946–1976, l'espérance déçue*. Port-au-Prince: Deschamps.
Price, Hannibal. 1900. *De la Réhabilitation de la race noire par la République d'Haïti*. Port-au-Prince: N.p.
Price-Mars, Jean. 1983. *So Spoke the Uncle*. Trans. Magdaline Shannon. Washington, D.C.: Three Continents. First published in 1928 (*Ainsi parla l'oncle*).
———. [1979?]. *Anténor Firmin*. Port-au-Prince: Séminaire Adventiste.
Trollope, Anthony. [1859] 1985. *The West Indies and the Spanish Main*. Gloucester, Eng.: Sutton.
Trouillot, Michel-Rolph. 1986. Review of *So Spoke the Uncle*, by J. Price-Mars. *Research in African Literatures* 17:596–597.
———. 1990. *Haïti: State against Nation: The Origins and Legacy of Duvalierism*. New York: Monthly Review Press.
———. 1993. Jeux de mots, jeux de classes: Les Mouvances de l'indigénisme. *Conjonction* 197:29–44.
———. N.d. Historiography of Haiti. In *General History of the Caribbean*. UNESCO, forthcoming.

SOHEIR A. MORSY

Beyond the Honorary "White" Classification of Egyptians: Societal Identity in Historical Context

[I]n the UN you have the Afro-Asian-Arab bloc. Now a lot of Arabs might like for you to think that they are white, but whenever you see them involved in the international picture, they are lined up with the dark world . . . Afro-Asian-Arab. They can come around here and pose as white. But when they get back home, they're not white. . . . We call ourselves Muslim—We don't call ourselves Black Muslims. This is what the newspapers call us. . . . We are Muslims. Black, brown, red, and yellow.

Malcolm X

The current U.S.-centered discussion surrounding the role of Egypt in the development of "Western" civilization (Adler et al. 1991; Begley et al. 1992; Bernal 1987; Yurgo 1991) suggests that although history may well belong to the victorious (Chomsky 1980), it is never too late for those who have been dispossessed to reclaim their heritage. In the U.S. context of color consciousness it is not surprising that the attempt at ancestral reappropriation on the part of African Americans has been linked to the question of Egyptian racial identity.

While popularized scholarship "[put] ancient Nubia back on the map" (Begley et al. 1992) and its imagery on T-shirts, Mostafa Hefny, a naturalized U.S. citizen from Egypt, remained bound by established racially defined differences. Hefny, a Detroit school teacher, is contesting U.S. Department of Immigration Directive Number 15, the basis of his classification as "White." According to this directive (also known as "Race and Ethnic Standards For Federal Statistics and Administrative Reporting"), people of European, northern African, and Middle Eastern origin are collectively designated "White." In rejecting this ascribed racial designation in favor of an African cultural identity, Hefny explains, in the November 1990 issue of *Jet*, under the headline "Black 'White' Man

Challenges Federal Race Identity Law," "My complexion is as dark as most Black Americans. My features are clearly African. . . . Classification as it is done by the United States government provides Whites with legal ground to claim Egypt as a White civilization. . . . We are fools if we allow them to take this legacy from us."

Aside from exhibiting a form of political consciousness and sense of African identity familiar to those of us who grew up in Nasserist Egypt, the case of Mostafa Hefny exemplifies Peter Worsley's conception of racial and ethnic categories as part of "social praxis."[1] As social identities these forms of differentiation are relative and situational, not absolute. They take on different meanings in different contexts, depending on who uses them and for what purpose (Worsley 1984:242–243). Thus Hefny's "racial" identity, irrelevant to him and others in their dealings with the Egyptian bureaucracy, now gains prominence in the social context of his new homeland and in the very process of his *natural*ization. Similarly, Arab identity, which prompts hate crimes against U.S. citizens of Arab descent in this country, was readily affixed to the Egyptian regime by the Bush administration in its attempt to camouflage the imperialist character of the 1991 war against the Arab people of Iraq.

Focusing on the recent history of Egypt from the colonial period to the Sadat years and drawing on experiential knowledge derived from Egypt and the United States, I address in this essay current anthropological concerns with the historical contingency and social construction of societal identity (Segal 1991; Williams 1989). Specifically, I examine U.S. racial categorization and foreign policy as these may now prompt Egyptians to stress their national or religious affiliation over identification as African and Arab.

From British Colonial Rule to an Open-Door Egypt

In the nineteenth century Egyptian national identity gained significance in opposition to European political economic hegemony and its associated Eurocentrist cultural orientation (Amin 1989; see also Abdel Malek 1963; Said 1978). With the 1841 military defeat of Muhammad Ali at the hands of the European powers, Egypt's own state-directed industrialization project was shattered. By 1879 Egypt had become a debtor nation under the rule of the Khedive Ismail, and hostage to European control. An international body decreed the appointment of the British and French to regulate the Egyptian treasury. Objection to foreign control by Ismail led to his dethroning and replacement by his son. This proceeded with the aid of the Ottoman sultan, who aspired to reestablish sovereignty over Egypt.

In periods of foreign control, as during the era of Ottoman rule, the historian al-Jabarti records that Egyptians distinguished themselves from other ethnic groups by the term *awlad al-balad* (people of the country) or *ahl al-balad* (literally, kin of the country). As is the case at present, these terms excluded Europeans, collectively known as Ifrang.[2] As designators of collective Egyptian identity these terms masked class differences, referring to the masses and to the rich Egyptian merchants and the learned, propertied religious leadership (El-Hamamsy 1985:41). Merchants and religious leaders had once played a significant role in cross-class communication in resistance to foreign political, economic, and cultural intrusion (Gran 1979). Among themselves, Egyptians distinguished Coptic Christians, Jews, and Muslims. Contrary to orientalist scholarly wisdom, religion did not constitute an immutable essence of identity. Then, as now, people assumed or were imputed with multiple identities in the context of social intercourse (El-Messiri 1978). As a subjugated people under the Turks and Circassians, Muslim Egyptians distinguished themselves from these coreligionists; like the Europeans, these foreign Muslims were not considered *awlad balad*. Also excluded from the "people of the country" category were Westernized Arabic-speaking groups with commercial, professional, or bureaucratic ties to non-Egyptian hegemonic social groups.

In 1882 protest against foreign domination erupted into open revolt involving large segments of the Egyptian population, including the peasantry (Brown 1990). This revolt, led by an Egyptian army officer and his comrades, is considered "the First Egyptian National Movement." While the Egyptian identity of these officers is beyond dispute, some Arab nationalists from Egypt cherish the additional significance of this revolt as the expression of a resurgent Arab national consciousness. As the late Fathi Radwan pointed out to me, "ᶜUrabi," the appellation by which the 1882 revolt is known, was not the original name of its leader. The adoption of this name (which derives from the Arabic root ᶜArabi, meaning Arabic) was used later to denote the Arab nationalist consciousness of the revolt's leadership (personal communication, 1986).[3]

While manifestations of Arab national consciousness are not documented for the Egyptian masses of the nineteenth century, Muhammad Ali's military expeditions into Syria and Palestine seem to have left his son Ibrahim, the commander of these military campaigns, with a highly developed sense of Arab identity:

> Ibrahim spoke of himself as Arab and liked to be regarded as one. . . . He spoke openly of his aims and exerted himself to spread his ideas among the

> humble as well as the influential in Syria. . . . Ibrahim made no secret of his intention to revive Arab national consciousness and restore Arab nationhood, to instill into the Arabs a real sense of patriotism, and to associate them in the fullest measure in the government of the future empire; that he regarded his father's ideas as narrow and merely imperialistic, and more suited to the state of enslavement into which the Arab world had sunk than to the politically independent status to which he proposed, on Muhammad Ali's death, to lead the Arab[s]. (Antonius 1947:29)

Contrary to Ismail's dream, it was not Egypt that assumed the leadership of the Arab nationalist movement in opposition to Turkish hegemony, which culminated in the Great Arab Revolt of 1916. The struggle for Arab unity then and during the two decades that followed was led by the Arabs of Greater Syria. Although Cairo had provided refuge to many Syrian intellectuals and experienced the renaissance of Arabic literature of the preceding century, the country's early independence from Ottoman rule left its people's sense of Arab identity underdeveloped relative to other parts of the Arab region under Ottoman control. In confronting British domination Egyptian national identity was more relevant. The nationalists' demands for reunification were restricted to Egypt and Sudan. It was not until the 1920s that Egyptian solidarity with surrounding Arab populations began to escalate and Cairo eventually came to assume a central role in the Arab region's intellectual life and its popular culture. With the formation of the Arab League in 1945, Egypt, the most populous of the Arab states, assumed leadership, a position that took on greater meaning with the coming to power of Nasser (Mussallam 1983:7–10).

The Arabic language itself gained significance in Egypt as a symbol of indigenous cultural identity much earlier. Following the crushing of the 1882 ᶜUrabi Revolt by the British, the appointment of Lord Cromer as consul general in 1883 initiated a policy of anglicization in education (Tignor 1966). Attendance at private French or English schools provided the children of privileged indigenous social groups with a European-style education.

Until the nationalization of educational institutions after the 1952 Free Officers' coup, those of us who attended foreign-language schools remained distanced from our multilayered cultural heritage. Afaf Mahfouz, an Egyptian friend, recalled in a conversation in 1991 how the nun at her French school in Upper Egypt chastised her for using a green coloring pencil. To the frightened little girl's surprise this color was banned because the teacher saw it as a symbol of Islam. In the British school that I attended in Alexandria the Italian schoolmaster who taught us art had no problem with this color. Whether this was a result of his tolerance of alien religions or because he was not well versed in symbolic analysis I do not know.

The curriculum of that British school, however, was as alienating as that of other European-language schools. We were encouraged to excel in French, Latin, and of course English, while Arabic instruction remained rudimentary. Students who sat for their Oxford and Cambridge School Certificate Examination possessed Arabic reading and writing skills that hardly surpassed those of a third-year primary school pupil in the public schools. In these schools, the efforts of colonial-era nationalist activists to reverse the colonial anglicization program had borne fruit. The emphasis on Egyptian national identity by Copts and Muslims during the 1919 Revolution (El Rafᶜi 1968) had forced the British to concede to some nationalist demands for educational reform.

Private European-language schools remained insulated from these reforms. In the British school I attended, speaking Arabic on the school grounds could result in "punishment." This often meant having to write the sentence "I must not speak Arabic in school" as many as several hundred times. In contrast to the restrictions imposed on the use of our native tongue, English was offered in abundance in its literary and scientific variants. I recall waking up early in the morning to memorize the long soliloquies of one famous Shakespearean character or another. As I reviewed the passages on the way to school, in preparation for their recital in class later in the day, I would hear the driver cursing the native pedestrians and their religion (also mine) in Italian.

In class we learned much about ancient Greece and Rome; we read British and other European histories, including passages about the problematic "barbaric" Moors, with whom our identification was anything but forthcoming. In science many of us were particularly impressed by Avicenna, whom I assumed to be a European, like all of the other scientists that we read about. In geography class we learned about a lake in Africa named after a British queen and marveled at how a Britisher had "discovered" the sources of the Nile in Africa. This "dark continent" was familiar to us through Tarzan movies. Needless to say, I did not identify with the natives in these films. In short, nationalism, whether Egyptian or otherwise, had no place in the London-made curriculum of our school. Unlike our compatriots in what were known as the Arabic schools, who demonstrated against both the British and those identified as their local allies, for us the development of our nationalist political consciousness was clearly an extracurricular activity in which friends and members of our extended families, including brothers and male cousins (who were less likely to be sent to European-language schools) played important parts.

As Egyptians struggled against foreign domination, the country's resident foreigners (who often distinguished themselves as such even when they came from families that had resided in Egypt for more than one generation) continued to exhibit a sense of superiority over indigenous social groups. As Egyptian anthropologist Laila El-Hamamsy observes for the Turks:

> They boasted of their Turkish blood and retained a sense of social superiority over the Egyptian, or the "fellah" as they often called him. Standards of personal beauty emphasizing Turkish standards, such as lighter shades of skin, eyes, and hair . . . [continued to be] prevalent. Egyptian reaction against this residue of Turkish superiority could be seen in the lampooning that the Turks suffered in popular jokes and plays, and in the tribute that novels and folk songs repeatedly paid to the dark beauty of the Egyptian. (1985:52)

In spite of such forms of popular cultural resistance, many Egyptians themselves came to aspire and acquiesce to the culture of the hegemonic groups, sometimes referring to indigenous products and customs by contemptuous terms such as *baladi,* which literally means "my country." In my mother's generation, the desirable attributes for a bride among the upper classes were a fair complexion and the ability to speak French and to play the piano. As for Egyptians who did not approximate the standards established by the hegemonic culture, their sense of alienation remains a topic of conversation to this day. Older compatriots speak of their feeling that Egypt "was not our country." Material wealth did not serve to overcome this feeling. Without appropriate European dress and linguistic skills, even rich Egyptians suffered disdain from the French-speaking clerks at movie theaters and department stores bearing European names such as Rivoli, Royal, Hannaux, Salon Vert, L'Enfant Chic, and Petite Reine. (I accompanied my mother to these locations, and I recall the discriminatory treatment to which Arabic-speaking patrons of these establishments were subjected at the hands of the French-speaking attendants, whether Egyptian, Italian, Greek, or otherwise.) This situation changed drastically after the 1952 Nasserist Free Officers' coup (popularly known as "the July Revolution"), when the anticolonial nationalist cry "Egypt for the Egyptians" came to be replaced by the idea of "Egypt for *all* Egyptians" (El-Hamamsy 1985:53, emphasis added).

As Egyptian nationalism was replaced during the 1950s and 1960s by the state ideology of Pan-Arabism and the companion banner of Arab socialism, we witnessed the nationalization of the *grands magazins* along with numerous other commercial and financial enterprises, schools, and hospitals. All these establishments acquired new titles, which contained such terms as the Arabic words for "victory," "people," "unity," "public sector," and most significantly the designation "Arab." Indeed it was Arab identity that came to center stage in Nasserist Egypt, subordinating Egyptian nationalist loyalties to aspirations of an encompassing Arab nation, unfettered by the nation-state boundaries established by colonial authorities (S. Amin 1978).

Among many changes brought about by the July 1952 army coup, the nationalization of European-language schools had a most profound effect on those of us who had been deprived of our cultural heritage in the name of quality education. As the administration and curricula of our school came under scrutiny by the Ministry of Education, those of us with "Egyptian" features became particularly valuable to the European staff of our school. We were deliberately assigned positions of heightened visibility in school activities to which officials were invited. For the first time school became a place where we read Egyptian history, including accounts of our compatriots' struggle for independence from Ottoman rule and European colonialism. Simultaneously the notion of "the unity of the Nile valley" was expanded to accommodate Pan-Africanism. Egypt's partnership in the Non-Aligned Movement also nourished African-Asian solidarity; the Afro-Asian Solidarity Committee provided a framework for people-to-people international collaboration.

From the early days of the July Revolution Nasser himself played an important role in highlighting the connectedness of Egyptians, through time and space, to Arab, African, and Muslim communities and causes. In his outline of "The Philosophy of the Revolution" he went well beyond "Egypt's history under the Pharaohs . . . , the interaction between the Greek culture and ours . . . , [t]he Roman invasion and the Islamic conquest . . . , [and] the waves of Arab migration" (1960:39). Turning to contemporary linkages, he described these associations as "a group of circles." Beginning with the first and "most important of these circles" he wrote

> [The] Arab Circle surrounding us is as much part of us as we are part of it . . . our history has been merged with it and . . . its interests are linked with ours. . . . [T]he . . . ties that bind our peoples together . . . make our homeland an integral indivisible whole, which should be defended as such and not as an isolated unit. (52, 68)

Referring to the second circle, which involves Africa, Nasser states

> [W]e cannot under any condition . . . stand aloof from the terrible and terrifying battle now raging in the heart of that continent between five million whites

> and two hundred million Africans. . . . We cannot stand aloof for one important reason—we ourselves are in Africa. . . . I shall continue to dream of the day on which I shall see in Cairo a great Africa Institute seeking to reveal to us the various aspects of the Continent, to create in our minds an enlightened African consciousness, and to associate itself with all those working in all parts of the world for the progress, prosperity and welfare of the peoples of Africa. (69, 70)

Finally, for the third circle, that which encompasses Muslims worldwide, the Egyptian leader reflected,

> As I contemplate the eighty million Moslems in Indonesia, the fifty million in China, the few millions in Malaya, Thailand and Burma, the hundred million in Pakistan, the well nigh over hundred million in the Middle East, the forty million in the Soviet Union, and the millions of others in the other remote and far-flung corners of the earth . . . I come out increasingly conscious of the potential achievements cooperation among these millions can accomplish—cooperation naturally not going beyond their loyalty to their original countries. (72)

While it is not possible to accurately determine the extent to which state ideology pertaining to societal identity came to be integrated into popular political culture (Salame 1990:46), there is no doubt that Cairo's role as center for an untold number of encounters between peoples of the three circles had significant consequences. Egyptians' visibility in international political activities increased dramatically, as did student politics abroad. Informed by the state's expanded definition of societal identity, Egyptians sent on education missions to the United States contributed to the work of the Organization of Arab Students, the Muslim Student Association, and campus chapters of the Organization of African Students, often assuming the leadership of the first. In solidarity with the struggles of African peoples, their support extended beyond their home continent to the diaspora. In 1962 Egyptian students, along with other Africans, Arabs, and Muslims, met with Malcolm X at Harvard University. The group's discussion extended to the racial dimension of social identity, demonstrating the evolution of Malcolm's thinking on the issue (Ashraf El-Bayoumi, personal communication, 1962).

As is evident from Malcolm's accounts of his trips to Africa and the Arab world, where he met with Nasser and made a pilgrimage to Mecca, he came to realize that the racial classificatory scheme with which he grew up in the United States was far from universally relevant. Describing his pilgrimage experience where he met people "of all colors," Malcolm writes,

> Being from America made me intensely sensitive to matters of color. I saw that people who looked alike drew together and most of the time stayed together. This was entirely voluntary; there being no other reason for it. But Africans were with Africans, Pakistanis were with Pakistanis and so on. I tucked it into my mind that when I returned home I would tell Americans this observation; that where true brotherhood existed among all colors, where no one felt segregated, where there was no "superiority" complex, no "inferiority" complex—then voluntarily, naturally, people of the same kind felt drawn together by that which they had in common (Malcolm X and Haley 1965:344).[4]

The common bond that Malcolm spoke of in reference to African peoples translated politically into Egyptian support for the civil rights struggle in the "pure white democracy" of the U.S.; using this phrase as his title, Richard Nolte documents Egyptian reactions to the 1956 attempt by the Black student Autherine Lucy to enroll at the University of Alabama, which included the offer of "a full all-expense Government scholarship for study in Egypt" (1956:8). Among the many reactions gathered by Nolte from the Egyptian press and individual Egyptians, the following are noteworthy:

> "The girl lives, eats, and sleeps guarded by armed police, night and day, while the Negro population meets together on how to oblige the Pure Whites—who believe in Peace and Democracy and Equality and Freedom and Humanity and Justice—how to compel them to honor the ruling of their Supreme Court which a few months ago at long last allowed colored Americans to attend the universities of the white Americans."
>
> "If I were an American Negro, I would claim a decent compensation for all Negroes; and it would not be less than one hundred million dollars. And I would prosecute this matter in every international conference and by every possible means."
>
> "Ohhh!! If I were in her place, I would offer my blood as ransom for the cause."
>
> "Greetings to the Free Negroes from Free Egypt, and from all free men!" (1, 2)

Of his response to this vilification of U.S. society, Nolte writes:

> I said I thought it was deplorable, most unfortunate, wrong . . . [but] pointed out that in the U.S., for Negroes as for everyone else, there were means of redress. . . . After all, she had been able to hire a lawyer and bring suit against the University Trustees. My unspoken question was, what redress did

> the several thousand Egyptians "detained" by government order in their own country have? But skepticism, not sympathy, was in every face. For them the issue was clear: the girl had been forced out of school because of the color of her skin.
>
> Egyptian society has its full share of discriminatory prejudices [and] inequalities. But racial prejudice is not a factor. There is no observable color bar. . . . [S]lavery as an institution in Mameluke and Ottoman Egypt was by no means limited to Negroes but included Whites in even greater numbers. . . . Skin color in Egypt is no clue to a previous condition of servitude, or to a lack of it. (6–7)

Ironically, Egyptian students who studied in racially segregated regions of the United States during the 1950s and early 1960s were generally assigned to "white" schools. We were welcomed as "foreign students"; rarely were we subjected to harassment, except in cases of "mistaken identity." At Florida State University, where I had my undergraduate training, Egyptian students' "integration" into activities on this white campus stood in contrast to our "segregation" from the activities of other African and African-American students at nearby Florida A&M, a "Negro school." So strict was the separation that a Yankee graduate student in physics was expelled from the university for inviting some Nigerian students from A&M to his off-campus apartment.

While affiliation with a "white" university endowed Egyptian students with this honorary racial status, it did not always shield us from the racism of the surrounding community. Our experiences ranged from the anecdotal to the offensive. Ashraf El-Bayoumi, then an Egyptian student, recalls that, when first confronted by the water fountain marked "colored" in the land of "technological miracles," he assumed the designation to be a reference to the water itself. Still under the impression that "Lincoln had freed the slaves," he tried to convince a landlady that his Coptic companion who wanted to rent her apartment "resembles Jesus Christ." The woman's response was unequivocal: "Christ or no Christ, I do not believe in integration" (personal communication 1957).

In my case, even after two years of U.S. residence, I was not immune to race-related surprises. Following a 1958 presentation on Egypt that I made with another Egyptian student at a black school, we learned that our photo would be appearing in the "colored edition" of the *Tallahassee Democrat*. Oblivious of racial implications, we blamed ourselves for missing it by having subscribed to the black-and-white version of the paper.

Aside from problems with housing for those of us of darker shades, and occasional aggravations such as my own experience of being told to sit at the back of the bus, which I refused to do, Egyptian students in the segregated South generally "passed." This changed with the intensification of the civil rights struggle in the early 1960s when sit-ins became a popular form of resistance. For the first time some of us were refused service in restaurants, often after long consultations among waitresses who were audibly debating our racial identity.

The period between 1967 and 1975 witnessed major changes in Egypt and its surrounding region. With the 1967 Arab military defeat, Egypt lost its position of leadership in the struggle against Zionism and imperialism. Subjected to a growing oil wealth–fueled Saudi influence, Egyptian society succumbed to the culture of the region's rentiers petro-Islamists (Beblawi 1990). Simultaneously, under Sadat the country became fully integrated politically, economically, and militarily within the U.S. orbit. Egyptian officials signed the U.S.-sponsored Camp David Accord, implemented its companion economic liberalization policies known as the Open Door Economic Policies (ODEP), and placed military bases at the disposal of the U.S. government.

As victory was declared by the champions of free enterprise and their belated allies who had flourished in the bosom of Nasserist state capitalism, the 1970s saw major shifts in definitions of societal identity, stressing those that were compatible with the newly forged alliances. These included state-sanctioned emphasis of our "pharaonic" identity, efforts to highlight our "Mediterranean heritage" (as exemplified by Farag Foda's program for his proposed new political party), as well as official promotion of Islamist rhetoric (exemplified by the description of Sadat as "the pious president," and his own repeated references to "science and faith").

As the three circles of the antecedent era lost their significance, Egyptians spoke of a sense of identity crisis [*daya*ᶜ, or loss], well expressed by the very title of President Sadat's 1978 autobiography, *In Search of Identity.* By the time of the president's assassination in October 1981, Pan-Arabism had been dealt a serious blow, Pan-Africanism was but a historical memory, the country was in the thrall of unprecedented sectarian strife between its Muslim majority and Coptic minority, and the economic turn northwestward came to be expressed in cultural terms, reminiscent of the period of European domination. In a culturally informed study of Egypt's ODEP, economist Galal Amin shows that "[j]ust as factors of production as well as purchasing power have [been] diverted from the domestic products towards foreign goods, national culture also . . . [gave] way in the interest of the culture from which these goods originate. . . . In a word: in order to create reliable customers for western goods, you are well advised to have those customers 'westernized' " (1981:433).

Within the framework of the ODEP, even the Pyramids were threatened with Westernization. A North American tourism prospector found "[no] bigger challenge than to tackle the pyramid. I mean to take a little water and a little shit and make an oasis of green where there's only been sand for 5,000 years, *to create a golf course*" (Fuad 78:135, emphasis added). The national campaign launched by Dr. Niᶜmat Ahmad Fuad shattered this arrogant adventurer's dream, thereby protecting a prominent symbol of Egyptian identity.

Efforts to create what Ali Mazrui described as "culturally relevant markets" for Western products restored to those who possessed European linguistic skills and looks the esteem they had enjoyed before the July Revolution. Egypt's "openness" was accompanied by a marked proliferation of English-language training programs, which were eagerly pursued by groups ranging from bank tellers to high-ranking army officers. Of the many advertisements that appeared in the national press two will suffice to illustrate the role of multinational firms in the promotion of neocolonial anglicization. From the February 17, 1985, issue of *Al-Ahram:* "AN AMERICAN FIRM in Cairo seeks ambitious young men and women for its challenging job. Candidates must have: high education, fluent English, excellent appearance, managerial personality, age between 20–28. English school graduates and car owners will have priority." And from a typical 1975 issue of *Al-Akhbar:* "Foreign Trade Office immediately requires young charming female secretary. . . . English typing with fluent English language . . . recent graduate or one/two years experience."

The mass information media, particularly its electronic forms also promote "excellent appearance," a standard of physical attributes that defines fair skin, light eyes, and blond hair as admirable. TV commercials, many of which are prepared in the West, feature blond women. When local actresses are involved, many of them either have their hair dyed or wear blond wigs. Indeed, in urban areas, a noticeable correlate of the ODEP is the increased number of women with dyed light hair. The influence of the fashionable beauties of locally broadcast North American TV series such as *Dallas, Knots Landing, Flamingo Road,* and *Falcon Crest* even extends to some fashion-conscious women who don the so-called Islamic-style dress but are also eager to wear colored contact lenses. Petro-Islamic modesty also takes the form of "Islamic" outfits bearing the label "imported from London" (Abdel Fadil 1989). Aside from promoting Euro-American standards of beauty, Egypt's "open-door" world of advertisement partakes of the Madison Avenue definition of diversity. Multiracial Benetton-type ads now appear in Egypt, sensitizing consumers to hitherto irrelevant U.S. racial archetypes.

Turning to the politics of the Sadat regime as it pertains to societal identity, it is noteworthy that while the official pro-Western stance was accompanied by suppression of the "vocabulary of Arabism," there were contravening forces that could not be easily vanquished. Prominent among these was the persistent support by members of the Egyptian opposition of the Palestinian resistance movement (cf. Owen 1983:22). Arab nationalists reasoned that the ineptitude of individual Arab states in support of the Palestinians could be overcome by Arab citizens "work[ing] at a . . . pan-Arab . . . level and transcend[ing] the local state phenomenon," as K. Hassib editorialized in *Al-Mustaqbal al-'Arabi* in 1985 (qtd. in Salame 1990:50). Acting on this premise, members of the Egyptian opposition committed to preserving the priority of Arab identity were confronted with the power of the regional petro-economy. This proved to be a monumental force in domesticating Arab nationalism. As Beblawi notes, "Pan-Arabism and Arab money [became], to a great extent, and in different hands, the stick and the carrot, used to bring about a very subtle equilibrium in sharing oil rent" (1990:96).

Although Egypt's integration in the regional petro-economy as a labor exporter contributed to the establishment of a vast pan-Arab institutional network (Owen 1983:22), the resulting intra-Arab cooperation in no way approximates earlier conceptions of Arab unity. Neither does it challenge the institutionalized *kafil* (sponsorship) system of privilege, which mocks the notion of Arab kinship by legitimizing exploitation of noncitizens by citizens. Indeed, the situation during the 1970s and 1980s differed fundamentally from that of the 1950s and 1960s, when Egyptians working in the petroleum-exporting countries were recruited primarily to contribute to a "unitarian [pan-Arab] construction" (Amin 1982). The ideological framework of this construction was clearly antagonistic to Arab reactionary regimes, and decidedly anti-imperialist.

During the 1970s and 1980s the integration of Egypt within a Gulf-led pan-Arab formation coincided also with the accentuation of Muslim identity. In contrast to Arab nationalists who seek the elimination of existing state structures and their integration into an encompassing Arab state, proponents of the Islamic *umma* (community) advocate the adoption of Islamic law (*shari^ca*) by the individual states and promote solidarity among the existing independent Islamic nations (Salame 1990:50). Not only does oil wealth–financed Islamism polarize Muslim and Coptic compatriots, it also incorporates the former in a new "circle" that is in many ways coterminous with the interests of multinational corporations and financial institutions, as evident from the 1991 Bank of Credit and Commerce International (BCCI) saga, to give but one example.

While some Islamist groups are decidedly anti-Western, it is important to guard against neo-orientalist scholarly alarm over "Islamic fundamentalism." This threatens to blind us to the harmonious relations that obtain between petro-Islamists, their Egyptian supporters, and international capital. In the Egyptian context, political-economic cum cultural expression of this partnership takes various forms. These include the state's own unceasing pursuit of Gulf and Western private capital investments (to the detriment of the productive public sector), individual contributions to deposits in the Bahama-based "Bank of Piety," and the recital of the Quran *in English* by children attending the Al-Rayan "Islamic" kindergarten in Cairo.

The compromised significance of the Nasser-era Arab circle in light of the post-1967 Americanization/Saudization of Egypt has a counterpart in relation to the African circle. Egypt's latter-day support of reactionary African regimes, whether that of Mubutu in Zaire or Hassan in Morocco, stands in contrast to earlier forms of solidarity. On a personal level, President Sadat's acknowledgment of his own African identity was anything but forthcoming. In fact, in one of his earlier interviews with Barbara Walters, his complaint about the Soviets ended with an objection to their treatment of Egypt as a "central African country." Where the Sudanese parentage of Egypt's first president, Muhammad Naguib, had been highlighted as a symbol of "the unity of the Nile valley," and where Nasser was proudly described as "the dark giant," Sadat himself was highly uncomfortable with his dark pigmentation (Heikal 1983:8, 13, 25).

Sensitized to the centrality of racial differences as attributes of social status in the United States, pro-Sadat Egyptians took offense when the African-American actor Lou Gossett portrayed the president in a 1984 TV film. Some of the Egyptians who saw this English-language film believed that the choice of a member of a subjugated group to portray Egypt's president was part of a Hollywood plot to undermine the significance of Sadat's peace mission.[5] By that time the struggle of African Americans no longer enjoyed formal support. As allies of the U.S. government, Egyptian officials had no doubt noted that African Americans are generally marginal in the halls of power where Sadat had met with people like "my friend Henry," as he used to refer to Secretary of State Kissinger. Neither the behavior nor the physical attributes of African Americans appearing in the many shows imported from the United States (including *Roots,* which highlighted the slave heritage of African

Americans) approximated the idealized image of North Americans as rich, powerful, and of course blond.[6]

Egyptians and the Politics of Identity in the United States

As visitors, permanent residents, and increasingly as citizens, Egyptians in the United States, as elsewhere, have multiple identities. Whether self-assigned or ascribed, these are informed not only by the societal divisions of the new homeland and the categories of social differentiation operative in the country of origin, but also by matters of foreign policy and international relations.

Unlike Mostafa Hefny, the Detroit schoolteacher, most Egyptians residing in the United States today are not likely to identify themselves either as African or African American. In a society where the melting-pot ideology provides but a transparent veil for an underlying "chosen people" of European origins (Gran N.d.:10), new immigrants who want to succeed in racially stratified U.S. society may well try to distance themselves from socially debased categories. With the increasing underdevelopment of the once significant internationalist consciousness in their country of origin, most Egyptians in the United States today are not likely to identify with the struggles of other racially or ethnically differentiated groups.

For these Egyptians, the honorary "white" classification, in conjunction with the identification of ancient Egypt as the origin of Western civilization, facilitates affiliation with the hegemonic social group. Hence the determination on the part of some Egyptians to monopolize the claim to the heritage derived from our ancient ancestors, and to exclude African Americans from such association. Illustrative of this stance is the indignation that marked the reaction of an Egyptian professor to my comments in 1991 following an event celebrating African History Month. I had pointed out that although I am in disagreement with the current attempts to impose on ancient Egypt an irrelevant racial typology derived from a historically specific Euro-American experience, I am nevertheless convinced that the Sahara has not been a barrier to genetic and cultural exchange among the peoples of the African continent. In response, my compatriot's protest targeted what she described as the attempt on the part of the African-American community to "steal our heritage" as a means of overcoming its "slavery complex." Ironically, and in contrast to such reaction, some Egyptians readily check off the ethnic minority category "African American" when they or their children apply to programs of academic training.

In addition to some Egyptians' opportunistic detachment from African identity, U.S. residents of Egyptian origin are also likely to shun their Arab identity in favor of nation-state, Islamic, or Coptic affiliation. While the emphasis on religious identity is an extension of post-1967 developments in Egypt and the surrounding region, the suppression of Arab identity is also understandable in light of U.S. foreign policy.

Whereas Arabs, as "colored" and "foreign," *did* experience their share of U.S. racially motivated hatred in the earlier part of the century, the present antagonism with which we are targeted is primarily informed by the tenor of U.S. foreign policy. As Helen Samhan, deputy director of the Arab American Institute explains,

> In the present period anti-Arab attitudes and behavior have their roots, not in the traditional motives of structurally excluding a group perceived as inferior, but in . . . political racism [the origins of which] lie in the Arab-Israeli conflict and, as such, constitute an ideological struggle more than an ethnic one. Arab Americans who choose not to be active in Palestinian or Arab issues or organizations are not, in most cases, victims of this political racism. Conversely, non-Arab Americans sometimes are. (1987:11)[7]

The withdrawal of Egyptians from activities pertaining to Palestinian and Arab issues coincided with the beginning of negotiations that led up to the 1979 U.S.-orchestrated Camp David agreement. Egyptian involvement in the Organization of Arab Students almost came to a halt, and a separate Egyptian student organization was formed. A similar decline occurred in relation to the Pan-Arab professional organization, Arab-American University Graduates. Some Egyptians who were once active in this organization became founding members of the Organization of Egyptian-American Scholars. Headed by a personal friend of President Sadat, this group gained significance, particularly for those who stood to benefit from their status as dual Egyptian-American citizens.

As Egypt was admitted to the hall of civilized nations under U.S. auspices, we witnessed a drastic modification of the country's U.S. media image. Egyptians are now usually excluded from the pervasive vilification of Arabs (Morsy 1986). This insulation generally extends to hate crimes against Arabs, such as those that followed the 1985 TWA hijacking in Lebanon and the 1986 U.S. raid on Libya. In conjunction with the 1991 Gulf War, when Japanese Americans gave council and comfort to the most recent victims of FBI harassment, many Egyptians distanced themselves from their victimized Arab "kin."

By identifying with the Egyptian regime, a key Desert Storm coalition partner, Egyptians in the United States were generally spared the violence that befell many other Arabs. According to the 1990 report of the

American-Arab Anti-Discrimination Committee (ADC), a civil rights organization founded by Senator James Abourezk in 1980,

> Violence against the Arab-American community is at an all-time high. Throughout the crisis in the Gulf, . . . and since the United States and Iraq went to war . . . the number of attacks against Arab-American individuals and organizations has spiralled. . . . Although acts of racism and discrimination occur on a regular basis, since its founding, ADC has noted a significant increase in hate crimes and violence directed against Arab-Americans whenever the United States or its interests are involved in a Middle Eastern crisis. . . . Even as this report goes to press, the FBI is questioning over 200 Arab-American community leaders regarding their political views and their knowledge of possible terrorist threats in the U.S. . . . In addition, Palestinian and Lebanese political activists and organizers in the peace movement report that they are under surveillance by the FBI. Such actions are viewed as an attempt to "chill" the legitimate political activities of U.S. citizens and residents. It is a paradox that the overzealous policies designed to prevent terrorist attacks are directed in an indiscriminate manner against a community when it is itself the victim of hate crimes. (ADC 1991:1, 3–4)

Ironically, after a "victory" in the Gulf War, neither the honorary "white" label nor the shedding of Arab identity can provide protection against economic recession, attendant homelessness, cuts in education and health care, and increasing antagonism toward foreigners among the growing numbers of unemployed "true" Americans. As economic racism comes into play, Egyptians, along with other recent immigrants, may well be defined as enemy in the same way that even lighter-skinned Lebanese and Turks, as well as North Africans, have been targeted by antiforeign neo-Nazi groups in Germany, and the right-wing Front Nationale in France.[8]

For Europe, Sivanandan has observed the movement "from an ethnocentric racism to a Eurocentric racism, from the different racisms of the different member states to a common market racism" (qtd. in Webber 1991:11). Similarly, in the absence of concerted efforts to combat the divide-and-conquer strategies of U.S. rulers and their multinational allies, we can expect the not-so-new "New World Order" (Chomsky 1992) to generate a compatible global system of exclusion, as now restored in "Free Kuwait."

> [R]ather than . . . mere manifestation of exceptionalism and non-conventionality . . . the attempt to elaborate a more relevant, valid and significant body of social theory is constantly related, at each step and stage, to the real

> concrete world of our times, to its historically constituted specificities in their rich diversity and across their powerful contradictions. (Abdel Malek 1981:iv)

> The pyramids were built for the rulers of Egypt, but the Aswan High Dam for the good of the people. Nasser will continue to be a big force in the Arab world. I myself rather like and admire him. (Malcolm X 1989:103)

The 1960s witnessed the proliferation of intellectual productions of decolonization that took such varied forms as Anouar Abdel Malek's critique of orientalist scholarship and Frantz Fanon's demystification of colonial medicine. The restructuring of African societies and rewriting of their histories by Africans on the continent and in the diaspora extended to the fragmented Western representation of Africa wherein ancient Egypt is separated out and designated the origin of Western civilization (Pieterse 1992). The struggle for political unity of the continent prompted scholarly investigations of the extent to which Egypt's relations with the rest of Africa obtained historically (Mokhtar 1981).

More recently, the connection of Egypt to Africa has been brought back into prominence by Martin Bernal, albeit with a decidedly Eurocentric emphasis—African Egypt's impact on ancient Greece, and by extension on Western civilization. Informed by an "intrigue" with his own ethnic "roots" (1987:xiii), Bernal's search led him to "Black" Athena. Although accurately reflecting a historically specific context of discovery wherein racial identity is central, this designation is contradicted by the fact that in the world of antiquity, including North Africa and Greece, skin color did not play a significant role (Pieterse 1992:23).

While the notion of a "Black" origin of civilization may well enhance some Africans' sense of pride, not to mention the Egyptomania of U.S. consumer culture, it does not translate into a political project of African independence and internal unity. Still intact are impeding structures of global power relations, expressed, inter alia, in anti-African racism in the United States, and neocolonial policies that thwart the political and economic unification of the African continent. As Talal Asad has observed for Britain, "[A]n account of origins tells us nothing about how . . . unity is structured" (1990:472), or about the reaction of dominant social groups to derivative expressions of collectivity. Thus in contrast to the British liberal establishment's tolerance of immigrant popular culture as testimony to a "rich and diverse heritage" and "wealth of culture and tradition" is the perception of threat posed by Muslim immigrants to established authority, notably in its determination of primary homogeneities and differences. Similar to Malcolm X's

Islamic Afrocentric project, Muslim immigrants' politicization of their religious traditions constitutes a challenge to the fundamental notion of the nation-state with its legal prerogatives and totalizing cultural projects (Asad 1990:474; see also Kilani, N.d).

In contrast to political mobilization around culturally meaningful elements of social identity, the mere transformation of racial attributes from stigma to badge of honor amounts to nothing less than perpetuation of ahistoric stereotypic representations with attendant simplification and generalization (Pieterse 1992:12). In contemporary Egypt the highly developed sense of national pride (repeatedly expressed in the familiar reference to Egypt as mother of the world) has not deterred subjugation at the hands of contemporary architects of world orders, whether colonial or "new." At present, as in ancient times, social identity remains a historically specific social construct, inextricable from prevailing power relations. As Pieterse has observed, "[I]n ancient Egypt alone (a period of almost 3,000 years) we witness a virtually complete cycle of images of blacks ranging from normal (in the sense of everyday) and warrior images to enemy images and images of defeat, images of servants and entertainers, and finally, at the other extreme, to images of black or 'mixed' Pharaohs" (1992:23).

Many of the very Westerners who idolize ancient Egyptians do not extend to their living descendants even common courtesy. Sometimes tourists extend insult, and injury, even to ancient Egyptian monuments (Ives 1990). In the realm of popularized scholarship one is sometimes astounded by the muted voices of living Egyptians who specialize in the study of their ancient homeland. For example the PBS *Nova* program "This Old Pyramid" leaves one with the impression that Egypt has no Egyptologists, and that only white Western men are "bent on solving the mysteries of pyramid-building" as a news item in *Washington Home*, October 29, 1992, suggests. As for the living Egyptians portrayed in the *Nova* program, their role is that of beasts of burden subjected to insults from an arrogant North American stonemason, whom we see enjoying the vibrating body of an Egyptian belly dancer as he delivers a token expression of appreciation of Egyptian culture.

As for Bernal's scholarly construction of "Black" Athena's Egyptian heritage, while his very limited reference to contemporary Egyptians is made in a much more civil tone than that expressed by *Nova*'s stonemason, it remains illustrative of orientalist essentialism. Reducing the dynamic of societal identity to religious affiliation, Bernal asserts that, with the exception of Copts, contemporary Egyptians lack interest in their ancient heritage. Furthermore, implying uninterrupted "acceptance of the massive power of Western scholarship," Bernal alleges that "Egyptian scholars have not challenged the orthodoxy on the world role of Ancient Egypt or investigated its influence overseas" (1987:401).

In an oral challenge to Bernal's assertions, Angela Gilliam reminded the audience of a 1991 American Anthropological Association invited session devoted to *Black Athena* of the roles of the Egyptian government of an earlier era, UNESCO, and certainly Egyptian and other African scholars in rewriting the history of the African continent; Brackette Williams questioned the relevance of Bernal's findings for contemporary struggles.

The challenge to the authoritative Western discourse on Africa articulated at the many politically motivated conferences devoted to African history held in Nasserist Egypt, also noted by Gilliam, were not designed to address Professor Bernal's interest in Egypt's contribution to ancient Greece, and by extension Western civilization. Instead, participants traced the linkages, whether linguistic, religious, economic, or political, within the continent itself, and more generally, the relation of the African "circle" to other indigenously defined significant struggles, including that of African Americans. More recently, a review of Nabil Ragheb's *Alexandria's Golden Age: An Egyptian Scientific Perspective* published in the Egyptian daily *Al-Ahram,* August 6, 1993, cites the work of Taha Hussein, "the dean of Arabic literature," which describes the Greeks as "pupils of the Egyptians." Presenting elaborations of this theme, the reviewer makes the point that "Taha Hussein was ahead of Martin Bernal by half a century."

The struggle for African unity involved much more than scholarly challenge to Western representations of Egypt as separate from Africa. Attempts at intellectual decolonization were themselves inseparable from political and armed struggle against foreign domination throughout the continent. Although neglected in Hollwood's imagery of Malcolm X as tourist at the foot of the Pyramids, it was Egypt's leadership role in the anti-imperialist struggle, not its ancient temples, that left a lasting impression on this African-American leader.

Egypt of the period of decolonization witnessed the emphasis of the Arab, African, and Muslim dimensions of its people's multifaceted societal identity. This contrasted with the de-emphasis of the Mediterranean dimension, which connects the once subjugated Egyptian population to those who enslaved its members. With identity conceptualized as a historically specific social construct, today's Egyptian society is logically expected to exhibit interest in those facets of identity that are, to one degree or another, compatible with the country's recent reintegration into the Western political-economic-cultural orbit. A recent conversation with a relative in Alexandria lent credence to this expectation. In bringing our conversation to a close he said that he was on his way to a lecture on ancient Greek culture, adding, "This is a sign of the times." Indeed, so it is.

Notes

The Malcolm X quote in the epigraph is from Malcolm X 1989: 54–55, 102–103.

1. During Nasser's rule the Egyptian regime's support of Pan-Africanism extended to the training of African National Congress cadres and affiliates of other African liberation movements. On a personal level, the marriage of an Egyptian woman to the president of Ghana was often noted as symbolic of the unity between Egyptians and other Africans.

2. As markers of collective identities, the designations noted for Egyptians and Europeans were, and remain, cultural rather than racial. These terms continue to be used to refer to behavior, life-style, and inanimate objects such as clothes and furniture (El-Messiri 1978).

3. Radwan was a prominent member of the original Nationalist party and opposed British colonial rule for many years prior to the 1952 July Revolution. Following the overthrow of the monarchy and his release from prison he was appointed minister of culture under Nasser.

4. A challenge to Malcolm's conclusion is found in Bernard Lewis's work (1971, 1990). With typical white-master arrogance, Lewis corrects Malcolm's alleged misconception, informing his readers that "the beliefs which [Malcolm] had acquired and still cherished at [the] time [of his pilgrimage] prevented him from realizing the full implications of what he saw" (1971:4). Without disclosing his own "cherished" beliefs (Nyang and Abed-Rabbo 1984), Lewis goes on to comment on how the African-American leader had reached his allegedly misguided conclusion: "The Middle East is an ancient land of myths in which the mythopoeic faculty—the ability to create myths, to believe in them, and *to make others believe*—has by no means died out. It would be wise to subject any widely held assumption regarding this area to critical scrutiny" (1971:3, emphasis added). When undertaken by Lewis himself, "critical scrutiny" involves the familiar reminder about the Arab slave trade, reducing this economic relation, which included the subjugation of fair-skinned peoples, to a racial question (Gran N.d.:9). Lewis goes on to assert the "Alabama-like quality" of Arab/Muslim societies (1971:5).

5. Anthropologist Seteney Shami informed me that the less-than-favorable portrayals of African Americans in the TV programs imported from the United States leave many Jordanians with the impression that "the scary thing about America is the Blacks" (personal communication 1991).

6. In sharing with my spouse, Ashraf El-Bayoumi, who is Egyptian, his recent experience as a tourist in Egypt, an African-American professor complained of

the less than courteous treatment he was subjected to at the Cairo Nile Hilton. In response my spouse remarked, "They treated you like they treat us [locals] . . . ; you see, Americans are supposed to look different [from you]."

7. Samhan's examples of the infliction of this "political racism" on non-Arab Americans extend to academia. Among other illustrations she cites the case of SUNY professor Ernest Dube, a South African antiapartheid activist accused of anti-Semitism for having lectured on the issue of Zionism as racism (1987:21).

8. Ironically, in France racism proceeds under the guise of preserving the progressive and rationalist values of the 1789 Revolution (Lloyd and Waters 1991).

References

Abdel Fadil, Mahmoud. 1989. Islamic Dress "Imported from London." *Sut Al-Arab,* April 26. [In Arabic.]

Abdel Malek, Anouar. 1963. Orientalism in Crisis. *Diogenes* 44:107–108.

———. 1981. *Social Dialectics: Nation and Revolution.* Albany: State University of New York Press.

Abdel Nasser, Gamal. 1960. *The Philosophy of the Revolution.* N.p.

ADC [American-Arab Anti-Discrimination Committee]. 1991. *1990 ADC Annual Report on Political and Hate Violence.* Washington, D.C.: ADC.

Adler, J., with H. Manly, V. E. Smith, F. Chideya, and L. Wilson. 1991. African Dreams. *Newsweek,* September 23.

Amin, Galal. 1981. Some Economic and Cultural Aspects of Economic Liberalization in Egypt. *Social Problems* 28:430–441.

———. 1982. External Factors in the Reorientation of Egypt's Economic Policy. In *Rich and Poor States in the Middle East,* ed. M. H. Kerr and S. Yassin, 285–315. Boulder, Colo.: Westview.

Amin, Samir. 1978. *The Arab Nation.* London: Zed.

———. 1989. *Eurocentrism.* New York: Monthly Review Press.

Antonios, George. 1955. *The Arab Awakening.* Beirut: Khayat.

Asad, Talal. 1990. Multiculturalism and British Identity in the Wake of the Rushdie Affair. *Politics and Society* 18:455–480.

Beblawi, Hazem. 1990. The Rentier State in the Arab World. In *The Arab State,* ed. Giacomo Luciani, 85–98. Berkeley and Los Angeles: University of California Press.

Begley, Sharon, with F. Chideya and V. Minor. 1992. Of Pygmies and Princes: Scholars Put Ancient Nubia Back on the Map. *Newsweek,* October 19.

Bernal, Martin. 1987. *Black Athena: The Afroasiatic Roots of Classical Civilization.* Vol. 1, *The Fabrication of Ancient Greece, 1785–1985.* New Brunswick: Rutgers University Press.

Brown, Nathan J. 1990. *Peasant Politics in Modern Egypt.* New Haven, Conn.: Yale University Press.

Chomsky, Noam. 1980. Preface to *Palestinians: From Peasants to Revolutionaries,* by Rosemary Sayigh. London: Croom.

———. 1992. "What We Say Goes": The Middle East in the New World Order.

In *Collateral Damage: The "New World Order" at Home and Abroad,* ed. Cynthia Peters, 49–92. Boston: South End.

El-Hamamsy, Laila. 1985. The Assertion of Egyptian Identity. In *Arab Society: Social Science Perspectives,* ed. Nicholas S. Hopkins and Saad Eddin Ibrahim, 39–63. Cairo: American University in Cairo Press.

El-Messiri, Sawsan. 1978. *Ibn Al-Balad: A Concept of Egyptian Identity.* Leiden: Brill.

El-Rafᶜi, Abdel Rahman. 1968. *The 1919 Revolution.* Cairo: Dar al-Shaab. [In Arabic.]

El-Sadat, Anwar. 1978. *In Search of Identity.* Cairo: Al-Maktab Al-Masri Al-Hadith. [In Arabic.]

Fuad, Niᶜmat A. 1978. *The Pyramid Plateau: The Dangers of Attacking Egypt.* Cairo: World Book.

Gran, Peter. 1979. *Islamic Roots of Capitalism.* Austin: University of Texas Press.

———. N.d. Readings from the Text: Political Economy in Anglo-American Middle Eastern Studies. Manuscript.

Heikal, Mohamed. 1983. *Autumn of Fury: The Assassination of Sadat.* New York: Random House.

Ives, Tom. 1990. Stepping on Karnak. *World Monitor,* December.

Kamel, Abdel Aziz A. 1971. *Islam and the Problem of Discrimination.* Paris: UNESCO. [In Arabic.]

Kilani, Modher. N.d. France and the Veil: Universalism, Comparison, Hierarchy. Manuscript.

Lewis, Bernard. 1971. *Race and Color in Islam.* New York: Harper and Row.

———. 1990. *Race and Slavery in the Middle East: An Historical Enquiry.* New York: Oxford University Press.

Lloyd, Cathie, and Hazel Waters. 1991. France: One Culture, One People? *Race and Class* 32(3): 49–66.

Malcolm X. 1989. *Malcolm X: The Last Speeches,* ed. Bruce Perry. New York: Pathfinder.

Malcolm X and Alex Haley. 1965. *The Autobiography of Malcolm X.* New York: Ballantine.

Mokhtar, G., ed. 1981. *General History of Africa.* Vol. 2, *Ancient Civilizations of Africa.* Paris: UNESCO.

Morsy, Soheir. 1986. The Bad, the Ugly, the Super-Rich, and the Exceptional Moderate: U.S. Popular Images of the Arabs. *Journal of Popular Culture* 20(3): 13–30.

Musallam, Basim. 1983. *The Arabs.* London: Collins/Harvill.

Nolte, Richard H. 1956. Pure White Democracy: Egyptian Reactions to the Affair of Autherine Lucy. *American Universities Field Staff Reports,* Northeast Africa Series 4(1): 1–8.

Nyang, Sulayman, and Samir Abed-Rabbo. 1984. Bernard Lewis and Islamic Studies: An Assessment. In *Orientalism, Islam, and Islamists,* ed. Asaf Hussein, Robert Olson, and Jamil Qureshi, 259–284. Brattleboro, Vt.: Amana.

Owen, Roger. 1983. Arab Nationalism, Arab Unity, and Arab Solidarity. In *The Middle East,* ed. Talal Asad and Roger Owen, 16–22. New York: Monthly Review Press.

Pieterse, Jan Nederveen. 1992. *White on Black: Images of Africa and Blacks in Western Popular Culture.* New Haven, Conn.: Yale University Press.

Said, Edward. 1978. *Orientalism.* New York: Random House.

Salame, Chassan. 1990. "Strong" and "Weak" States: A Qualified Return to the Muqaddimah. In *The Arab State,* ed. Giacomo Luciani, 29–64. Berkeley and Los Angeles: University of California Press.

Samhan, Helen. 1987. Politics and Exclusion: The Arab American Experience. *Journal of Palestine Studies* 16(2): 11–28.

Segal, Daniel A. 1991. "The European": Allegories of Racial Purity. *Anthropology Today* 7(1): 6–9.

Tignor, Robert. 1966. *Modernization and British Colonial Rule in Egypt, 1882–1914.* Princeton: Princeton University Press.

Webber, Frances. 1991. From Ethnocentrism to Euro-Racism. *Race and Class* 32(3):11–18.

Williams, Brackette F. 1989. A Class Act: Anthropology and the Race to Nation across Ethnic Terrain. *Annual Review of Anthropology* 18:401–444.

Worsley, Peter. 1984. *The Three Worlds: Culture and World Development.* Chicago: University of Chicago Press.

Yurgo, Frank. 1991. Egypt's Link to Greece Overstated, Misused. *Chronicle of Higher Education,* September 4.

PATRICIA ZAVELLA

Reflections on Diversity among Chicanas

Second-wave feminists have been attempting to create a scholarship and conduct research in ways that no longer "privilege" the concerns of white, middle-class, or heterosexual women, or take their experiences as the norm (di Leonardo 1991; Ginsburg and Tsing 1990; Morgen 1989). This agenda has often been born from struggle with those women seen as "other." Women-of-color theorists have argued that race, class, and gender—including sexuality—are experienced simultaneously, and to use only a gender analysis for understanding women's lived experience is reductionist and replicates the silencing and social oppression that women of color experience daily (Anzaldúa 1990; Davis 1981; hooks 1984; Hurtado 1989; Joseph 1981; Swerdlow and Lessinger 1983). The response by feminist theorists who see women's common biologically based experiences as the basis for the construction of theory has often been to include women's "many voices." Highly influenced by French feminist theory, this view sees that women from diverse class, ethnic, or racial groups have very different perspectives on so-called universal feminine experiences, and the project within feminist studies is to document, listen to, validate those voices. This viewpoint has produced somewhat of a quandary: on the one hand, we have an understanding that all women's experiences are highly complex and that there is variation among women on the basis of race, ethnicity, class, sexual preference, age, or abilities. Yet simply recognizing the richness of diversity can lead to an atheoretical pluralism where diversity seems overwhelming, and it is difficult to discern the bases of commonality and difference among women. Moreover, expanding the feminist canon to include other women can sometimes replicate stereotypes about internal similarities among the category of women being integrated. I believe we need to reflect on how women within a particular group vary from one another, and to research women's lives in ways that identify the sources of diversity without resorting to mechanistic conclusions that class, race, or gender alone gives rise to difference. That is, we should analyze how race, class, or gender are socially constructed yet not essentialize any of the categories of oppression (Sacks 1989).

Further, I believe we must begin our analysis with the historically specific structural conditions constraining women's experiences. We can then link these conditions to the varieties of ways in which women respond to and construct subjective representations of their experiences. This suggestion helps us to avoid the problematic assumption of much recent feminist scholarship: beginning with historical material conditions rather than with "experience" embeds "women's diversity" as a theoretical priority and frees us from the artifical task of deriving diversity from prior commonality. In a sense, then, feminists of color are challenging one of the basic assumptions in women's studies—the notion that feminist theory should be grounded in women's experience in which there are commonalities. Instead, we ask that the structure in which women's experiences are framed become the primary analytical locus, which may generate profound differences between white women and women of color, and among Chicanas or women of Mexican origin in particular.

The diversity among Chicanas can initially be seen by the terms of ethnic identification we have claimed for ourselves. When referring to ourselves within a white context, we often prefer more generic terms. like *Las Mujeres* or the combination *Chicana/Latina,* in opposition to *Hispanic,* which is often seen as inappropriate because of its conservative political connotations. When speaking among ourselves, we highlight and celebrate all of the nuances of identity—we are *Chicanas, Mexicanas, Mexican Americans, Spanish Americans, Tejanas, Hispanas, Mestizas, Indias,* or *Latinas*—and the terms of identification vary according to the context. This complexity of identification reflects the conundrum many Chicanas experience: on the one hand, together we are seen by others as a single social category, often Hispanic women. Yet the term *Hispanic,* imposed by the census bureau, is seen as inappropriate by many women who prefer to identify themselves in oppositional political terms. As Chicanas, we have common issues and experiences with other women of color in the United States and therefore often feel a strong sense of affinity with their struggles. On the other hand, we are a very diverse group of women, with different histories, regional settlement patterns, particular cultural practices, sexual preferences, and occasionally radically different political outlooks, and our solidarity as Chicanas can be undermined by these differences among us.

My purpose here is to contextualize the notion of diversity among Chicanas and sketch out a conceptual framework for making sense of the commonalities and diversity among us. My discussion will have two parts: in the first I concentrate on the structural commonalities among Chicanas, based on the subordination engendered by the intersection of race, class, and gender but different for particular groups of women; later, I discuss how we Chicanas have constructed our sense of selves in opposition to the many forms of subordination. We must also examine how Chicano culture is socially constructed in ways that are misogynist or homophobic, or that internalize racism and class prejudices.

I suggest that our understanding of difference among Chicanas will be enhanced through close attention to women's (and men's) social location within the social structure, that is, in looking at the social spaces created by the intersection of class, race, gender, and culture (Zavella 1991a). The term *social location* differs from and complements that of Renato Rosaldo's (1989) useful concept of "positioned subject," where the observer-writer-ethnographer is self-reflective of her own social status and takes responsibility for uncovering the power relations within the culture being studied—including her own participation within changing cultural processes. Rosaldo cautions us that cultural analyses by positioned subjects are always provisional, subject to revision by other positioned subjects who may be of a different racial status than those being studied. My use of social location also differs slightly from the notion of "crossing borders" suggested by Gloria Anzaldúa (1987), who emphasizes how Chicanas construct a sense of self, a liberating critical consciousness, in oppositional terms highly influenced by processes on both sides of the U.S.-Mexican border. Instead, I am emphasizing the dialectical process in which historical conditions, including cultural traditions, and the social construction of self occurs. That is, I am emphasizing the processes that constrain Chicanas' sense of self, the structures of oppression that make being a "positioned subject" or "crossing borders" problematic. I hope that this preliminary framework will help us to make sense of the racial identity of people of Mexican origin and will contextualize the sources of diversity of experience that global racial categories often obscure.

To begin formulating a framework on diversity among Chicanas, it is important to first deconstruct the stereotypic thinking that often comes to mind among outsiders. Stereotypes sometimes have a grain of truth but mask gross generalizations or ignorance of the diversity not only among but within different groups of women of color. Some of these stereotypes include the assumption that Chicanas all speak Spanish or that we have such a rich culture—when our culture has been repressed. Other assumptions that I've heard include that Chicanas have such loving, big families; in fact, like other groups, Chicanas experience familial breakdown or abuse toward women.

Probably one of the most insidious stereotypes regarding Chicanas is the notion that culture is determinant of behavior. Because Chicanas are racially distinct and have Spanish language as an ethnic signifier, we seem obviously culturally different from white North Americans. This often leads to the assumption that there is a coherent Chicano culture heritage: that the values, norms, customs, rituals, symbols, and material items (such as women's religious altars) form part of a "tradition" that all Chicanos are socialized into. Moreover, this thinking goes, Chicanos mechanistically base their behavior and decisions on these traditional norms. This stereotype was given life with Oscar Lewis's notion of a "culture of poverty" based on fieldwork with Puerto Rican and Mexican families, in which people were said to have a whole host of maladaptive cultural traits (Ybarra 1983). The equation of racial status and poverty conditions with culture has been critiqued for being static, ahistorical, and simplistic. More importantly, this view of culture as determinant is really a different version of blaming the victim, where Chicanas' own cultural heritage is seen as limiting their educational, social, or political aspirations.

It is unfortunate that this view has cropped up more recently in seemingly progressive thinking as well. Some researchers suggest that the official high rate of intact nuclear families among Mexican immigrants is an indication of "stable" families and "good family values," and they argue that, in contrast to poor Black Americans, family ties are all-important to Mexicans, teenage pregnancy is a source of opprobrium, and young men are pressured to marry and form nuclear households (Hayes-Bautista et al. 1992; Hurtado et al. 1992; Taub 1991; Testa and Krough 1990). The evidence is usually statements by Mexicans who agree that a couple *should* get married when the woman gets pregnant, or who state that family is very important to them. With this data, researchers conclude that stable behavior follows. It seems that Mexicans are becoming the new "model minority," and our so-called good values are contrasted with the supposed dysfunctional values of poor African Americans and others in poverty. Yet as feminist research shows so well, the "intact" Mexican nuclear family can range from the fiction of common-law marriages with "husbands" in name only (Del Castillo 1993), to women who are *solitas* in circumstances but not norms (Goodson-Lawes 1992), to women who can only migrate with male sponsorship because of discriminatory U.S. hiring practices (Chavira 1992). Moreover, Latinas sometimes migrate to the United States to *escape* dysfunctional families (Arguelles and Rivero 1993). Once again, the cultural model of "good, stable nuclear families" says more about conservative political ideology than the conditions in the United States and Latin America under which migrants live.

A way to move beyond stereotypic views and reconstruct how Chicanas have common experiences is through a historical perspective. History helps us to understand how particular stereotypes became hegemonic, and how Chicanas have become marginalized and invisible in the popular, political, and scholarly discourses. While I cannot go into historical detail here, I would like to sketch out a framework that helps us to understand the similarities among Chicanas, and helps clarify the sources of diversity among us, based on class, race, gender, and culture.

Some initial historical reorientations are important to point out: Spanish colonizers "discovered" America and the civilizations of indigenous peoples, and Spanish soldiers settled in what is now northern New Mexico in the early sixteenth century, long before the so-called original settlers landed on Plymouth Rock. The history of the Americas, then, is of Spanish—not English—origin. Secondly, the conquest and racial mixtures with indigenous peoples set in motion the "colonized" status of Chicanos today. An important conceptual point is that Chicanos did not enter the United States the same way that many white immigrant groups did. European immigrants were pushed out of their countries of origin for important economic and political reasons and then, depending on where they settled and the historical period, found more or less receptive communities in which to settle. As nonracialized peoples, Euro-Americans had more choice regarding the ethnic signifiers that were important to retain.

Chicanos, on the other hand, have been integrated into U.S. society through involuntary means, and internal class, racial, ethnic, and gender divisions within Spain (Guriérrez 1991) and then within the colonies have been reconstituted through industrial development (Almaguer 1994). Mexican women became U.S. citizens by default after the U.S.-Mexican war, where the border literally migrated to them—imposing a foreign language and sociolegal system. Through a variety of legal and informal mechanisms, Mexicans were displaced from their land and propelled into the bottom of the working class, disenfranchised and segregated into barrios, their language and customs denigrated or even outlawed (Barrera 1979; Camarillo 1979). Many of the mechanisms that institutionalized racism, sexism, and working-class status as Chicanos were incorporated into North American society continue today. This common historical legacy is a powerful basis of solidarity among Chicanas.

Attention to history, though it does point out the sources of common experiences, also begins our exploration of diversity among Chicanas. History helps us understand the regional settlement patterns of different groups of Chicanas, which were then replenished through waves of migration: historically, women of Mexican descent originally settled in south Texas, northern New Mexico, and California in the Southwest, and later migrant streams that began in the early twentieth century created settlements in the Midwest and Pacific Northwest coast. More recently Mexican migrants have established communities on the East Coast in New York City, Washington, D.C., or rural areas—so that Chicano communities are becoming more dispersed throughout the nation. Settlement and migration history also helps us to understand the intraethnic relations—both conflictual and cooperative—between groups of Chicanos. For example, in California researchers have found that Mexican immigrants who settled in that state in previous waves of migration have established economic "niches," in particular industries or occupations, and then felt threatened by compatriots who migrated more recently (Cornelius et al. 1982).

Closely related to settlement patterns is the notion of culture-region, a geographic and sociopolitical area where historical processes—including isolation, waves of industrialization, urbanization, and discrimination toward racialized others—have segregated racial/ethnic groups and enabled historical actors to construct particular terms of ethnic identification in opposition to the dominant society (Galarza 1972). The notion of culture-region helps highlight the particular racial mixtures that occurred—the mestizas from the unions of Spanish men and Indian women in the Southwest, the African and Spanish mixtures near the Caribbean—and helps us to understand the contours of cultural syncretism: women from the East Coast or Gulf region show Puerto Rican, Cuban, and African influences, whereas Chicanas from desert regions will have more indigenous influences. There are also regional differences regarding the preferred terms of ethnic identification among women—*Chicana* in California, *Mexican American* or *Mexicana* in Texas, *Spanish American* in New Mexico—although there is a good deal of mixing of terms as well (Anzaldúa 1987; Garcia 1981; Gutiérrez 1989; Keefe and Padilla 1987; Limón 1981; Metzgar 1974; Moraga 1983; Zavella 1993; Zinn 1981).

One implication of culture-region is that generation is important: whether women are of the first generation (that is, born in Mexico), of subsequent generations born in the United States, or recent immigrants has implications for language use, cultural knowledge, and the process of identification. A Chicana's generation affects whether she feels a sense of identification and solidarity with other Chicanas, whether she feels marginalized, or whether she feels as if she is more "American" than Chicana.

Beyond historical settlement patterns, this framework attends to important internal differences within Chicano populations. Class is clearly an important demarcation: the overwhelming majority of Chicanos are of working-class origins, although with the recent economic crisis in Mexico, a few more middle-class and professional women are migrating to the United States. These women often have higher median incomes and higher educational levels, in contrast to those women who have migrated from rural, underdeveloped areas of Mexico. The class status of Chicanas can take on insidious overtones: foreign-born Chicanas from elite, upper-class backgrounds clearly have very different life chances than those from the working class yet are often categorized as Hispanic and inflate the affirmative action statistics about the presence of underrepresented minorities. Class is often the source of tensions among Chicanas, coinciding with political disagreements.

Racial physical features are also important: whether women have fair or dark skin and hair; Indian, African, or European features; or some combination thereof bears upon how Chicanas are treated and how they reflect upon their racial/ethnic status. Although some change is occurring regarding the preferred body image, U.S. society still values images of women who are white—and blond in particular—and who have European features. Research shows that women who have dark skin, especially with indigenous features, face the worst treatment from society at large. Individuals within Chicano communities may reflect this devaluation, or even internalize it, so that physical features are often noted and evaluated: skin color in particular is commented on, with *las gueras* (light-skinned ones) receiving appreciation, while *las prietas* (dark-skinned ones) are devalued and admonished to stay out of the sunlight so they won't get darker. In contrast to white ethnic women, it is impossible for most Mexican women to "blend in" and opt out of their racial/ethnic status and pass for white. Thus we see examples of U.S. citizens being mistaken for undocumented immigrants and being deported because of the color of their skin.

Sexuality is also a significant demarcation of social location. Whether women establish lesbian, heterosexual, or bisexual relationships is central to their identity and experience. Within our heterosexist society, Chicana lesbians and bisexuals—particularly those of working-class origin—face extreme marginalization from both the dominant and Chicano society. Paraphrasing Cherríe Moraga (1983): being queer and of color is "as rude as women can get." Sexuality, then, forms the basis of, and identity in which, community building is necessary against physical assaults and for survival. Sexual preference has generated political disagreements and conflict among lesbian, bisexual, and heterosexual Chicanas, and some lesbians are creating what Emma Perez (1993) calls a lesbian "uninvited discourse" with a separate "*lengua y sitio*" (language and space).

These aspects of social location—class, gender, race/ethnicity, and sexual preference—all are indications of social inequality and reflect power relations in which Chicanas are often relatively powerless. Yet specifying women's social locations also means taking into consideration various ethnic or cultural attributes that create "borders" over which women cross in their daily lives. These attributes include nativity—whether Chicanas were born in the United States (and, if so, what generation) or in Mexico, and whether immigrants arrived as children and were socialized in the United States or received their education, socialization, and sense of identity in rural villages or urban centers of Mexico. Language use is critical and closely related to nativity. If Chicanas are born in the United States, particularly if they are reared in integrated communities, they are more likely to speak mainly English and without a Spanish accent, whereas Chicanas reared in Mexico or in segregated barrios in the United States are likely to be bilingual, predominantly Spanish speakers, or have heavy Spanish accents when speaking in English. Whether one was reared in the barrios or grew up isolated from other Chicanos has great implications for cultural knowledge and sense of self. Religion is also significant: the majority of Chicanas come from a Roman Catholic heritage in which religious rituals and practices are often the center of women's social activities and are forms of social control of women's sexuality. Finally, women's sexuality, in particular, but other activities as well are controlled through Chicano cultural values involving the polar opposities of macho male aggressive sexual license and passive female chastity.

To understand how culture has placed constraints on the experiences of Chicanas, we need to distinguish between "traditional culture"—cultural knowledge as ideology—and culture in process. Cultural ideologies, as Rosaldo (1989) points out, often are forms of social control that seem most brittle when under attack. When "culture" is evoked to remind recalcitrant women to be proprietous (for example, when working mothers are reminded of the importance of familism), Chicanos are orchestrating cultural ideology as cultural determinism (Pesquera 1986).

In contrast to a view of culture as determinant, scholars have formulated a view of Chicano culture that is much more fluid and is embedded in a U.S. historical context in which differential power relations between classes, Anglos and Chicanos, men and women, or heterosexuals and homosexuals are taken into consideration. This perspective also critiques the ways in which Chicano culture is exoticized and devalued. Further, this view sees culture as socially constructed by actors who are influenced by both "traditional" cultural norms and the audience of cultural "performances," so that culture is always interactive within particular situations (Paredes 1977). This perspective focuses on cultural variation and the nuances of culture in process, particularly in daily life by "ordinary" Chicanas. In other words, I am calling for a perspective that sees the dialectics of how the social structure and culture provide a context for the ways that Chicanas construct their identities. The implications are that ethnographic work should focus on particular subcultural groups and communities among Chicanos. Some of the more recent Chicano ethnographic work has had this focus—on lesbians and gay Chicanos who contest heterosexist traditions (Almaguer 1991), on the elderly of northern New Mexican villages who construct oppositional discourse (Briggs 1988), on gangs and lowriders in southern California who form alternative support systems (Vigil 1988), on high school youth in South Texas who resist authority (Foley 1990), on South Texas men who resist ethnographic characteristics (Limón 1989), or on middle-aged women workers in northern California who consider alternative work and family-based culture (Zavella 1987). Comparisons between Chicanos within these different social locations reveal important variations of experience. More ethnographies of various communities of Chicanas would heighten our sense of diversity.

I am suggesting that in addition to class, race, and sexual preference, "traditional" culture provides a context in which Chicanas are in positions or situations in relation to other women and men that allow greater or lesser autonomy. Further, these women strategize within this context to construct a sense of self, and they try to live their lives in opposition to these constraints. Although the limitations on Chicanas' lives can delineate "borders" by which women construct a sense of self, I am emphasizing that there are "locations" created by the intersection of class, race, gender, sexuality, and culture and that women sometimes cannot "cross" some "borders" that constrain their lives.

I believe that we should construct feminist studies that reflect the myriad of social locations among Chicanas, which specify relationships—both personal and structural—that sustain them. I believe that this is the starting point for understanding the social and cultural symbolic representations and consciousness that women express through literature, art, and daily activity.

It might be helpful to use my own experience to illustrate how culture-region and culture in process is integral to one's social location. I have been told repeatedly, "You're so different from other Mexicans"—a puzzling, objectifying idea, especially to a child. I am the fourth generation born in the United States in a working-class, predominantly English-speaking family. My cultural heritage is from the northern New Mexico culture-region, my family descended from peasant farmers who migrated from Tierra Amarilla, New Mexico, to Trujillo Creek in southern Colorado. My grandparents were coal miners and farmers. I remember that when I was a child my grandmother used to say we were "Spanish-American" (often used synonymously with "Hispano"), the term used in the northern New Mexico culture-region to distinguish Mexican Americans from Indians, whites, and Mexicans from Mexico. Although my parents' native language was Spanish, they were punished as children for speaking Spanish in school and eventually used mainly English, which became the language we learned at home. (Some of us eventually took Spanish classes and attempted to regain "our" language.) The Spanish language was all around us, but it was mainly the language of adult kin, who used it when speaking of things they wanted hidden from the children—unfortunately a common occurrence under conditions of language repression.

My father joined the U.S. Air Force to escape racism and lack of economic opportunities in Laredo, Texas, on the border between the United States and Mexico. An "air force brat," I was born on an air base in Tampa, Florida. My grandmother had by now relocated to the city of Colorado Springs, and her home became our base, but we made year-long forays to rural Maine and rural South Dakota (twice) before my family migrated to southern California. We were often one of a few Mexican families on a base, so I never lived in barrios. With many experiences of racism (particularly in schools, where I heard the refrain that I was so different from other Mexicans), I grew up feeling marginalized from whites and isolated from other Chicanos. Because we moved so much, I was often the new kid in school, and teachers assumed that because I was Mexican I would be a Spanish speaker and not perform well. My schooling, then, was in contesting the racist and sexist assumptions about my abilities, and I became a "scholarship girl" (Cuadráz 1992). I was often puzzled at being called a Mexican: although my racial features are clearly Mexican, I had never been to Mexico, nor did I know of any relatives who were living there. Yet my grandmother and mother are staunch Catholics, and part of my sense of being Chicana comes from chafing at the misogyny of Catholic rituals and doctrine.

I am part of the limited class mobility occurring among Chicanos: I am of the first generation that received a higher education, the only Ph.D. among my large extended family, the only writer. I was fortunate to take part in the Chicano movement and Chicana movement, which shaped my consciousness and identity as a Chicana feminist. My social location, then, of working-class, English-speaking Hispana of Catholic background, clearly demarcates my experiences from those of other Chicanas. My experiences in constructing culture in process (feminist parenting, for example) embody the contradictions generated from my now privileged social location.

If anything, the heterogeneity of Chicanas will only increase in the future. Stepped-up migration from Mexico and some class mobility means that class polarization will become more pronounced. More Chicanas are entering higher education and professional occupations; others—women from rural Central American and Latin American countries, often without documentation, are entering this country at the bottom margins of the social structure. In California, but also in other international settlement areas like Washington, D.C., New York City, or Chicago, Chicano communities are becoming niches within multiethnic neighborhoods, and Chicanos are forming their own businesses and organizations.

Let me conclude by returning to the notion of identity, which captures the heart of the problematic of understanding Chicanas. I have suggested that we pay attention to the history of particular groups of Chicanas, where they settled or migrated to, how their communities were formed, how there are key, structurally based differences among Chicanas. For each woman, this means understanding her social location structurally and culturally. Instead of lumping all Chicanas together into separate sections of a course on women, we might better ask, What purpose does it serve to categorize all of these very disparate groups? Whose interests get served? When is it appropriate to think of these women as Chicanas, and when it better to specify a particular regional form of identity?

Regarding curriculum development, I have found that "social location" is helpful for white and other students as well. In trying to develop feminist curricula to include Chicanas, we might think about when it is useful to make comparisons between women with different cultural backgrounds but in similar social locations. In a course on women and work, for example, we might contrast Chicana and Jewish working-class factory workers. At other times, our strategy might be to contrast women from very different social locations: the poetry and novels of an Alice Walker and Ana Castillo, both women who searched for their historic roots. More importantly, what identity does a particular Chicana claim, and why? It is obvious that we have much work before us in understanding diversity among all women, and in struggling to develop solidarity with women of different social locations. Yet it is exciting to envision a feminist studies in which women "on the margins" are demanding that the "center" be reconstituted.

Notes

This is a slightly revised version of an article originally published in *Frontiers, a Journal of Women's Studies* (1991b). Thanks to Micaela di Leonardo, Louise

Lamphere, and the anonymous reviewers of *Frontiers* for their helpful comments, as well as to Steven Gregory and Roger Sanjek for their helpful suggestions for revisions on this version.

References

Alarcon, Norma, Ana Castillo, and Cherrie Moraga, eds. 1989. *The Sexuality of Latinas,* Special issue of *Third Woman* 4.

Almaguer, Thomas. 1991. The Cartography of Homosexual Desire and Identity among Chicano Men. *Differences* 3 (2): 75–100.

———. 1994. *Racial Fault Lines: The Historical Origins of White Supremacy in California.* Berkeley and Los Angeles: University of California Press.

Anzaldua, Gloria. 1987. *Borderlands/La Frontera: The New Mestiza.* San Francisco: Spinsters/Aunt Lute.

———. 1990. *Making Face, Making Soul: Haciendo Caras.* San Francisco: Aunt Lute.

Arguelles, Lourdes, and Anne Rivero. 1993. Violence, Migration, and Compassionate Practice: Conversations with Some Women We Think We Know. *Urban Anthropology* 22 (3–4): 259–275.

Barrera, Marrio. 1979. *Race and Class in the Southwest: A Theory of Racial Inequality.* Notre Dame, Ind.: University of Notre Dame Press.

Briggs, Charles L. 1988. *Competence in Performance: The Creativity of Tradition in Mexicano Verbal Art.* Philadelphia: University of Pennsylvania Press.

Camarillo, Albert. 1979. *Chicanos in a Changing Society.* Cambridge, Mass.: Harvard University Press

Chavira, Alicia. 1992. The Female Undocumented Experience. Paper presented at the American Anthropological Association Annual Meetings, San Francisco.

Cornelius, Wayne A., Richard Mines, Leo R. Chavez, and Jorge G. Castro. 1982. *Mexican Immigrants in Southern California: A Summary of Current Knowledge.* San Diego: University of California, Center for U.S.—Mexican Studies, Research Report Series, No. 40.

Cuadráz, Gloria Holguin. 1992. Experiences of Multiple Marginality: A Case Study of Chicana "Scholarship Women." *Journal of the Association of Mexican American Educators,* 31–43.

Davis, Angela. 1981. *Women, Race, and Class.* New York: Random House.

Del Castillo, Adelaida. 1993. Negotiating the Structure and Cultural Meaning of Sex/Gender Systems: Mexico City's Women-Centered Domestic Groups. *Urban Anthropolgy* 22 (3–4): 237–258.

di Leonardo, Micaela, ed. 1991. *Gender at the Crossroads of Knowledge: Feminist Anthropology in the Postmodern Era.* Berkeley and Los Angeles: University of California Press.

Foley, Douglas E. 1990. *Learning Capitalist Culture, Deep in the Heart of Tejas.* Philadelphia: University of Pennsylvania Press.

Galarza, Ernesto. 1972. Mexicans in the Southwest: A Culture in Process. In

Plural Society in the Southwest, ed. Edward H. Spicer and Raymond H. Thompson, 261–297. New York: Interbook.

Garcia, John A. 1981. "Yo Soy Mexicano . . . Self-Identity and Sociodemographic Correlates." *Social Science Quarterly* 62 (1): 88–98.

Ginsburg, Faye, and Anna Lowenhaupt Tsing, eds. 1990. *Uncertain Terms: Negotiating Gender in American Culture.* Boston: Beacon.

Goodson-Lawes, Julie. 1992. Changes in Feminine Authority and Control with Migration: The Case of One Family from Mexico. *Urban Anthropology* 22 (3–4): 277–297.

Gutiérrez, Ramón A. 1989. Ethnic and Class Boundaries in America's Hispanic Past. In *Intersections: Studies of Ethnicity, Gender, and Inequality,* ed. Sucheng Chang, 47–63. Lewiston, N.Y.: Mellen.

———. 1991. *When Jesus Came the Corn Mothers Went Away: Marriage, Sexuality, and Power in New Mexico, 1500–1846.* Stanford: Stanford University Press.

Hayes-Bautista, David E., Aída Hurtado, R. Burciaga Valdez, and Anthony C. R. Hernández. 1992. *No Longer a Minority: Latinos and Social Policy in California.* Los Angeles: UCLA, Chicano Studies Research Center.

hooks, bell. 1984. *Feminist Theory from Margin to Center.* Boston: South End.

Hurtado, Aída 1989. Relating to Privilege: Seduction and Rejection in the Subordination of White Women and Women of Color. *Signs* 14: 833–855.

Hurtado, Aída, David E. Hayes-Bautista, R. Burciaga Valdez, and Anthony C. R. Hernández. 1992. *Redefining California: Latino Social Engagement in a Multicultural Society.* Los Angeles: UCLA, Chicano Studies Research Center.

Joseph, Gloria. 1981. The Incomplete Ménage à Trois: Marxism, Feminism, and Racism. In *Women and Revolution: A Discussion of the Unhappy Marriage of Marxism and Feminism,* ed. Lydia Sargent, 91–108. Boston: South End.

Keefe, Susan E., and Amado M. Padilla. 1987. *Chicano Ethnicity.* Albuquerque: University of New Mexico Press.

Limón, Jose E. 1981. The Folk Performance of Chicano and the Cultural Limits of Political Ideology. In *"And Other Neighborly Names": Social Process and Cultural Image in Texas Folklore,* ed. Richard Bauman and Roger D. Abrahams, 197–225. Austin: University of Texas Press.

———. 1989. *Carne, Carnales,* and the Carnivalesque: Bakhtinian Batos, Disorder, and Narrative Discourses. *American Ethnologist* 16: 471–486.

Metzgar, Joseph V. 1974. The Ethnic Sensitivity of Spanish New Mexicans: A Survey and Analysis. *New Mexico Historical Review* 49: 49–73.

Moraga, Cherríe. 1983. *Loving in the War Years, lo que nunca paso por sus labios.* Boston: South End.

Morgen, Sandra, ed. 1989. *Gender and Anthropology: Critical Reviews for Research and Teaching.* Washington, D.C.: American Anthropological Association.

Paredes, Americo. 1977. On Ethnographic Work among Minorities: A Folklorist's Perspective. *New Scholar* 6(1/2):1–32.

Perez, Emma, 1993. Speaking from the Margin: Uninvited Discourse on Sexuality and Power. In *Building with Our Hands: Issues in Chicana Studies,* ed. Beatriz Pesquera and Adela De La Torre, 57–71. Berkeley and Los Angeles: University of California Press.

Pesquera, Beatriz. 1986. Work and Family: A Comparative Analysis of Professional, Clerical, and Blue-Collar Chicana Workers. Ph.D. diss., University of California, Berkeley.

Ramos, Juanita, ed. 1987. *Companeras: Latina Lesbians (An Anthology).* New York: Latina Lesbian History Project.

Rosaldo, Renato. 1989. *Culture and Truth: The Remaking of Social Analysis.* Boston: Beacon.

Sacks, Karen Brodkin. 1989. Toward a Unified Theory of Class, Race, and Gender. *American Ethnologist* 16:534–550.

Swerdlow, Amy, and Hanna Lessinger, eds. 1983. *Class, Race, and Sex: The Dynamics of Control.* Boston: Hall.

Taub, Richard. 1991. Differing Conceptions of Honor and Orientations toward Work and Marriage among Low-Income African Americans and Mexican-Americans. Paper presented at the Chicago Urban Poverty and Family Life Conference, University of Chicago, 1991.

Testa, Mark, and Marilyn Krough. 1990. Nonmarital Parenthood, Male Joblessness, and AFDC Participation in Inner-City Chicago. Final report prepared for the Assistant Secretary for Planning and Evaluation, Department of Health and Human Services.

Vigil, Diego. 1988. *Barrio Gangs: Street Life and Identity in Southern California.* Austin: University of Texas Press.

Ybarra, Leonarda. 1983. Empirical and Theoretical Developments in Studies of the Chicano Family. In *The State of Chicano Research on Family, Labor, and Migration: Proceedings of the First Stanford Symposium on Chicano Research and Public Policy,* ed. Armando Valdez, Albert Camarillo, and Tomas Almaguer, 91–110. Stanford: Stanford Center for Chicano Research.

Zavella, Patricia. 1987. *Women's Work and Chicano Families: Cannery Workers of the Santa Clara Valley.* Ithaca, N.Y.: Cornell University Press.

———. 1991a. Mujeres in Factories: Race and Class Perspectives on Women, Work, and Family. In *Gender at the Crossroads of Knowledge: Feminist Anthropology in the Postmodern Era,* ed. Micaela di Leonardo, 312–336. Berkeley and Los Angeles: University of California Press.

———. 1991b. Reflections on Diversity among Chicanas. *Frontiers* 12(2): 73–85.

———. 1993. Feminist Insider Dilemmas: Constructing Identity with Chicana Informants. *Frontiers* (special issue on feminist ethnography) 13(3): 53–76.

Zinn, Maxine Baca. 1981. Gender and Ethnic Identity among Chicanas. *Frontiers* 5(2): 18–24.

RENATO ROSALDO

Race and Other Inequalities: The Borderlands in Arturo Islas's *Migrant Souls*

When decision-making rooms suddenly include people who represent gender and racial diversity, people who once worked in those rooms with an exclusive sense of entitlement can feel uncomfortable. In contexts where long-term inhabitants of decision-making rooms once voiced opinions unchallenged, they now find that the new people in the room talk back. Professors, for example, find that new students do not laugh at their old jokes. Where certain individuals once enjoyed a monopoly on authority, they now show symptoms of relative deprivation because they have been asked to share authority. Even when not recognized as such, privilege quickly becomes so habit forming, rather like a vested right, that it is (mis)recognized as pure merit or as the natural order of things, which must be passionately defended.

One symptom of the present moment's lawlike tendency for white authority to defend a monopoly status has been the resurgence, across the political spectrum, of the dream of a unified culture. A number of neoconservative writers have claimed the "Great Books" as "our heritage," the *unum* that will pull together the *pluribus* of the United States. Diversity of color and creed, they claim, will dissolve in an educational solvent that teaches all citizens to honor, as this nation's common culture, a shelf of "Great Books" from Plato through Shakespeare to Tolstoy. In the name of universal values and high culture, women and people of color have no place on this list.

One can only wonder, however, that in the United States there has been no groundswell of popular opposition to the frequent exclusion of U.S. authors from the "Great Books" list. Literary theorist Mary Louise Pratt (N.d.) is probably right in arguing that in the United States the decolonization of culture has lagged far behind that of politics and economics. Is this nation condemned to believe that the world's most significant culture happened back then and over there (in ancient Athens and western Europe), but that the here and now is a cultural wasteland?

Certain centrist authors have spoken about the dangers of divisive multiculturalism and the need to restore the liberal consensus that purportedly once governed the United States. Such admonitions seem oblivious to viewpoints other than those of their speakers. Can one empower people without consulting them, let alone without recognizing that they can speak for themselves? The liberal consensus, such as it was, failed to empower members of racialized minorities, even as it claimed to look after "their" interests. From this perspective, the old liberal consensus appears to be part of the problem, not part of the solution. Its consensus marginalized people of color who now insist on speaking for ourselves.

Certain leftist writers have argued that the restoration of the concept of *class,* a term that unites all movements, will combat the present-day fragmentation into interest groups and identity politics. For better and for worse, they seem to forget that old-style class politics often was fraught with sectarian divisions. Such conflicts were not born today or even yesterday. Nor will they end tomorrow. Arguably, and more to the point, strict class analysis tacitly endorses an identity politics whose central figure is the working-class white male. How will such an exclusive class politics mobilize groups concerned both with class *and* with such other sources of subordination as white supremacy, misogyny, and homophobia? If the vanguard group combatting white supremacy is all white, it seems to have a practice-what-you-preach problem.

Recurrent dreams of a common culture, whether from the Left, Right, or Center, often betray the perhaps unconscious wish to become the CEO or manager of the new consensus. One must ask by whom, and for whom, the new consensus has been drawn. Who was and who was not in the decision-making room when the new consensus was reached?

Issues at the level of institutional politics derive in certain respects from those of the nation-state that has so long attempted to create a bounded internally homogeneous space (Anderson 1983; Fox 1990; Gilroy 1987; Handler 1985). Within the national space, equality among citizens putatively derives from their sameness with respect to such attributes as language, culture, and race. The classic late-nineteenth-century model tacitly assumes that the macrocosm of the national community is mirrored in the microcosm of the individual monolingual monocultural citizen.

Although the nation-state emphasizes its capacity to enfranchise certain citizens, it maintains a discreet silence about how it simultaneously disenfranchises others. Think of the popular slogan of the French Revolution: liberty, equality, fraternity. Who was not included in the national fraternity? Women, for beginners, and, in the United States, non whites and non–property holders (Landes 1988). The late-eighteenth-century egalitarian fraternity probably excluded more people than it included. Although the scope of formal citizenship has expanded, informal matters (often addressed along the spectrum from full to second-class citizenship) remain unresolved.

Issues of enfranchisement have special resonance in the United States, where the Constitution's exclusions set in motion movements for women's suffrage, the abolition of slavery, and civil rights. The long-term goal of movements for social justice has been the full enfranchisement of all the citizenry, particularly in relation to certain social identities that have suffered systemic marginalization and exclusion (Hall and Held 1990; Rosaldo 1994).

In my view, the national contract in the United States is now in a process of renegotiation, with the eventual outcome still uncertain. Will the concept of rights be expanded to include new identities over the course of the current crisis of the national community? Can one uncouple the historically forged link between equality and sameness and thereby find equality and solidarity, rather than threatening divisiveness, in social differences?

In the context of national debates about diversity, consider the ideological concept of race. By ideological I mean that racial characterizations lack empirical validity as descriptions of what X-group is really like, but that they can be a powerful objective social force because people often behave, whether consciously or not, as if such characterizations were true. Anthropologists have often made similar arguments, for example, about witchcraft. Witchcraft gossip or killings of alleged witches can be studied as powerful social forces, whether or not the analyst gives credence to local claims of witchcraft's supernatural potency.

Ideologically speaking, race functions in contexts of domination by one categorical sameness group over another as if it were a border, a policed divide separating two countries. At the same time, *race* is a complex term that appears different from relatively subordinate positions than it does from relatively dominant ones. In considering the dynamics of race from both dominant and subordinate positions I have found enlightening a 1990 work called *Migrant Souls* by the late Chicano novelist Arturo Islas, who died of AIDS on February 15, 1991. Set in Del Sapo, Texas (Del Sapo, "from the toad," is a playful anagram of El Paso), the novel breaks a taboo and addresses matters we, as Chicanos, all know but don't talk about. It speaks to the dynamics of racial differentiation within the Chicano community as well as the categorical divide separating Chicanos and Anglos.

My purpose in this essay is twofold: first, to provide an alternative reading of the text, because most reviewers have failed to notice either the novel's pervasive comic spirit or its exploration of the dynamics of race in Chicano communities; second, to illustrate how, in the absence of other data, the novel can serve as a source of evidence for thinking conceptually about how race works among certain Chicanos. For example, I am developing initial formulations from the text in an ethnographic research project on Latinos in San José, California (Rosaldo et al.: n.d.). Imaginative literature thus becomes the stimulus for model building in social analysis.

In making explicit what is presented richly but obliquely in Islas's novel, I read selected passages of *Migrant Souls* against a dominant North American notion of race that anchors racial identity in biology or in physical appearance. In the dominant version, one that holds social analysts in its grip even as it is the object of critical thought, race is written definitively, once and for all, on the skin, and it is a binary, as in black versus white or Chicano versus Anglo. The binary opposition does double duty: it elevates one disparate group, whose members are ideologically united in their whiteness, and subordinates another disparate group, whose members ideologically united in their blackness, brownness, or whatever. Each group is treated as if it were a color-coded species rather than, as it actually is, one more member of the human species. I argue here that social analysis must take into account, in local and specific contexts, a number of competing dominant and subordinate norms to which people adhere in varying degrees.

Race in *Migrant Souls*

Dominant Anglo white supremacy perhaps becomes most evident in Arturo Islas's *Migrant Souls* when the narrator describes the context of domination in which crossing the racial border becomes a sign less of its premeability than of its status as a policed divide separating Anglos and Mexicans: "Crossovers from one group to another were noticed and talked about later, for each race guarded its own and had been taught to fear the consequences of mixing cultures. An undeclared borderline existed between Mexicans and Anglos that only a few dared to cross in the name of love" (67–68). Aside from the occasional courtship and marriage, the line between Mexicans and Anglos appears hard and fast. In the most encompassing context of domination, the two races ideologically comprise distinct monolithic worlds, each bent on maintaining its boundaries in a manner not accidently reminiscent of a nation-state determined to maintain an equality that derives from a condition of purity—that is, linguistic, cultural, and racial sameness (Williams 1989).

Passing from the lower-status Chicano world into the higher-status Anglo, one can never be easy. One character in Islas's novel, Ricardo, tried to assimilate and, as the narrator says, "brought up his children to ignore their Mexican heritage and to live according to the myths of North America" (204). His hopes for the next generation were conditioned by Anglo efforts to keep Mexicans in their place. "Ricardo's dream was to be a respected member of the middle class on the north side of the river. He was determined to see his children enjoy lives free from the prejudice against Mexican Americans who rose too high above their place in the second largest state of the Union" (202). Suffering his family's contempt as a result of his rejection of their heritage, Ricardo appears determined to use social mobility and economic success in what he judges to be the probably vain hope of liberating his children from the social effects of prejudice. Even as he changes his name from Ricardo to Richard to Dick, his dilemma reveals the coercive nature of the racial border he can only ambiguously cross.

It may clarify matters to say that Chicano racial dynamics are pervasively conditioned relative to, rather than entirely determined by dominant Anglo white supremacy. The conditioning force of white supremacy becomes evident throughout Islas's novel in depictions of housing segregation, the exploitation of labor, the glass ceiling on job advancement, and schooling that renders Chicanos invisible and seemingly incompetent. Speaking of a woman named Eduviges, for example, the narrator notes: "For the most part, Mexican Americans like her and her children were ignored or exploited. When they were educated into the lower middle class, their school lessons contained no mention of their heritage or contributions to history. Those in the working class remained desperate and poor despite their citizenship" (43). The combination of poverty, exploitation, and miseducation gives a justifiably bleak sense to Chicano life chances in the novel. Subordination by race is pervasive and systemic.

Although in *Migrant Souls* cultural borders can become sites of transculturation and creative play, the literal border exists as an absolute policed divide between two nations. The separation is defended through state violence, inflicted literally by the border patrol and more figuratively by stories Chicano adults tell their children. "The Angel children were brought up on as many deportation stories as fairy tales and family legends. The latest border incident had been the discovery of twenty-one young Mexican males who had been left to asphyxiate in an airtight boxcar on their way to pick cotton in the lower Río Grande Valley" (23). The policed dividing line that is the border and the pervasive anxiety about deportation come to stand for the harsh relations of dominance and subordination between Anglos and Mexicans.

An analysis of the dynamics of race in *Migrant Souls* could easily become earnest and utterly miss the novel's comic spirit and its use of irony in revealing the complexity of racialized dominance and subordination. The nature and impact of white supremacy become vivid through comic narratives of border crossings, weddings, and holiday meals. In 1947, for example, Eduviges precipitates a border crossing by deciding to prepare her daughters an Anglo-style Thanksgiving meal, complete with turkey. The family's efforts to follow North American customs ironically lead them to cross into Mexico and buy a turkey to smuggle back to their home in the United States. They form a two-vehicle caravan, Sancho leading in a pick-up with his daughter Josie in the cab and her sister Serena seated in back on the turkey's crate; his wife Eduviges follows with their eldest daughter, Ofelia. On their way to the border, the bridge over the Río Grande, Sancho and Josie engage in an extended and humorously presented conversation about the use and abuse of the term *alien.*

> On the way to the bridge, Josie made the mistake of asking her father if they were aliens. Sancho put his foot on the brake so hard that Eduviges almost rear-ended the truck. He looked at Josie very hard and said, "I do not want to hear you use that word in my presence again. About anybody. We are not aliens. We are American citizens of Mexican heritage. We are proud of both countries and have never and will never be that word you just said to me."
>
> "Well," Josie said. Sancho knew she was not afraid of him. He pulled the truck away from the shoulder and signaled for his wife to continue following them. "That's what they call Mexican people in all the newspapers. And Kathy Jarvis at school told me real snotty at recess yesterday that we were nothing but a bunch of resident aliens."
>
> After making sure Eduviges was right behind them, Sancho said in a calmer serious tone, "Josie, I'm warning you. I do not want to hear those words again. Do you understand me?"
>
> "I'm only telling you what Kathy told me. What did she mean? Is she right?"
>
> "Kathy Jarvis is an ignorant little brat. The next time she tells you that, you tell her that Mexican and Indian people were in this part of the country long before any *gringos,* Europeans (he said 'Yurrup-beans') or anyone else decided it was theirs. That should shut her up. If it doesn't, tell her those words are used by people who think Mexicans are not human beings. That goes for the newspapers, too. They don't think anyone is human." She watched him look straight ahead, then in the rearview mirror, then at her as he spoke.
>
> "Don't you see, Josie. When people call Mexicans those words, it makes it easier for them to deport or kill them. Aliens come from outer space." He paused. "Sort of like your mother's family, the blessed Angels, who think they come from heaven. Don't tell her I said that" (29–30).

When the family feels in grave danger during this border crossing, their comic conversation comments obliquely on the risk they run even as they speak. For all this humor, the passage makes it clear that the U.S.-Mexico border, not unlike that between Anglos and Chicanos, comprises a site of state violence and personal vulnerability.

Further complexities concerning the definition of race in Anglo-Mexican relations become apparent when one steps outside the confines of the novel. Precisely what will count as race and racism in vernacular usage cannot be readily predicted, for this is a matter of socially varying dynamics of race and not cultural window dressing. In an interview conducted as part of an ongoing project on cultural citizenship in San José, for example, one man described an incident that happened to him the first time he worked in the United States. A contract laborer during World War II, he was spat upon by a trainload of G.I.s as he laid rails. Yet he described the incident not in the idiom of race but in that of a lack of *respeto*. For him, respect and social humiliation emerged paradigmatically from the social relations between workers and foremen on haciendas. Compliance and resistance revolved around such gestures as how high one should lift one's hat or how loudly one should speak to the foreman. Rather than make assumptions about what constitutes race and racism, studies of racial dynamics should explore and specify the divergent intersubjective worlds inhabited by the Mexican laborer and the Anglo G.I.s.

Returning to Islas's novel, the bifurcated vision of Anglos versus Mexicans, each striving for racial and cultural purity, does not exhaust the semiotics and politics of race. Nor does its dichotomy of domination, Anglo over Chicano, even acknowledge the presence of mestizo notions of race in the text.

The novel's opening sentence is: "In their mother's eyes, Josie Salazar knew, she and her sister Serena were more like the Indians than the Spanish ladies they were brought up to be" (3). This is a curious sentence. Although Indian and Spanish are racial categories, they appear to be determined not only by the seemingly dichotomous choice between heredity (whether biological race or phenotype) and environment (socialization), but also by a third factor. In order to register its presence without defining it prematurely, let us call the third factor "something more." In opposing Spanish and Indian, the narrator conceives them along a continuum differentiated by degrees (more and less) rather than as a dichotomous opposition (either/or). The two sisters can be more like one racially encoded heritage than the other and yet they can partake of both. Such, one supposes, is the nature of mulatto or mestizo notions of race.

The nature of the "something more" and the most succinct challenge to the phenotypical view of race is voiced by Josie's mother who, speaking in exasperation, scolds her daughter. "She's simply acting like an Indian, that's all," their mother said. "Everyone knows they don't talk and can't answer politely when someone asks them a question" (5). Far from the genetic fatality of being Indian, race in this passage becomes a form of conduct. Such behavior usually is encoded by parents or other adults with Spanish pretensions who reprimand children for failing to conform to the norms of a distinctive set of religious convictions and class aspirations.

It probably goes without saying that the categories *Spanish* and *Indian* refer not to existing Spaniards or Native Americans but to in-group canons of prestige based on codes of conduct complexly related to forms of religiosity, assertions of aristocratic heritage, affirmation of linguistic purity, and claims to middle-class status. "Serena, get that braid out of your mouth," her mother admonishes. "Do you want to be taken for an Indian?" Or, "Josie, how many times do I have to tell you that a young lady does not cross her legs like an Indian?" (3). Indian demeanor in the novel consists of putting a braid in one's mouth, not talking, having stringy hair, not answering questions politely, crossing one's legs indecently, being late, and wearing loud or immodest dress. Such behavior is regarded as Indian, that is, rustic and uncouth, rather than Spanish, that is, polite and refined. Being Indian thus derives as much from behavior as from phenotype.

Such an analysis must be located, however, in relation to the position of the speaker. It derives not from the culture in general, but from a particular putatively high-status category of person, *la gente decente* (decent people). Late in the novel the narrator describes gente decente (or at any rate their class aspirations, though probably not their socioeconomic reality): "Manuel and Ricardo knew that the phrase 'decent people' meant middle-class Catholics" (201). Ascent into the category of decent people in the novel, one should add, often involves the deliberate concealment of personal history and past identity. Concerted efforts to pass (one passes up, not down) reveal both the existence of a social boundary and personal insecurities about a lifetime of negotiating which side of the line one stands on. Even racial identities can be multiple, unstable, and painfully contested.

The novel describes the construction of racial status even for the seemingly most secure, the male bearers of the Angel family name, in ways that derive more from culture than from phenotype. The family myth long ago elevated a venerated senior male, Jesús Angel, into being more Spanish than Indian in heritage. And then, by a few short steps of mythic revisionism, his ancestors were said to have reached Mexico in the sixteenth century. "And," the narrator says, "the legend continued, if his ancestors had not been in the army of *conquistadores*, they certainly had sailed in shortly thereafter" (9). The invention of family tradition thus canonizes the founding family patriarch.

Jesús Angel's wife rose through marriage and baptism to her elevated status as a person of Spanish descent, an Angel (a bilingual pun on the word *angel* in English): "The girls' only surviving grandparent—Encarnación Olmeca, or Mama Chona as she instructed them to call her—may have had the Indian origins her maiden name suggested, but she had married Jesús Angel. By this act, as well as by her baptism into the Church of Rome, Mama Chona felt herself and her children to have been elevated into civilization for all time" (8). Marriage, the gift of the Angel family name, and religious devotion eventually transform Mama Chona, who probably was once more Indian than Spanish, into the reigning matriarch who frequently exhorts her descendants to follow (sacred) Angel family norms.

Mama Chona's daughter Eduviges once was "a small child with dark eyes, a prominent brow, and cheekbones she learned to powder later on in life so that she might appear as light-skinned as her sisters Jesús María and Eufemia María" (36). Shc alters her phenotype daily, or at any rate she powders it every morning, because she has inherited the racialized class and religious aspirations of her family, the Angels, who epitomize Spanish religious, class, and racial pretensions of socially elevated purity. They set the standards for Eduviges and her eldest daughter, Ofelia; they also set the standards with which her two younger daughters, Josie and Serena, fail to conform. A range of strategies, from powdering one's cheeks through intermarriage and baptism to rewriting the past, appear to be the price of admission into the sometimes unstable and contested category of gente decente.

The world of *Migrant Souls* is governed by multiple and competing norms. By no means everyone directs their energies toward the same official version of status mobility. The official version imagines that dominant social norms act as a magnet and pull everyone upward. They appear to have a monopoly status that obliterates all other norms. Contrary to many theories that view social norms only from a top-down perspective, however, not everyone wants to assimilate. The goal of becoming gente decente, whether Spanish in conception or Anglo in aspiration, fails to move a number of characters in the novel. The refusal to conform to Spanish or Anglo norms of status mobility can be viewed not only, from a high-status vantage point, as a failure to achieve, but also, from a putatively lower-status position, as a positive effort to pursue alternative norms. Sancho Salazar, the father of Josie and Serena, for example, loves to hunt and fish in Mexico where, as the narrator says, "his Indian blood came to life and made him feel at home with the land and sky" (4). Described in positive terms, rather than in the negative terms of Angel family values, the two sisters and their father enjoy a yearning for Indian norms of behavior.

The alternate norms entail race not in isolation, but as it interacts with other dimensions of inequality and identity, such as religion, gender, and sexual orientation. For example, Josie, whose behavior so often is coded as Indian, violates gender and status expectations by returning to Del Sapo as a divorced woman with two daughters. Her sister, Serena, who also appears Indian, loves and lives with another woman. Their cousin Miguel Chico was once one of Mama Chona's favorites (that is, he was regarded as Spanish when he was a child), but he becomes socially defined as more Indian in adulthood when it becomes evident to others that he is a man who loves men. Family members know about the sexual orientation of their gay and lesbian kin, but, following the code of the public secret, they rarely speak about such matters. Miguel Chico shows, however, that being gay, often recoded as being Indian in Del Sapo, is a game that those subordinated by the local official pecking order can knowingly play back. He deliberately delays his arrival for Christmas dinner by taking his cousin Josie and her daughters to a sleazy strip joint: "It is our duty to be late," Miguel Chico said. "The Angels expect us to be rude and we mustn't let them down. It's all part of the ceremony" (206). Through his excessive conformity, by seeming to live up to (or, rather, down to) the expectations of his gente decente cousins, Miguel Chico flaunts their norms and actively asserts his own.

In its own self-conception, the Angel family sits in judgment on its less-than-respectable ("sinning") members, Miguel Chico and Josie, but appears oblivious to how severely it is judged in turn. Miguel Chico sees the gente decente of the Angel family as small-minded, uptight, and pathetic. His canons of pride and respect are at least as fierce and demanding as theirs.

In recognizing the presence of alternative norms one must not be too celebratory. Coercive dominant norms have the capacity to punish the disobedient. Miguel Chico drinks far too much, and his pride is often self-destructive; his lesbian cousin, Serena, pays the price of her sexuality and must keep up appearances by attending mass daily; Josie lives with the locally costly stigma of being a divorced woman. Within the sphere of Spanish norms under Anglo domination, Mama Chona's only success story is bittersweet. She raised her daughter's illegitimate son, Ricardo, as if he were her own son. Yet she, the matriarch who insists on Spanish-language purity, lives with the pain of knowing that her adopted son rejects her heritage and achieves linguistic purity by having his children speak, not Spanish, but English only. Even in insisting on following alternative norms, subordinated people suffer as they contend with the coercive force of dominant norms.

On Being in the Same Room

In attempting to enfranchise all citizens, being in the same room certainly helps, but it seems unlikely to erase ideologically dichotomizing dynamics of race that divide the world into a dominant monolithic group and a subordinate monolithic group. Nor will more subtle mestizo rankings, with codes of conduct socially interpreted as racial categories and the recoding of one basis of inequality as if it were another, evaporate in such rooms. Once people get in the same room, complex racial dynamics of dominance and subordination can determine matters feminist theorists have long taken into account, such as who speaks more, who interrupts whom, and who listens to whom. The politics of speech and everyday interactions require an exploration of the implications of doing a social analysis of race as a complex category that varies with other sources of inequality and produces at times contested and unstable hierarchical relations.

One immediate implication for the politics of being in the same room is that it will not do for people in relatively dominant positions to embark on processes of democratic inclusion by self-righteously engaging in self-criticism. People speaking from positions of privilege often live in socially determined ignorance of how the world looks, feels, and is lived from subordinate positions. Thus, challenging white supremacy and working to change related hierarchical relations that do so much damage in everyday life requires that people in positions of relative privilege behave not unlike ethnographers and listen attentively in order to better apprehend subordinated people's aspirations and grievances.

Social analysts and other relatively empowered people must recognize that relatively subordinated people's apparent failure to conform to dominant norms may result from their desire to follow other norms rather than from moral turpitude. Chicanos need not be viewed, for example, as failed Anglos. The code of race may shape and in turn be shaped by other forms of inequality, such as caste, class, religion, gender, and sexual orientation. Thus when it becomes evident that Miguel Chico is gay, homophobia inhibits talk about sexual orientation and recodes his homosexuality as his becoming more Indian and less Spanish than he was as a child. By the end of *Migrant Souls,* being more or less Spanish, Indian, or Anglo involves not a simple dichotomy (either brown *or* white) written once and for all on the skin, but a painful adjudication of phenotype, behavior, class, religion, being divorced, being gay, and being lesbian.

Read as social analysis, the novel presents evidence of variegated Chicano efforts to survive, both under white supremacy and within the mestizo relative ranking of being more Spanish or more Indian, without having to give up being who one is. The characters face pressures to become decent people, both Anglo and Spanish (itself, in this complex social space, often a putatively Spanish-style racially motivated denial of Indian heritage and at the same time a determined antiassimilationist refusal to become Anglo). Some people attempt to rise along the official social scale while others navigate other trajectories with compromises and resistance born of a conviction that, if the price of admission to relatively high-status rooms is that one's identity must be left at the door, they will refuse to enter and will struggle to create other spaces within which to survive and perhaps someday thrive.

When people declare that a consensus emerged from the decision-making room, whether now or in the past, whether from the Right, Left, or Center, one should remember to ask: Who was in the room when the consensus was reached? And who spoke, and who was listened to? And who is the "we" in whose name the consensus was reached? When people invoke the happy dream of a unified culture (as opposed to "divisive multiculturalism"), one should ask: Who is excluded from or marginalized by such Edenic visions of the past or utopian visions of the future?

When social analysts speak of national character, whether invoking individualism versus community or belonging in everyday life settings, Chicanos, among others, cannot help but notice that we are not in the picture. Who does belong in America? The politics of inclusion and full citizenship have long animated dissident traditions of struggle in the United States. Processes of change, especially around the enfranchisement of identities based on class, race, gender, and sexual orientation, are certain to cause short-run discomfort for the relatively privileged, but one should keep in mind that in the long run the nation's ideals of democratic inclusion hang in the balance.

References

Anderson, Benedict. 1983. *Imagined Communities: Reflections on the Origin and Spread of Nationalism*. London: Verso.

Fox, Richard G., ed. 1990. *National Ideologies and the Production of National*

Cultures. American Ethnological Society Monograph Series, No. 2. Washington, D.C.,: American Anthropological Association.

Gilroy, Paul. 1987. *There Ain't No Black in the Union Jack: The Cultural Politics of Race and Nation.* London: Unwin Hyman.

Hall, Stuart, and David Held. 1990. Citizens and Citizenship. In *New Times: The Changing Face of Politics in the 1990s,* ed. Stuart Hall and Martin Jacques, 173–188. London: Verso.

Handler, Richard. 1985. On Having a Culture: Nationalism and the Preservation of Quebec *Patrimoine.* In *Objects and Others: Essays on Museums and Material Culture,* ed. George W. Stocking, Jr., 191–217. Madison: University of Wisconsin Press.

Islas, Arturo. 1990. *Migrant Souls.* New York: Morrow.

Landes, Joan. 1988. *Women and the Public Sphere in the Age of the French Revolution.* Ithaca, N.Y.: Cornell University Press.

Pratt, Mary Louise. N.d. Decolonizing Cultural Theory. In *Borders/Diasporas,* ed. James Clifford and José Saldívar. Berkeley and Los Angeles: University of California Press. In press.

Rosaldo, Renato. 1994. Social Justice and the Crisis of National Communities. In *Colonial Discourse/Postcolonial Theory,* ed. Francis Barker, Peter Hulme, and Margaret Iversen, 239–252. Manchester, Eng.: Manchester University Press.

Rosaldo, Renato, William Flores, and Blanca Silvestrini. N.d. Identity, Conflict, and Evolving Latino Communities: Cultural Citizenship in San José, California. Manuscript.

Williams, Brackette. 1989. A Class Act: Anthropology and the Race to Nation across Ethnic Terrain. *Annual Review of Anthropology* 18:401–444.

Persisting Dilemma:

Sites of Racism

DANA Y. TAKAGI

Post–Civil Rights Politics and Asian-American Identity: Admissions and Higher Education

The Los Angeles riots that erupted after the Rodney King verdict in 1992 represent a watershed in U.S. race relations—a major consequence of which has been to place, if only temporarily, the issues of race, racism, and race relations a notch or two higher on the list of the country's domestic issues. This is, of course, a positive outcome, especially when one considers that the subject of race has been trivialized in most writing about U.S. history. By trivialized I mean our understanding of racism—its discourses, its practices, and its material foundations—has been shallow and grossly underexamined. I do not mean to suggest that the topic of race has not been studied in a variety of academic disciplines and by a number of policy analysts, but rather, that the past century or so of the study of race has progressively relegated the subject of racial identities to the category "epiphenomenon."

For example, in my own field of sociology, late-nineteenth- and early-twentieth-century thinkers who were frank in their acknowledgment of class divisions in society were far less willing to grant the category "race" the same theoretical status. The early U.S. sociologists either adopted biology-based notions of race, at times even promulgating eugenicist solutions toward nonwhites, or, in a few instances, were outright racists who lobbied for exclusion of "lesser" races—blacks, Asians, and Native Americans—from "their" society. Thus, the topic of race, partly as a result of the way the founders of U.S. sociology cloaked the topic with determinism and the bias of assimilation, has been reduced to a "factor" or, in the language of much sociological research, a discrete "variable," like sex.

Our inattention to issues that are racial is pandemic even in much contemporary talk about race relations. Part of the problem, I think, is that the process of trivializing race has resulted in a propensity to think of the variable race as phantasm—to view race or racism as a displacement, most often for class, or perhaps for something more "real" or "structural," as if only things that are defined as structural can be real.

One way that race has been trivialized has been through the stubborn and persistent frameworks in race relations discussions that construct race, racism, and race relations in terms that are black on the one hand and white on the other. And I mean that quite literally and figuratively. Even though the events in Los Angeles offer a recent and glaring indicator that race relations are more than black and white, tremendous uncertainty remains over how to theorize "multiracial" race relations.

Recognition is growing that race is a fundamental and constituent element of U.S. political discourse (Goldberg 1990; Omi and Winant 1986; Waters 1990). Issues of racism, race relations, and racial identity are widely diffused in contemporary discussions of U.S. domestic frontiers: education, crime, the family, housing, welfare, and poverty. Occasionally, the racial dimensions of these social issues is made explicit, as in Senator Bill Bradley's (1991) plea for "more straight talk about race," or in rap artist Ice Cube's (1991) song about Black/Korean conflict in the inner city. More often, issues of race are hidden in political discourse but easily recognizable through key phrases that connote racial meaning without explicit mention of race. For a majority of Americans, code words like "busing" or "affirmative action" conjure up images of unqualified minority students (often assumed to be black), while phrases like "the drug epidemic" and "the gang problem" project images of menacing young men in hooded sweatshirts on wilding sprees (assumed to be black or Hispanic).

In short, race is an inescapable element of the national politic. In the fall 1990 elections, Governor Pete Wilson of California and Senator Jesse Helms of North Carolina made the issue of "quotas," a thinly veiled reference to racial preferences, a core piece of their opposition to Democratic competitors (Toner 1990). And in the first six months of 1991, numerous issues of national interest told of conflicts steeped in accusatory and finger-pointing racial politics: the beating of Rodney King by Los Angeles police officers; the confirmation controversy surrounding Supreme Court Justice Clarence Thomas; statewide political battles, particularly in California and New York, over apportionment and redistricting in the wake of the 1990 census counts; and a second year of debate over a Democrat-backed national civil rights bill.

In contrast to the 1960s and early 1970s when issues of race were securely held inside the political domain of liberal Democrats, race has become a part of Republican and conservative political currency. As a result important changes in the politics of race have taken place since the peak years of the Civil Rights movement and the Johnson administration's much celebrated Voting Rights Act of 1965. Political winds have changed considerably, and in the 1980s and 1990s conservatives are blaming the Civil Rights movement and its federal legacy, the War on Poverty, for the decline of the family, the creation of a permanent underclass, a spiraling federal deficit, and an ethos of entitlements that, according to some, has eaten away at the moral and political fabric of U.S. society.

Several characteristics of contemporary race politics, I think, dramatize the retreat from a civil rights agenda, or at least from the belief in its viability. For example, ethnic coalitions have undergone crucial shifts since the 1960s. Political cooperation between black organizations and white ethnics, in particular Jewish organizations, to define and lobby for civil rights issues has been substantially weakened by conflict between Black Americans and Jews over Jewish entrepreneurship in Black communities, community control of schools, the subject of Palestinian homeland rights, and Israel's trade with South Africa. Also, the emergence of a vocal sector of minority conservatives (Carter 1990; Chavez 1992; Rodriguez 1982; Steele 1990) who articulate a vision of race and rights that is more consistent with the views of George Bush than those of Jesse Jackson has signaled a turning point in discussions about racial issues. Compared with the 1970s, much contemporary debate and conflict about affirmative action, for example, is as intraracial as interracial and, most important of all, is no longer a conflict between white conservatives and black liberals. Instead, much of the conservative grit on racial politics is produced by leading minority conservatives such as Thomas Sowell, Shelby Steele, Glenn Loury, and Linda Chavez. A corresponding development is that in the 1970s and 1980s, demographic changes, mainly immigration from Asia, the Caribbean, and Latin America, dramatically altered the composition of racial "minorities" and changed the proportion of "minorities" to "whites" (Barringer 1991).[1] In California for example, nonwhites—blacks, Asians, Latinos/Chicanos, and Native Americans—who used to comprise the "minority" will soon become the "majority."

Taken together, I suggest these changes be conceived as part of a post–civil rights politics that features the departure of some blacks and many whites from the old civil rights coalition; increasing multilateral interethnic or interracial conflict; and an ever-growing pastiche of interests and cultures that make up and destabilize the category "minority."[2] While it is far beyond the scope of this essay to analyze the origins or implications of these changes, I think it imperative to begin to identify the constituent pieces of contemporary racial politics.

In this essay I explore the relationship of Asian Americans to a post–civil rights politics. Given that our notions of "racial" have broadened into "multiethnic," that "politics" is no longer black and white, how should we situate Asian Americans in contemporary race politics? How do Asian-American issues affect, and how are they affected by, the changing nature of racial politics? These questions concern the relationships between Asian-American identity and contemporary race politics.

Issues that confront Asian Americans offer a revealing window through which to view broader changes in racial politics. For the most part, Asian Americans, whether they like it or not, are seen as being on the periphery of racial politics. Stereotypic myths of Asian Americans as a model minority who outwhite the whites have often resulted in their being sidelined in discussions of racial problems in the United States. Indeed, Asian Americans are rarely viewed as a problem minority group. Their educational and occupational achievements—particularly among second- and third-generation Japanese Americans and Chinese Americans, and among the sons and daughters of recent Korean and Southeast Asian immigrants—have often been held up as examples to other racial minorities.

The squeaky-clean image of Asian Americans as good minorities led to their being dropped from most university affirmative action programs during the 1970s. Not considered members of "underrepresented" or "disadvantaged" minorities, Asian Americans were said to be competitive students who no longer needed racial preferences to gain admission to the university.

The controversy over the admission of Asian-American applicants to the nation's most selective colleges and universities during the 1980s is a good example of both the location of Asian Americans in racial politics and the complexity of the post–civil rights politics of race. In particular, there is a paradox about the Asian admissions controversy that nuances one aspect of a changing racial politics. That is, Asian admissions features lengthy and technical debate about the merits of Asian-American applicants to college while simultaneously narrating the awkwardness of fitting Asian-American concerns into a highly polarized climate of race relations between blacks and whites.

Between 1983 and 1990, Asian-American complaints that the most selective universities in the United States—Berkeley, UCLA, Brown, Stanford, Harvard, Yale, and Princeton—set quotas or ceilings on Asian-American enrollment sparked one of the most explosive debates in higher education since the 1978 *Bakke* decision (Bunzel and Au 1987: Mathews 1987; Takagi 1990; Wang 1988). Like *Bakke,* the political controversy over Asian-American admissions replayed themes of race discrimination and affirmative action. However, the Asian-American admissions controversy went beyond Bakke, disclosing significant changes in the politics of race: shifts in ethnic coalitions, reconstruction of affirmative action discourse, and the emergence of vocal minority conservatives. In the closing years of the 1980s, the full repercussions of these changes would unfold within the context of embittered public debate between conservatives and liberals over "the canon," P.C. or political correctness, and multiculturalism.[3]

Most important of all, the controversy over Asian admissions signaled a crucial change in post-Bakke understanding of racial politics, articulated in such discursive practices as advocacy for the withdrawal of racial preferences in affirmative action, a development I characterize as "the retreat from race" (Takagi 1993). While racial preferences are still employed at most of the top universities, there have been significant changes. For example, at the Berkeley and Los Angeles campuses of the University of California, admissions officers announced in the late 1980s that guaranteed admission of underrepresented students (Black Americans, Hispanics, and Native Americans) who met minimum eligibility requirements would be cancelled. Admissions officers at many private universities, such as Harvard and Stanford, sensitive to charges that they have turned away better-qualified whites to make room for less-qualified blacks, emphasize the use of class or socioeconomic disadvantage in their admissions process.

Beyond the university, some researchers, politicians, and policy analysts claim that the use of racial preferences, in employment practices for example, has not been an effective means of bringing working-class blacks into the economic mainstream (Wilson 1987).[4] Racial preferences, argue the critics, have tended to benefit middle-class blacks, leaving working-class blacks virtually shut out of white-collar job markets. As a result, there is some discussion among policy analysts of shifting the organizing principle of affirmative action away from racial preferences toward class preferences.

Allan Bakke, a white man in his thirties, sued the University of California at Davis because he felt that his application to its medical school had been unfairly rejected. According to Bakke, his chances of admission to the university were diminished by the fact that he was white, and therefore ineligible to be considered for sixteen admission slots reserved for minority applicants. In a historic 1978 decision on race and admissions policy, the Supreme Court ordered the University of California to admit Bakke. The Court, while deciding that the university's set-aside program for minorities violated Bakke's civil rights, did not close the door on racial preferences in admissions policy. Rather, Justice Lewis Powell, whose comments on the case have been considered the controlling opinion, affirmed the use of such preferences, saying that although race could not be the sole criteria, it could be one among several factors determining admission.

In the ten-year aftermath of the *Bakke* decision, opinions about affirmative action remain sharply divided. Advocates contend that *Bakke* brought affirmative action to a virtual standstill while opponents suggest that *Bakke* did not go far enough in outlawing racial preferences. The result, according to some, has been that affirmative action has been largely ineffectual ever since. As one official in higher education, Mary Gray (1988), commented in the *Chronicle of Higher Education,* "The most that can be said about *Bakke* is that while it failed to lead to real change or even much progress, it may have kept the revolution from grinding to a halt."

In 1982 when the *New York Times* reported that minority access to higher education had "flattened out," the concern focused on black, Hispanic, and Native-American enrollment (Fiske 1982). Asian Americans, however, presented a different story. At about the same time the Supreme Court ruled in *Bakke,* the demographic warning signals of an impending debate on Asian-American access to higher education were already in place. In the 1970s, the Asian-American population, already the fastest-growing sector of the U.S. population, more than doubled in size. Correspondingly, the numbers of Asian Americans seeking entry to the nation's most selective colleges increased in dramatic proportions. For example, between 1979 and 1988, Brown University reported a 750 percent increase in the numbers of Asian-American applicants (Asian American Student Association 1983).

In spite of the spectacular growth in Asian-American applicants to college, actual Asian-American enrollment at many universities, particularly the elite private schools, was far less dramatic. At Harvard, Asian enrollment rose from 5.5 percent in 1979 to 8.5 percent in 1982. At Stanford, figures for Asian Americans were unavailable before 1983, at which time Asians constituted 7 percent of the first-year class. In the next two years, Asian enrollment remained steady at 8 percent. At Berkeley in 1984, Asian enrollment dropped 20 percent from the previous year.

A short five years after *Bakke,* changing population demographics brought different political realities to Asian Americans. In the early 1980s, Asian-American civil rights organizations that a half-decade earlier had filed amicus briefs on behalf of the University of California in the *Bakke* case, poised themselves to confront the university over Asian admissions (Asian American Task Force 1985). For example, in the San Francisco Bay Area, a group of Asian-American community leaders formed the Asian American Task Force on University Admissions to monitor and investigate the effect of the University of California admissions policy on Asian-American applicants.

It was within the context of declining black enrollments and rising numbers of Asian-American applicants that Asian admissions became a flash point for renewed debate about race, rights, and admissions. Many of the top schools, with more qualified applicants than admissions slots, were forced to turn away qualified and competitive applicants. Some Asian-American applicants who found themselves rejected from the top schools wondered if their racial background was being used against them in the admissions process.

Yat-Pang Au, the son of Vietnamese immigrant parents, does not think of himself as another Allan Bakke. An outstanding student at San Jose's Gunderson High School, Au scored an impressive 1,320 on the SAT, accumulated a 3.9 GPA, and in his spare time ran track, headed the school math club, and tutored disadvantaged children. Yet in 1986, when Au was rejected from the University of California at Berkeley, he too complained that he was the victim of race discrimination. Unlike Bakke, Au did not charge the University of California with "reverse discrimination." Instead, Au worried that his rejection from Berkeley might be the result of stereotypic myths about Asian Americans held by university officials who made admissions decisions. Some evidence supports his fear. For example, in a review of Harvard undergraduate admissions by the federal Department of Education's Office of Civil Rights, investigators found that admissions officials' comments on extraordinary achievements by Asian immigrant applicants were greeted with comments like, "A typical bootstrap case" (U.S. Department of Education 1990). Au was keenly aware of popular stereotypes of Asian Americans as "curve-raising nerds" threatening to "overrun" the university. "I am not a nerd," declared a defiant Au in response to the contention by one Berkeley official that Yat-Pang Au was a "good but not excellent" student (Mathews 1987).[5]

Both Bakke and Au felt their rejections from the University of California were based on their racial backgrounds, but the logic of discrimination in each case could not have been more different. Whereas Bakke argued that his rejection was the result of racism *against* white applicants, Au and his supporters contended he was the victim of discrimination *by* whites against Asians. For Bakke, the issue was "reverse discrimination." To Au and his supporters, the issue was good old-fashioned discrimination. In both cases, the rejected applicant insisted he was "qualified" for entry to the university. But whereas Bakke indicted "racial preferences" for minorities as the reason for his rejection from Davis, the Au case suggested that it was racial preferences for whites that accounted for his failure to gain entry to Berkeley.

The Au case at Berkeley dramatizes how issues of race and racism have increasingly become a politics of competing interpretations, rooted in our assumptions about what policies and visions are equitable and just. Though Au never went to court to press his claims against the university, his story, which was widely publicized by the media, made him a cause célèbre of the Asian-American admissions debate. Sympathetic media coverage portrayed Au as an applicant with impeccable qualifications and puzzled over his rejection from Berkeley. Asian-American students and faculty cited Yat-Pang Au as evidence of de facto discrimination against Asian-American applicants at Berkeley and elsewhere.

But university officials saw it differently. According to them, Yat-Pang Au was less qualified than applicants offered admission to Berkeley. Many officials argued that admissions officers faced an impossible situation: increasing demands for Asian-American access to higher education amid mounting pressure to increase, or at least maintain, existing levels of black and Latino enrollments. Hence, popular discourse about Asian admissions emphasized an oppositional relation between Asians and diversity. Berkeley officials contributed to this opposition and then, in their efforts to counter the negative publicity generated by the Au case, succeeded only in further eroding the public trust when two faculty committees took several years to investigate Asian-American complaints.[6]

The first faculty committee at Berkeley disbanded after it was revealed that the chair of the committee had written and circulated a report without discussion with the members of the committee. The report, never publicly released, cleared the university of discrimination charges and described media coverage of Yat-Pang Au's rejection from Berkeley as a case of "slanted journalism." The second committee also exonerated the Berkeley administration of discriminating against Asians in the admissions process. But a California state legislative hearing on admissions at the University of California critically assailed both the committee and the Berkeley administration for "putting rhetorical flourishes" on what it concluded were discriminatory policies against Asian Americans.

Officials' arguments that students like Au were rejected so that the university might maintain "racial balance" provided an irresistable invitation to conservatives who demanded to know if "diversity" justified "discrimination" against the so-called model minority. Neoconservatives paraded Au as the newest minority victim of affirmative action and racial preferences, hence suggesting that Au's complaint was an updated version of Bakke's. In the neoconservative reconstruction of debate over affirmative action, discrimination against Asian Americans was the logical consequence of affirmative action and racial preferences for blacks.

But in contrast to *Bakke,* which pitted whites against minorities, the Au case suggested a different kind of racial politics. The fact that Au was a racial minority was interpreted by neoconservatives to mean that the debate about affirmative action had moved *beyond race* to focus on issues of fairness and equity.

Claims and counterclaims about Asian admissions opened a political discourse on admissions in which conservatives sounded like Asians, liberals sounded like conservatives, and some conservatives sounded like liberals. For example, claims that Asian-American students were as well qualified but less likely than whites to gain entry to the elite schools set in motion a tedious debate over the definitions of "excellence" and "merit" and "diversity." Groups like the Asian American Task Force on University Admissions argued that Asian-American students were both "excellent" and "diverse"; university officials contended that Asian-American students while perhaps "excellent" were not "diverse"; and neoconservatives—among them, many minorities—argued that Asian-American students were simply "excellent" and that the notion of "diversity"—that is, racial diversity—was irrelevant. In one stunning example of how political interests no longer paralleled racial group interests, Arthur Hu, a Chinese-American computer programmer whose intellectual heroes include Nathan Glazer and Thomas Sowell, on May 22, 1989, filed a written complaint with Gary Curran in the Office of the Assistant Secretary for Civil Rights, Department of Education, accusing Berkeley of discriminating against whites through preferences for blacks.

Post–Civil Rights Politics: The Retreat from Race

The cases of Allan Bakke and Yat-Pang Au illustrate a significant and widespread change in how we define and talk about racial issues in the United States. As others (Edsall and Edsall 1991; Omi and Winant 1986) have already noted, racial topics have been increasingly coded in U.S. political discourse. In higher education, a string of recent controversies—for example, political correctness—is heavily laden with racial imagery in which black "bullies" square off against white "Truth." In the case of Asian-American admissions, the encoding of race into discussions of qualification, fairness, and merit at Berkeley has produced sharp conservative criticism of affirmative action and racial preferences by neconservatives.

But a key difference between the cases of Allan Bakke and Yat-Pang Au is that whereas Bakke challenged the *policy* of racial preferences, debate over Asian-American admissions demanded a reworking of the *discourse* of racial preferences. Race became more embedded and coded in conservative challenges to liberal politics—quotas, affirmative action, and civil rights—and solutions to racial problems have been increasingly cast in terms of class, not race. A linchpin of this shift has been the reconstruction of affirmative action debates in which Asians replacing whites as sympathetic victims of racial preferences has shifted the debate from one about race to one about fairness. Indeed, the very subject of racial preferences continues to fade in both policy and discursive practices involving minorities in higher education. In October 1990 for example, Michael Williams, the assistant secretary of the Department of Education and one of the highest-ranking black officials in the Bush administration, announced plans to stamp out race-based scholarships in higher education on the grounds that such programs violate the civil rights of whites. According to Williams, those schools with race-reserved scholarships, such as NAACP-sponsored awards, would risk losing their federal aid.[7]

In the early 1990s, a good deal of discussion by liberals and conservatives, policy analysts and intellectuals, has focused on shifting the basis of affirmative action from racial preferences to class preferences. While it may be a bit early for full-blown predictions, it is absolutely crucial to begin to anticipate what the effects of such changes might be. For example, how will the new emphasis on class affect admission rates of working-class blacks and middle-class blacks compared to equally qualified whites?

There are important political considerations as well. For example, what exactly are conservatives talking about when they argue for class-based preferences? Or more importantly, what should we make of this fresh concern for class by conservatives? Are conservatives really concerned with equalizing class differences in admissions or employment practices or with ossifying them?

A slightly different but related vein of questions might be posed for liberals who are also touting class preferences as a replacement for racial preferences. Given that liberals and Democrats have historically been aligned with the interests of minorities, is the policy of replacing racial preferences with class preferences consistent with, or a retreat from, past coalitions between liberals and nonwhites? Also, if both white liberals and conservatives support this policy initiative, what differentiates liberalism from conservatism on matters of race? Or put differently, is this a strategic and temporary intersection of liberal and conservative thinking, or does it represent a deeper convergence between the two?

If the controversy over Asian admissions exemplified a retreat from race in terms of policy and discursive practices, it also narrates a central problematic of Asian-American identity. That problematic, as Lowe (1991) has pointed out, is that the term *Asian-American identity* encompasses on the one hand a strategic politics, and on the other a limiting trap for the expression of diverse ethnic cultures. As a strategic politics, the articulation of Asian-American identity is a useful position or location from which to challenge hegemonic understandings of racial identity. Asian-American complaints of discrimination, such as the one raised by Yat-Pang Au, illustrate how the "model minority" still considers itself a "minority" and hence may be subject to discriminatory policies. But categories like Asian-American identity, while sufficiently broad to articulate a political position, can also be overarching, consuming, and restrictive.

At its worst, Asian-American identity suggests a unified political view or essence of being that is culturally or racially unique. However, such a notion fails to distinguish between the acts of individuals like Arthur Hu, the computer programmer who worried that whites were being discriminated against at Berkeley, and Yat-Pang Au, who worried that he was discriminated against by whites. More generally, such a notion does not recognize that the construction of Asian-American identit*ies,* by Asian Americans as well as by non-Asian Americans, is intimately tied to racial politics. For example, in this era of post–civil rights politics, conservatives have culled Asian-American experiences in their efforts to recode and recast the sides and terms of debate about affirmative action. Thus, while debates about affirmative action are not about Asian-American students per se, Asian-American educational experiences are frequently enrolled in such debates with great consequences for other minorities, in particular, blacks and Hispanics.

I suggest that the position of Asian Americans in contemporary race relations—a post–civil rights politics that is increasingly multiethnic but that remains dominated in analytic terms by the tendency to view race in frameworks that are largely black and white—has been grossly undertheorized. Studying racial minorities who are neither black nor white presents us with an opportunity not just to "correct" history but also to critically reevaluate and reassess the very terms—theoretical and analytical—on which to understand new multicultural realities.

Where does the imperative to go beyond black and white lead? Of course such an outline at this historical juncture is at best preliminary but I would argue there are at least two salient points. First, a revisioning of racial politics requires more than a simple acknowledgment of the diversity of racial experience in contemporary society. The inclusion of group experiences that have often been overlooked or perhaps intentionally left out of historical narratives on race, such as those of Asian Americans, is an important first step. The act of "including" Asian-American experiences in racial politics forces us to reconsider the ways in which such experiences are uniquely different from both white experiences and black experiences. Second, as this essay has documented, the racialized nature of the Asian-American experience in the admissions debate illustrates the usefulness of a "constructivist" theoretical approach to the study of race. A constructivist theoretical approach to race analyzes the heterogeneity and instability or racial meanings and identities—and it does not assume that such meanings and identities are historically fixed or culturally given. Moreover, as the debate over Asian-American admissions has shown, racial politics are never static but instead are routinely contested and discursively reworked. Determining through which social and political interests and under what historical conditions such reworkings occur is crucial for understanding racial meaning, racial identities, and race relations.

Notes

I wish to thank the editors of this volume, Roger Sanjek and Steven Gregory, for their helpful comments on an earlier draft of this essay.

1. In some cities in California, the demographic future is already here. For example, in the city of San Francisco, 50 percent of all elementary school children are of Asian heritage.

2. I first heard the term *post–civil rights* in a public presentation on postcolonial discourse by Ruth Frankenberg and Lata Mani (1993) at UC Santa Cruz. A brief version of their argument is that the corollary space to postcolonial discursive formation in the world economy would in the United States be more accurately described as a "post–civil rights" era of politics.

3. A spate of books and articles appeared early in the 1990s arguing for the neoconservative view that multiculturalism in higher education has led to decline in excellence, lower standards, and rising racial tensions on college campuses (D'Souza 1990; Kimball 1990; Smith 1990; Steele 1990).

4. Wilson's (1987) position resonates with some corners of conservative disaffection with racial preferences as well. For example, Sleeper (1990) has suggested that the core problem in New York City race relations is economic, not racial.

5. Gary Trudeau (1989), *Doonesbury* cartoonist, offered a humorous portrayal of white anxiety about Asian-American student achievement in a series

of strips during the late 1980s. One strip shows Kim, a National Merit finalist, being congratulated by her high school teacher, who says that her achievements are a good example of the fruits of persistence and hard work. A nonplussed-looking Kim responds that not everyone in the community agrees. The final box shows white parents at Kim's doorstep, pleading with her parents, "Couldn't you get her to watch more TV? She's throwing off the curve for the whole class!"

6. The first committee report was confidentially passed to me by an official close to the University of California, Berkeley. The second committee report (Shack 1989) is available through the University of California at Berkeley.

7. Public outcry in 1991 over Williams's announced ban on race-based scholarships forced the Department of Education to further study and evaluate the legality of the policy. If the Bush administration was unresolved on this issue, the Clinton administration was not. In February 1994, the proposed ban was rescinded by Secretary of Education Richard Riley.

References

Asian American Students Association. 1983. Asian American Admission at Brown University. October 11. Mimeograph.

Asian American Task Force. 1985. *Report of the Asian American Task Force on University Admissions.* San Francisco, June.

Barringer, Felicity. 1991. Census Shows Profound Change in Racial Makeup of the Nation. *New York Times,* March 11.

Bradley, Bill. 1991. Race and Civil Rights in America. Speech given at the National Press Club, July 16, Washington, D.C.

Bunzel, John, and Jeffrey Au. 1987. Diversity or Discrimination? Asian Americans in College. *Public Interest,* Spring, 49–62.

Carter, Stephen L. 1990. *Reflections of an Affirmative Action Baby.* New York: Basic.

Chavez, Linda. 1992. *Out of the Barrio: Toward a New Politics of Hispanic Assimilation.* New York: Basic.

D'Souza, Dinesh. 1990. *Illiberal Education.* New York: Free Press.

Edsall, Thomas, and Mary Byrne Edsall. 1991. *Chain Reaction.* New York: Norton.

Fiske, Edward. 1982. Fewer Blacks Enter Universities: Recession and Aid Cuts Are Cited. *New York Times,* November 29.

Frankenberg, Ruth, and Lata Mani. 1993. Crosscurrents, Crosstalk: Race, 'Postcoloniality' and the Politics of Location. *Cultural Studies* 7: 292–310.

Goldberg, David Theo, ed. 1990. *Anatomy of Racism.* Minneapolis: University of Minnesota Press.

Gray, Mary. 1988. The Tragic Legacy of the Supreme Court's 1978 Bakke Ruling Is That Affirmative Action Has Been Ineffectual Ever Since. *Chronicle of Higher Education,* January 29.

Kimball, Roger. 1990. *Tenured Radicals*. Chicago: University of Chicago Press.
Lowe, Lisa. 1991. Heterogeneity, Hybridity, Multiplicity: Masking Asian American Differences. *Diaspora,* Spring, 24–44.
Mathews, Linda. 1987. When Being Best Isn't Good Enough. *Los Angeles Times,* July 19.
Ice Cube. 1991. *Death Certificate*. Priority. Compact disk.
Omi, Michael, and Howard Winant. 1986. *Racial Formation in the U.S.* New York: Routledge and Kegan Paul.
Rodriguez, Richard. 1982. *Hunger of Memory*. Boston: Godine.
Shack, William. 1989. Report of the Special Committee on Asian-American Admissions. University of California, Berkeley. February.
Sleeper, Jim. 1990. *The Closest of Strangers: Liberalism and the Politics of Race in New York*. New York: Norton.
Smith, Page. 1990. *Killing the Spirit*. New York: Penguin.
Steele, Shelby. 1990. *The Content of Our Character*. New York: St. Martin's.
Takagi, Dana. 1990. From Discrimination to Affirmative Action. *Social Problems* 37: 578–592.
———. 1993. *The Retreat from Race: Asian American Admissions and Racial Politics*. New Brunswick: Rutgers University Press.
Toner, Robin. 1990. Issue of Job Quotas Sure to Affect Debate on Civil Rights in the 90s. *New York Times,* December 10.
Trudeau, Gary. 1989. *Read My Lips, Make My Day, Let Them Eat Quiche*. Kansas City, Mo.: Andrews and McMeel, Universal Press Syndicate.
U.S. Department of Education, Office of Civil Rights, Region I. *Statement of Findings (Harvard University)*. Compliance Review. #01-88-6009. October.
Wang, L. Ling-chi. 1988. Meritocracy and Diversity in Higher Education. *Urban Review* 20: 189–210.
Waters, Mary. 1990. *Ethnic Options: Choosing Identities in America*. Berkeley and Los Angeles: University of California Press.
Wilson, William Julius. 1987. *The Truly Disadvantaged*. Chicago: University of Chicago Press.

EVELYN HU-DEHART

P.C. and the Politics of Multiculturalism in Higher Education

A war is being waged on our campuses, and it is getting more heated and vicious by the day.[1] It is a curious sort of battle, because one side does not really want to fight, but the other is acting very bellicose. It pits a group of administrators, faculty, students, staff, and concerned members and leaders of the community, whom I shall call "multiculturalists," against another group made up of mostly neoconservatives, but also some traditional, or longtime, liberals, who are high federal government officials, political commentators, academics, and students. These are the antimulticulturalists, or "triumphalists."[2] In the late 1980s, with enormous support from the media (always prone to sensationalism), the triumphalists invented a clever weapon called P.C. (for *political correctness,* ironically a term appropriated from the Old Left, which used it as a check on its own ideological dogmatism), and they have since used it effectively to persuade an innocent public that higher education is being destroyed by the multiculturalists. Their targets, more specifically, are multiculturalists in higher education, and especially in elite universities such as Berkeley, Stanford, Michigan, Duke, and Wisconsin. They are so fervent because they believe they are battling for the heart and soul of America. Triumphalists argue that there are fundamental (or inherently superior), universal, immutable values that should always undergrid this society.

The funny thing is, the multiculturalists believe that they too are working for the good of this country, whose ethnic/racial minority populations are growing demographically; in another fifty years they will become the numerical majority in a world that is globally more interdependent. According to the multiculturalists, education must take major steps to keep up with these changes. Furthermore, in this post–civil rights era, when legal apartheid has finally been dismantled in the United States, education can and must take the lead toward the realization of an authentic, pluralistic democracy. In practice, this means ensuring the total and equal accessibility to educational opportunities for all Americans, at all levels and in all fields. It must also entail reorienting scholarly endeavors to begin the long process of recovery and restoration of the place and significance of Americans historically excluded from the project of defining the history and culture of this nation. In the end, how we teach, whom we teach, and what we teach will all be transformed. Multicultural education is an educational and social reform movement.

Obviously some very profound differences exist in the way each camp views the past, the present, and the future of this country. It is a question of perspectives, of values, of ideology. It is an explosive political issue, potentially the hottest political issue for the rest of this century, because the outcome will have profound impact on how this country continues to see and define itself. Underlying this heated debate is the question of "race"—historically constructed to separate those desirable European immigrants ("whites") from nonwhite peoples in American society ("people of color") deemed unassimilable or plain undesirable in the formation of U.S. nationhood and democratic culture and hence excluded. It is not coincidental that this debate was fueled by the 1992 Columbus Quincentennary, which divided this nation into opposing camps of those who saw it as an opportunity to celebrate the triumphs of Western civilization in the United States, and those who preferred to use it as an opening to investigate the forgotten aspects of our national history and to question the validity of the deeply rooted triumphalist view of it.

Multiculturalists begin with an alternative view of U.S. history fundamentally different from the version most often taught in our schools. Every school child in America learns the "fact" that the United States was built by immigrants, along with the widely and uncritically held metaphor of America as the "melting pot." But not every child is equally attuned to the fact that the country was already populated by a great diversity of peoples numbering in the millions, speaking many languages and practicing many cultures, nor the fact that the European settlers took the land and waters from these native peoples, destroyed their environments and nearly destroyed their cultures. and slaughtered them by the tens of thousands when they resisted.

Furthermore, when thinking of immigrants who built the nation, powerful, moving images of Europeans processed through Ellis Island under the shadow of the Statue of Liberty immediately come to mind. Consequently, we think of the United States as a white nation culturally defined by European or Western civilization, speaking the English language. Our educational curricula from kindergarten through graduate school reflect this deeply ingrained notion. Our holidays and celebrations reinforce this vision. When we celebrate Columbus Day and Thanksgiving, we are really celebrating the triumph of Europe and the "white man" in America; we are celebrating the European conquest of the New World.

This vision of the United States as white and European and English speaking and democratic, successfully passed down from generation to generation, is not an accident, I and other multiculturalists maintain, but the result of conscious, deliberate decisions taken by the "Founding Fathers," then carefully nurtured by our educational enterprise. For example, in order to sidestep the obvious contradiction between the existence of slavery and the statement that "All men are created equal," they simply decreed blacks and slaves to be less than complete human beings. Freed from slavery after the Civil War, African Americans endured another century of legal apartheid that barred them from full participation as equal citizens. Today, persistent barriers to economic and educational mobility have continued to segregate them, relegating a disproportionate number to the "underclass" of multigenerational poverty and hopelessness.[3]

When it comes to Native Americans, the federal government did not grant them citizenship until 1924, shamed into doing so only after many had served and died in defense of this country during World War I. By then, most Native-American nations had lost their land and water; many had been destroyed by war and disease; still others had been relocated far from their original homelands. Confined to reservations on desolate land in remote places, unemployed, and unable to scratch out even a decent living, they have been conveniently placed out of our sight, and therefore out of our minds and out of our consciences and consciousness.[4]

During the nineteenth century, the United States of America won by force or bought at bargain-basement prices vast chunks of land from Mexico, amounting to almost half of Mexico's national territory at that time. Although according to the Treaty of Guadalupe Hidalgo of 1848 the largely Spanish-speaking residents of the greater Southwest were promised citizenship and the right to retain their languages and cultures, the United States has not observed these commitments with honor but rather has incorporated the brown-skinned Mexican Americans as another disenfranchised, disadvantaged minority group, the "Hispanics," whose ranks have been swelled by other dark-complexioned Spanish-speakers on U.S. soil, such as the Puerto Ricans.[5]

Finally, the history of Asians in the United States has been one of repeated exclusion and special treatment. In 1790, as part of the scheme to keep this nation white and European, the Federal Naturalization Law was enacted to deny citizenship to nonwhite immigrants. Thus, when tens of thousands of Asian workers were brought to the American West druing the nineteenth century to build the railroads and work the mines, they found themselves barred from full political participation and social integration into society. From 1882 to World War II, the Chinese and later other Asian groups were barred from entering the country at all. During World War II, thousands of Japanese residents on the West Coast and their U.S.-born children were interned in camps behind barbed-wire fences, when not one of them had committed an act of disloyalty or sedition.[6]

Thus, from the vantage points of Native Americans, African Americans, Mexican Americans and other Hispanics, and Asian Americans, the triumph of Western civilization in the United States—of an unrelenting march toward freedom and democracy—unfortunately does not describe the essence of their experiences. This fundamental contradiction—between the nation's multiracial origins and continuing reality on the one hand and its dominant self-identity as white and European on the other, between freedom and democracy for all alongside a racialist social order that historically relegated peoples of color to an immutable inferior status as cheap labor but not citizens—is what multicultural education confronts and attempts to eventually resolve.

Since the 1960s, several dramatic developments have taken place in this country to create the political base for a broadly defined social movement for cultural pluralism and democracy, and to provide the impetus to implement multicultural education as a concrete project. The Civil Rights movement and the antiwar movement gave rise to political awakenings within all the ethnic minority communities. Changes in the naturalization law as well as in the immigration law, both of which had favored Europeans over immigrants from Africa, Asia, and Latin America, have resulted in dramatic rises in the numbers of nonwhite Americans, many of whom are no longer quiescent about their second-class status. Joining cause with women, who have also had a history of exclusion from certain institutions, they want change, and they want a fair shot and an equal chance to enjoy the opportunities traditionally limited to white males.

To the credit of many colleges and universities, their leadership has responded to the clamor by women and minorities for greater access to higher education. Public-policy initiatives such as affirmative action, more aggressive recruitment efforts, enhanced scholarship opportunities, and a frank reconsideration of what had traditionally constituted merit have brought encouraging results. In the 1990s our campuses are far more diverse by gender and especially by race than when I was an undergraduate twenty-five years ago. Leading the way is the University of California at Berkeley, with about two-thirds minority enrollment. Along with recruiting a more diverse student population, colleges and universities are also emphasizing a more diverse faculty and, as the last part of this transformation of higher education, embarking on serious curriculum revisions.

Twenty-five years ago, when minority students began entering universities in significant numbers, they also demanded new courses that spoke to their experiences and needs. Women students demanded the same. Thus was born ethnic studies and women's studies programs.[7] The faculties and students of such programs have been primarily, though rarely exclusively, people of color and women. Degrees and variations of such programs probably exist on most campuses today. They have produced an impressive body of scholarship and, like any intellectual endeavor, have their share of mediocrity and brilliance. If women's studies challenge the patriarchical paradigm, ethnic studies interrogate the material and ideological bases of U.S. racism and, by extension, other forms of institutionalized discrimination. These are the academic origins of multicultural education, and although controversial at various moments of their short history, and although they continue to struggle for full acceptance and legitimacy within the academy, they have nevertheless been allowed by and large to do their work.

However, all hell broke loose when ethnic studies and women's studies left the confines of their respective quarters on campus to invade other departments and disciplines, specifically to influence the general curriculum, and when white, especially male, faculty from traditional disciplines crossed into forbidden territory to consult with ethnic studies and women's studies colleagues about how best to update their course content, to change the way they teach given the changing nature of their students, and even, in some rare cases, to transform their perspective.[8]

The attack began in earnest when a coalition of broad-minded professors and students, whites and minorities, at Stanford University, after much discussion and debate, agreed to open the traditional required freshman course in Western civilization to include more works by people of color and women from the United States and around the world. Contrary to media reports and neoconservative depictions that Stanford jettisoned Western culture wholesale, the new program, renamed "Cultures, Ideas, Values," retained the core readings of Western culture while introducing students to representative works from other cultures. Machiavelli, the Bible, Freud, Marx, Shakespeare, Aristotle, Descartes, St. Augustine, Rousseau, Aquinas, Plato, Homer, Dante, Montaigne, Nietzsche, Galileo, Conrad, and Mill continue to be taught in three or more of the eight tracks students can select from. In one or more of the tracks, students are also exposed to the thought and writing of Frederick Douglass, Toni Morrison, Virginia Woolf, and other new names. The faculty remained the same and, as before, had the responsibility of choosing the texts.

Apparently, this minor tinkering was too much for some very powerful and influential public voices, including the then secretary of education William Bennett. Using the power of his office, Bennett descended on Stanford to denounce the action by a community of scholars and students who were going about a rather normal business of reexamining and revitalizing the curriculum, something that happens every day on college campuses and usually would not have aroused any outside attention.[9]

By the time of the Stanford incident, Bennett had already joined forces with University of Chicago professor Allan Bloom, who had written the best-selling book *The Closing of the American Mind* (1987) to flail at changes in higher education curricula he was uncomfortable with, such as women's studies and ethnic studies. To uphold the virtues and preeminence of Western culture and the established canon in literature and other traditional studies against the invasion of these multiculturalists, the two men founded the Madison Institute to aggressively promote Western civilization and the traditional curriculum.

Encouraged by the success of Bloom's book, a slew of other attacks on higher education soon followed, including E. D. Hirsch's *Cultural Literacy* (1987); Charles Sykes's *The Hollow Men: Politics and Corruption in Higher Education* (1990); Roger Kimball's *Tenured Radicals: How Politics Has Corrupted Our Higher Education* (1990), which was especially harsh on what Kimball saw as the radicalization of the humanities; and culminating with Dinesh D'Souza's *Illiberal Education: The Politics of Race and Sex on Campus* (1991). Sensing they are on losing ground on the campuses, where most of the faculty and administrators know their jobs well and, at least up to now, are committed to some degree of multiculturalism in education, these polemicists are clearly aiming to influence the vast and mostly uniformed public outside the academy. In this, they have been ably abetted by most of the mainstream press and national media, all of which have helped spread their alarmist message of campuses run amok with multiculturalism, which by now has become synonymous with the destruction of Western civilization and, by extension (given their narrow, Eurocentric worldview of U.S. history), with anti-Americanism.

These political diatribes served as bibles and launching pads for several powerful institutions. The Madison Institute, founded by Bloom and Bennett, merged with the Institute of Educational Affairs, headed by Irving Kristol, publisher of the leading neoconservative magazine, the *National Interest,* to become the Madison Center for Educational Affairs, based in Washington, D.C., and headed by Chester Finn, former undersecretary of education under Bennett and onetime professor of education at Vanderbilt University.

Kristol's main project at the Institute of Educational Affairs, which was then carried on by the Madison Center, was to encourage, advise, and train conservative students to establish, fund, write, and produce conservative student periodicals, such as the notorious *Dartmouth Review,* in 1980 the first of its kind, whose first editor was Dinesh D'Souza. Along with the *California Review* at UC Berkeley and the *Florida Review* at the University of Florida, there were in the early 1990s some sixty such campus papers, which together formed the Collegiate Network (Butterfield 1990; Dodge 1991).[10] Their primary financial benefactor has been the Olin Foundation, whose chair is William Simon, treasury secretary under Ronald Reagan. Like their elders, the student writers focus their sharp (often plain nasty) racist and sexist attacks on all aspects of multiculturalism, from women and minority students and faculty to the changing curriculum.

The presence and rhetoric of such papers also encourage the formation of "white student unions" on various campuses, including the University of Florida and the University of Minnesota. The Minnesota group's president, a senior majoring in ancient history and Greek and Latin, was quoted in the September 11, 1991 issue of the *Chronicle of Higher Education* as asserting that black students are not as capable of succeeding academically as whites. This is reminiscent of a statement made by D'Souza when he was editor of the *Dartmouth Review:* "The question is not whether women should be educated at Dartmouth. The question is whether women should be educated at all" (Henson 1991).

Another institutional base for the attack on multiculturalism appeared within the academy. Calling themselves the National Association of Scholars (NAS), a cadre of predominantly white, male, middle-aged professors, with a smattering of women and minorities, formed a support group to combat and repel what founding member Alan Kors, historian at the University of Pennsylvania, described viciously as "the barbarian in our midst." Based in Princeton, New Jersey, this outfit also received funding from Olin, Coors, and other conservative foundations and in 1991 listed seventeen hundred members and twenty-five state chapters.[11]

The Madison Center and the NAS obviously have very similar agendas and are in close communication with each other; familiar figures in government and academia serve as their liaisons with other conservative think tanks, such as the Heritage Foundation (founded during the early Reagan years and heavily supported by Coors) and the Hudson Institute in Indianapolis. Notable among the liaison figures is Lynne Cheney, former director of the National Endowment for the Humanities, whom the neoconservative commentator George Will, a devout supporter and mouthpiece of their cause, aptly described in his *Newsweek* column, April 22, 1991, as the secretary of domestic defense, presumably while her husband, Dick Cheney, continued as the secretary of external defense.[12] Lynne Cheney actively spread horror stories about multiculturalists on campuses across the land, such as black students and feminist colleagues hounding defenseless white male professors from their classrooms when they refused to toe the P.C. line—specifically Stephen Thernstrom of Harvard's History Department and Alan Gribben of University of Texas at Austin's English Department, both NAS members or sympathizers (Gamarekian 1991).[13] She also gained notoriety when she denied funding to a highly regarded project put together by a group of noted scholars to examine the Columbus encounter from different perspectives (Winkler 1991).

Another critic is Diane Ravitch, sometime coauthor with the Madison Center's Chester Finn and Bush administration Secretary of Education Lamar Alexander's assistant in charge of research and curriculum. Ravitch acknowledged diversity in U.S. society and professed support for multicultural education, but only if it did not become "particularistic," that is, challenge the centrality of Western civilization, the glue that she and other triumphalists maintain binds this nation together (Ravitch 1990a, b).[14] When the Madison Center held a national conference in early 1991 with many of its celebrity members in attendance, they decried the "anti-Americanism" of a small but vocal core of academics who "have allowed their political agenda to taint their scholarship and teaching," and who have made "race, class, and gender" central to their intellectual work. By contrast, Madison Center members describe themselves as upholding the study of Western culture and "objective" (as opposed to P.C.) scholarship.

When the NAS held its founding conference in New York City in 1988 with five hundred in attendance, it described itself as a "national movement" to "reclaim the academy." The conference charged that a "radicalization" of U.S. higher education—a reference to the new curriculum—has led to a "decline in academic standards" (Mooney 1991, 1988).

Although the founders and many of the stalwarts of both organizations are neoconservatives with close ties to the Reagan and Bush administrations, several well-known traditional liberals have lent their voices and clout to the attack on the "barbarians" on their campuses. James David Barber, professor of political science at Duke University and former president of Amnesty International, organized an NAS chapter on his campus to call attention to the "politicization of higher education" and to the "new orthodoxy" and "rising hegemony of politically correct" education (Rabinowitz 1990).

Other longtime liberals such as Eugene Genovese (1991) and C. Vann Woodward (1991), both noted for major scholarly works on slavery and the South, have published extremely favorable reviews of D'Souza's book in leading liberal magazines such as the *New Republic* and the *New York Times Book Review.*

Even Arthur Schlesinger of Camelot fame was obviously pained and baffled by the challenge to the hegemony of Western civilization when the New York State Curriculum Task Force, charged with revamping the public school curriculum of a state heavily populated by minorities and Third World immigrants, ignored his admonition to preserve the centrality of Western civilization in the curriculum. Echoing Diane Ravitch, he has since warned in numerous books and articles against the "cult of ethnicity," asserting that multiculturalism threatens the ideal that binds America (1991). Along with other triumphalists, Schlesinger has also frequently touted the idea that the "Western tradition is the source of the ideas of individual freedom and political democracy to which most of the world now aspires." He was joined in this sentiment by neoconservatives such as Ravitch, and by many other "old liberals" like himself, in a protest published in *Perspectives* by the American Historical Association (1990) against the proposed revision of the state of New York's history curriculum. Schlesinger was a dissenting member of the committee chaired by the eminent African-American psychologist (and retired Yale University professor) Edmund Gordon, under whose name the New York State report was issued (1991).

During the early 1990s, almost all the critics of multiculturalism jumped on the P.C. wagon. Futhermore, as propagated and popularized by the press and media, P.C. has become an easy handle and a catchall phrase for denouncing everything about recent developments in U.S. society that conservatives, traditional liberals, and especially neoconservatives of the Reagan-Bush era dislike: affirmative action; women's studies, especially feminist theories; black and other ethnic studies; gay and lesbian studies; cultural studies; and new trends in literary criticism, such as deconstructionism and new historicism.

Instead of engaging their colleagues in serious, reasoned debate about their differences in understanding and teaching history and culture, they resort to hysterical and nasty rhetoric, calling feminists and multiculturalists a "thought police" spreading a "new McCarthyism" that stifles freedom of expression on our campuses.

The intensity of this antimulticultural movement is rooted, I believe, in the inability to confront the truth of U.S. history as experienced by those of non-European heritage. When Schlesinger, a historian, declares categorically that historically the United States has been a nation of "individuals making their own choices" and that the "historic American goals" have been "assimilation and integration" of its peoples, this interpretation is one with which African Americans, Native Americans, Latinos, and Asian Americans cannot resonate. Declaring, as he also has, that Europe has been "the unique source of the liberating ideas of democracy, civil liberties and human rights," he denies that other cultures have their own sources of human liberation and ignores another historical fact: that Europe has also been a unique source of racism, sexism, social inequality, exploitation of other human beings, and general human suffering.

Similarly, when the professor of history and classics and dean of Yale College Donald Kagan gives his interpretation of early U.S. history, it may be valid for European immigrants: "Before long [after the arrival of the first English-speaking settlers], however, people of many different ethnic, religious, and national origins arrived with different cultural traditions, speaking various languages. Except for the slaves brought from Africa, most came voluntarily, as families and individuals, usually eager to satisfy desires that could not be met in their former homelands. *They swiftly became citizens and, within a generation or so, Americans*" (1990, emphasis added). But for Native Americans and nonwhite immigrants, Kagan's version of history is noteworthy more for its continuous exclusion, if not outright ignorance, of their historical experiences.

Unfortunately, in the post–civil rights era, just when peoples of color are rising up to reclaim their proper place in U.S. history, culture, and institutions, powerful triumphalist forces choose to succumb to their fears and cling to the old social and ideological order instead of shedding their defensiveness and arrogance. Contrary to the triumphalists' shrill charges, multiculturalists understand that diversity and assertion of differences need not lead to divisiveness if there is no social inequality based on constructed and imposed racial and gender categories.[15] Unless we eliminate these basic barriers to equal opportunity, what does a "common culture" mean, and how do we forge unity and a genuinely democratic American future?

Notes

1. This piece was written in late 1991, as the P.C. debate was at its height, and thus, I believe, provides a good framework for examining the early history of the P.C. controversy, particularly as it revolves around issues of multiculturalism,

which can be understood as part of the new racial politics of the late twentieth century.

2. I borrow the idea of characterizing mainstream U.S. scholars as "triumphalists" from Gene Bell-Villada's biting and incisive 1990 review of Bloom and Hirsch.

3. In *The Rise and Fall of the White Republic* (1990), historian Alexander Saxton bluntly states that America's supposed openness to newcomers throughout most of its history has been "racially selective." While there are too many books on the African-American experience to mention here, I recommend Marable 1983.

4. Among the too few good books on Native America, the best reader currently available is Jaimes 1992.

5. Still probably the single best and most widely read and consulted interpretative history of Chicanos is Acuña 1988.

6. Recently several good histories of Asian Americans have been published, including Chan 1991 and Takaki 1989.

7. For good discussion of how women's studies and ethnic studies have helped transform the curriculum, see Butler and Walter 1991.

8. See the essays assembled in Gless and Smith 1992.

9. Much too much has been written about the reforms of the Stanford Western civilization course: chapter 3 of D'Souza's *Illiberal Education* represents the extreme of exaggeration and is rebutted in an article by Byers (1991). The December 1991 issue of *Stanford* magazine contains sober, analytical essays by John Wagner and Lance Morrow about this campus curriculum issue.

10. The Intercollegiate Studies Institute, based in Bryn Mawr, Pennsylvania, also produces two publications. The first, *Campus: America's Student Newspapers,* feeds many stories to these conservative student papers regularly denouncing, deriding, and trivializing women's studies, ethnic studies, new cultural studies, affirmative action, campus speech codes, minority programs and scholarship, and all issues preceived as P.C. The second publication, the *Intercollegiate Review,* is in journal format. Both can be obtained free by writing Intercollegiate Studies Institute, 14 S. Bryn Mawr Avenue, Bryn Mawr, PA 19010-3275, or by calling 1-800-526-7022. The Madison Center for Education Affairs in 1992 launched yet another journal. Edited, written and aimed at college-age readers, it has the politically correct title *Diversity: A Critical Journal of Race and Culture.*

11. The *Chronicle of Higher Education* first focused attention on the NAS in Mooney 1988. Since then, the *Chronicle* has reported on the NAS numerous times. Another substantive exposé is Weisberg 1991. Regarding funding for NAS and related groups, including the conservative student newspapers, see Butterfield 1990, McMillen 1992, and Wiener 1990. The NAS publishes the journal *Academic Questions;* a representative article is one by Thomas Short, philosophy professor at Kenyon College (1988).

12. Will even asserted that the "foreign adversaries" that Cheney's husband, Dick, faced were "less dangerous, in the long run, than the domestic forces with which she must deal." Who were these dangerous forces? Professors of literature

(in this case mostly white) running amok in elite U.S. universities brainwashing unsuspecting students, professors like those included in Gless and Smith 1992.

13. The "incidents" surrounding Thernstrom and Gribben are typical of the kind of so-called P.C. horror stories that Cheney, Bennett et al. like to recite ad nauseum. Thernstrom's story, as originally recounted by D'Souza in chapter 4 of *Illiberal Education,* then recycled by other journalists, is also exemplary of the kind of gross exaggeration that P.C. bashers freely use to make their point. Wiener (1991) did a masterful job of exposing the Thernstrom story; unfortunately, the mass media has not bothered to pick up and recycle his version, thus letting the damage perpetrated by D'Souza, Cheney et al. stand in the public's perception.

14. A cursory reading, with no information on Ravitch's background, might suggest that Ravitch supports multiculturalism. But see Ravitch 1990b, which discloses her real attitude toward multicultural education and the multicultural project.

15. Typically, the mass media has mindlessly latched onto this neoconservative–old liberal view that equates multicultural perspectives of U.S. history with divisiveness; for example, the July 8, 1991, cover story of *Time* proclaims that "American kids are getting a new—and divisive—view of Thomas Jefferson, Thanksgiving and the Fourth of July."

References

Acuña, Rodolfo. 1988. *Occupied America: A History of Chicanos.* 3d ed. New York: Harper and Row.

Bell-Villada, Gene. 1990. Critical Appraisals of American Education: Dilemmas and Contradictions in the Work of Hirsh and Bloom. *International Journal of Politics, Culture, and Society* 3:485–511.

Bloom, Allan. 1987. *The Closing of the American Mind.* New York: Simon and Schuster.

Butler, Johnnella, and John C. Walter, eds. 1991. *Transforming the Curriculum. Ethnic Studies and Women's Studies.* Albany: SUNY Press.

Butterfield, Fox. 1990. The Right Breeds a College Press Network. *New York Times,* October 24.

Byers, Bob. 1991. Machiavelli Loses Ground at Stanford; Bible Holds Its Own. *Chronicle of Higher Education,* June 19.

Chan, Sucheng. 1991. *Asian Americans: An Interpretive History.* Boston: Twayne.

Dodge, Susan. 1991. A National Network Helps Conservative Students Set Up 58 Newspapers on College Campuses. *Chronicle of Higher Education,* May 9.

D'Souza, Dinesh. 1991. *Illiberal Education: The Politics of Race and Sex on Campus.* New York: Free Press.

Gamarekian, Barbara. 1991. Grants Rejected; Scholars Grumble. *New York Times,* April 10.

Genovese, Eugene D. 1991. An Argument for Counterterrorism in the Academy: Heresy, Yes—Sensitivity, No. *New Republic,* April 15.

Gless, Darryl J., and Barbara Herrnstein Smith, eds. 1992. *The Politics of Liberal Education.* Durham, N.C.: Duke University Press.
Gordon, Edmund. 1991. *One Nation, Many Peoples: A Declaration of Cultural Interdependence.* Report of the New York State Social Studies Review and Development Committee.
Henson, Scott. 1991. The Education of Dinesh D'Souza: How an Angry Young Man Parlayed Right-Wing Money into National Attention. *Texas Observer,* September 20.
Hirsch, E. D. 1987. *Cultural Literacy.* Boston: Houghton-Mifflin.
Jaimes, M. Annette, ed. 1992. *The State of Native America: Genocide, Colonization, and Resistance.* Boston: South End.
Kagan, Donald. 1990. The Role of the West. *Yale Alumni Magazine,* November, 43–46.
Kimball, Roger. 1990. *Tenured Radicals: How Politics Has Corrupted Our Higher Education.* New York: Harper and Row.
Marable, Manning. 1983. *How Capitalism Underdeveloped Black America.* Boston: South End.
McMillen, Liz. 1992. Olin Fund Gives Millions to Conservative Activities in Higher Education; Critics See Political Agenda. *Chronicle of Higher Education,* January 22.
Mooney, Carolyn J. 1988. Conservative Scholars Call for a Movement to "Reclaim the Academy." *Chronicle of Higher Education,* November 23.
———. 1991. Scholars Decry Campus Hostility to Western Culture. *Chronicle of Higher Education,* January 30.
Rabinowitz, Dorothy. 1990. Vive the Academic Resistance. *Wall Street Journal,* November 13.
Ravitch, Diane. 1990a. Multiculturalism: E Pluribus Plures. *American Scholar,* Summer, 337–354.
———. 1990b. Multiculturalism Yes, Particularism No. *Chronicle of Higher Education,* October 24.
Saxton, Alexander. 1990. *The Rise and Fall of the White Republic.* London: Verso.
Schlesinger, Arthur. 1990. New York State: Statement of the Committee of Scholars in Defense of History. *Perspectives* 28(7): 15.
———. 1991. The Cult of Ethnicity, Good and Bad. *Time,* July 8.
Short, Thomas. 1988. "Diversity" and "Breaking the Disciplines": Two New Assaults on the Curriculum. *Academic Questions* 1(3): 6–29.
Sykes, Charles. 1990. *The Hollow Men: Politics and Corruption in Higher Education.* Washington, D.C.: Regnery Gateway.
Takaki, Ronald. 1989. *Strangers from a Different Shore: A History of Asian Americans.* New York: Penguin.
Weisberg, Jacob. 1991. N.A.S.: Who Are These Guys Anyway? *Lingua Franca,* April, 34–39.
Wiener, Jon. 1990. The Olin Money Tree: Dollars for Neocon Scholars. *Nation,* January 1.

———. 1991. What Happened at Harvard? *Nation,* September 30.

Winkler, Karen. 1991. Humanities Agency Caught in Controversy over Columbus Grants. *Chronicle of Higher Education,* March 13.

Woodward, C. Vann. 1991. Freedom and the Universities. *New York Review of Books,* July 18.

ROBERT R. ALVAREZ, JR.

Un Chilero en la Academia: Sifting, Shifting, and the Recruitment of Minorities in Anthropology

In any academic discipline the recruitment and filling of the ranks sets its tone, nature, and trajectory. This process demonstrates not only the maintenance of hierarchies but the ultimate manner in which the discipline defines acceptable knowledge and accepts the bearers of that knowledge. With this essay I merely hope to raise questions about the current recruitment of minorities into the academy and to begin dialogue about what this recruitment means to the replication of professional hierarchies.

In recent readings on power and knowledge I have been taken by methodology suggested by Foucault that seems particularly appropriate here. Examining the structures of knowledge and power, Foucault states that in any discipline it is the most disassociated realm found "at the extreme points of its exercise" where power and knowledge installs itself "and produces its real effects" (1980:97). Recruitment in anthropology illustrates a gatekeeping quality that not only neglects the epistemological contributions of minority scholars but maintains both our discipline's hierarchy and its canon in a status quo situation.

The examination of recruitment at our margins—that is, minority recruitment—might tell us something about the nature of our hierarchies and their maintenance. Regardless of the attention and visibility given to "target of opportunity," "action now," and "cultural diversity" hires, the recruitment of women and U.S. minorities into the academy remains at the most disassociated and extreme points in the discipline's exercise of power.

My reentry into academia in late 1989, after a five-year hiatus in the "real world," provides the basis for a firsthand account of the recruiting process. While some would argue that this is too personal and not objective, it is in line with current anthropological trends: "Any autobiography by the anthropologist, while emerging from a unique and personal experience, evokes resonances of recognition among others. There are solidarities as well as contrasts to be examined and systematized for the enrichment of the discipline. The autobiography is not a linear progress of the lone individual outside history, let alone outside cultures and the practice of anthropology" (Okely 1992:8).

Before I left academia in 1984 I was practicing anthropology and teaching only part-time, but I was nonetheless attached to the academy. I then left to pursue work in agriculture and the produce industry along the border of the United States and Mexico. I had grown up in that world and returned to fulfill a familial obligation. But I also returned to immerse myself in the U.S.-Mexican border region, an area that I had specialized in during my graduate studies. My graduate years at Stanford University, 1972–1978, and my postgraduate career had included work in migration and border-community studies, primarily focused on the town of Lemon Grove in southern California, and the extended kin-network that reached across the border into Baja California, Mexico, of which I was a part (see Alvarez 1985, 1986, 1987a, b).[1] I conducted research for a Ph.D. along the U.S.-Mexican border, pursuing issues that had been framed by current literature on migration theory. But my main career trajectory was that of an applied anthropologist working in settings that were oriented toward social change, particularly among indigenous Americans—Chicano, Latino, Black, and Native. This work took me to the Institute for Urban and Minority Education at Teachers College in New York City and back again to my native state, where I became engaged in bilingual and leadership training in Chicano, Indian, and Pacific Island communities at the Cross Cultural Resource Center, California State University, Sacramento. However, in 1984, I looked at my reentrance into the border world as an opportunity to be engaged full-time in a cultural milieu that I had only partially examined in my role as an anthropologist. I welcomed the change and the challenge.

I worked primarily along the California-Arizona-Mexico border, centered first in Tijuana, Baja California Norte, and later in San Luis Rio Colorado, Sonora, just south of Yuma, Arizona. I became thoroughly involved in the chile pepper trade on both sides of the international line, eventually moving throughout the Republic of Mexico as a bona fide *chilero* (chile specialist), obtaining and distributing chile peppers in the world of Mexican fruit entrepreneurs. I first worked in the Los Angeles Wholesale Produce Terminal, receiving chile peppers and learning the logistics of the market and the export demands of the trade, but I was soon located in Mexico, working out of Tijuana in a totally Mexican entrepreneurial environment. I became the Mexico-U.S. connection for a Mexican chile-packing business and represented its packing shed, as do other Mexican chileros, in sales to and negotiations with large U.S.

wholesale firms. I, like other chileros, would visit the market daily, maintain contacts with U.S. buyers, and stand in line on Friday afternoons waiting for the payments that would keep our venture in operation. Along with a Mexican colleague, I also made frequent trips into Mexico to negotiate buying contracts with farmers, and to visit other chileros who were involved in the trade. Each day was an exciting cycle of ups and downs in a world described by the chilero as a "rollercoaster ride" and a life of strong emotions. I had become totally immersed in *la vida del comerciante,* the life of the entrepreneur.

It was a mind-opening experience and renewed my interest and energy in the anthropological endeavor. Where in the past, like other anthropologists, I had entered Mexican markets equipped with my camera and notepad, during my border tenure I traveled behind the scenes. More than once I thought about this change in roles. On one occasion in the Guadalajara market, I can remember the irony I felt as I sat among bundles of tamale leaves with a group of *fruteros* (Mexican fruit entrepreneurs), drinking *mezcal.* As an anthropologist, I had been on the other side of the looking glass, peering in on such activity. The anthropologist observes vendors and group activities but rarely participates as a bona fide member. In this case, I remember thinking that as a student of human behavior I had been impressed with colorful products, the bantering and negotiating of market folk, and had wondered what thoughts and activities defined the behavior I was witnessing. Now I was part of a group of carousing fruteros drinking tequila in the morning hours. From within the market stall, I saw other vendors and their clientele hurrying by or joining our group. My friend and I were visitors from the north, and we were participating emotionally and physically as part of this frutero group.

Although my graduate specialty was Mexico and the border, in many senses as an anthropologist I had missed the richness and complexity that I was now encountering. The anthropologist in me was alive and well, rekindled and reoriented by these real-world experiences, emotions, and sentiments. I was to learn that this involvement would be viewed by academics as questionable activity because it was not performed within defined institutional parameters.

Toward the end of this five-year period, I had a variety of experiences with a number of anthropology departments that were seeking minority candidates for positions through action-now, target-of-opportunity, and cultural diversity hires. These types of hires are intended to help increase the alarmingly low and often nonexistent representation of minority and women faculty in campuses throughout the nation. Primarily because of community and affirmative action pressure, most campuses conduct special searches for high-profile and qualified candidates of minority background. Ideally, once hired, these folks filled needed quotas as well as complementing course offerings and department specializations. As I began to respond to the targets-of-opportunity calls, instead of open doors and opportunity I found intrigue, secrecy, manipulation, misused power, and reasserted hierarchy. In speaking to other colleagues of color and to women anthropologists, I learned that the experiences I had were unique only in the specific form they took.

Individuals who underwent both junior- and senior-level hirings told of similar processes. First, candidates are sifted, that is, processed through unusual departmental and university procedures. (I stress that many others than I see such processes as different from the "normal" experiences of white male job candidates). In all hiring procedures, candidates go one by one through an elimination process, but when there are only a few new Ph.D.s in the pool—Chicano anthropologists in this case—many candidates are also actively recruited from positions in other institutions. Thus, there is also a shifting of individuals from one institution to another, something I would discover only after my experiences with being sifted. While I have not succumbed to any shifting myself, the experiences of others in my small pool suggest that there the sifting starts again.

Here, at this periphery of the discipline, the established hierarchy reveals its efforts to reproduce itself. Although an extreme and marginal activity for most departments, the recruitment of racial minorities has become highly symbolic of fulfilling wider institutional needs and demands, such as university requirements to diversify faculties and represent the growing numbers of people of color and women in U.S. society. But in fact, all this has little to do with the incorporation into the discipline of new knowledge and perspectives from such persons. Rather, their recruitment and the hires that may result are subordinated by the departments to academic hierarchy and value commitments.

During my tenure in the chile pepper trade, I visited a major research institution in a state and region historically populated by Mexicanos and Chicanos through a long history of migrant farm labor. I went there primarily to investigate new developments in cold-storage laboratories for perishable fruits and vegetables. At the same time, I visited the anthropology department, which I was told was seeking a target-of-opportunity hire. I met with several faculty and had formal and informal interviews. Calls of inquiry already had been made about my experience and work; individuals had sent letters of support. Thus naively inspired, I had also already sent a formal letter of interest in the position and a resume. I was informed that the department did indeed have an open position and was in search of a qualified and appropriate candidate.

I would learn when I met with the department chair that he and the department faculty believed my interests and background were precisely what was needed there. They had no faculty that taught the ethnography of Mexico, Mesoamerica, or the U.S.-Mexico border, and no Chicano-related courses. Both my formal training in migration and Mexico, as well as my recent practical experience in agriculture and marketing, were perfect for this institution and position, he and other faculty members reiterated. They needed a Mexicanist, and they needed Chicano representation. Within the next weeks after my visit I received letters from the department, both from faculty members and the chair, stating that "I was their man," and that I would be asked to give a formal presentation in the near future.

That was the last I heard from the department. More than a year later, on attending my first American Anthropological Association annual meeting after my return, I ran into the search committee head, and behind elevator doors he asked, "What happened to you?" When I responded "What happened to *you?*" I was informed that the department had advertised for a position in political anthropology, not for a Mexicanist, not for a border scholar. They had waited for my new application, something I had assumed was already in their hands. Piecing together the course of events from discussions I had with both anthropology faculty and other friends at this university, I concluded that specific members of the anthropology department had opposed any target-of-opportunity hire, out of a belief that any position should be available to all candidates, not just those of minority background. A "regular" search was made, in order to get the "best possible candidate." Hence, the position was advertised in "normal" channels and the pool developed from all available candidates. I was sifted out. But they had also accomplished what the university had set out to do. In the words of that anthropologist in the elevator, they hired a person who "passed as Chicano." I had been ignored and never offered the job. I relate this episode with no personal vendetta to settle, but to illustrate the resistance of established hierarchical values to both new knowledge and experience, and to university directives.

This experience is indicative of more than a sloppy and mismanaged search and a lack of professional courtesy. It reflects a widespread process that is exhibited in much of minority recruitment. I first asked myself if mine was a typical experience. How were other individuals faring in similar recruitment processes? And most important, was this case representative of the nature of affirmative action recruitment in the discipline?

After this initial encounter, I was cautious in investigating other job possibilities. Let me share two examples, one from a major Southwest university, and another in the Midwest. Both of these universities were "powerhouses," as I was told by faculty members there.

I received a number of calls from one of these institutions through its Center for Mexican American Studies, which was acting as a recruitment broker for the anthropology department in the search for a Chicano anthropologist. The calls were almost clandestine in that I spoke to only one individual at the center and never communicated with the anthropology department directly. However I *was* told informally by colleagues there, and by others who were in contact with the anthropology department, that I was being considered seriously. I sent a resume and was told by the center that I was a short-list candidate in anthropology and would be asked to visit the campus and deliver a lecture. After this brief but intensive round of communication, all officially through the Center for Mexican American Studies, I heard nothing. I called again after a three- or four-month period had passed, curious about the silence. I was told that there was indeed strong interest in my candidacy, but when it came down to it, I had "done too much." I was told I would be considered again in the future. I later discovered informally through colleagues that several positions had been filled in the department, all at the junior level. The one position for which I had been considered, a senior-level associate professorship, had not been filled. Sifted once again.

My third experience illustrates a totally different attitude. On arriving at this institution, I was put under extreme scrutiny about my involvement in the chile pepper trade, defined by a few in this department as "agribusiness," and thus contrary to all anthropological ethical canons. In my interviews with faculty, I quickly realized that I had been brought in because of ethnic hiring pressure from above, and that my own work and interests were of little concern within the department. As I went from office to office speaking with faculty members, I was told by more than one person that they "already had a Chicano" on the faculty. They "really couldn't understand what I would do."

This experience is almost comical in retrospect. The reception I was given was all negative: I was viewed as a capitalist agrimonger by a few key faculty, and the others saw me as a typecast Chicano. I cut my talk to the shortest possible time and hurried on to a plane home. Again, the point here is not the personal abuse or injustice that may or may not have occurred. In these cases it was not, I believe, any personal antagonism toward me, but rather a structural and hierarchical script played out with me in a predesigned role. Furthermore, it is only fair to state that there was strong support for my candidacy from a few faculty at this third department.

In 1990, I joined the faculty at Arizona State University. This was an action-now position in the Department of Anthropology, where the faculty had itself defined the need to hire a person who would contribute to a growing Mesoamerican and Mexicanist program. My credentials were evaluated on this basis, in addition to my work in border scholarship and applied anthropology. Given my previous experiences, I believed the faculty to be sincere in considering me for the job they wanted to fill. I was able to outline a program of teaching that suited my interests and career trajectory in applied anthropology, Mexico, and the border region. I was indeed recruited because of community and university pressure for Chicano representation, but I was hired because of my record as an anthropologist.

Since being back on the academic inside, I have myself been on a number of cultural diversity search committees, in and outside my own department. This experience has added to my view and interpretation of the sifting and shifting process. Viewed from these perspectives, and based on my discussions with other colleagues, affirmative action recruitment appears to be an ad hoc procedure that varies not only from university to university, but also from search committee to search committee. In the University of California, for example, "target of opportunity positions" are made available by the administration campuswide, with anthropologists competing with candidates from other disciplines. In the universities of Arizona, departments originate affirmative action searches, and individual candidates are then evaluated in each discipline, rather than in a universitywide pool. In most of these situations, the novel or fresh theoretical perspectives that candidates offer are rarely the reason they are considered. If they fulfill the required criteria of ethnicity or gender, the department's evaluation simply concerns how closely the candidate fits into the existing theoretical, area specialization, and methodological venues of the department.

The resulting sifting of individuals is frequently more manipulative than affirmative action guidelines would suggest. The polite and humane considerations one expects in the hiring process are often lacking. Initially, affirmative action was meant not only to diversify recruitment, but also to insure that minorities are not treated differently from other candidates in a hiring pool. This second goal of affirmative action hiring is rarely honored in searches aimed specifically at minorities and women. The assumption of departments today seems to be that since the hire will be a person of color or a woman, affirmative action criteria are satisfied simply by considering such candidates. However, as my own experiences and those of colleagues would suggest, fair and equal treatment in the sifting process is a rarity. In effect, the special conditions of target-of-opportunity and similar hiring programs release both institutions and departments from practicing equity and fair treatment. Standard procedures followed in "regular" hires are often abandoned, and each affirmative action candidate is evaluated on unique and occasionally even contrasting measures.

The following examples of reasons given for not hiring persons of color illustrate this lack of equity and common courtesy. These examples came from both my own experience in universitywide committee work and from discussions with colleagues in universities throughout the United States.

1. There is not enough space in the department for the new faculty member. (Like the remaining reasons, such statements are rarely made about successful white male candidates in a "regular" job search.) "Where will we put them?"

2. "The candidate does not look ethnic enough." In one case, this phenotypical excuse was actually stated! Here the fact that the candidate was blue-eyed, fair skinned, and did not fit the image of the department's ethnic category became a live issue in the rejection process.

3. The individual does not meet the federal category of an unrepresented minority. In this situation, it was suggested that a highly qualified candidate of Asian background would not be considered. No case for hiring the person was made, even though this institution has very few Asian faculty.

4. The individual is "too ethnic." In these cases, people have been viewed as tied too closely to their communities, and therefore lacking the "theoretical" detachment required of "real" anthropologists.

5. "We already have one." (Again, this is never a reason not to hire a white male.)

Overall, the results of such affirmative action recruitment and hiring have been rather bleak. Let me contextualize the present situation through a brief review of the numbers of women and minority faculty in the academic world. In a 1988 national survey of 450 colleges and universities, women comprised only 27 percent of the full-time faculty nationwide (compared with more than 50 percent of the population). Minorities accounted for only 11 percent of the faculty at four-year institutions. Of this 11 percent, Asians comprised 5 percent, African Americans, 3 pereent; Hispanics, 2 percent; and American Indians, 1 percent (Russell 1991).

Perhaps surprisingly, the numbers for minority representation among full-time anthropology faculty are even lower than this national 11 percent figure. According to the American Anthropological Association 1989 Survey of Departments, minority professors at all levels make up only 7 percent of full-time anthropology faculty in the United States, and Euro-Americans are 93 percent (AAA 1990:12). This 7 percent is broken down as follows: American Indians, 0.6 percent; Asians/Pacific Islanders, 2.2 percent; Afro-Americans, 2.3 percent; Hispanics, 2.2 percent.

In terms of specific universities and their state's Chicano populations, the ratios of representation in departments of anthropology are appalling. In California, with 33 percent of the total (enumerated) "Hispanic" population of the United States, and with Hispanics now close to 25 percent of the state population (U.S. Bureau of the Census 1990), the eight-campus University of California boasts only two tenured Chicanos in its departments of anthropology.[2] Similarly, in Texas, with 21.5 percent of the total U.S. Hispanic population, and with Hispanics, primarily of Mexican origin, comprising 11.2 percent of the state's total population, the leading research institution, the University of Texas at Austin, has no full-time tenured Chicano anthropologist.

From my perspective, these numbers clearly illustrate that the current spate of cultural diversity hiring searches has done little to change the composition of faculty in postsecondary education, or in the discipline of anthropology. The numbers illustrate dramatically the continuing marginality of racial minorities to the academy. They also suggest the minor role that the epistemological concerns and research-based contributions of these scholars currently play in academia.

Although most anthropology departments and their individual faculty members verbally endorse the concept of diversifying and recruiting individuals from so-called minorities, it is in the actual techniques and tactics of recruitment that the maintenance of race and gender hierarchy persists. My own return to academia is but one example of this process. When I left academia I thought that my future employment possibilities would be very good. I had rich fieldwork experience and a good record of publications and scholarly activity. But when I began actively to respond to job inquiries, I found unexpected barriers. Many faculty exhibited caution because of my community-based work experience outside of the discipline, that is, outside of the academy. That I had not been in an academic institution itself became a reason for misgivings. The question, for example, "Where have you been before coming here?" really means "What university and what department have you been affiliated with?" My not having come from any institution was met with suspicion. People kept referring to my absence from academia as synonymous with having severed a tie to anthropology. The *content* of my experience and the expansion of my knowledge base, all highly relevant to my research and career goals, were not taken seriously.

A question I was asked continually by individuals in a number of departments was: "But have you kept up with the literature?" I wondered at the assumption that it is "the literature" that defines the parameters of the discipline rather than the subject of our inquiries. (I also wonder how they gauge keeping up with the literature in "normal" career-trajectory candidates.) The point is that individuals coming into departments are evaluated in terms of the deeply rooted academic perceptions that function to maintain existing hierarchies. It is not the training or experience that engender our epistemologies and guide our choice of inquiry that comes under scrutiny. Rather, it is our comformity to the existing structures and canons.

Once I had survived the sifting, the shifting process began. After I was fortunate enough to regain a position in a department of anthropology and reentered academic life, I immediately began to receive recruitment calls from departments in other universities. They had a slot for a Chicano, or a minority, and wanted to place my name on their search lists. I had again been granted membership in the club and was now perceived as a bona fide contender for the shifting game. But, I wondered, did my newfound popularity reflect any more of an interest in my intellectual perspectives and research interests than did the suspicions raised when I was undergoing the departmental siftings of the hiring process?

In none of these events was there any awareness that minority scholars may bring new epistemologies and research strategies that challenge current orthodoxy. Instead, we hear the standard and much echoed refrain in search committees that the work of minority scholars is "not theoretical." Much current work being done by minority anthropologists does illustrate epistemological choices that are antithetical and contrary to establish career tracks with the discipline. This work often springs from personal history, or from an identification with and emotional attachment to the population studied. Worst of all, our research is often "applied," that is, geared toward solving practical social problems. These specific characteristics have been shunned by the discipline—until recent years.

It is no accident, I contend, that many anthropologists of color are engaged in such research. Carlos Velez-Ibañez's work (1992) on the "funds of knowledge" in a Chicano neighborhood in Tucson aims at the democratization of knowledge and is conducted in a neighborhood in which he grew up. It is not by chance that Diego Vigil, who is from the Chicano neighborhoods of downtown Los Angeles, has focused on barrio gangs in that city (1989), or that Bea Medicine has for years been both spokesperson and researcher among many Native American peoples, including her own Lakota (e.g., 1987). And there is Leith Mullings's work in ethnicity and urban anthropology (1977, 1978, 1987), George Bond's research on the black intellectual tradition and the Black American middle class, Sylvia Yanigisako's work (1989) on Japanese Americans and gender, Renato Rosaldo's confessions of truth as a Chicano (1989), Leo Chavez's research on cancer among Latina women (1992; Martinez and Chavez 1992), Edmund Gordon's anthropology of liberation (1992)—indeed the entire volume *Decolonizing Anthropology,* an Association of Black Anthropologists monograph (Harrison 1992)—the list is much longer. My own research on the border and in the community of my parents and grandparents was not merely a good anthropological project but stemmed from the need to set the record straight and to provide illumination about the community of which I am a part (Alvarez 1985, 1986, 1987a, b).

My goal is to not place blame on the profession, to throw rocks at academic institutions, and certainly not to cry on any shoulder about wrongs done. And neither do I suggest it is only minority scholars who are engaged in an epistemological struggle. My intent here has been to begin to investigate and unravel the knowledge base—that *savoir* that Foucault discusses—of our discipline by looking at the marginal, by looking at the extremities of our recruitment process. "Minorities" are the extreme group, the outsiders, those most disassociated. Change will come with our physical presence, but also from our perceptions and our interpretations, and from the uses to which we put the structures of knowledge of the academic profession.

Notes

I first presented a version of this essay at the session "Scholarly Canons and the Replication of Hierarchies: Race, Gender, and National Origin," organized by George C. Bond, at the 90th Annual Meetings of the American Anthropological Association in Chicago in 1991. I thank Professors Bond, Faye Harrison, George A. Collier, Mel Firestone, Roger Sanjek, and Karen Hesley for editorial and supportive comments.

1. Two Public Broadcasting System films, "The Lemon Grove Incident" and "The Trail North," were based on research I conducted in the border region and in the community of Lemon Grove. I participated as executive consultant and associate/coproducer, with Paul Espinosa of KPBS-San Diego.

2. I use the term *Hispanic* here because this is the category utilized by the American Anthropological Association. However, this term glosses the variation

and historical differences in this population in the United States. People of Cuban, Dominican, Puerto Rican, Mexican, and Chicano descent, as well as people from throughout Central and South America, are not clearly delineated with this term.

References

Alvarez, Robert R. Jr. 1985. The Border as Social System. *New Scholar* 9: 119–135.

———. 1986. The Lemon Grove Incident: The Nation's First Successful Desegregation Court Case. *Journal of San Diego History* 32:116–136.

———. 1987a. *Familia: Migration and Adaptation in Alta and Baja California.* Berkeley and Los Angeles: University of California Press.

———. 1987b. The Foundations and Genesis of a Mexican American Community: A Sociohistorical Perspective. In *Cities of the United States,* ed. Leith Mullings, 176–197. New York: Columbia University Press.

American Anthropology Association (AAA). 1990. *1989 Survey of Departments.* Departmental Services Program Report. Washington, D.C.: American Anthropological Association.

Chavez, Leo F. 1992. Etiologies of Breast and Cervical Cancer: A Comparison of Latina's and Physician's Perceptions. Paper presented at the American Anthropological Association Annual Meetings, San Francisco.

Foucault, Michel, 1980. *Power and Knowledge.* Pantheon: New York.

Gordon, Edmond T. 1992. The Anthropology of Liberation. *In Decolonizing Anthropology,* ed. Faye Harrison, 149–167.

Harrison, Faye, ed. 1992. *Decolonizing Anthropology.* Association of Black Anthropologists Monograph. Washington, D.C.: American Anthropology Association.

Martinez, Rebecca, and Leo Chavez. 1992. Cancer, Knowledge, and Power: Case Studies of Mexican Immigrant Women in the U.S. Paper presented at the American Anthropological Association Annual Meetings, San Francisco.

Medicine, Bea. 1987. Learning to be an Anthropologist and Remaining "Native." In *Applied Anthropology in America,* ed. E. M. Eddy and W. L. Partridge, 282–296. 2d ed. New York: Columbia University Press.

Mullings, Leith. 1977. The New Ethnicity: Old Wine in New Bottles. *Reviews in Anthropology* 4:615–624.

———. 1978. Ethnicity and Stratification in the Urban United States. *Annals of the New York Academy of Sciences* 318:10–22.

———, ed. 1987. *Cities of the United States.* New York: Columbia University Press.

Okley, Judith. 1992. Anthropology and Autobiography: Participatory Experience and Embodied Knowledge. In *Anthropology and Autobiography,* ed. Okley, 1–28. London: Routledge.

Rosaldo, Renato. 1989. *Culture and Truth: The Remaking of Social Analysis.* Boston: Beacon.

Russell, Susan H. 1991. The Status of Women and Minorities in Higher Education: The Findings from the 1988 National Survey of Postsecondary Faculty. *College and University Personnel Association Journal* 42:1–11.

U.S. Bureau of the Census. 1990. *The Hispanic Population in the U.S., 1989.* Current Population Reports. Washington, D.C.: U.S. Government Printing Office.

Velez-Ibañez, Carlos, and James Greenberg. 1992. Formation and Transformation of Funds of Knowledge among U.S.-Mexican Households. *Anthropology and Education Quarterly* 23:313–336.

Vigil, James Diego. 1989. *Barrio Gangs.* Austin: University of Texas Press.

Yanagisako, Sylvia. 1989. Transforming Orientalism in Asian American History. Paper presented at the American Anthropological Association Annual Meetings, New Orleans.

MICHAEL L. BLAKEY

Passing the Buck: Naturalism and Individualism as Anthropological Expressions of Euro-American Denial

This essay concerns the role that physical anthropologists have continually played in the support of ideologies of human inequality. This professional trajectory began with the overt espousal of polygenist racism in the nineteenth century and finds expression today in current, often obscurantist, research orientations that privilege individualist over social, cultural, and political explanations. By examining this history, I seek to show how mainstream biological and biomedical anthropology have been influenced by and had an influence upon Euro-America's denial of its participation in a racist and classist social order.

This pattern of denial partly originates in longstanding Euro-American conservative beliefs that nature and individuals—not social institutions—are ultimately responsible for a society's social ills, which, therefore, cannot or should not be solved by public policy initiatives requiring economic redistribution. No dominant societal group or exploitative social, political, or economic structures are at fault. Something may be wrong, but no one has been wronged. Justice and individual liberty are believed to prevail within a natural order that is sometimes unkind. These ideas, in which physical anthropologists are socialized and against which they must struggle, legitimate the status quo conditions of life in the United States and in other capitalist societies.

Aristotle comments in *Politics* that some philosophers and jurists "detest the notion that, because one man has the power of doing violence and is superior in brute strength, another shall be his slave and subject." Aristotle then proceeds to resolve the contradiction between a virtuous but slaveholding society by explaining that this condition is *natural.* He argues what his teachers knew to be false (Gould 1981:19–20): some were born to be slaves, while others were *natural* masters; dominion over *natural* slaves enhanced a natural master's virtue. This justification of inequity as natural would remain endemic, untested, and marginal compared to other justifications throughout much of European history.

Only with the convergence of "scientific" biology and U.S. slaveholding some millennia after the philosopher's death did naturalism advance to center stage and become a powerful ideological tool.

During the period of U.S. slavery, as Gould (1981) has amply demonstrated, theories of racial ranking (whites on top, blacks on the bottom) and polygenic origins (separate for each "race") were central concerns of U.S. anthropology. The creation of a biological ideology of white supremacy in the craniometry of Samuel Morton and the theorizing of Louis Agassiz were not at the periphery but were the very mainstream of nascent anthropological *science* (see also Bieder 1986; Harris 1968: chap. 4). The scientific justification for slavery and the inhuman treatment of Native and African Americans supplanted an earlier religious justification that made slavery and genocidal colonialism consistent with Christian charity—the souls of the conquered and enslaved would be saved. As the religious rationale weakened under the weight of its own contradictions (the success of Christianization), biological theories emerged to give a natural basis for white dominance over "the other" so-called racial groups.

The African-American statesman and abolitionist Frederick Douglass disputed the anthropological claims of Morton, Nott and Glidden, and Harvard's Agassiz in 1854, in "The Claims of the Negro Ethnologically Considered" (1950). He showed their analysis to be an attempt to make blacks out to be less than human, and he pointed to evidence against their misappropriation of ancient Egypt as a demonstration of European rather than African accomplishment and intellectual capacity. Douglass outlined the importance of social and environmental "circumstances upon physical man" in opposition to the reverse argument made by these establishment biological determinists. Indeed, Douglass emphasized the effects of social and economic inequity in the similarities of social behavior and physical condition of Irish manual laborers and African-American plantation slaves. Thus, the kinds of antiracist (and social science) arguments that would later be taken up by Franz Boas and others in the twentieth-century nature-nurture debate were used much earlier by Douglass, at the very origins of racial determinism. Douglass's argument, however, placed less emphasis on individual change through acculturation than Boas's, and more on persisting socioeconomic inequity.

With the end of U.S. slavery, the vigor of mainstream physical anthropology declined. As the discipline regrouped, Ales Hrdlicka, the leading professional physical anthropologist during the first third of the twentieth century, lamented the lapse in U.S. craniometry that followed the Civil War (Hrdlicka 1918; Brace 1982). Hrdlicka's own craniometric research sought to account for the unequal social and economic attainments of new immigrant groups from southern and eastern Europe, of African Americans, and of women as results of inferior brains (Hrdlicka 1925, 1928). He also explained the high mortality of indigenous peoples under the press of colonial expansion as a natural process of evolutionary advance. "We see that the higher civilized white man has already in some respects outdistanced others," Hrdlicka wrote, "that he is rapidly diversifying, and that all about us those who cannot keep the accelerated pace are being eliminated by *nature*" (1915, emphasis added; see also Blakey 1987).

Hrdlicka's general view of the bearing of evolution on his contemporary society is epitomized in a 1921 lecture he gave at American University:

> There is no question that there are today already retarded peoples, retarded races, and that there are advanced and more advanced races, and that the differences between them tend rather to increase than to decrease. . . . And there is no acceptable possibility, there is nothing that we can conceive or accept unless it be some unforseen calamity . . . that would make the white man wait upon the Japanese or Chinaman who is only a little bit behind, or the Negro who is a long way behind. . . . From the scientific point of view there is no such prospect at all according to all indications and simply through the continuous process of evolution that the order of the world in the future will be quite different from what it is today. (1921:12–14)

Hrdlicka's reasoning was typical of, not peripheral to, mainstream physical anthropology in the early part of this century. Racist biological determinism continued to be espoused by the leading figure to succeed Hrdlicka during the 1930s, Harvard's Ernest Hooton (see Hooton 1939a, b; cf. Gould 1981: 109–110).

Much of physical anthropology as it pertained to living populations focused on racial, ethnic, class, and gender differences and justified as natural their inequalities in the urban industrial United States. Hrdlicka sought to use evolutionary science to promote U.S. progress through eugenic research. More politicized eugenicists such as Charles Davenport (the Cold Spring Harbor human geneticist who headed the National Research Council Anthropology Committee beginning in 1918), Madison Grant, Lothrop Stoddard, and others enjoyed a significant impact on racially restrictive immigration policy. This body of ideas also gave scientific justification to racial segregation, antimiscegenation laws in most states, and the ideology of the Ku Klux Klan (see Allen 1975; Patterson 1970 [1951]). These same ideas fostered fascism worldwide.

The main difference between the eugenics activists and Hrdlicka was that he resisted the idea of immediate application in favor of programs to accumulate extensive empirical data, thus necessitating further professionalization of his field. Although convinced of the superior objectivity of his approach, Hrdlicka produced research no different from that of the eugenicists. His research results, in fact, were often presented in spurious ways in order to support his a priori belief in white, American, and male superiority (Blakey 1987).

This history of anthropological racism is almost never mentioned in introductory texts in physical anthropology. More often, it is psychology that is pointed to as having a racist history through its biased use of IQ testing. One prominent physical anthropology text (Nelson and Jurmain 1991) gives Hrdlicka and Hooton their due as founders of the field but says nothing of their racist work. In connection with the issue of the repatriation of Native-American burial remains, these authors flatly state, "Anthropologists are not racists" (114–115), a generalization that reflects a wholly uncritical view of Euro-American anthropology. When scientific racism is discussed in histories of physical anthropology, racist figures are often characterized as odd pseudoscientists, or as methodologically primitive, and without bearing on the discipline in general, or on its institutionalization as a science.

Nowhere in the leading research on Hrdlicka's life and work (Spencer 1979, 1982; see also Brace 1982), for example, is there an examination of the racism, class elitism, and sexism that I found so frequently in Hrdlicka's work (Blakey 1987, 1991; Rankin-Hill and Blakey 1994). Indeed, Hrdlicka's most extensive obituary (Schultz 1945) characterized him as an antiracist because he opposed Nazi Aryan supremacy. Yet he clearly believed in and wrote about white racial supremacy, male supremacy, Anglo-American supremacy, and the biological superiority of academics.

A sterilized institutional history that peripheralizes physical anthropological work before 1930 may predispose us to repeat the mistakes of the past. That the founders of physical anthropology promoted racist and eugenic views that were eclipsed in the wake of the Nazi program or the Civil Rights movement needs to be taught today, as biological determinism based on misconstrued data again gains currency in the political climate of the 1990s (see Leslie 1990).

In the forefront of the liberal reaction to naturalism was Franz Boas, undoubtedly the most potent opponent of the Harvard-Washington axis, as Spencer (1979) describes Hrdlicka and Hooton. Boas emphasized the biological plasticity in head form, stature, and other traits of southern and eastern European immigrants in New York. Boas showed that their biology and behavior was influenced by U.S. acculturation (1912). Despite his empiricism, Boas was influenced by the integrationist politics of his youth in Germany and by his experience as an American Jew, making the mainstream racial hierarchies unpalatable (Glick 1982). His students and those he had influenced (Mead 1928; Benedict and Weltfish [1943] 1986; Klineberg 1935; Montagu 1941) elaborated upon the Boasian antiracist/antibiodeterminist tradition from the late 1920s onward, and these liberal views began to capture the imagination of the U.S. public.

The application of Boas's approaches was consistent with liberal ideology, emphasizing the need for intercultural understanding and nonintervention in the affairs of other cultures. It was only indirectly a critical indictment of the social organization and domestic policies of the United States. The Boasian emphasis on nurture over nature bolstered the idea that inequities could be eliminated through individual and group acculturation. This did contribute to undermining the ideological hegemony of the mainstream naturalism that served to legitimate inequality. In Nazi Germany, Boas's *Kultur und Rasse* was burned (Herskovits 1953:4) while at home he advocated U.S. pacifism.

Among the opponents of the biological deterministic view was T. Wingate Todd, who wrote that cases of defective cranial development resulting from (and not creating) poverty were being misinterpreted to show the inferiority of blacks. Todd warned that anthropology was "a powerful tool that, if not carefully used, damaged both those who wielded it and those upon whom it was inflicted" (1930). Todd influenced African-American physical anthropology (Drake 1980; Rankin-Hill and Blakey 1994) through his mentorship of W. Montague Cobb.

African-American scholars, however, had initiated the nature-nurture debate in North American anthropology during slavery, criticizing biological determinism while posing socioeconomic explanations for biological and social effects (Douglass 1950 [1854]). African-American antiracist critiques of biological determinism focused on social and economic differences, prominently including those resulting from institutional racial discrimination (Douglass 1950 [1854]; Du Bois 1967 [1899]; Cobb 1939). Their analyses gave scientific rationale for the development of human and civil rights struggles, calling for policy correctives. Two recent historical studies (Rankin-Hill and Blakey 1994; Baker 1994) show that, among African-American anthropologists and sociologists, Boasian culturology stressing the potential for acculturation, while useful, was considered inadequate as an explanation of the social and health problems of African Americans (Baker 1994). The Boasian approach was not sufficiently critical to adequately inform the anti-discrimination policy initiatives that were essential to applied or activist African-American scholarship.

From the 1930s to the 1960s, opposition to nazism and fascism, disgust with the eugenically motivated Holocaust, labor unrest, and the rise of the African American–led Civil Rights movement all created a political and intellectual climate conducive to liberal science (Drake 1980; Stocking 1968). Yet naturalism surrendered only conditionally to liberal environmentalism. One condition was the retention of the continuing belief that nature as an ultimate cause of biological variation made a research program more scientific or objective than did the study of social or economic causal variables. Increasingly for physical anthropology (or human ecology) "environmental" influences would mean the *natural* ecology, and not social and economic conditions (Blakey 1987).

"Race" was also retained, even as the very concept of biological races was shown by leading anthropologists to be unnatural, analytically bankrupt, and (at best) a form of folk-scientific classification (Livingstone 1962; Montagu 1967). The continuing scientific need for biological categories to fit naturalist theories, however, and the continued use of folk racial classification in an institutionally racist society meant that physical anthropologists in fact remained split on the question of the utility of racial classification (Lieberman and Reynolds 1978). In that study, the social backgrounds of anthropologists were shown to account for their choices of racial or nonracial typology.

In the new physical anthropological emphasis on evolutionary and ecological theory, studies of major urban and industrial populations were peripheralized. While racial hierarchy, genetic determinism, and eugenic application were rejected, the continuing adherence to naturalism pressed the human ecologists of the 1960s and 1970s to seek out the extreme environments (high altitude, deserts, etc.) and the seemingly isolated, traditional populations where natural science theories of human physical difference had the most explanatory power. Little attention was paid to the biological and health effects of inequitable political and economic institutions. This continuing emphasis on nature, like racial determinism, avoided intellectual confrontation with social inequality. Theories and research agendas serving the purposes of denial have remained, although their forms have become more subtle and obscure.

As physical anthropologists largely abdicated responsibility for conducting research in the industrial West and turned to societies where they could study nature as they defined it, an appreciation for physical plasticity (a Boasian concern) had grown considerably. In fact, naturalism took on an increasing emphasis in the international focus on physiological adaptation and human adaptability that developed by the 1960s. Influences of culture on biology (in a Boasian sense) were considered, but these were of interest mainly as a necessary control of statistical "noise" interfering with an analysis of the direct relationship between the natural ecology and human biology—the real, objective, and scientific variables. For example, during formulation of the Human Adaptability Program in 1962, Paul Baker wrote, "The primary correlation may be between climate and body size, or malaria and hemoglobin C, but the discovery of why these correlations exist also requires a knowledge of the similarities and differences in cultures of the people involved" (1962:19).[1]

An alternative approach, resisting naturalism, does exist. Goldstein, Tsarong, and Beall (1983), for example, emphasize the integration of high-altitude Himalayan and Andean communities into international political and economic systems whose effects are more powerful than, or negate, the causal variables considered important within the naturalist program. Similar studies by other physical anthropologists are rare. Not only has the naturalist tendency promoted a disregard for physical health conditions in the urban industrial societies once studied by Boas, Hrdlicka, and other early bioanthropologists, but the primacy of natural environment stressors over national and international economic integration have only been reified by the focus on supposedly isolated "traditional" societies. Modernization studies attempt to return to industrial society but carry with them an evolved brand of denial based on notions of individualism.

Individual (versus social) explanations for persisting "racial" and group differences have had an increasing impact on public attitudes in recent decades, and I argue that this is also connected to shifts in physical anthropological perspectives. As more liberal views began to dominate in the years following World War II and at the height of the Civil Rights movement, both anthropologists and the general public increasingly disavowed a biologically fixed hierarchy among races, genders, or classes.

Major trends in Euro-American and African-American racial attitudes between 1942 and 1983 were summarized in the National Research Council study, *A Common Destiny: Blacks and American Society,* in 1989 (Jaynes and Williams 1989: chap. 3). Based on national surveys by the Institute for Social Research, National Opinion Research Center, Gallup, and others, these data showed little change in black attitudes favoring *principles* of integration and social equality; these attitudes were held by the vast majority at the beginning of the survey period, as they were during the latest survey. Euro-American support for principles of integration and racial equality had improved remarkably but lagged slightly behind that of African Americans.

In the two most directly comparable data sets, 90 percent of whites favored multiracial access to the same schools in 1982 (a 58 percent increase since 1942), and 88 percent favored open residential choice in 1976 (up 23 percent since 1963). Black figures were 96 percent and 99 percent respectively. Other data on Euro-American attitudes revealed a 52 percent increase in support for the principle of equal job access between 1944 and 1972, when 97 percent answered in support.

Attitudes about *implementation,* however, were often contrary to those of principle. Data on support for federal job intervention showed that only 36 percent of whites answered favorably in 1974, down 2 percent since 1964. Blacks during the same period showed 82 percent in support, down 10 percent. Most dramatically, while only 26 percent of whites supported government appropriations for blacks, and 18 percent supported aid to all minorities, 80 percent and 49 percent of blacks favored these measures.

The National Research Council report attributes much of this difference between principle and implementation to competing values of equality and individual freedom. According to surveys in 1972, most whites (60 percent) explained black-white inequality as a matter of individualistic or personal responsibility, or they emphasized a lack of effort among blacks. These whites supported "the view that government [and their tax dollars] has no role to play in improving the status of blacks." Survey data from 1980 showed that blacks tended to view discrimination as resulting both from "prejudiced individuals and broader social processes." In that year 53 percent of blacks, but only 26 percent of whites, felt that blacks face significant racial discrimination.

In the early 1990s, a carefully controlled experimental study by the Urban Institute (Turner, Fix, and Struyk 1991) showed racially based job discrimination to be biased three times as much against blacks as against whites, and even more biased against Latinos. Pairs of specially trained black and white male college students were matched for age, speech, education, work experience, demeanor, and physical build. They individually answered classified advertisements for 476 randomly selected entry-level private-sector jobs in Washington, D.C., and Chicago. Whites were advanced farther than blacks in the hiring process (given interviews) 20 percent of the time, while blacks were advanced farther than whites 7 percent of the time. Also, whites received job offers three times more often than their equally qualified black counterparts (15 percent compared to 5 percent). Blacks waited longer for interviews, their interviews were shorter, and they received fewer encouraging comments. "In some cases, the blacks were steered toward jobs for which they did not apply. In Washington, a man applied for a job as a hotel desk clerk, but was offered a job as a bellboy" (*Washington Post,* May 15, 1991).

Notwithstanding this and numerous similar studies, where most blacks see persisting discrimination, most whites see individual failure to succeed. In 1981, only 35 percent of blacks but 60 percent of whites accepted "the claim that a lack of motivation or effort was responsible for black-white inequality." Overlying these contrasting social and individualist explanations for inequality, nonetheless, is the overt racism entailed in the desire expressed by many Euro-Americans to maintain social distance from blacks (Jaynes and Williams 1989: chap. 3)

Individualism contributes to ahistorical and social context–free explanations of inequality, to overly narrow definitions of racial discrimination (as merely racial epithets or other openly racist personal acts), to victim blaming, and to the denial of institutional racism and racially linked class barriers. The survey data indicate that most Euro-Americans believe that freedom and equality exist for all Americans. It is policies of redistributive justice (such as affirmative action) that seem unfair to whites, given those assumptions. Individualism feeds the denial of continuing racial discrimination. This denial leads to the conclusion that the fault lies with those who would otherwise be recognized as oppressed.

Some biomedical researchers during the 1970s and 1980s did in fact begin to return to the study of urban and industrial societies by undertaking *modernization* or acculturation studies. Here the Boasian emphasis on the individual effects of acculturation melds with evolutionary ideas. Migrant populations from the rural Pacific, Africa, and elsewhere were shown to experience social stress from adjustments to a "modern lifestyle" in an urban host environment (see Brown 1982; Harburg, Glieberman, and Harburg 1982; McElroy and Townsend 1989:291–384; McGarvey and Baker 1979).

A leading medical anthropology text of the period indicates that modernization means "emulating the lifestyle of people—colonists, soldiers, diplomats, the urban elite—who have material goods, leisure, and privilege" (McElroy and Townsend 1989:343–344). "Successful acculturation" in a Westernized industrial capitalist society (i.e., *modernization*) is also described as synonymous with acquiring the "middle-class" life style in which traditional and transitional individuals have yet to fully participate (cf. Brown 1982; Spindler 1977). I contend that *all* social groups of any society participate "fully" in that society (if not in its middle class). They participate in different ways, through the varied social and economic roles and relations that actually define the society. The stresses of "acculturation" and "modernization" are in larger measure stresses of frustrated aspirants for class mobility in societies in which they already participate, on unequal terms (Blakey 1985). The connotations of the concept "modernization" confound upward socioeconomic mobility with social and technological change and in turn suggest, falsely, the inevitability of class mobility.

In modernization studies, measurable psychosocial and psychophysiological stress effects such as hypertension or alcoholism are attributed to the victim's resistance to acquiring (or lack of participation in) modern culture. They are not attributed to economic insecurity in class-stratified societies, or to the inaccessibility of upward economic mobility. One recent reassessment of modernization reveals its individualist ideology clearly. "Dressler and his associates (1987) found that it was not modernization itself but modernizing beyond one's means that affected blood pressure" (McElroy and Townsend 1989:344). Here Brazilian "life-style stress" is viewed to result from a discrepancy between economic resources and bad individual choices about markers of modern life-style (color television, stereo, vacation travel, newspaper reading).

If one were to explain the stress-related high blood pressures of economically disadvantaged blacks and whites in the United States (Harburg, Glieberman, Roeper et al. 1978; Harburg, Glieberman, Ozgoren, et al. 1978) in the same terms used to describe the Brazilians discussed above, the obfuscation of the stresses of class inequality with individualist modernization rhetoric would be obvious. "Modernizing beyond one's means" is an epistemologically and politically loaded alternative to characterizing such populations as striving for a socioeconomic status and security that is for the most part unattainable because of socially organized economic exploitation and racial discrimination. To posit instead that life-style choice (social mobility) is *at the discretion of individual's* in a modern society, and to blame their cultural or individual ill preparation for failure, is to embrace the conservative philosophy of individualism completely, and to disavow the existence of structural barriers of racism and class.

Naturalism and individualism give plausibility to the idea of a just and free meritocracy in which no one oppresses, despite the obvious inequity about us. They have served to legitimize the United States in terms of the revolutionary principles upon which it was founded, and they provide a convenient protection for individual egos whose identities are rooted in those values. Not surprisingly, these attitudes can be found among any U.S. subgroup; they characterize a majority of Euro-Americans, and a minority of African Americans. What is more, corresponding attitudes about *implementation* of these principles through redistribution policies and safeguards do not differ by income, education, or region (see Jaynes and Williams 1989). They are no doubt part of the socialization experience of the majority of U.S. anthropologists, varying proportionately in relation to their social identity (as evinced by our field's intellectual history). While overt racial determinism has been displaced by individualist explanations of racial inequity, fortunately for the process of social change and the development of physical anthropology, we do not all accept these ideas to the same extent. Still, individualist interpretations apparently form the dominant Euro-American viewpoint.

Most anthropological research since Boas has been too much an uncontested terrain, safely nestled in apology between what might be considered either liberal or reactionary ideas. Critiques of naturalism and of pervasive individualism are needed to contest this safe terrain and to expose past and present supports of a racist and classist social order. Unless all sides of the field's history are examined, future anthropologists will be unable to determine the difference and make informed choices for themselves.

Physical anthropology's history has been marked by an epistemology of denial. Naturalism, as biological and racial determinism, denies human responsibility for social inequity. In its ecological form, naturalism denies human responsibility for the social etiology of major organic health problems, and biological variation in the urban industrial world is left unstudied. By its very insistence on objectivity, naturalism denies that the study of human biology is an intrinsically political pursuit. Human responsibility for scientific interpretation and ideological production is denied.

Individualism, as a major tendency of thought within U.S. society, denies the pervasiveness of its racism, and the impact of discrimination on African-American and other oppressed communities. In its modernization guise, individualist analysis in the physical and biomedical anthropology of Third World societies reduces international and national systemic forces to the good or bad choices of individuals. Finally, there is a tendency within the profession of anthropology for its practioners to deny the pervasiveness of racism in its own history and to attribute racist thinking to aberrant individuals.

In each instance, denial is used to disguise conflicts or contradictions between what are perceived to be lofty values and base behaviors. Its effect is to perpetuate assumptions that lead to racist conclusions about the causes of obvious social, economic, and biological differences. It constrains the development of more adequate societal solutions to societal problems and the kinds of biocultural studies that could reveal them.

Notes

1. This tendency is reflected in the research on genetic, physiological, and health studies of the Human Adaptability Section of the International Biological Program sponsored by the National Science Foundation and the National Institutes of Health (see Baker and Eveleth 1982:43–44). It should, however, be noted that physical anthropologists made a contribution to descriptive studies of U.S. health as consultants and analysts for the National Center for Health Statistics, Centers for Disease Control, and Health and Nutritional Examination Surveys during the same period. Those analyses, however, did not address the systemic impact of broader social and economic inequities on health differences.

References

Allen, Garland. 1975. Genetics, Eugenics, and Class Struggle. *Genetics* 79: 29–45.

Baker, Lee D. 1994. The Role of Anthropology in the Social Construction of Race, 1896–1954. Ph.D. diss., Temple University.

Baker, Paul T. 1962. The Application of Ecological Theory to Anthropology. *American Anthropologist* 64:15–21.

Baker, Paul T., and Phyllis M. Eveleth. 1982. The Effects of Funding Patterns on the Development of Physical Anthropology. In *A History of American Physical Anthropology, 1930–1980,* ed. Frank Spencer, 31–38.

Benedict, Ruth, and Gene Weltfish. 1986 [1943]. *The Races of Mankind.* Revised ed. New York: Public Affairs Committee.

Bieder, Robert E. 1986. Samuel Morton and the Calculations of Inferiority. In *Science Encounters the Indian, 1820–1880: The Early Years of American Ethnology,* 55–103. Norman: University of Oklahoma Press.

Blakey, Michael L. 1985. *Stress, Social Inequality, and Culture Change: An Anthropological Approach to Human Psychophysiology.* Ph.D. diss., University of Massachusetts.

———. 1987. Skull Doctors: Intrinsic Social and Political Bias in the History of American Physical Anthropology, with Special Reference to the Work of Ales Hrdlicka. *Critique of Anthropology* 7:7–34.

———. 1991. Man and Nature, White and Other. In *Decolonizing Anthropology,*

ed. Faye V. Harrison, 8–16. Association of Black Anthropologists Monograph. Washington, D.C.: American Anthropological Association.
Boas, Franz. 1912. *Changes in Bodily Form of Descendants of Immigrants.* New York: Columbia University Press.
Brace, C. Loring. 1982. The Roots of the Race Concept in American Physical Anthropology. In *A History of American Physical Anthropology, 1930–1980,* ed. Frank Spencer, 11–30.
Brown, D. E. 1982. Physiological Stress and Culture Change in a Group of Filipino-Americans: A Preliminary Investigation. *Annals of Human Biology* 9:553–563.
Cobb, Montague. 1939. The Negro as a Biological Element in the American Population. *Journal of Negro Education* 8:336–348.
Douglass, Frederick. [1950]. The Claims of the Negro Ethnologically Considered. In *The Life and Writings of Frederick Douglass,* ed. Philip S. Foner, 289–309. New York: International Publishers.
Drake, St. Clair. 1980. Anthropology and the Black Experience. *Black Scholar* 11(7): 2–31.
Dressler, William W., José Ernesto Dos Santos, Philip N. Gallagher, Jr., and Fernando E. Viteri. 1987. Arterial Blood Pressure and Modernization in Brazil. *American Anthropologist* 89:398–409.
Du Bois, W.E.B. 1967 [1899]. *The Philadelphia Negro: A Social Study.* New York: Schocken Books.
Glick, Leonard B. 1982. Types Distinct from Our Own: Franz Boas on Jewish Identity and Assimilation. *American Antrhopologist* 84:545–564.
Goldstein, Melvyn G., Paljor Tsarong, and Cynthia M. Beall. 1983. High Altitude Hypoxia, Culture, and Human Fecundity/Fertility: A Comparative Study. *American Anthropologist* 85:28–49.
Gould, Stephen Jay. 1981. *The Mismeasure of Man.* New York: Norton.
Harburg, E., L. Glieberman, and J. Harburg. 1982. Blood Pressure and Skin Color: Maupiti, French Polynesia. *Human Biology* 54:283–298.
Harburg, E., L. Glieberman, F. Ozgoren, et al. 1978. Skin color, Ethnicity, and Blood Pressure II: Detroit Whites. *American Journal of Public Health* 68:1184–1188.
Harburg, E., L. Glieberman, P. Roeper, M. A. Schork, and W. J. Schull. 1978. Skin Color, Ethnicity, and Blood Pressure I: Detroit Blacks. *American Journal of Public Health* 68:1177–1183.
Harris, Marvin. 1968. *The Rise of Anthropological Theory: A History of Theories of Culture.* New York: Crowell.
Herskovits, Melville J. 1953. *Franz Boas: The Science of Man in the Making.* New York: Scribners.
Hooton, Ernest A. 1939a. *The American Criminal.* Vol. 1. Cambridge, Mass.: Harvard University Press.
———. 1939b. *Crime and the Man.* Cambridge, Mass.: Harvard Universitty Press.
Hrdlicka, Ales. 1915. Evolution in the Light of Recent Discoveries, and Its Rela-

tions to Medicine. Paper read at joint meeting of the Medical and Anthropological Societies, October 12, 1915. Hrdlicka Papers, National Anthropological Archives, Smithsonian Institution.

———. 1918. Physical Anthropology: Its Scope and Aims; Its History and Present Status in America. *American Journal of Physical Anthropology* 1:3–34.

———. 1921. Lecture Number 27, delivered at the American University, May 27, 1921. Hrdlicka Papers, National Anthropological Archives, Smithsonian Institution.

———. 1925. *The Old Americans.* Baltimore: Williams and Williams.

———. 1928. The Full-Blood American Negro. *American Journal of Physical Anthropology* 10:205–235.

Jaynes, Gerald David, and Robin M. Williams, Jr., eds. 1989. *A Common Destiny: Blacks and American Society.* Washington, D.C.: National Academy Press.

Klineberg, Otto. 1935. *Race Differences.* New York: Harper.

Leslie, Charles. 1990. Scientific Racism: Reflections on Peer Review, Science, and Ideology. *Social Science and Medicine* 31:891–912.

Lieberman, Leonard, and Larry T. Reynolds. 1978. The Debate over Race Revisited. *Phylon* 4:333–344.

Livingstone, Frank. 1962. On the Nonexistence of Human Races. *Current Anthropology* 3:279–281.

McElroy, Ann, and Patricia K. Townsend. 1989. *Medical Anthropology in Ecological Perspective.* Boulder, Colo.: Westview.

McGarvey, Steven, and Paul T. Baker. 1979. The Effects of Modernization on Samoan Blood Pressures. *Human Biology* 51:461–479.

Mead, Margaret. 1928. *Coming of Age in Samoa.* New York: Morrow.

Montagu, Ashley. 1964. The Concept of Race in the Human Species in the Light of Genetics. In *The Concept of Race,* ed. Montagu, 1–11. New York: Free Press. First published in 1941, *Journal of Heredity* 23:243–247.

———. 1967. *Man's Most Dangerous Myth: The Fallacy of Race.* Cleveland: Meridian.

Nelson, Harry, and Robert Jurmain. 1991. *Introduction to Physical Anthropology.* 5th ed. St. Paul, Minn: West.

Patterson, William L., ed. 1970 (1951). *We Charge Genocide: The Historic Petition to the United Nations for Relief from a Crime of the United States Government Against the Negro People.* New York: International Publishers.

Rankin-Hill, Lesley M., and Michael L. Blakey. 1994. W. Montague Cobb (1904–1990): Physical Anthropologist, Anatomist, Activist. *American Anthropologist* 96:74–96.

Schultz, A. H. 1945. Biographical Memoir of Ales Hrdlicka, 1869–1943. *National Academy of Sciences Biographical Memoirs* 23:305–338.

Spencer, Frank. 1979. *Ales Hrdlicka, M.D., 1869–1943: A Chronicle of the Life and Work of an American Anthropologist.* Ph.D. diss., University of Michigan.

———, ed. 1982. *A History of American Physical Anthropology, 1930–1980.* New York: Academic Press.

Spindler, Louise S. 1977. *Culture Change and Modernization*. New York: Holt, Rinehart and Winston.

Stocking, George M., Jr. 1968. *Race, Culture, and Evolution: Essays in the History of Anthropology*. New York: Free Press.

Todd, T. Wingate. 1930. The Folly of Complacency. Address to the Association for the Study of Negro Life and History, Washington D.C. Published as An Anthropological Study of Negro Life. *Journal of Negro History* 16 (1931): 36–42.

Turner, M., M. Fix, and R. Struyk. 1991. *Opportunities Denied, Opportunities Diminished*. Washington, D.C.: Urban Institute.

ROBERT PAYNTER,
SUSAN HAUTANIEMI, AND
NANCY MULLER

The Landscapes of the W.E.B. Du Bois Boyhood Homesite: An Agenda for an Archaeology of the Color Line

Next to a highway in the Berkshires of Massachusetts is a National Landmark/National Register site, the Boyhood Homesite of William Edward Burghardt Du Bois. Du Bois was born in Great Barrington in 1868, became one of the foremost scholar-activists of the twentieth century, and died at the age of ninety-five in Ghana. He spent some early years of his life at this site, and in the 1930s he vacationed here. During the nineteenth century this homesite was part of a small neighborhood of African Americans, people who by the twentieth century were dispersed throughout North America and Africa. This place and these people, and some of their white neighbors, nurtured the young Du Bois, inspired some of his philosophical commitments, and were among his reference points throughout his life.

A stop at the site today teaches one little about Du Bois or his life in Great Barrington or in any of the many other places around the globe that he influenced. The visitor sees an abandoned field encroached upon by shrubs and brambles, pines, cedar, and sugar maples, a land parcel now undergoing New England old-field ecological succession. Attached to a wooden fence post is a small plaque proclaiming official National Landmark status, but giving virtually no other information. Walking through the parcel one encounters poison ivy; an abandoned cellar hole; a chimney base; shards of white and rose decorated dinner plates and of blue, green, and brown glass; and the metal pieces of tools, barrels, fences, hardware, and household appliances.

A place of historical significance on the contemporary landscape should be a site for remembering. Places like Independence Hall in

Philadelphia or the Washington Monument in the District of Columbia or Mount Vernon in Virginia exist today to remind people of the individuals and groups who shaped history and gave birth to the present. Historical places exist to teach our world about the past in a different way from textbooks. They tempt us to experience the past, to touch, feel, and connect with the past, to try to imagine eating, washing, raising a family, debating issues great and small, in short to identify with people in the past. The learning that happens at historical sites is among the most powerful for signaling the significant people, groups, and events of this culture's history and thereby underlining the dynamics driving the unfolding drama of American life.

The Du Bois Boyhood Homesite, albeit duly listed on the National Register of Historical Places, does none of this. It is not a place to learn about Du Bois and his numerous contributions to American life, to remember his relatives, to confront the long history of African Americans in New England, to inquire about the historical depth and distinctive shape of northern racism. Instead, the Du Bois Boyhood Homesite is, for the majority of the American citizenry, a place of forgetting, yet another site on our contemporary landscape that by omission of African Americans from the historical record contributes to a racially constructed ignorance about the place of African Americans as transformative agents in the history of the United States. It is only a poison ivy patch by the side of the woods.

How is it that the Du Bois Boyhood Homesite stands mute to Du Bois's significance in U.S. history? This is a complex question about the dynamics of remembering and forgetting in the racial formation that is U.S. culture (see, e.g., Wallace 1990). It has, in part to do with the conjunction of the character of Du Bois, the texture of northern racism, and the depths to which white racism is rooted in the practice and ideas of historical disciplines, such as our own historical archaeology. Along with colleagues at the University of Massachusetts, Amherst, we are engaged in a project to bring the Boyhood Homesite of W.E.B. Du Bois to a prominent place on the landscape of historical places, to help realize the potential power of this place to challenge racist constructions of Du Bois and African-American life in the North.

As archaeologists our task is to call attention to the site and its objects and thereby the people responsible for them. The first step involves establishing the historical presences, including Du Bois's, who built, transformed, and eventually abandoned this landscape. What we have learned about these people and how we have used objects to come to these conclusions are the subjects of much of this essay. But to truly unlock the potential of the site requires deeper readings of the objects that disclose the workings of the color line in the past and present of western Massachusetts. Achieving such readings is hampered by the blind spots white racism imposes upon the practice of archaeology. In our conclusion we point to some of these and develop caveats, drawn from Du Bois's work, for scholars seeking to work through these issues. The essay is thus part of a work in progress, and it documents some of the forces and struggles that have shaped the formation of the Du Bois Boyhood Homesite.

Our encounter with the site began in 1983 when Ernest Allen, chair of the W.E.B. Du Bois Department of Afro American Studies at the University of Massachusetts, Amherst, and Homer Meade, a lecturer in the department, approached Robert Paynter with artifacts from the site. They asked if archaeological investigations might provide more information. Utilizing as a documentary base the extensive holdings of Du Bois's papers in the University of Massachusetts Archives, and Du Bois's own voluminous writings, Paynter organized two archaeological summer field schools at the site. Nancy Muller joined the project as a student in one of these field schools. Susan Hautaniemi later helped analyze some of the twelve thousand shards recovered in the two field seasons.

As archaeologists seeking to understand African-American lifeways, we have tried to identify biases we bring to our study. For us, the biases include the personal and institutional ignorances of the white sector of a racially divided society, and the difficulties that archaeologists encounter in moving from identifying the functions of recovered objects to understanding what they mean to the people who used them. For the historical archaeologist looking at things not so different from those in our own everyday life, the step to interpretation can occur too quickly if the significance of racial identity and racism is not probed carefully. Did patent medicines advertised with exclusively white models have the same meaning and use for white American women and African-American women in the Jim Crow nineteenth century? Does the use of European housing forms and mass-marketed commodities point to the social or cultural assimilation of African Americans into white New England society? A moment's reflection should suggest quite probably not, but without reflection a white historical archaeologist might misinterpret or reinforce misunderstandings. A strategic pause is needed to consider how "race" may mark an interpretive divide in the way one approaches material records. Unfortunately, studies that consider the implications of "race" in historical sequences and theoretical perspectives are not central in the literature of archaeology.

The absence of such viewpoints in our disciplinary common sense has to do, in part, with essentialist constructions of the notion of "race." Barbara Fields (1990:97) points out that for most Americans implicitly "there is really only one race, the Negro race." Hence, studies of "race" in the historical archaeology of the United States are, in effect, studies about African Americans, and not about the overarching significance of racism and racial identity for Euro-Americans and for Asian Americans, Native Americans, and all others. The importance of a system of racial inequality is rarely raised in interpretations of Euro-American sites.

Race, as a social construct, operates within a context of concepts and actions. St. Clair Drake's (1987, 1990) historical overview of racial discrimination demonstrates that no simple causal chain leads from color symbolism to social prejudices based on skin pigmentation and to socially structured inequality. The concept of race as we know it today—appearing within a system of significant social division, based indirectly on, and sometimes explained by, ancestral biological traits—arose in the ideological structures of plantation production and the Atlantic slave trade. From there it worked its way into the hegemonic ideologies of the political economies of the Western Hemisphere (see also Cox 1948; Robinson 1983; Smedley 1993). Political economies in which race figures as an important social division, such as the United States, are *racial formations,* or sets of ongoing relations in "which social, economic and political forces determine the content and importance of racial categories and by which they are in turn shaped by racial meaning" (Omi and Winant 1986:63).

Appiah parses the ideologies of such societies with a series of related concepts. *Racialism* is the conviction "that there are heritable characteristics possessed by members of our species, that allow us to divide them into a small set of races, in such a way that all the members of these races share certain traits and tendencies with each other that they do not share with members of any other races" (1990:4–5). Such racialist understandings can be the foundation for more elaborate notions of the significance of biological differences and their implications for social practice, policy, and morality. These are referred to by Appiah as *racisms*. Believers in racism hold *racial prejudice,* "the deformation of rationality in judgement that characterizes those whose racism is more than a theoretical attachment to certain propositions . . . [and is characterized by] an inability to change your mind in the face of appropriate evidence" (1990:8).

In the United States, the racialist, racist, and racially prejudiced ideology of white superiority has been a continually transmuting set of ideas seeking to justify Euro-American political and economic dominance (Epperson 1990, N.d.; Gossett 1963; Jordan 1968). One of the dominant effects of this racism on subordinated subjects was captured by Du Bois in his notion of the veil: "[T]he Negro is a sort of seventh son, born with a veil, and gifted with second-sight in this American world, a world which yields him no true self-consciousness, but only lets him see himself through the revelation of the other world" (1969:45). The veil is imposed by white racism and makes the experience of African Americans opaque to mainstream white culture. Stereotypes inform the dominant group, which remains ignorant of life beyond the veil. Reports by African Americans about life on their side, or about how the dominant culture appears to them, have no place in hegemonic white discourse (Valentine 1968; Wallace 1990). Invisibility and ignorance are especially marked when studying African-American communities in New England, a region that historically has been the home of relatively few African Americans, and in which scholarly studies only infrequently pierce the veil (Greene 1942; Kaplan and Kaplan 1989; Piersen 1988).

Historical archaeology as a discipline aims to bring to light lives (across all "races") that are invisible, or only barely visible, in the documentary record (Deetz 1977:7–8; Singleton 1990). Deetz argues that material culture holds "the promise of being more democratic and less self-conscious in its creation than any other body of historical material. . . . Although relatively few [persons] wrote, and what was written captured the personal biases of the recorder, in theory almost every person who lived in Anglo-America left behind some trace, however slight, of their passing" (1988b:219).

A major goal of African-American historical archaeology has been to uncover lifeways of people whose presence in historical documents is distorted by white racism (Cowan-Ricks 1991; Singleton 1988:348).[1] The plantation colonies have been prime areas for work seeking to extricate the lifeways of African Americans and African Caribbeans under slaveholding regimes (Orser 1988, 1990; Singleton 1985). Such research has brought to light "detailed information on topics such as the existence of a [distinctive African-American] pottery tradition, building technologies, food procurement techniques, culinary practices, household equipment and personal possessions. Such topics have received little or no attention in the historiography of slavery and emancipation" (Singleton 1988:348).

At the Du Bois site there is no problem of documentary invisibility. Du Bois wrote two autobiographies, tape recorded his reminiscences, and composed short articles on life in the Berkshires. If we seek to read objects as well as texts, it is because documents and objects do not always tell the same story; we benefit from treating the material and the documentary records as independent, distinctive, sometimes complementary, and sometimes contradictory sources of evidence on elusive pasts (Leone and Crosby 1987; Leone and Potter 1988:14–19). For Du Bois, there is also the reality that document-based biographical studies (Lester 1971; Rampersad 1990; Lewis 1993) lead away from Great Barrington and follow their subject around the globe. We pursue the historical archaeology of the homesite to make more visible the presence of Du Bois and the African-American community of which he was a part.

Recreating the Homesite

On the day after Du Bois's death in Ghana in August 1963, Roy Wilkins informed the 250,000 people assembled for the March on Washington "that at the dawn of the twentieth century, [Du Bois's] was the voice calling you here today" (Lester 1971:147; Marable 1985:93). The Du Bois Boyhood Homesite commemorates a person of local, national, and international import.

After graduating from high school in Great Barrington, Du Bois received a bachelor's degree from Fisk University and a B.A., M.A., and doctorate degree from Harvard; but for racist academic politics, he would have received another doctorate from the University of Berlin (Du Bois 1968:146, 149, 175). His dissertation, *The Suppression of the African Slave Trade to the United States of America, 1638–1870* (Du Bois 1896), was the first number in Harvard's Historical Studies series. *The Philadelphia Negro* (Du Bois 1899) is arguably the first urban ethnography in the United States. As a professor at Atlanta University, he oversaw one of the earliest and most systematic sets of studies of African-American life, ranging over fifteen volumes.

Du Bois was a founder of the Niagara Movement, an important African-American civil rights organization that shaped the formation of the National Association for the Advancement of Colored People (NAACP). He served as the director of publications and research for the NAACP from 1910 to 1934 and edited and contributed to its monthly periodical, the *Crisis,* a widely distributed publication. Du Bois's ideas on most topics touching the lives of African Americans—from a description of the Alhambra in Spain, to critiques of Marcus Garvey, to considerations of Black separatism and of Marxism—were read by African Americans throughout the land. By the end of his life, Du Bois had written innumerable pamphlets and articles, more than ten scholarly books, numerous major works of fiction, and two autobiographies (Du Bois 1968, [1940] 1984; Lester 1971:55–113; Lewis 1993).

This all too brief synopsis of Du Bois's life calls attention to his significance for U.S. history. It is also a story derived largely from the study of documents by and about Du Bois. Coming to Du Bois through the objects at the Boyhood Homesite in Great Barrington brings other people and other struggles into view, people and struggles that have largely disappeared from historical memory.

To get to the stories locked in the things of the Boyhood Homesite requires some understanding of what the things of the homesite are and how they are studied by archaeologists. This excursis on methodology does have the benefit of also showing how the discipline itself highlights some issues and ignores others, thereby contributing in its own way to the perpetuation of a silence about the position of African Americans in U.S. history.

In the summers of 1983 and 1984, the University of Massachusetts at Amherst's Anthropology Department's summer field school conducted preliminary archaeological surveys of the Du Bois homesite to assess the extent and condition of its archaeological remains. We sought to determine which features associated with the farmstead were still visible, to locate extant caches of artifacts and to estimate their number, and to gauge whether full-scale excavation was warranted.

From documentary sources, we first mapped the prominent surface features (fig. 1). We laid in a grid in meters (indicated by ticks along the borders of the landscape maps) with concrete datum points at the origin of the grid (N00, E00) and at the point we entered the site (N00, E42). Our subsurface testing concentrated on the area north of the house foundation to locate home-lot features, such as trash pits, middens, privies, fields and gardens, and outbuildings. We used magnetometer, resistivity, and soil phosphate survey remote sensing methods to identify these features. We further studied areas of interest identified by these techniques with .5m × .5m test pits. In addition to finds in these subsurface exposures, many artifacts were visible on the surface; we collected these, primarily to deter the interest of unauthorized amateur collectors. We also tried to retain much of the surrounding underbrush to avoid calling attention to what was shaping up as a rich archaeological site.

Figure 1 shows some of the major features identified during the archaeological survey. The foundations for the house and a well to the southwest were uncovered but not excavated at this stage. The test pits disclosed a plow zone to the rear of the house, at some points as near as fifteen meters from the house. Three trash pits were identified with the test excavations. And, finally, surface artifacts from the two large middens, approximately fifty to one hundred square meters each, were collected, although the middens were not excavated. These midden collections yielded most of the twelve thousand artifacts recovered from the site.

The focus of our studies has been on the artifacts from the two surface

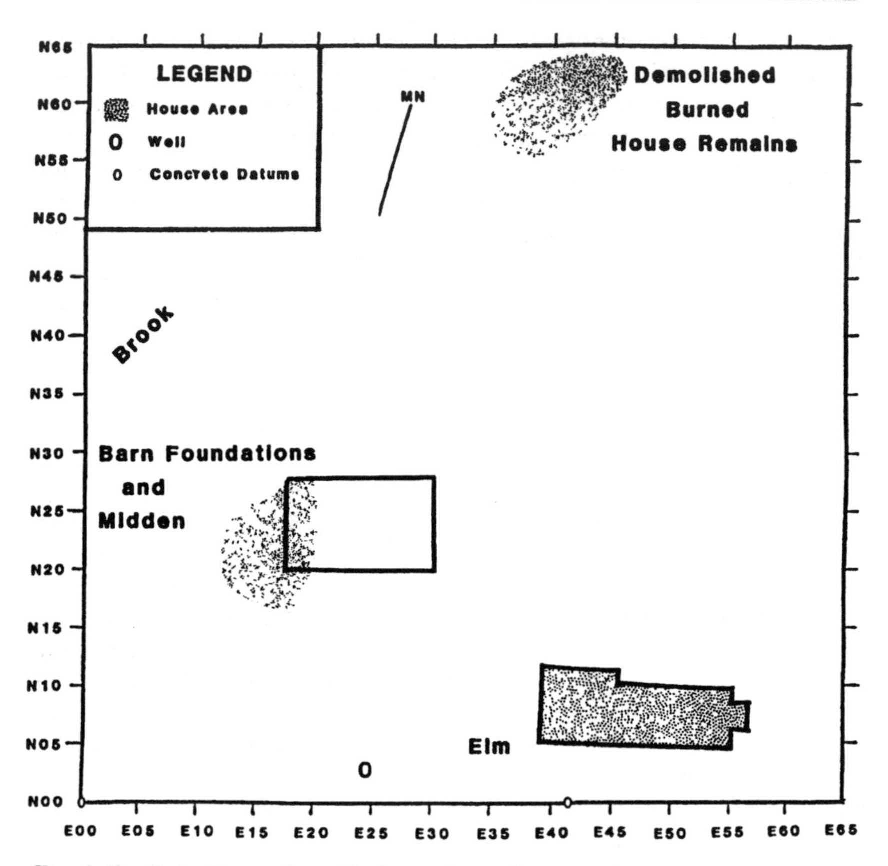

Fig. 1. Du Bois Homesite—Features from documentary sources.

middens, Midden A adjacent to the barn foundation, and Midden B next to the remains of the burned house. What activities led to the deposit of these artifacts? When were the artifacts deposited? Answers to these questions would enable us to fit these middens into a general reconstruction of the landscape that would include the less enigmatic house foundation and plow zones.

The middens are to the north of the site, behind what would have been the house. Artifacts appear quite densely on the surface of the middens, hundreds per square meter. The gap between them of some twenty meters has virtually no artifacts on the surface. This separation suggests that the middens were created by different activities at different times. In fact, we have found no pieces of any artifact that occur in both middens.

Closer analysis bears out this suspicion and leads us to interpretations of the middens. Midden A is the remains of a barn used in the 1800s for agricultural activities. Gradually, the barn became more of a depository for old and worn-out things (shoes, coal-stove refuse, and garbage from meals), and by the 1920s it had collapsed on itself and virtually disappeared from the landscape. Midden B is the remains of the superstructure of the house itself, the place where the dilapidated frame was bulldozed and burned in the 1950s. The objects in this midden were most likely used by Du Bois in his visits to the site between the 1920s and the 1950s.

We studied the question of the activities represented by the middens by comparing and contrasting the assemblage from the two middens (Hautaniemi 1989; Prunier 1983). The inventory of 10,430 objects was assigned to various functional types (table 1) (Orser 1988:233; South 1977). The frequency of different kinds of objects—say, kitchen utensils versus horse harness pieces—informs one about the kinds of activities that people on the site were engaged in and, in this case, the places on the site where the trash from these activities found its resting place.

Most of the objects in Midden A are related to foodways activities (33 percent) with storage-related objects (pieces of crocks, canning jars, etc.) comprising the most frequent of these. Objects associated with food service (plates, platters, etc.) and food remains (bones) are also found in Midden A. Clothing comprises almost 14 percent of the objects in Midden A, almost all of which are shoe parts. A surprisingly large percentage of objects in Midden A is related to household activities and parts of the structure of a building; almost 40 percent of these are waste from coal stoves. Personal objects comprise a very small percentage of the shards in Midden A, three-quarters of which are parts of patent medicine bottles and other medicinal receptacles. Tools related to agricultural activities (e.g., barbed wire, horsehoes) are another very small percentage, as are the objects associated with bicycle transportation.

Midden B has some interesting contrasts to Midden A. Foodways objects comprise 58 percent of the shards in Midden B; though storage vessels are most frequent, food service objects make up more than a third of the foodways objects, and virtually no food remains were found in Midden B. Clothing is a very small percentage of the objects in Midden B; though shoe parts predominate, the forty pieces in B are far fewer than the nearly nine hundred pieces in A. Household/Structural objects are about 13 percent of Midden B. As with Midden A, window glass, bricks, and nails are found, indicating a structure. However, in Midden B we found plaster, floor tile, roofing paper, and wallboard, as well. Personal items are a small percentage of Midden B, with cosmetic

Table 1. Functional Analysis of material from Middens A and B

	Midden A		Midden B	
Category	Items	% of Category	Items	% of Category
Foodways				
Procurement	—	—	—	—
Preparation	3	.14	6	.26
Service	321	14.89	767	33.44
Storage	1567	72.68	1471	64.12
Remains	228	10.58	23	1.00
Unknown	37	1.72	27	1.18
Total	2,156 (33.24%)		2,294 (58.16%)	
Clothing				
Fasteners	4	.45	2	4.35
Manufacture	3	.34	1	2.17
other (shoe)	885	99.10	40	86.96
other	1	.11	3	6.52
Total	893 (13.77%)		46 (1.17%)	
Household/Structural				
Arch/const	567	47.81	290	55.66
Hardware	13	1.10	11	2.11
Furnish/access	137	11.55	199	38.20
Furnish/access (heat)	469	39.54	17	3.26
Unknown	—	—	4	.77
Total	1,186 (18.29%)		521 (13.21%)	
Personal				
Medicinal	106	77.94	7	14.00
Cosmetic	17	12.50	31	62.00
Recreational	7	5.15	2	4.00
Monetary	—	—	—	—
Decorative	2	1.47	7	14.00
Other (weapon)	1	.74	—	—
Other	3	2.21	3	6.00
Total	136 (2.10%)		50 (1.27%)	
Labor				
Agricultural	132	100.00	28	100.00
Industrial	—	—	—	—
Total	132 (2.04%)		28 (0.71%)	

Table 1. Continued

Category	Midden A		Midden B	
	Items	% of Category	Items	% of Category
Transportation				
Automotive	—	—	4	100.00
Bicycle	3	100.00	—	—
Horse	—	—	—	—
Total	3 (0.05%)		4 (0.10%)	
Unknown	1,980 (30.53%)		1,001 (25.38%)	
Grand Total	6,486 (100.02%)		3,944 (100%)	

rather than medicinal items predominating. A very small percentage is agricultural-related items and an even smaller percentage is automobile parts.

Both middens appear to be the remains of structures and their associated trash. Midden A is the simpler structure and seems to have been the repository for objects associated with agricultural practices, foodways objects representing an emphasis on storage rather than service, and general household trash (worn-out shoes, coal-stove refuse, and garbage from meal preparations). Midden B is the more complex structure in which food service was emphasized and is a site that did not attract the refuse from everyday life.

The problem of dating these middens becomes critical. Who wore out and deposited the shoes? Who ate from the dinner service? And who used the patent medicines? We know from documents that the property passed out of the hands of the Wooster family (Du Bois's maternal relatives) and into Du Bois's hands in 1928. So we were interested to see if one of the middens related more to the Woosters' use of the property before 1928, and the other to Du Bois's use after 1928.

We are able to date the middens by close study of the ceramics and the glassware. The vast majority of the ceramics from both middens were plain whitewares, difficult to date on the basis of stylistic patterns. However, thirty ceramic shards contained maker's marks with identifiable dates of production. Study of these confirms that Midden A is the earlier of the two. Of ten ceramic lines with identifiable maker's marks found in Midden A, eight ceased being produced prior to 1928. The two remaining lines terminate in the 1930s or continue into the present; both of these begin by 1909. Thus, the Midden A maker's marks were from ceramics most likely available before 1928. For Midden B, only five of twenty identified ceramics maker's marks terminate production before 1928; the remaining fifteen were produced after 1928, and nine of these are produced up to the present. Thus, Midden B has many lines of pottery available after 1928 and only a few from before that period. (Of course, working with dates of termination is problematic, because people can still be using a piece after its line has ceased being produced. But studies by South [1977:226] show that there is usually no lengthy curation of all common items, a result that supports associating Midden A with pre-1928 inhabitants and Midden B with post-1928 people.)

Thousands of glassware shards were recovered from the site, of which only a very few could be associated with dates of manufacture. Still, analyses of various datable marks on glassware provide additional information on the dates and associations of the middens. Generally there is considerable overlap in the date ranges of the two middens: the earliest possible production date in Midden A is 1850 and in Midden B is 1820, with both middens containing objects that might have been made quite recently. The overlap in part results from the extremely wide production ranges for glassware, some spanning a century. Despite the similarity in date ranges for the two middens, there is evidence that supports associating Midden A with pre-1928 occupations and Midden B with post-1928 occupations.

Of the twenty-eight datable types of glassware in Midden A, only one begins its manufacture after 1928; so virtually all of the datable glassware in Midden A was available before 1928. Of the thirty-five datable types in Midden B, only three ended their production runs prior to 1928, so virtually all of the datable glassware in Midden B was available for Du Bois without lengthy curation. An average date for the glassware that takes into account the prevalence of shards from various times also yields a temporal separation. The mean date for Midden A is 1919, and for Midden B, 1928 (Hautaniemi 1989).

In sum, the ceramics and the glassware suggest that the material from Midden A was deposited beginning in the third quarter of the nineteenth century, with most of it being manufactured in the late nineteenth and early twentieth centuries. Midden B contains objects deposited from the second quarter of the twentieth century until recently. Thus, not only are the middens distinct in function (barn versus house), they are distinct in time.

The middens also tell us something about the historic landscapes of the site. A barn (Midden A) was part of an agricultural way of life during the 1800s. Toward the end of the twentieth century, like many barns and attics, it began to collect the detritus of everyday life—remains from meals, worn-out clothing, coal-stove ash, and so on. All this marks the demise of an agricultural way of life and the continuance of domestic activity at the site. Domestic life in the house persisted sporadically through the 1950s. Objects of daily life in the house awaited the return of W.E.B. and Shirley Graham Du Bois and remained there when it was sold and demolished in the 1950s.

But how did the house come to rest so far from the foundation itself? And how did the barn come to fall into disrepair? These are issues about the middens that can best be understood by turning to documents about the site. Combining the insights from the documents and the objects creates a more complete picture of home-lot change over time.

The site's National Register nomination document (Parrish 1981) drew on local oral history and a site walkover to identify the approximate locations of a house foundation, barn, and well. The barn area correlates with Midden A. Indeed, the evidence of a structure with relatively few furnishings, lacking interior decorative items, and holding a number of agricultural items, seems consistent with the remains of a barn.

The National Register form also notes that the house was reported as "collapsing" in 1954. The structure was bulldozed to the rear of the site and the remains burned, forming Midden B. The artifacts in this midden are indeed those of a demolished and burned house with more complex architecture than the barn's and with the remains of cosmetics bottles and without the daily refuse, such as coal stove waste or food remains, one would expect from a site under continual occupation.

A second documentary source is Du Bois's own remembrance of the site, which he recorded in "The House of the Black Burghardts" (1928).

> On this wide and lovely plain, beneath the benediction of grey-blue mountain and the low music of rivers, lived for a hundred years the black Burghardt clan. Up and to the east of a hill of rocks was Uncle Ira; down and to the South was Uncle Harlow in a low, long, red house beside a pond—in a house of secret passages, sudden steps, low, narrow doors and unbelievable furniture. And here right in the center of the world was Uncle Tallow, as Grandfather Othello was called. It was a delectable place—simple, square and low, with the great room of the fireplace, the flagged kitchen, half a step below, and the lower woodshed beyond. Steep, strong stairs led up to Sleep, while without was a brook, a well and a mighty elm.

The neighborhood inhabited by the Burghardt clan extends along Route 23 between Great Barrington and South Egremont. An 1876 atlas (Beers 1876) identifies Harlow's, and Ira's houses, as well as Othello's (today's Du Bois site), then owned by W. Piper.

We also consulted newspapers, vital statistics, maps, the U.S. Manuscript Census for Great Barrington at the Great Barrington Town Hall

Table 2. Principal Owners of the Du Bois Boyhood Homesite

Dates of Ownership	Owners
1820 or 1833–1857	James and Lucinda Freeman
1860–1873	Henry W., Harlow, and Albert D. Burghardt
1873–1909	William and Martha Piper
1909–1928	Lena Wooster
1928–1954	W.E.B. Du Bois

and the Du Bois Archives in the University of Massachusetts library. Finally, we conducted a title search of the property, which revealed the names of the principal owners. Apart from persons who held the land in mortgage or acted as intermediaries in transfers, these are listed in table 2. The 1830 to 1910 U.S. Manuscript Censuses provided the names of the past residents of the property and often included household members' ages, race, sex, and occupations (table 3). A genealogy of the Burghardts (fig. 2) is based on Du Bois's first autobiography, *Dusk of Dawn* ([1940] 1984:113), supplemented by our research (Pomerantz, Gumaer, and Paynter 1984).

The data on site owners, residents, and their kin can be woven together with the archaeological data on the barn, the house, and the agricultural fields to construct a landuse history of the site. There is still much we would like to know in greater detail, but we can now sketch the general contours of change at the site as affected by shifting race, class, and gender lines in Great Barrington over a century and a half.

Historical Landscapes of the Du Bois Homesite

Period 1 (1820–1873). Land use at the site can be divided into five major periods. The first begins in the early 1820s when James Freeman and Lucinda Burghardt Freeman, Du Bois's mother's uncle and aunt, purchased the land from Horace Church. It ends in 1873 with the sale of the property to William Piper. About these years Du Bois recalled, "[I]n my family, I remember farmers, barbers, waiters, cooks, housemaids and laborers" (1968:63). He described the farmers living in his neighborhood on Egremont Plain as people who "long earned a comfortable living, consorting usually with each other, but also with some of their white neighbors" (1968:63). During this time the site was occupied to the 1850s by James and Lucinda Freeman, and afterwards by Lucinda's brother Othello Burghardt and his family.

Table 3. Residents of the W.E.B. Du Bois Boyhood Homesite

Year	Residents	Age	Occupation
1830	James Freeman (head)	n.a.	
	1 male	36–55	
	1 female	36–55	
1840	James Freeman (head)		1 person in agriculture
	1 male	36–55	
	1 female	36–55	
1850	Lucinda Freeman	55	n.a.
	James Freeman	65	
	Robert Blake	n.a.	
1860	Othello Burghardt	70	Laborer
	Sally Burghardt	68	Housewife
	Francis Jackson	15	
	Ines Burghardt	6	
	James F. Burghardt	31	Barber
	Charles Jackson	9	
1870	Othello Burghardt	80	
	Sally Burghardt	78	Keeping house
	Inez R. Burghardt	16	At home
	Adelbert Burghardt	8	At home
	William E. Burghardt	2	At home
	Isiah Buckley	57	Farm laborer
	Elizabeth Buckley	56	Keeping house
	Lucinda Buckley	30	
	Matilda Buckley	4	At home
1800	Edward C. Wooster	50	no entry
	Lucinda B. Wooster	45	" "
	Bertha Wooster	7	" "
	Edward Wooster	5	" "
	Florence Wooster	4	" "
	Willis E. Wooster	1	" "
	Silas Mitchell		Boarder and clergyman
1900	Edward C. Wooster		Farm laborer who rents a house
	Lucinda B. Wooster		
	Edward B. Wooster		Farm laborer
	Willis E. Wooster		Farm laborer
	Howard Darling		Boarder

(*continued*)

Table 3. *continued*

Year	Residents	Age	Occupation
1910	Edward Wooster	29	Farm laborer who rents a house
	Lena Wooster	24	
	Kenneth Wooster	8	
	Bessie Wooster	7	
	Olive Wooster	5	
	Marietta Wooster	4	
	Florence Wooster	2	
	Lena Wooster	1	

NOTE: All are identified as "Black" except James Freeman, who in the 1850 census is identified as "Mulatto," and the Buckleys, who appear only in the 1870 census and are identified as "White."

The contemporary manuscript censuses disclose that African Americans in Great Barrington were then employed in a variety of jobs, including servant, freeholding farmer, laborer, and tradesperson. Both women and men sold labor power or the products of their labor, and women also did the work of maintaining households with boarders. When Lucinda and James Freeman first appeared in the public records, James was employed in agriculture, as was Lucinda's brother and neighbor, Harlow Burghardt. Brother Othello, who later moved to the site, was identified in 1840 as a whitewasher, a poorly paid trade at that time. The 1850 census was the first to list by name all household residents, and in that year Lucinda was keeping house for herself, James, and a boarder, Robert Blake. On the 1860 census, Othello was listed as an agricultural laborer, as were his African-American neighbors. By 1870, eighty-year-old Othello had no listed occupation, and his wife, Sally (or Sara, now seventy-eight), was in charge of a household that included her granddaughter Inez, grandsons Adelbert and William Edward Burghardt Du Bois (listed as Burghardt in the census), and the Buckley family of white boarders (table 3).

The reconstructed landscape for the period (fig. 3) includes agricultural fields in the plow zone areas, a barn work area for agricultural and craft production, and the house area, with activities of self-presentation, play, food preparation, washing, and heat provision. Othello may have practiced his trade of whitewashing near the barn (shell is found in the early Midden A), and Lucinda or Sally may have participated in service outwork as laundresses. This landscape reveals the agriculturalists, artisans, and homemakers of a small New England farmsite.

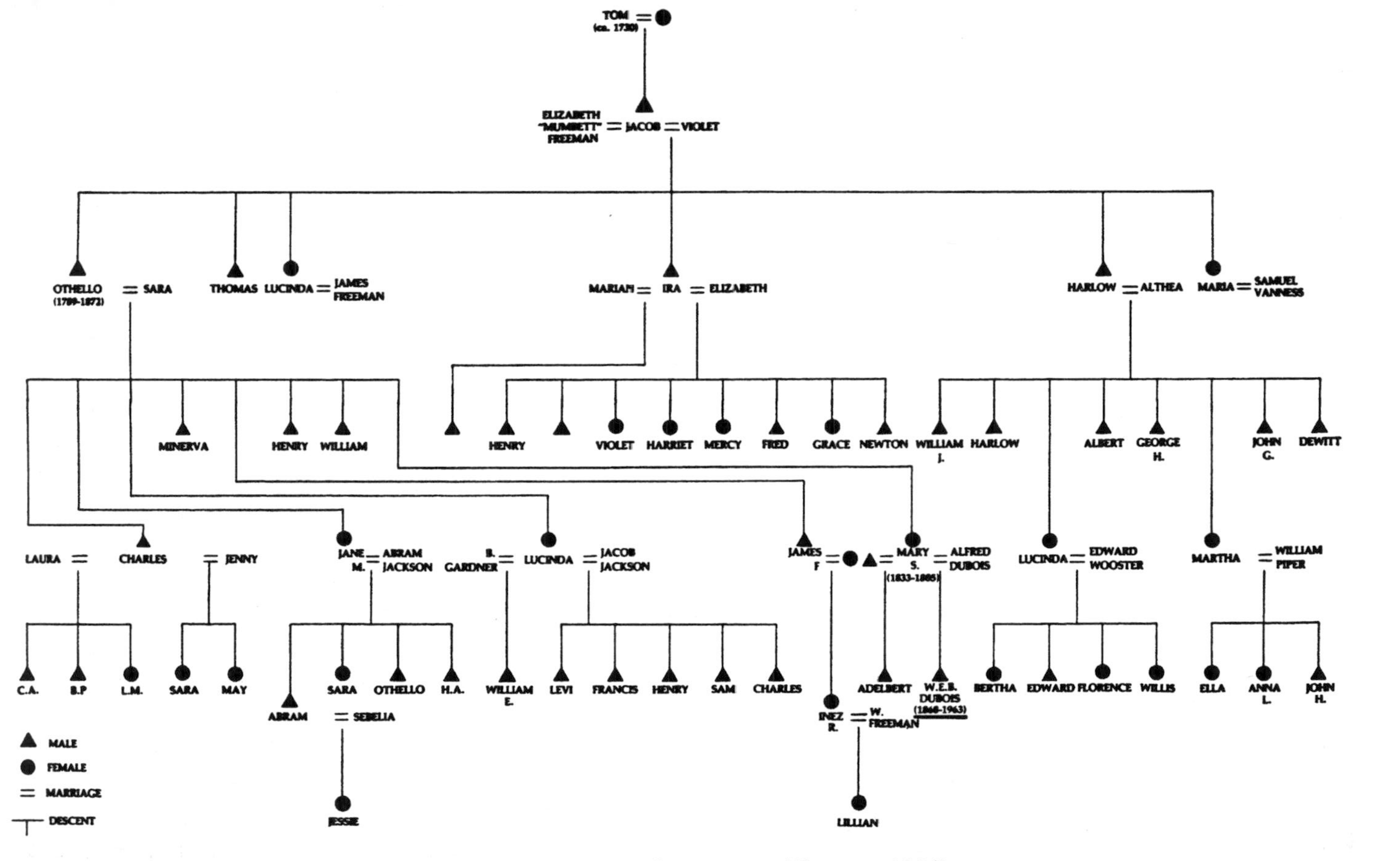

Fig. 2. Genealogy of the Black Burghardts (from Pomerantz, Gumaer, and Paynter 1984).

Period 2 (1873–1928). Though early in period 1 the residents of the house retained a degree of control over the means of production, by the end of it they were increasingly involved in the sale of their labor power. By 1880, occupations had changed; the men of the site and the neighborhood were all laborers, and the women were laundresses and servants, as well as wives and caretakers of boarders. To quote Du Bois, "The living to be earned on the farms gradually became less satisfying, and the group began to disintegrate: some went to the Connecticut Valley; some went West; many moved to town and city and found work as laborers and servants" (1968:63).

Great Barrington was a growing commercial and industrial town in the mid-nineteenth century. A firm, if not overtly hostile, color line (Du Bois 1968:94, 96; [1903] 1969:44) excluded African Americans from the professions, better paying trades, and factory work. As wage work became more common for all residents, African Americans found paid service work in the houses of the professional classes and well-to-do farmers, in the hotels, dining rooms, and laundries serving the growing summer trade, and in vacation homes of the nation's elite.

An 1886 guidebook (Bryan 1886:100) notes that Great Barrington "is coming into greater prominence than ever as a summer and autumn resort; and while it is sought more than ever by appreciative tourists . . . it is also becoming highly valued, by people who retire from work or leave the city, as a most perfect location for Country Homes." William Cullen Bryant helped to spark elite interest in the Berkshires by writing about his frequent visits beginning in 1825. The Berkshire House was built in 1840 to receive guests, and David Leavitt, a New York merchant, bought what was reputed to be the area's first "country home" in 1852. In the 1880s, Mrs. Mark Hopkins, wife of the San Francisco railroad builder, oversaw the building of the Searles Castle mansion at a cost of $1 million, and Du Bois himself worked as a timekeeper on its construction (Bryan 1886:82–90; Du Bois 1968:102).

The class divisions in Great Barrington by the later nineteenth century included those between agrarian workers and landowners, and between industrial workers and factory owners, all indigenous to Great Barrington. In addition, because the area had attracted the country's newly rich, a division between those who enjoyed the "comfortable life" and their servants existed along with the other two class divisions. Racist constructions of African Americans by whites relegated them to service either for the local well-to-do or for vacationing white elites.

The occupation of the site by the Wooster family during period 2 was a product of the changing class, race, and gender relations of the late nineteenth century. In 1873 the estate of Othello Burghardt sold "the

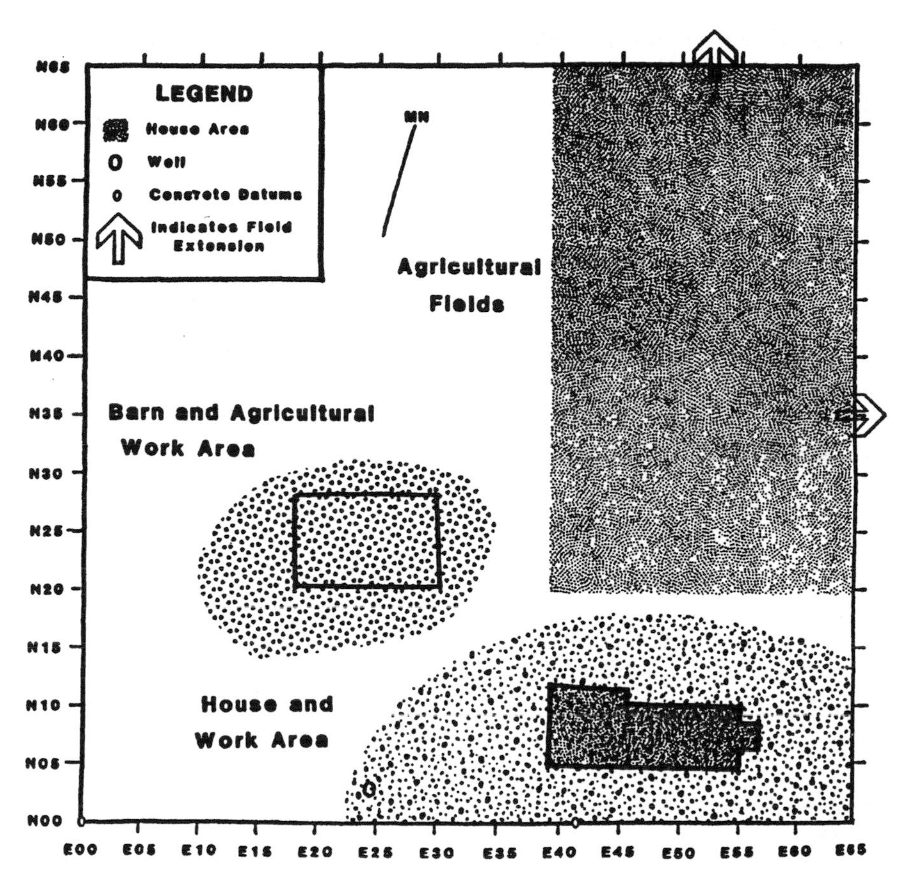

Fig. 3. Du Bois Homesite—Period 1, 1820–1873, Freeman-Burghardt agro-artisanal landscape.

house of the Black Burghardts" to William Piper, scion of an African-American family from Sheffield, one town south of Great Barrington. Piper had married into the Burghardt family, to Martha, daughter of Harlow and Althea. Though owners of the site from 1873 to 1909, the Pipers resided in Sheffield, according to the manuscript censuses. During these years censuses list the Wooster family as residents of the site. In 1909, title to the house and land was sold by Martha Burghardt Piper to Lena Wooster.

The relationship between Woosters and Pipers is of some interest. Martha Burghardt Piper (wife of the post-1873 owner of the site and later its owner herself) was the sister of Lucinda Burghardt Wooster (wife of

Edward Wooster). This couple, with their children, resided at the site during period 2 (fig. 4). Upon Othello Burghardt's death in 1872, the title passed to Harlow, Henry W., and Albert D. Burghardt, in accordance with Lucinda Freeman's will. It is likely that Harlow, now over age seventy, was too old to keep up two farmsteads. Henry W. and Albert, in their late thirties and forties, no longer resided in Great Barrington. The sisters Martha Piper and Lucinda Wooster, however, were still in the area, and apparently in need of land. Husband William Piper was (we suppose) in a position to buy out the Burghardt men's interests in the land and then rented it to his brother-in-law Edward Wooster.

We would like to know more about why this particular course was taken. Was it the only available and affordable property at the time? Was the sale easily arranged because it was in the family? Was the Burghardt family connection to the property an overriding consideration? When Du Bois received the property as a gift in 1928, the "House of the Black Burghardts" had tremendous significance to him. Did this earlier transaction point to a similar symbolic significance of the family property for his ancestors and especially his great aunts? And, what role did the sisters, Lucinda and Martha, play in the arrangements between the Pipers and the Woosters? We suspect that it is because of these two Burghardt women that the property stayed in possession of Burghardts into the twentieth century. (When we enquired in 1983 of Great Barrington white residents about the Pipers and Woosters, we were told that Piper, the site's 1873 purchaser, was a poor white farmer; at least some had forgotten the historical association of the property in Great Barrington with the Black Burghardt family.)[2]

The black Wooster men listed at the site in the 1900 and 1910 censuses are Edward and his son Edward. Both are shown as renting a house, rather than renting a farm. In 1900 Lucinda Wooster kept house for her family as well as for an African American, Howard Darling, a boarder (see table 3). Like her neighbors, Lucinda Wooster may have done service-related outwork during period 2, or her daughters may have been servants. One clue that suggests such scenarios is the large number of hotel-ware ceramics found in late-nineteenth-century Midden A.

Although we do not know how these ceramics arrived on the site, there are several possibilities. First, they may have been purchased to use in either the course of domestic life or catering. Du Bois indicates that his relatives included waiters and people who operated dining rooms. Bower and Rushing's (1980) work on the African Meeting House in Boston discloses that early nineteenth-century African-American caterers owned the dining ware they used in their trade. Second, the ceramics may represent a form of compensation to persons employed in the area's hotels,

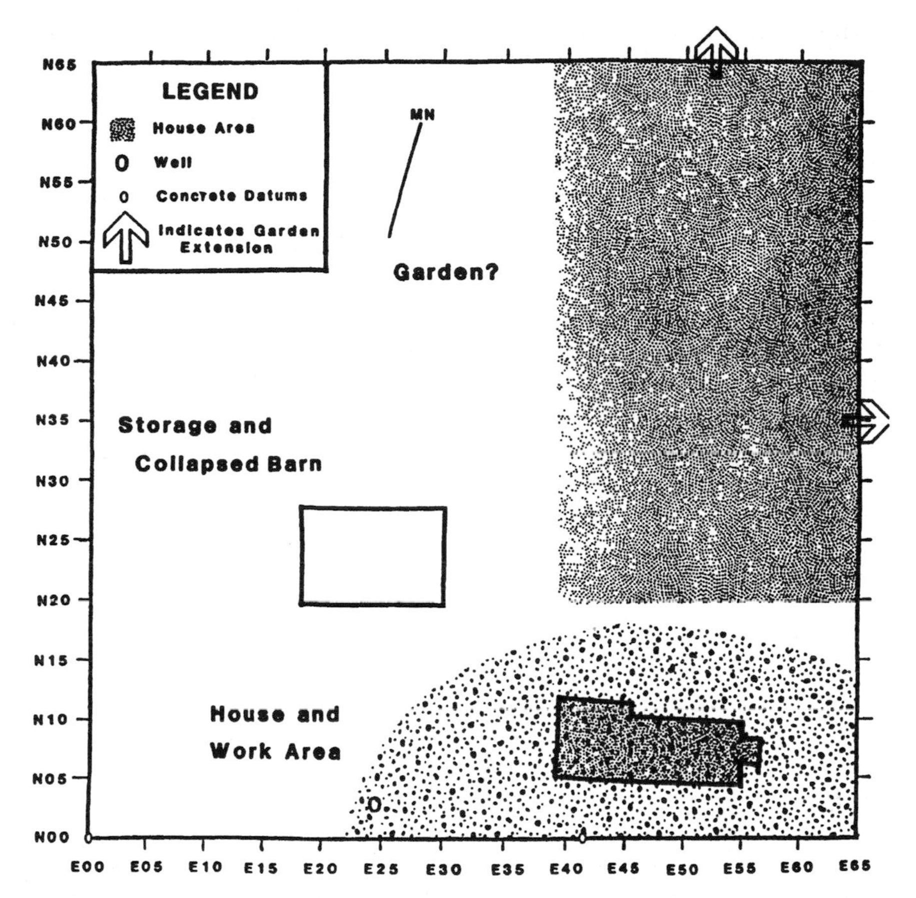

Fig. 4. Du Bois Homesite—Period 2, 1873–1928, Wooster laborer and service worker landscape.

paternalistic in-kind "gifts" from employers of out-of-style or incomplete set items to workers or "fringe benefits" pilfered by these underpaid employees.

The reconstructed landscape for this period (fig. 4) is one in which the land may have carried symbolic value for Burghardt family continuity. It certainly was a site of the reproduction of domestic life and may have been a location of service industry outwork by women. As agricultural production at the site became less important, the barn became a place to store or dispose of seldom used objects, such as the shoes and ceramics found in Midden A. Du Bois, writing in 1928, describes many features of the site but does not mention a barn. By then the barn had already collapsed.

Not all the Burghardts remained in Great Barrington or worked in the service industry. Du Bois notes, "The fate of my various relatives among the black Burghardts I do not know very well. . . . Others have prospered as western farmers, one became a singer and teacher of music and another was head of the home economics department in the colored school system of a large border state city" (1968:96–97). Most notably, Du Bois himself left.

In 1885, with savings from work at Searles Castle and the assistance of four local churches, Du Bois traveled to Nashville and enrolled in Fisk University. There he observed the color line of the South. The lynchings, personal insults, rigid segregation, and lack of education for African Americans were horrifying to this Black Yankee. But he enjoyed his discovery of the cultural integrity that a large and thriving African-American community offered. His understandings of the richness of African-American culture, of its African foundation, of the history and contributions to world civilization of people of African descent, and of the struggle against the brutalities of white racism all crystallized during his years at Fisk (Du Bois 1968:101–131; [1903] 1969:96–108). He went on to earn degrees at Harvard, to study at the University of Berlin (Du Bois 1968: 146, 149, 438), and to teach and do research at the University of Pennsylvania, Wilberforce College, and Atlanta University. By the early decades of the twentieth century, Du Bois had become an increasingly prominent leader in the emerging Civil Rights movement.

Period 3 (1928–1954). During Du Bois's NAACP years a committee of benefactors and admirers, including Clarence Darrow, John Hurst, Mary McLeod Bethune, James A. Cobb, Lillian A. Alexander, and Arthur B. Spingarn, raised funds to purchase and present to him on his sixtieth birthday in 1928 the homesite of Lucinda and James Freeman, Sally and Othello Burghardt, and the Woosters. Du Bois, a world traveler, a sophisticated member of New York's African-American literati, and a social activist, wanted something quite different from the homestead in Great Barrington than his ancestors had. The house represented a tie to his past, a retreat from the city, and a symbol of his position in society. In a 1928 article in the *Crisis* he wrote that "riding near on a chance journey I suddenly was homesick for that house. . . . [However] country estates and limousines are not adapted to my income" (360–361).

Left out of his description in that article, "The House of the Black Burghardts," was any reference to production: the barn, fields, or work areas for craft production. Du Bois was primarily interested in the house and its bucolic setting as a site of past and future social reproduction. Thus, the reconstructed landscape for this period (fig. 5) includes the

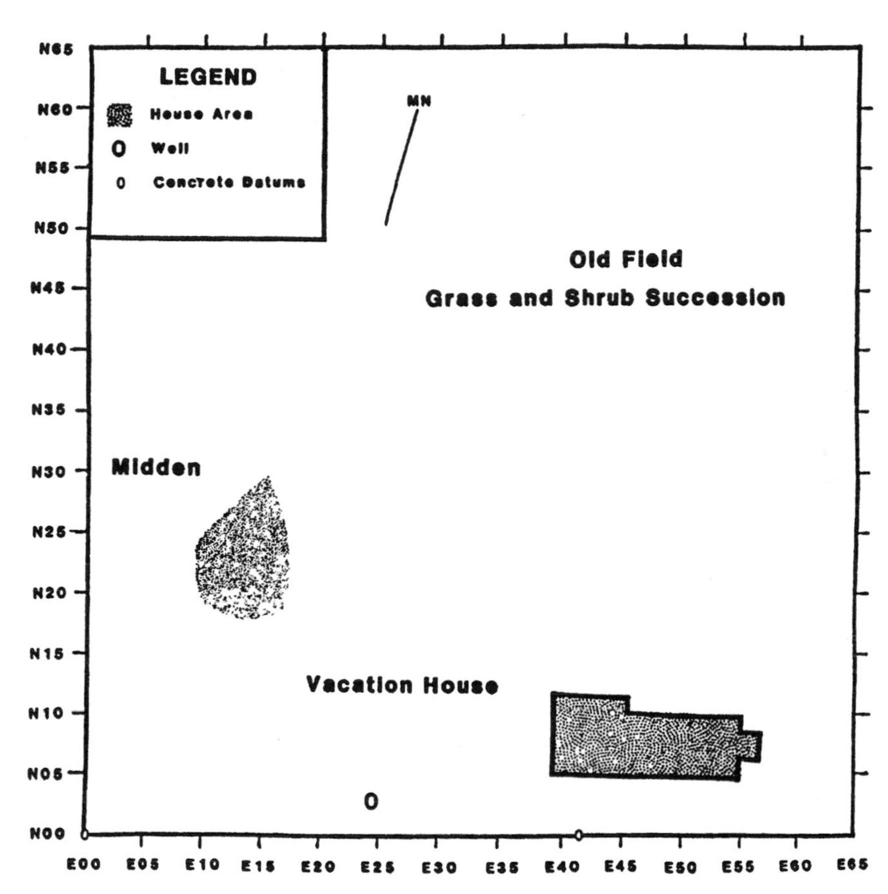

Fig. 5. Du Bois Homesite—Period 3, 1928–1954, Du Bois vacation landscape.

house, the well, and the field in early stages of ecological succession. The area of the former barn may have still been a midden for trash disposal, or perhaps merely an overgrown part of the landscape. Some additional evidence of Du Bois's interest in the site are blueprints found in Du Bois's papers in the University of Massachusetts Archive. Drawn by the architect J. McA. Vance of Pittsfield, Massachusetts, in response to Du Bois's instructions, they reveal the cottage of a person of letters, with bedrooms for family and guests, and a library–music room.

How many of these planned improvements were completed is not clear. Du Bois received the site at the beginning of a period that would take him away from the Northeast. He differed with the board of the

NAACP on the role of nationalist strategies in the struggle for African-American equality and resigned from the *Crisis* in 1934 (Du Bois 1968:297–300; Lester 1971:100–113). He returned to Atlanta University to chair its sociology department until his forced retirement at the age of seventy-six in 1944 (Du Bois 1968:308–325; Lester 1971:113–119). From 1944 to 1948 he worked for the NAACP in New York again, and he was its representative to the founding of the United Nations. After more disputes between Du Bois and the NAACP leadership, the board dismissed him in 1948. He was then eighty (Du Bois 1968:326–339; Lester 1971:113–119).

Du Bois remained active in public life. "In 1950 he became chairman of a new organization, the Peace Information Center, whose purpose was 'to tell the people of the United States what other nations were doing and thinking about war' " (Lester 1971:121). Banning the atomic bomb was a goal of the PIC, a politically dangerous one in McCarthyite America. In 1951, Du Bois and other PIC officers were indicted for failing "to register as agent for a foreign principal" (Lester 1971:123). Defending himself taxed Du Bois's resources and tried his patience, even though he was acquitted and the judge declared that the prosecutor had failed to support the charge (Du Bois 1968:385–386). Time and funds to improve the Berkshire homesite must have been subordinated to more pressing issues. Although the chimney was restored, and reroofing and some interior work had been ordered in the late 1920s, what improvements were made can only be determined by future excavation of the house area.

Period 4 (1954–1968). In 1954, Du Bois sold the property. He left Great Barrington as a part-time resident, though photographs show him at the site even after he sold it. During the later 1950s, Du Bois remained active in intellectual and political life. In 1961, he joined the Communist party (Du Bois 1968; Robinson 1983). That same year he accepted Kwame Nkrumah's invitation to move to newly independent Ghana and oversee the production of the proposed *Encyclopedia Africana.* Du Bois died in Ghana on August 27, 1963, ninety-five years after his birth in a rural New England town.

Sometime during the 1950s the new owners of the homesite demolished the rundown house (Parrish 1981). New England old-field succession set in, and the home-lot reverted to shrubs and trees. The house of the Burghardts now underlay a copse of trees beside a New England highway (fig. 6).

Period 5 (1968–present). Though the house was gone, its significance was not forgotten. In October 1969, a year after the assassination of Martin

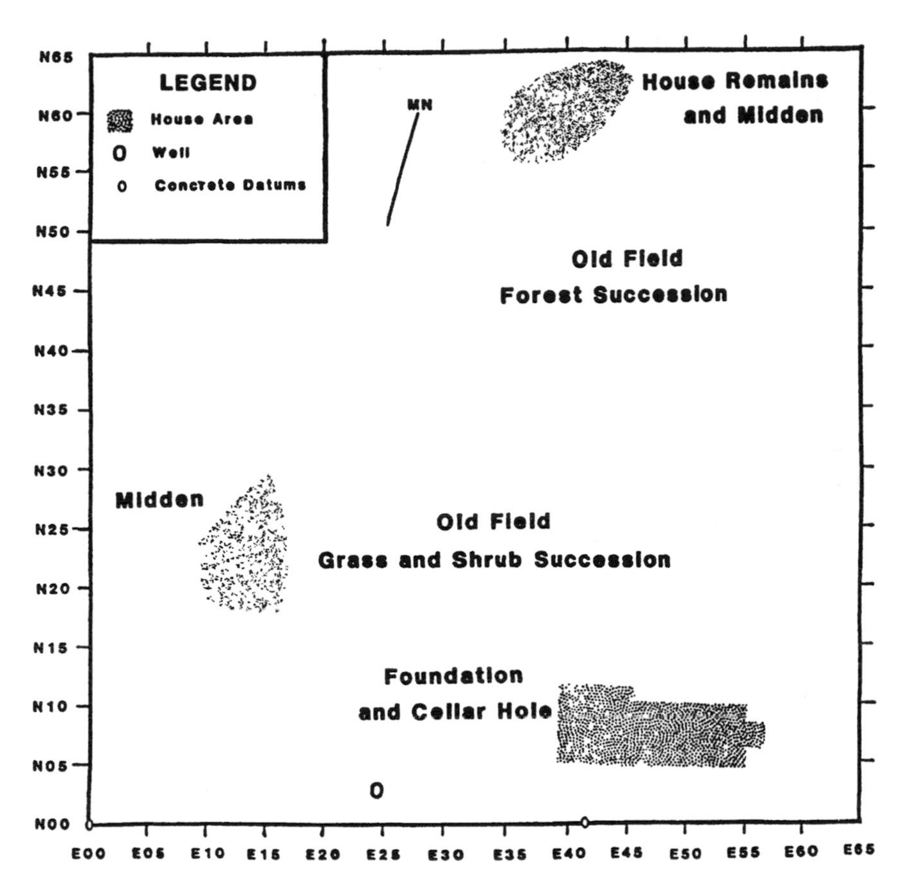

Fig. 6. Du Bois Homesite—Period 4, 1954–present, abandonment landscape.

Luther King, Jr., a dedication ceremony was held at the site. In attendance were, among others, Julian Bond, Horace Mann Bond, Ossie Davis, and the ambassador from Ghana. The meaning of this new cultural landscape was contested, however, for not all believed that Du Bois deserved this honor. Residents of the town sought to block the dedication ceremony and even threatened physical violence. Town officials delayed the dedication by questioning the legality of the use of the site as a park. Police and dissidents were formidable presences at the ceremony.

The mood of some in the town was captured in the *Berkshire Courier's* editorial of October 16, 1969, which supported the stand of a neighbor who sought to block the ceremony.

> We agree with his arguments and we admire the Selectmen for standing up and attempting to ward off this honor being bestowed on a Communist. . . . [However] blocking the dedication now would only mean trouble. . . . A cool head must be kept in dealing with the situation, for the slightest spark could touch off an inferno which would bring the town into the focus of the rest of the nation as have New York, Chicago and Detroit. Any attempt at blocking the actual ceremonies through physical efforts would certainly mean a confrontation and that is one thing which surely no one wants. . . . Let the memorial committee have its day and leave the monument to those who will undoubtedly take out their wrath on it in the weeks to come.

Those seeking to honor Du Bois prevailed, and the dedication was held. Mention of Du Bois can provoke hostility among some residents to this day (Johnson 1993). Others have changed their minds. The October 18, 1979, issue of the *Berkshire Courier* carried a rather different editorial written by the same editor:

> Ten years have passed. We have learned that this country's involvement in Vietnam was questionable at best. We have lived through Watergate and our faith in the country's leaders has been drastically changed. . . . Today we recognize Dr. Du Bois for the contribution he made in his writings and through education for the betterment of mankind. The people of Great Barrington should be proud that their home town was the birthplace of this remarkable man.

It would be encouraging to report that such recognition is reflected in the creation of a cultural landscape that carries the message of Du Bois's place in U.S. history to the general public. It has attracted archaeological and historical scholars, and the site has been purchased by the Commonwealth of Massachusetts, with the University of Massachusetts, Amherst, as custodian. But otherwise it remains neglected, presenting no message to any but persons knowledgeable about Du Bois's personal history who seek out this site in the Berkshires.

Reading Objects from Multiple Points of View

We have been able to mesh artifacts, archaeological features, documents, and reminiscences to establish the history of the W.E.B. Du Bois Boyhood Homesite. Any such history is necessary to unlock the potential of historical places to inform the present. Beyond such chronology, however, lies the texture of life at the site: what was it like to live there as a member of the Burghardt family, a member of the African-American community of Great Barrington, and within the political economy of

Western Massachusetts? Du Bois's writings provide one source of insight. Particular objects at the site provide another.

Archaeological method is most likely to fall afoul of embedded racism at the level of reading objects to render meanings. One striking characteristic of the artifacts from the Du Bois site is their similarity to objects from Euro-American sites. The late 1800s was the period of the explosive growth of the mass market and its accompanying consumer culture. The objects of that expanding market cover all archaeological sites of the period. But did participation in the same market, in the purchase, use, consumption, and deposition of the same kinds of items, have the same meaning for people on both sides of the color line? In other words, does participation in the same market result in participation in identical cultures of consumption (Mullins 1993)? This is one more aspect of racialism, that different meanings may be masked by a veil of material similarities. Race thus can limit archaeological interpretations if they are made only from the vantage point of white consumer culture. Though we do not have the key that unlocks the multiple meanings of material life for participants in a mass culture, we would like to consider a common object of the turn of the century, the patent medicine bottle, to disclose how multivalency must be taken into consideration when looking for the meanings material objects held for residents of historical places.

We found nine identifiable types of patent medicine bottles in Midden A, and eight in Midden B. The patent medicines used at the Du Bois site included "Ayer's Sarsaparilla," a blood renovator that also claimed to cure "scrofulas affections and diseases arising from changes of the season, climate or of life." Three "Warner's Safe Diabetes Cure" bottles were recovered. Warner stressed the safety of its product in both its brand name and in its advertising copy. A "Fink's Magic Oil" bottle was also discarded at the site. Fink's promised to cure, among other things, "colic, cholera, sore throat and neuralgia." "Pe-ru-na," a cure for catarrh, was also represented, as was "Musterole," a commercial mustard plaster for colds and congestion.

Today, we tend to think of such patent medicines as hoaxes and cons. However, at the time that patent medicine use boomed, it was one response by the general public to very real increasing morbidity and mortality rates. In the late nineteenth century, these rates were increasing with the rise of laissez faire industrial capitalism, and attendant social conditions of contagion, contamination of water sources, industrial work-related hazards, and malnutrition (see Eyer and Sterling 1978; McArdle 1986; Starr 1982). At that time no one, including physicians, understood fully the cause and treatment of disease (Rosenberg 1962; Starr 1982). The germ theory was not very well understood by researchers, physicians, or the general public and was of no practical use in the treatment of disease until the early twentieth century (Preston and Haines 1991:8–9).

One response was a strong movement for health reform as people turned to self-care—from diet and life-style changes, to relegitimation of traditional methods of care, to widespread use of patent medicines (Donegan 1986; Ehrenreich and English 1978; Nissenbaum 1980; Starr 1982). Patent medicine proprietors capitalized on the public's concern about disease, distrust of doctors, general misunderstanding about the germ theory, and traditions of self-care and community healing. Some companies offered herbal and vegetable compounds and used imagery of Native Americans to symbolize traditional, natural healing. Some stressed claims of safety in their advertisements, in response to fear about the effects of medicines prescribed by doctors. Other companies played on newfound fears of germs by advertising that their products would eliminate these unseen but deadly enemies. Many advertisers sought to establish a shared sense of identity between the purchaser and the individuals portrayed in their advertisements.

Who, specifically, were the people responsible for self-doctoring? Usually women, who were targeted by patent medicine advertising as the persons responsible for their families' health. The cult of "true womanhood" defined white middle-class women as primary health consumers and administrators. However, high morbidity and mortality also drove poor white and black women to self-care remedies. We know that many African Americans used these patent medicines. We have recovered the bottles from the Du Bois site, just as pharmaceutical bottles have been recovered from other African-American sites (Mullins 1992; Orser N.d.). Du Bois also mentions patent medicines when discussing the health of African Americans in *The Philadelphia Negro* (1899).

The patent medicine companies, however, portrayed only whites in their advertisements; images of African Americans did not appear. Even personal care products marketed specifically for African Americans were advertised with images of refined white women. Yet at the same time, racist, negative, African-American stereotypes were widespread in the advertising industry and were used to sell many other products. Helán Page suggests that such advertising was a constant reminder to whites of their racial superiority, and to African Americans that their race rendered them unacceptable and demeanable (personal communication 1992). Advertising helped construct monolithic racist identities in the post-Emancipation United States that were increasingly legitimated by job, housing, and social discrimination, and by violence.

From the presence of patent medicine bottles in the Du Bois Homesite middens, we can infer that some of its residents experienced ill health and resorted to self-care. But we must resist the easy step to assuming that we already understand all that the presence of these medicines means. Here we must pause and ask questions intended to help us past the limits of our discipline's current understandings. Did Lucinda Wooster, as wife and mother, purchase the patent medicines? How did she respond to the Pe-ru-na, Ayer's Sarsaparilla, and Warner's Safe Diabetes Cure advertising, which featured idealized white women? Did these images evoke for her the "double-consciousness" that Du Bois speaks of in his writings, "this double-consciousness, this sense of always looking at one's self through the eyes of others, of measuring one's soul by the tape of a world that looks on in amused contempt and pity" ([1903] 1969:45)? Did Lucinda Wooster receive the message that she was invisible or an unacceptable caricature; did she resist this essentialization?

Knowledge about African-American women's perspectives on such specific objects as medicine bottles is not yet part of an archaeological disciplinary matrix, nor can we now do more than raise questions about their meanings to the women of the Du Bois homesite. But we need to remember that the archaeological "facts" do not speak for themselves. We lack important understandings of how identity formed among African Americans in nineteenth- and early-twentieth-century New England, and of how mass consumption was experienced in the African-American community at a time when insult and debasement were a major feature of product advertising (Mullins 1993).

That we are only partially able to bring the Du Bois site to life exemplifies the power of racism in structuring the scholarship and everyday common sense in a racially divided society. Du Bois offers a chilling image that may assist archaeologists of all colors to remember the power of the veil of race in America as they attempt to bring African-American consciousness into the mainstream of culture history. In *Dusk of Dawn,* written some forty years after he offered the metaphor of the veil in *Souls of Black Folk,* he presented the metaphor of the cave.

> It is as though one, looking out from a dark cave in a side of an impending mountain, sees the world passing and speaks to it; speaks courteously and persuasively, showing them how these entombed souls are hindered in their natural movement, expression, and development; and how their loosening from prison would be a matter not simply of courtesy, sympathy, and help to them, but aid to all the world. One talks on evenly and logically in this way, but notices that the passing throng does not even turn its head. . . . It

> gradually penetrates the minds of the prisoners that the people passing do not hear; that some thick sheet of invisible but horribly tangible plate glass is between them and the world. They get excited; they talk louder; they gesticulate. Some of the passing world stop in curiosity; these gesticulations seem so pointless; they laugh and pass on. . . . Then the people within may become hysterical. . . . They may even, here and there, break through in blood and disfigurement, and find themselves faced by a horrified, implacable, and quite overwhelming mob of people frightened for their own very existence. ([1940] 1984:130–131)

The plate-glass wall of racism is not impenetrable, Du Bois explains, and at times people from the outside seek to communicate with people in the cave, and to try to champion their cause in the outside world.

> But this method is subject to two difficulties: first of all, not being possibly among the entombed or capable of sharing their inner thought and experience, this outside leadership will continually misinterpret and compromise and complicate matters, even with the best of will. And secondly, of course, no matter how successful the outside advocacy is, it remains impotent and unsuccessful until it actually succeeds in freeing and making articulate the submerged caste. (132)

The lack of historical places on our contemporary landscape that remind all persons of the omnipresence of African Americans throughout U.S. history, even in rural New England, helps create a cultural amnesia and contributes to the recreation of racism. Even with such sites identified, without rich and textured stories these places will realize only a small portion of the power historical sites have to inform the public, create identifications, and combat racism. These stories will be recovered only as scholars reflect on the limits racism has imposed on their discipline, and seek, as part of their everyday scholarly business, to invent antiracist methods and theories that recover liberating understandings of the past. When the color line runs less deeply in our disciplines, when the theoretical imperatives that arise from a fuller appreciation of African-American existence in a racially divided society are accepted, and when one readily and regularly wonders about how places, people, and things were experienced by the full variety of structurally differentiated people who lived in the past and built the present, then veils may be pierced, and caves exited and entered.

Notes

We thank Roger Sanjek and Steve Gregory for their assistance with this paper. Paynter especially thanks Homer Meade, Jim Parrish, Linda Seidman, Ken

Fones-Wolf, John Kendall, Helán Page, Rita Reinke, Rick Gumaer, Paul Mullins, Jim Delle, Jim Garman, John Bracey, Ernie Allen, Bill Strickland, Kevin Sweeney, Tom Patterson and the many students who worked on the Du Bois collection, especially those in the 1983 and 1984 summer field schools. Hautaniemi thanks Helán Page, Alan Swedlund, and Paul Mullins. Muller thanks the folks mentioned above and includes Terry Epperson and Faye Harrison for their ongoing support in our work.

1. Singleton (1988:348; 1990) notes that another major focus of African-American archaeological studies has been the identification of Africanisms, culture traits found in the Western Hemisphere traceable to African cultures (see also Deetz 1988a; Emerson 1988, N.d.; Ferguson 1991, 1992; Mouer et al. N.d.). Though important, the search for Africanisms can obscure African-American creativity in a wide array of material constructions (Howson 1990; Paynter 1992; Perry and Paynter N.d.).

2. In a study of the relationship between historic houses and legitimating legends for local families, Anne Yentsch (1988:12–17) finds a similar pattern of "forgetting" patronymic family associations when continuity is through women, and when residents are African American.

References

Appiah, Kwame Anthony. 1990. Racisms. In *Anatomy of Racism,* ed. David T. Goldberg, 3–17. Minneapolis: University of Minnesota Press.

Beers, Frederick W. 1876. *County Atlas of Berkshire, Massachusetts.* New York: White.

Bower, Beth Anne, and Byron Rushing. 1980. The African Meeting House: The Center for Nineteenth Century Afro-American Community in Boston. In *Archaeological Perspectives on Ethnicity in America,* ed. Robert L. Schuyler, 69–75. New York: Baywood.

Bryan, C. W. 1886. *The Book of Berkshire.* Great Barrington, Mass.: Bryan.

Cowan-Ricks, Carrel. 1991. African American Cemeteries: Historical Symbols. Paper presented at the American Anthropological Association Annual Meetings, Chicago.

Cox, Oliver C. 1948. *Caste, Class, and Race.* New York: Monthly Review Press.

Deetz, James F. 1977. *In Small Things Forgotten.* New York: Anchor.

———. 1988a. American Historical Archeology: Methods and Results. *Science* 239:362–367.

———. 1988b. Material Culture and Worldview in Colonial Anglo-America. In *The Recovery of Meaning,* ed. Mark P. Leone and Parker B. Potter, Jr., 219–233.

Donegan, J. B. 1986. *"Hydropathic Highway to Health": Women and Water-Cure in Antebellum America.* Westport, Conn.: Greenwood.

Drake, St. Clair. 1987. *Black Folk Here and There: An Essay in History and Anthropology.* Vol. 1. Los Angeles: University of California, Center for Afro-American Studies.

———. 1990. *Black Folk Here and There: An Essay in History and Anthropology.* Vol. 2. Los Angeles: University of California, Center for Afro-American Studies.

Du Bois, W.E.B. 1896. *The Suppression of the African Slave Trade to the United States of America, 1638–1870.* Harvard Historical Series, No. 1. Cambridge, Mass.: Harvard University Press.

———. 1899. *The Philadelphia Negro: A Social Study. Together with a Special Report on Domestic Service, by Isabel Eaton.* Philadelphia: University of Pennsylvania.

———. 1928. The House of the Black Burghardts. *Crisis* 35(4): 133–134.

———. 1968. *The Autobiography of W.E.B. Du Bois: A Soliloquy on Viewing My Life from the Last Decade of Its First Century.* New York: International Publishers.

———. [1903] 1969. *The Souls of Black Folk.* With introductions by Dr. Nathan Hare and Alvin F. Poussaint, M.D. New York: New American Library, 1969.

———. [1940] 1984. *Dusk of Dawn: An Essay toward an Autobiography of a Race Concept.* New Brunswick: Transaction.

Ehrenreich, Barbara, and Deirdre English. 1978. *For Her Own Good.* New York: Doubleday.

Emerson, Matthew C. 1988. *Decorated Clay Tobacco Pipes from the Chesapeake.* Ann Arbor, Mich: University Microfilms.

———. N.d. African inspirations in a New World Art and Artifact: Decorated Clay Tobacco Pipes from the Chesapeake. In *"I, Too, Am America;"* ed. Theresa Singleton.

Epperson, Terrence. 1990. Race and the Disciplines of the Plantation. *Historical Archaeology* 24(4): 29–36.

———. N.d. Constructed Places/Contested Spaces: Contexts of Tidewater Plantation Archaeology. In *"I, Too, Am America,"* ed. Theresa Singleton.

Eyer, Joseph, and Peter Sterling. 1978. Stress-related Mortality and Social Organization. *Review of Radical Political Economy* 10:1–42.

Ferguson, Leland. 1991. Struggling with Pots in South Carolina. In *The Archaeology of Inequality,* ed. Randall H. McGuire and Robert Paynter, 28–39. Oxford: Blackwell.

———. 1992. *Uncommon Ground.* Washington, D.C.: Smithsonian.

Fields, Barbara J. 1990. Slavery, Race, and Ideology in the United States of America. *New Left Review* 181:95–118.

Gossett, Thomas F. 1963. *Race: The History of an Idea in America.* Dallas: Southern Methodist University Press.

Greene, Lorenzo. 1942. *The Negro in Colonial New England, 1620–1776.* New York: Columbia University Press.

Hautaniemi, Susan. 1989. Temporal Analysis of Glass Assemblages from Middens A and B, Du Bois Homestead, Great Barrington, Mass. Department of Anthropology, University of Massachusetts, Amherst. Typescript.

Howson, Jean. 1990. Social Relations and Material Culture: A Critique of the Archaeology of Plantation Slavery. *Historical Archaeology* 24(4): 78–91.

Johnson, Dennis Loy. 1993. Native Son, W.E.B. Du Bois. *Berkshire Magazine*, Autumn, 44–57.

Jordan, Winthrop. 1968. *White over Black: American Attitudes toward the Negro, 1550–1812.* Baltimore: Penguin.

Kaplan, Sydney, and Emma N. Kaplan. 1989. *The Black Presence in the Era of the American Revolution.* Rev. ed. Amherst: University of Massachusetts Press.

Leone, Mark P., and Catherine A. Crosby. 1987. Epilogue: Middle-Range Theory in Historical Archaeology. In *Consumer Behavior in Historical Archaeology,* ed. Suzanne Spencer-Wood, 397–410. New York: Plenum.

Leone, Mark P., and Parker B. Potter, Jr., eds. 1988. *The Recovery of Meaning: Historical Archeology in the Eastern United States.* Washington, D.C.: Smithsonian.

Lester, Julius, ed. 1971. *The Seventh Son: The Thought and Writings of W.E.B. Du Bois.* Vols. 1 and 2. New York: Vintage.

Lewis, David Levering. 1993. *W.E.B. Du Bois: Biography of a Race.* New York: Holt.

Marable, Manning. 1985. *Black American Politics: From the Washington Marches to Jesse Jackson.* London: Verso.

McArdle, Alan H. 1986. *Mortality Change and Industrialization in Western Massachusetts, 1850–1910.* Ph.D. diss., University of Massachusetts.

Mouer, L. Daniel, Mary Ellen N. Hodges, Stephen R. Potter, Susan L. Henry, Ivor Noël Hume, Dennis J. Pogue, Martha W. McCartney, and Thomas L. Davidson. N.d. "Colono" Pottery, Chesapeake Pipes, and "Uncritical Assumptions." In *"I, Too, Am America,"* ed. Theresa Singleton.

Mullins, Paul 1992. The Contradictions of Abundance: African American Women and Mass Consumer Culture. Department of Anthropology, University of Massachusetts, Amherst. Typescript.

———. 1993. The Contradictions of Consumption: An Archaeology of African America and Consumer Culture, 1850–1930. Department of Anthropology, University of Massachusetts, Amherst. Typescript.

Nissenbaum, Stephen. 1980. *Sex, Diet, and Debility in Jacksonian America.* Westport, Conn.: Greenwood.

Omi, Michael, and Howard Winant. 1986. *Racial Formation in the United States.* New York: Routledge and Kegan Paul.

Orser, Charles E., Jr. 1988. Toward a Theory of Power for Historical Archaeology: Plantations and Space. In *The Recovery of Meaning,* ed. Mark P. Leone and Parker B. Potter, Jr., 313–343.

———. N.d. Proprietary Medicines and Archaeological Meaning. Department of Anthropology, University of Massachusetts, Amherst. Typescript.

———, ed. 1990. Historical Archaeology on Southern Plantations and Farms. *Historical Archaeology* 24(4).

Parrish, James N. 1981. *House of the Black Burghardts: W.E.B. Du Bois Boyhood Home.* Boston: Massachusetts Historical Commission Historic Resource Survey of Historic Archeologic Sites.

Paynter, Robert. 1992. W.E.B. Du Bois and the Material World of African-Americans in Great Barrington, Massachusetts. *Critique of Anthropology* 12(3): 277–291.

Perry, Warren, and Robert Paynter. N.d. Epilogue: Artifacts, Ethnicity, and the Archaeology of African Americans. In *"I, Too, Am America,"* ed. Theresa Singleton.

Piersen, William D. 1988. *Black Yankees.* Amherst: University of Massachusetts Press.

Pomerantz, Frieda, D. Richard Gumaer, and Robert Paynter. 1984. The Black Burghardts. Department of Anthropology, University of Massachusetts, Amherst. Exhibit panel.

Preston, S. H., and M. R. Haines. 1991. *Fatal Years: Child Mortality in Late Nineteenth-Century America.* Princeton: Princeton University Press.

Prunier, Jesse T. 1983. Progress Report on Glass Analysis Project—Fall '83. Department of Anthropology, University of Massachusetts, Amherst. Typescript.

Rampersad, Arnold. 1990. *The Art and Imagination of W.E.B. Du Bois.* New York: Schocken.

Robinson, Cedric J. 1983. *Black Marxism: The Making of the Black Radical Tradition.* London: Zed.

Rosenberg, C. E. 1962. *The Cholera Years.* Chicago: University of Chicago Press.

Singleton, Theresa. 1988. An Archaeological Framework for Slavery and Emancipation, 1740–1880. In *The Recovery of Meaning,* ed. Mark P. Leone and Parker B. Potter, Jr., 345–370.

———. 1990. The Archaeology of the Plantation South: A Review of Approaches and Goals. *Historical Archaeology* 24(4): 70–77.

———, ed. 1985. *The Archeology of Slavery and Plantation Life.* Orlando, Fl.: Academic Press.

———. N.d. *"I, Too, Am America,": Studies in African American Archaeology.* Charlottesville: University of Virginia Press. In press.

Smedley, Audrey. 1993. *Race in North America.* San Francisco: Westview.

South, Stanley. 1977. *Method and Theory in Historical Archeology.* New York: Academic Press.

Starr, Paul. 1982. *The Social Transformation of American Medicine.* New York: Basic.

Valentine, Charles. 1968. *Culture and Poverty: Critique and Counter-proposals.* Chicago: University of Chicago Press.

Wallace, Michelle. 1990. *Invisibility Blues.* London: Verso.

Yentsch, Anne. 1988. Legends, Houses, Families, and Myths: Relationships between Material Culture and American Ideology. In *Documentary Archaeology in the New World,* ed. Mary Beaudry, 5–19. London: Cambridge University Press.

JOHN J. ATTINASI

Racism, Language Variety, and Urban U.S. Minorities: Issues in Bilingualism and Bidialectalism

Divergence from "standard" English is easily perceived. Dialect differences are frequently the instrument or excuse for discrimination along racial, ethnic, geographic, and educational lines. For two U.S. populations in particular, African Americans and Latinos, physical differences and socioeconomic indicators reinforce linguistic stigma, and all three are used to rationalize separation, prejudice, inequality, and more blatant forms of racism that are expressed in or linked to language. Among African Americans, dialect differences in English speech, writing conventions, and communication styles are used both to explain away differential treatment by outsiders, and to strengthen the group's cohesion in the face of devaluation and separatism. Similar language-based stigma and resistance are found among Latinos through Spanish and Latino varieties of English. In this essay I explore several aspects of language discrimination, especially its educational dimensions, and offer perspectives on the dynamics of clashes between vernacular and standard language forms in relation to Latino and African-American groups. Balanced against the external discredit of linguistic varieties, subordinate group resistance and self-respect help maintain ethnolinguistic vitality.

Verbal expressions accompany oppressive policy and acts. Persons are dehumanized when referred to as "those people," "males," or "females." Terms such as *underprivileged* and *non-English proficient* perpetuate a deficit theory regarding cultural diversity. The insistent anglicization of unusual names and the corrective repronunciation of accented speech send messages of devaluation regarding vernacular and non-native speech varieties.

In education, neglect and illegality are linked to race when funding for desegregation efforts is misdirected to receiving schools in "white" neighborhoods, leaving overcrowded and inner-city schools with Latino and African-American majorities underfunded and unchanged (Hess and Warden 1988). Using compensatory monies to bolster a bureaucracy rather than to teach children is more easily tolerated in a school system that is mostly nonwhite (Hess 1991:25–26). "Special education" disproportionately enrolls urban minority children. Unfortunately, those who need the most receive the least. Special programs suffer first in budget crises; unsettled urban school strikes disrupt the year for inner-city children. High teacher turnovers, the placement of inexperienced teachers in urban schools, and the continuation of noncertified persons in bilingual and special education are common practices, but overlooked. Racial correlates cannot be discounted in such educational situations. Multicultural subordinate populations (Latinos, African Americans, Native American Indians, and many Asian groups) are further victimized educationally by low expectations. The student is undereducated because the group is assumed to be incapable of more than the past low-achievement average scores. Students and teachers then enter a conspiracy of silence in which neither bothers to exert effort, and neither disturbs the other's very different school (and after-school) subcultures. The gap continues and widens. The prophecy fulfills itself, and a language is created to rationalize or mitigate the situation.

Beyond the classroom, other forms of institutional and personal linguistic discrimination need exploration. In schools, universities, and in the streets of cities, recent signs of bigotry and racist verbal assault have been, sadly, more open and injurious than ever. Police brutality erupted into a destructive aftermath in Los Angeles in 1992; it was clearly racial. Unfortunately, such violence continues, in Detroit and elsewhere. Polarizations "beyond black and white" to anti-Asian, anti-Latino sentiments, and tensions across groups compound longstanding patterns of white-to-black discrimination.

Also in 1992, Native Americans reminded others that ethnic oppression and racism in the Americas is five hundred years old. Being treated as less than human, less than "*cristiano*" or "*castellano,*" American Indian people have fathomed the links between language, group identity, and human dignity. The treatment of Latinos, who share a Native-American heritage, and African Americans, who were transported throughout the Americas as an alternative to the failed enslavement of indigenous peoples, are two more facets of one problem—racism. Today, racism is "dysconscious," embedded in the status quo (King 1991). It underlies fatalism in the face of hierarchy and paternalism that erupts into machismo and self-righteousness. Depending on its variety, racism perpetuates, or neglects, or quietly laments persisting inequality.

Several analyses of the linkages among language and discourse, discrimination, and racism have been undertaken. In the formative period of studying the sociolinguistics of Black English, sensitive white researchers explored the structural integrity and logic of this vernacular variety (Kochman 1972; Labov 1972a, b). More recently, African-American authors have collaborated with committed social scientists from other backgrounds to investigate the cultural dimensions of African-American discourse, and the sociolinguistic politics of exclusion (Gay and Baber 1987; Smitherman-Donaldson and van Dijk 1988).

> Language and discourse are vital in reproducing racial oppression and control of Blacks and other minorities. Whether in informational or institutional contexts, whether among the elite or the public at large, racial oppression becomes structural, rather than individual or incidental, when its conditions are shared by the dominant group. Reasons, motivations, goals and interests must be communicated. They are linked with opinions and attitudes, and [receive] expression, verbalization and persuasive formulation in various types of talk and text. (Smitherman-Donaldson and van Dijk 1988:17)

The difference between prejudice and racism is the power to enforce sentiments of bigotry. Therefore, discriminatory language used by minorities is inherently weaker than similar language directed by members of more powerful groups at subordinated people. If *X* hates *Y* but has little economic or political clout to affect the life of *Y*, he or she cannot do anything about it. *X* can lash out with an insult or a brick, but the effect is temporary and local. It is much different if *Y* can impede *X*'s employment, deny a home, or prevent him or her from enjoying an acceptable quality of life. In a classroom confrontation, a racial epithet against a white can be diffused by the prevailing relations of power and social climate; whereas the verbal devaluation of a minority person is reinforced by disparities in neighborhoods, housing, employment, mean test scores, school tracking, and treatment in public places. An educational system that excludes, discourages, or "can't find" certain groups of people participates in a web of racism, ranging from "color-blind" social invisibility and condescending smiles to epithets, vandalism, and violence.

The forms of inequality, from neglect to ugly racism, are structured and implemented through language. In linguistic interaction, issues of control over people and resources may surface overtly and undermine interaction covertly. The linguistics of racism extends beyond the legal squabble over "fighting words," that is, whether racist language should be protected as free speech unless it is directed at a specific person in a hostile way.

At elementary and secondary educational levels, children are frequently victimized with racial dimensions at both the core and surface of undereducation. Terms of reference, manner of address, inattention, low expectations, and lack of equity need to be explored and catalogued for their ethnic and racial dimensions. Thus, language manifests the unfinished business of emancipation from inequality and completing the civil rights agenda in a multitude of social contexts, nearly all of which have verbal expression or communicative interaction attached.

Focusing directly on language, there are three levels of current social practice in which racism is expressed by, or related to, language: overt racism, covert racism, and suppression of linguistic varieties. The rise of campus racism and the proliferation of skinheads, "Aryan" groups, and political catalysts such as David Duke have been seen by some as symptoms of something new, perhaps because many young people support such overt racism. Hate speech and nativist rallies, both in the United States and Europe, openly express superiority and inferiority based on race and ethnicity. The racial label or slur on a college campus, the stereotype, racist graffiti, and fighting words are erroneously considered new. Such expressions are simply old-fashioned hate: persistent bigotries from the Jim Crow and Nazi eras that have not died. Inaction to oppose such racism either is permitted because these expressions are thought to be too new and different for anyone to know how to combat them or is the result of a legal paralysis by which conservative libertarians invoke First Amendment rights of free speech. Less sophisticated people know that, despite legal injunctions and civil rights legislation, prejudice has continued unbroken throughout U.S. history in negative images and practices that suppress those outside the culture of power.

Covert racism flows as a softer current that exists in attitudes, in social interaction, and in the workplace. Privatized lives, personal defenses, and conservative enterprises result in an insidious disconnection from a diverse society. People seemingly cannot take the time, risk the investment—or jeopardize the deal—to work with people who are "other." Moreover, a refined "racism without racists" exists in many institutions, especially schools (Massey et al. 1975). It is characterized not so much by overt or covert acts as by quiet desperation. Nonracists perpetuate racism by being unaware or by simply giving up and retreating from the challenge to maintain, and follow through on, high expectations for children whose talents are clouded by societal circumstances. Combating such tendencies requires vigilance against longstanding stigmas, and the courage to challenge the racial stratification we all inherit as part of institutional cultural climates. But denial has its consequences. Acting "color-blind" in a color-conscious world results in a vicious ignorance of the social antecedents to, and present implications of, race and ethnicity.

The invisibility of persons of color progresses from "We are all the same" to "They just stopped participating."

Third, and related to overt and covert racism, is the muzzle. Dialogue is silenced through power relations that delegitimize arguments and ideas that are not articulated in acceptable discourse or fashionable jargon (Delpit 1986, 1988). The English-only movement attempts to degrade and repress the validity of ideas (and speakers) of over a hundred languages existing in the United States. Silence itself is also a powerful form of linguistic discrimination, especially when lack of response or long delays may repress or abort communication. If verbal communication does occur between powerful and subordinate groups, it can be interrupted by insistence on standard form and official languages that tend to diminish the message of the powerless by setting the rules of interchange in favor of the powerful.

"White-only" country clubs, blatant campus graffiti, racist jokes, blaming the victim, acting color-blind, and listening more to form than content are examples of the continuum from overt to covert sociolinguistic discrimination. As it becomes more indirect, racism does not become less devastating, only less tangible.

Overt Linguistic Racism

The significance of prejudice conveyed through speech merits careful analysis because language is socially pervasive and pointedly visible. Language variety acts as a "badge of ethnicity and symbol of social interaction," as sociolinguist Joshua Fishman has phrased it. Words are an ingredient of discrimination, not just its instrument. Overt racism in language is clearest in racial slurs—here language is a weapon. Epithets are hurled. Taunts constitute aggression. Words can be the bullets of political suicide. Racially hostile speech may have the force of assault, despite any freedom-of-speech protections.

Beyond prohibited threat and libel, a legal controversy rages concerning whether psychological injury through racist language passes beyond the protection of "free speech," or whether only direct inciting of violence may be punished (Cole 1991). An extreme civil liberties argument contends that offensive expression is constitutionally protected. The battle continues in local, state, and federal courts over the legality of expressions that stimulate anger or resentment related to race, and even the Supreme Court has considered the right of universities to censure racist expression (Ferrell 1992). A fear expressed by First Amendment absolutists is that speech control may be enforced more severely against minorities than against their oppressors. "The same first amendment that protects the right of a David Duke to speak freely on racial issues protects the same right for a Louis Farrakhan," according to a litigation counsel in a sexism case at George Mason University (Glasberg 1991). Another argument emphasizes the responsibility of educational institutions to set standards for an intellectual, civilized society and to promote learning by all groups. In that view, campus racism should not be allowed on the grounds that expressions of racist hate create a hostile environment. Even when they are indirect, slurs and racial devaluations are socially injurious and may threaten persons from groups underrepresented in higher education. Thus minority students sense discomfort and find it impossible to pursue an education in environments where bigotry is allowed. Educational institutions, as inclusive communities, have the right to set policy regarding acceptable intellectual dialogue, and to punish persons, fraternities, or other groups for speech that has racist, sexist, or other innuendos. (Swift and severe penalties in politics and sports are frequent.) The central issue in several university cases is the role of language in the responsibility of schools to balance constitutionality and free expression and to eliminate bigotry in order to promote equal educational opportunity and an ethical intellectual and social climate.

Explicit bigotry in language may be seen in its most blatant form in overt slurs, offensive jokes, and names. Derogatory ethnic labels abound, and at least eight types may be identified (Allen 1990). One type is based in shortened names: *Mex* for Mexican; *Spic,* from a mispronunciation of "speak," or from the attempt to pronounce the abbreviation *Hspc* for Hispanic; *Flip* for Filipino; and *Hunkie* (*Honkie*) for immigrants from the Austro-Hungarian empire. A second type derives from negative stereotypes: *swamp rat* for Acadian or 'Cajun; *pigsticker* for eastern Europeans who often worked in the packing industries of the Midwest; *wetback* for Mexicans who may have crossed the Rio Grande (or other land or water borders); *spear-chucker,* for African Americans, based on ignorance promoted by Tarzan-type movies about African nations; *spaghetti-bender, beaner,* or *greaser,* because of foods and the appearance of southern Europeans and Latin Americans. (I am kept from mentioning even worse epithets based on stereotypes only by the limits of bad taste.) A third type includes derogatory ethnic labels based in metaphor: *chocolate* and *white-bread* for dark and light skin color; *redskin, kike, coffee,* and others based on appearance. A fourth type is derisive ethnic nuances present in verbs: *to gyp* (Gypsy), *to jap* (Japanese), *to jew* (Jewish), *to welsh* (stereotyped behavior of persons from Wales). A fifth type comprises the many stereotypical nicknames: *Jan Kees* (Dutch version of John Doe) became *Yankee; Mick* (Irish); *Tony* (Italian); *Sapphire* (African American); *Hiawatha* (Native American). A sixth type includes limited-use slurs based on military experience or in-group beliefs in items such as *Charlie* (Vietnamese, in addition to the African-American generic for white man, *Mr. Charlie*); *Sally* or *Miss Ann* (generic name for white women); and *Kunta Kinte* (African person in the U.S.). A seventh type is made up of numbskull jokes based in ethnic slurs and stereotypes of the ignorant minority; for example, substitute an ethnic slur for "numbskull" in, *"How many numbskulls does it take to change a light bulb?"*

Finally, whereas it is clear that putting down another group attempts to reinforce or assert the superiority of those issuing the put-down, a more sensitive situation is found in the eighth type, the self-ascribed epithet. In-group self-ridicule, with varying degrees of humor and malice, is documented in epithets, jokes, and other overt language usage—for example, Italians who refer to themselves as *dagos,* or Black Americans who call each other *nigger.* Dick Gregory used the "n-word" as a book title in the 1970s but probably would not do so today. Numerous African-American comedians play fast and loose with the term, and poets are sensitive to the baggage that it carries in various pronunciations and contexts. Rappers find shock value without resorting to four-letter profanity in the frequent use of the word. When African-American entertainers use "niggah" in public, they create a double standard: black use of the term is not derogatory, but white usage is racist. There are two dangers in such an in-group/out-group dual standard: first, that permission for others to use the term is implied; and second, that the group tacitly accepts the stereotypes about itself through the facile use of the derogatory ethnic label.

Euphemistic terms abound that still seem racially loaded—*urban poor, culturally deprived, culture of poverty, underclass, disadvantaged, underprivileged, minority,* and *GI* (a person from Gary, Indiana, which is over 90 percent African American) have all been used to refer to nonwhite minority groups. Their offensiveness varies. So does the reception of supposedly neutral social science labeling. In *Drylongso: a Self Portrait of Black America,* an old-timer's skepticism spoke volumes: "Sometimes I think all this anthropology is just another way of calling me a *n*——" (Gwaltney 1980: xix).

Others have gone to greater lengths than I have reflected here to develop an appropriate analysis of overt linguistic racism (Allen 1983, 1990; Allport 1954; Greenberg et al. 1988). Lists of such terms are simply descriptive, and perhaps trivial, but the cumulative cultural and psychological effects of blatant, "humorous," and stereotyped racial language are not. We next turn to more subtle forms of linguistic discrimination.

Covert Racism

Today's climate of public concern with being politically correct channels most of the expression of discrimination to covert and symbolic levels, avoiding the blatant derogatory ethnic label. Instead, ethnic distinction and discrimination are reflected indirectly, in behavior, attitudes, reactions to speech and speakers, and "nonoffensive" linguistic expressions that may be voiced in polite company. Several areas of analysis can help clarify contemporary linguistic discrimination, including verbal codes, nonverbal communication, and language attitudes.

Overt racists are blunt and intolerable, but others who allow themselves to discriminate in order to maintain a quality of life that is insulated from racial intrusion, and undisturbed economically or visually, embody more antiseptic and socially acceptable racism. "Communicative apartheid" might serve as a label for this stance. A few examples may illustrate the phenomenon. Many professions and professional meetings remain mostly white; nonwhites are absent in "good neighborhoods" in the surburbs, and from most of the managerial levels of business. People in the corporate world (and elsewhere) prefer to work with people they know and trust. The infamous old boys' network lingers, despite affirmative action and set-asides for women and minorities. This segregated world can be rationalized by its participants, especially when money is involved. Trust is built by interaction and destroyed by breakdowns in communication. Delays, "dropping the ball," lack of performance without satisfactory explanation or petition for extension—in other words, the hard core of business negotiations—are more difficult when neither party can be sure of what the other is saying at verbal and nonverbal levels. People who speak the same language are able to establish trust and satisfactorily negotiate proposed tasks and their modification when things do not go as planned. If people cannot speak to and read the other, they are less confident in the business transaction.

This situation is interpretable in terms of the psycholinguistic concept of synchronicity, or "communicative mirroring." When people are having a rewarding conversation, verbal and nonverbal interaction synchronizes ("*That was a great meeting. We had a good talk. I think we got somewhere. We really speak the same language*"). Linguistic analysts note congruent body position among interlocutors. Eye-contact conventions, utterance length, nods, facial gestures, turn-taking cues, and intonation patterns further signal mirrored interaction.

Moreover, it is now clear from child development research that speech intonation is conditioned by dialect and family communicative patterns perceived even before birth. Speech patterns that are comfortable for acquiring information, negotiating, or socializing are learned and practiced. Socialization during youth reinforces linguistically separated subcultures, whether ethnically white, Latino, or African American, based on geographic region, religion, or social class. By adulthood, we have all come to feel comfortable with certain discourse conventions about the form of a discussion, the use of examples, or valid appeals to authority. Familiar vocabulary items may be repeated and have power. (Each microculture has its buzz words.) Question and request structures are internalized, and in the end, one knows how a decision has been reached or if a conversation has finished. (For some Native-American cultures, no conversation is finished, no decision is final.)

In brief, people often want to hear and be with their own, and they suspect the other. Formal sociolinguistic conventions are reinforced by cultural content. The message of the other is best delivered by in-group brokers of the "other" microculture. This is why men learn about feminism from enlightened men and why white performers like Mick Jagger, the Beatles, Elvis, and Vanilla Ice made millions off black music, selling it to general (white) markets. African Americans and Latinos may prefer to listen to Black or Latin singers and enjoy Black movie actors or Spanish television. Minority clients may more easily respond to and understand a salesperson or teacher from their respective group. A group is moved by preaching in Black American churches, or by the pageantry of the Roman Catholic religion. After five days of working for "the (white) man," an African American might be heard to say: "*I don't want to hear no white people today.*" Spanish speakers may react similarly, as did the Cuban mother on the Upper West Side of New York City, in the movie *El Super.* One morning, her daughter was listening to the radio in English, and the mother said: "*Apaga ese radio. Hoy no quiero escuchar el inglés.*" (Turn off that radio; I don't want to hear English today.) White Americans frequently react in the same way to Spanish and Black English on television, radio, or in public places: they don't want to hear it. (These are my own sociolinguistic observations, based on many years of observation of intergroup communication and interaction across languages, dialects, and settings.)

Such examples help us to identify the most subtle and unconscious forms of contemporary covert linguistic racism. A failure of mirroring between whites, blacks and Latinos results in linguistic mismatch, devaluation of ability and character, and a presentation of self across group borders that results in the reinforcement of the stratified status quo. This often occurs in educational and employment settings, even where liberal attitudes and affirmative action plans seek out racial equity. After a nonwhite person interviews before a mostly white panel, the following may be heard: "*The resumé was good, but they interviewed poorly.*" "*The committee did not feel confident.*" "*There's something that bothers me.*" "*I feel the other candidate could become a team player more successfully.*" "*I just don't think this will work.*"

The larger issue is that, together, communicative apartheid, linguistic conventions, privacy based in linguistic varieties, and mirrored synchronicity add up to a dysconscious climate of prejudice that is made concrete in interaction, conflict, or avoidance. Keeping marginalized people at the periphery is the essence of racism, and language often facilitates it.

The problem is two-sided. We value and respond to our own group, and our own dialect or language variety. Hence the value of role-model teachers, and the economic advantage of a diverse sales force and advertising campaign. On the other side, racial separation appears almost natural. Resistance among minority groups provides a safety zone against the climate of xenophobia. Separation is rooted in the deepest origins of our socialization, perhaps even in our speech perceptions before birth. Infant response to tone of voice and pitch contours emerges very early (Pérez and Torres-Guzmán 1992: 29). Weir (1966) has reported that five-to-eight-month-old babies of Chinese and American English-speaking parents had different intonation patterns in their babbling. Heath's study of language socialization in three U.S. sociolinguistic groups found clear differences in verbal inputs to, and interpretations of, infant vocalization (1983: 75–76, 344–354).

Our challenge is to overcome encapsulation within single language varieties (from which both the ghettoized purist and the isolated minority suffer), by expanding dialect-specific patterns to proficiency along a continuum of linguistic varieties. This amplification of repertoire would at once empower the marginalized, encourage multidialectal understanding, and promote communicative acceptance to enable communication between groups. Knowledge can change attitudes and influence behavior. We therefore need an understanding of the sociolinguistic dimensions of attitudes, based on the theoretical and empirical study of status differences among language varieties.

Covert racial discrimination patterns based on linguistic features such as accent and intonation have been classified through investigation of the persistence and status of language varieties by sociolinguists and social psychologists. This research enables us to raise the focus of discussion from explicit linguistic usage to implied metalinguistic levels (Gere and Smith 1979; Hecht and Ribeau 1988; Obudho 1976). In everyday interaction among ordinary people distinctions are not usually made among the content of speech, the manner of speaking, and the speakers themselves. Nonstandard features of speech stand out, seem to be intolerable, unsupportable, or just plain wrong, and are invoked to justify avoidance and exclusion. In effect, persons and their group, not just their speech, are excluded. The public imagines itself to be reacting to speech (with the rationale that it "sounds bad," is inaccurate, or unintelligible), but the net result is opposition to the speaker, discrimination against the group, and resistance to supposed infringement on the language and culture of power.

Discrimination may occur in tone of voice, choice of vocabulary, facial expression, gesture, and posture that encode attitude and engender reaction. Mutual linguistic antagonism may yield a mockery of dialect varieties and languages, or an exaggeration of dialect. In response, resistance culture develops, and vernacular forms persist and may seem overemphasized ("*loud jive talk*"). Non-English languages may be flaunted ("*They speak Spanish in front of you and make you wait*"). Aversion may originate from either the powerful or the powerless, since languages exhibit several dimensions of "prestige."

How do we order and compare linguistic varieties? Social psychology has the dubious honor of probing and analyzing commonly held conceptions, which are often stereotypes. In operationalizing the relationships among varieties, sociolinguistic power has been plotted along two dimensions: standardization and vitality (fig. 7). Standardization is the degree to which one variety of a language has been refined to become "standard," "a prestige variety used as an institutionalized norm in a community" (Crystal 1987:430). The development of a single spoken variety into a standard gives prestige to the source variety but actually involves differences from all spoken varieties. Possible opposite terms, *nonstandard* or *substandard,* seem negative, even pejorative, and imply grammatical elitism. *Vernacular,* as an objective term for the pole opposite the standard, places no judgment on the value of coexistent varieties. Rather, the term *vernacular* refers to "the indigenous language or dialect of a community" (Crystal 1987: 35).

In figure 7, boldface type indicates the varieties under discussion in this essay. Varieties are plotted on the chart with respect to their standardization and vitality. English as a worldwide linguistic phenomenon has great currency as both a first and second language. Media standards and major literary vehicles, such as Received Pronunciation of English, Parisian French and Castillian Spanish, are important standardized varieties. Second-tier varieties, both standardized and vital through official (though nonprimary) language status, include Guaraní, Catalán, Flemish and Québecois. Black English vernaculars are strong in vitality, though not standardized. Spanish in the United States is standardized through its hemispheric and global connections. Its vitality is undeniable, yet limited

Increasing Vitality

English as a World Language
RP in Britain Parisian French
Spanish in Spain and Latin America

Guaraní in Paraguay
Catalán in Spain

Black English Vernaculars in the U.S., Caribbean, Africa

Flemish in Belgium French in Canada

Spanish in the U.S.

Working Class Urban Dialects

Welsh

Irish

Vernacular — **Standard**

Language Mixtures

Immigrant Language Varieties in Most Countries

Regional Dialects in Most Countries

French in Africa

French in Asia

Classical Languages

Decreasing Vitality

Fig. 7. Two primary sociocultural factors affecting language attitudes (adapted from Ryan, Giles, and Sebastian 1982:6).

by controversy and unofficial status. Bilingual education, media, and public services, as well as demographic strength, nonetheless place it in the upper right quadrant. Similar situations may apply to Welsh and Irish, with less vitality. Colonial languages are becoming less vital, but neither extinct nor fossilized, as are standardized classical Latin and Greek. Regional dialects have limited vitality and nearly no standardization; immigrant varieties participate in the standard. Language mixtures (code switching, pidgins) and working-class urban dialects are vernaculars with little standardization, and varying elements of vitality. Plotting standardization and vitality of varieties in particular speech communities should be a determination based on empirical research and documentation.

Literary, political and institutional support have enabled dialects to become standardized through acceptance over time. In fact, there are several standards in operation for any language, despite royal academies and purist thinking that there is but one English, one Spanish, or one French. The operational habits of work, electronic media, and printed information enable several accepted conventions to coexist—societal (regional, class, occupational) standards, literary standards within genres, even publication-specific standards and broadcast standards—each appropriate to varying contexts.

The vitality dimension is dynamically interwoven with that of standardization. Originally conceived as a sociopsychological composite factor, vitality accounts for the sense within an ethnolinguistic group of being "a distinctive and active collective entity in intergroup situations" (Giles, Bourhis, and Taylor 1977: 308). The components of ethnolinguistic vitality help analyze various social aspects of intergroup strength in relation to the structure and usage of language varieties. Language vitality may be determined by analyzing sociolinguistic status, demography, and institutional support (fig. 8). Status factors reflect the group's economic and political power, its social and historical standing, and the international prestige of the language. Demographic factors relate to the size and dynamics of the linguistic community. Institutional support refers to the use of the variety in a wide range of social institutions, both formal and informal, including mass media (especially written forms), the home, houses of worship, social settings, and schools (Hamers and Blanc 1989:162–166).

These two dimensions, standardization and vitality, are useful in understanding the various types of prestige, loyalty, and devaluation that language varieties attract. Standardization is a relatively clear dimension related to written language norms, conventional spelling, and formal rules of grammar. Spanish has a standardized form that gives economic and literate status to the language of Latinos, even the nonstandard varieties, which may be developed into standard forms. On the other hand, Ebonic varieties (language usages derived from the African diaspora) are vernacular and are written only as approximations of speech (Gay 1987: 66). Nonetheless, vernacular varieties of English and other languages, urban and rural regional dialects, and sociolects based in class, economic, and educational status are dynamic and should be described for their vitality and validity without prejudgment. Many types of code switching and English varieties spoken by Latinos, in addition to

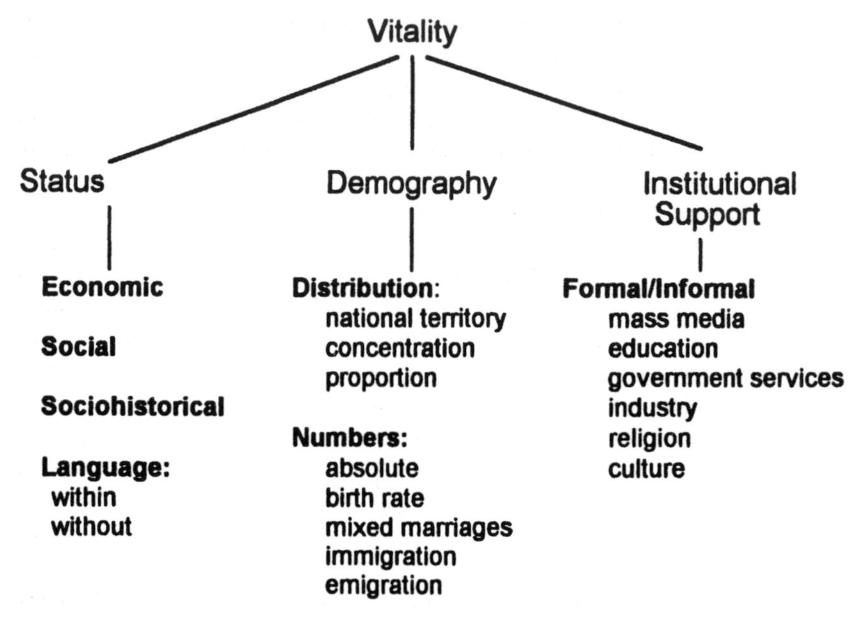

Fig. 8. Taxonomy of structural variables affecting sociolinguistic vitality (from Giles, Bourhis, and Taylor 1977:309).

regional spoken dialects of Spanish, might also be seen as "working-class vernaculars" (Flores, Attinasi, and Pedraza 1981).

The vitality of vernaculars has increased in status as a result of institutional support from the electronic media, which allow spoken varieties to be broadcast widely, and through the eloquent verbal language of orators who speak compellingly without compromising dialect features. For instance the status of Ebonic speech has been increased by the language of the Black-American clergy and public figures such as Rev. Jesse Jackson, the Chicago alderman Danny Davis, or the late mayor of Chicago Harold Washington. César Chávez and Russell Means speak in ways that evoke the voices of Latino and Native-American struggles. The population increases among Latinos in the United States and of African Americans strengthens the demographic support of vernacular varieties of Spanish and English. Institutions and media as diverse as churches, desktop publishing, salsa music, rap recordings, radio and television, and literary works of African-American, Latin American, and U.S. Latino writers have enhanced the institutional vitality of non-mainstream cultures and their accompanying language varieties.

No one denies the power of standard forms, especially in writing, as a means of access to a wider audience (Edwards 1982; Greene 1981: 66). This essay is written in standard English, not in Spanish, and with few strictly oral colloquialisms. Its purpose is to reach a wider audience who may only read English, or who use it as a second language. But spoken strategies beyond the controlled use of standard written English may be necessary for discussion, understanding, analysis, and application of this condensed written format. (Conversations about the ideas presented here, their application to practice for teachers, and discussions with students may necessitate a wider use of spoken language in varieties of Spanish, English, and other languages). It is neither logical nor legitimate to assume that all discourse in standard literate form is intelligent, or to insist that clarity or brilliance may be expressed only in standard form.

For most African-American Ebonic linguistic varieties, cultural conventions exist, but formal textual standardization does not, although Kréol in Haiti and Papiamentu in Curaçao do have standardized written forms. Vitality, on the other hand, seems to be increasing for African-American varieties, and aspects of vernacular are amplifying the standard through the fiction and poetry of African-American authors, from the classics of Langston Hughes and Paul Laurence Dunbar to the contemporary works of writers like Toni Morrison, Ishmael Reed, and Terry McMillan. Legal rulings (Smitherman 1981) and the development of cultural identity in language use (Gay and Baber 1987) have increased the status of and support for vernaculars, thus enhancing their vitality. To the chagrin of purists who claim to speak only what is in the dictionary, many topical phrases from wide sources, including Spanish and Black English colloquialisms, are becoming current in standard English as that language expands (and its dictionaries continuously incorporate new words and expressions).

Against this sociolinguistic backdrop, the evaluation of language varieties unfolds and evolves. Attitudes toward language varieties frequently express covert racial attitudes. Evaluations of dialects and accents do not reflect simply linguistic or aesthetic elements but rather couch expressions of the status and prestige accorded the speakers of these varieties. Social psychologists have explored how listeners rate speakers on scales of competence (e.g., job status, intelligence) and likability (e.g., friendliness, trust). The overall conclusion is that standard speech is preferred. Kalin (1982: 155), for example, reported that standard accent was rated higher on competence and likability scales by both in-group and out-group members; Hopper (1977) found a positive reaction to Black speakers who spoke standard English. On the other hand, a minimum nonstandardness was sufficient to elicit the stereotype of African-American speech. Progressive increases in

Ebonic nonstandard features of speech samples had little effect on raters' negative reactions. This is the language-variety correlate of the old race-conscious "one-drop rule"; one grain of Black speech and the person is categorically devalued.

In several attitudinal experiments regarding Mexican-American speech, the situation of esteem is similar: as accentedness increased, the value rating by Anglos descended (Carranza 1982). When looking at Latino raters, however, studies suggest that foreign-born Mexican-Americans ascribe more prestige to accented speech than do U.S.-born Mexicans (Baird 1969; Brennan, Ryan, and Dawson 1975). This implies that foreign-born Mexicans in the United States have a more positive self-image than do U.S.-born Mexican Americans. The hegemony of Anglo culture is reflected in the finding that self-concept among Mexican Americans became more negative as time in the United States increased. The implication from this work is that the U.S. experience engenders and reinforces biracially divided language attitudes (standard vs. all others), as pointed out by Rodriguez (1989: 50–51). Puerto Ricans and other Latinos in the United States who experience a multidimensional stratification in Latin America (based on economic status, partially on color, and with linguistic dimensions involving sociolects of Spanish) are pressed into a perplexing two-dimensional world where the educated professional, the nonliterate worker, and even indigenous American Indians who speak Spanish as a second language are considered "Hispanics," with no distinction made among them.

The discrimination against speakers of vernaculars and those who speak standard varieties of languages other than English seems to be the result of a monolingual view of prestige, at least in the Anglophone world. British "received pronunciation" seems to be at the top of the scale, confounding whites who speak U.S. dialects when they encounter black West Indians or Africans who speak prestige-attracting British varieties. The phenomena reviewed here, whether discrimination against vernaculars or devaluation of accentedness, are part of a covert scale that places a single group (and supposedly a single language variety) in a position of honor, at the expense of all others in a sort of pecking order. But the monolithic prestige scale has its contradictions, and nowhere are they more visible than in English-only nativism.

Suppression of Linguistic Varieties and the English-Only Movement

Silencing, or linguistic suppression, is the ultimate dehumanization through language. Both dialect suppression and language prohibition exclude speakers from dialogue with the culture of power. In this respect, discrimination against speakers of Black English vernaculars and exclusion of speakers of languages other than English have the same social effect. Vernacular speakers are disenfranchised or dismissed for not speaking standard English. This is taken to the extreme when English receives exclusive rights. Standard English elitism and English-only movements discriminate against bilingual persons for both of their languages, especially if they speak English with an accent or working-class vernacular English. The prestige of English does not need legal support, given the English origins of U.S. history and the currents of isolationism and nativism that have periodically arisen in the United States (Crawford 1992). Recognizing the danger of linguistic chauvinism, the National Council of Black Studies recognized that English-only policies could have a negative impact on black students, although it is evident that most African Americans are unaware of the personal or wider impact of the English-only movement (Smitherman 1992).

The legal, practical, and ideological consequences of English exclusiveness in the United States have been vigorously debated over the past decade, as nineteen states passed provisions giving official status to English (Piatt 1990). The ideological effect of such laws is to reinforce the mistrust of non-English languages, speakers, and cultures. In California's 1986 referendum on English (Proposition O), the English press implied that language minority groups were being manipulated by local politicians. Much of the rhetoric assumed that inability to speak English (not even thought of as "knowing other languages") could be equated with the inability to speak and even the inability to think (Woolard 1989: 277). The ideology was that non-English languages were cultural prisons and that English would liberate minorities and protect their rights; but the practical effect was to deprive language minorities of many avenues of social access, including access to learning English through bilingual methods. Such laws seem to impact most severely on the elderly and women, sectors that are the least bilingual among language minority groups. Continued divisiveness, not unity, has been the effect of English-only. Those who support language diversity are thought to be un-American, and those who speak other languages are seen as deviant and dependent, rather than as bearers of a precious human resource. Zentella (1988) offers an impassioned explanation of that ideology and defends multilingualism: "Language is not the real issue; it is a smokescreen. The browning of America is under way, and as the face of America changes, so must our definition of 'American.' The United States is not home only to English-speakers; the American dream is not dreamt in English only."

Whereas the suppression of languages other than English is a clear case of linguistic discrimination, the censure of dialects and what Delpit (1988) has called "the silenced dialogue" are more subtle. The silencing of linguistic variety frequently occurs in professional settings dominated by white males, and in discourse that frequently uses military and sports metaphors. Women's ways of knowing, Ebonic rhetorical styles, the accent of the English-as-a-second-language speaker, and the hesitance of disabled persons tend to be neglected and disempowered. It is doubly devastating when the speaker is both from a minority group and a woman. The setting might be a staff meeting. An issue is on the table. Various persons are giving presentations or opinions. When an African American, Hispanic, or Asian takes the floor and begins to speak, the focus of attention is broken. People refer to papers, move in their seats, get a coffee, begin a side conversation. Afterwards, they say that the person had a point but that it wasn't clear, couldn't be followed, was off the mark.

In schools and universities, the subtler forms of discrimination in the situations just described are compounded. Schools are stratified by a student-teacher-administrator hierarchy. In urban schools, the higher the stratum, the fewer the minorities (in suburban schools, minority representation is less overall). Even in integrated schools, more elite and higher-track programs contain fewer minorities. Schools are thus environments for covert racism, even if blatant derogatory ethnic labels are controlled. Speakers of languages other than standard English and of vernacular dialects suffer devaluation and negative language attitudes and their social-psychological consequences. These consequences, broadly, are societal and personal: the inequities of institutional racism without overt racists, and the silencing of inchoate ideas if they are not framed in accepted linguistic form. In the educational arena, this often results in polarization or communication breakdown, to the great detriment of the most innocent victims of all, schoolchildren.

In educational circles, despite years of analysis, the verbal-deprivation myth persists regarding both non-English speakers (chiefly Mexicans and Puerto Ricans, but others as well) and vernacular speakers of English (certainly African Americans, but others depending on geographic region). In all cases, the myth is accompanied by tenacious errors regarding cognitive deficiency or social deficit. First, the language system or psychophysical reasons are blamed for any inability to perform on standardized measures, and for the lack of achievement in the economic marketplace. Second, social environment and verbal interaction are blamed for lack of access to standard forms. These mind-sets persist today, even though Labov noted over two decades ago that "the myth of verbal deprivation is particularly dangerous because it diverts attention from the real defects of our educational system to imaginary defects of the child" (1972a: 202). In the 1990s, issues of Afrocentric curriculum, biliteracy, and language development have sparked a new debate, with emphasis on the cultural resources, funds of knowledge, and linguistic abilities that children bring to school. These resources may be seen as starting points for acquiring standard forms and succeeding in general academic subjects.

In the 1980s, moves to institutionalize Black English through preschool primers were correctly viewed as patronizing, a liberal idea that furthered the ghettoization of and discrimination against African Americans. Modeled on the bilingual education notion of home-language literacy first and transfer of skills later, the inept analogy fortunately did not gain wide adoption. No one has successfully reduced Black English to a definitive written form, primarily because of its verbal roots and wide variation (Goodwin 1990; Hewitt 1986; Smitherman 1977:70). Still, denial persists regarding the existence and sociolinguistic vitality of Ebonic language varieties, usually among standard-English purists with normative—not descriptive—frames of reference. The speech of African Americans cannot (and should not) be taught in a standard formulaic manner. Nonetheless, awareness of the vitality of vernaculars and a transformation back and forth between vernacular and standard English varieties provide essential strategies for valid and successful pedagogy. The same arguments have been advanced regarding other languages as the foundation of bilingual and bicultural education: analogical processes promote divergent thinking, respect for communicative skill builds self-esteem, and the transfer of ideas from vernacular variety to standard English strengthens both grammar and content.

Dialect awareness for teachers has been mandated by courts (*King v. Ann Arbor* 1979; Simpkins and Simpkins 1981; Smitherman 1981), and sociolinguistic concepts are emphasized in training sessions for teachers (Gere and Smith 1979). The challenge in such cases is clear: if workshops are provided by academic linguists, they may bore the audience with descriptive facts, antagonize practitioners who are purists, and ultimately neglect to provide concrete strategies for academic improvement. Such inservice sessions will not reduce language-based racial discrimination. The recommendations may remain mild and unsatisfying: know that these structural and discourse differences exist and have their own logic; respect your students and their family speech patterns; but you still have to—somehow—get them to speak and write in the standard form. Such admonishments are inadequate to overcome overt, covert, or suppressive linguistic racism.

One study of African-American linguistic patterns in mathematical problem solving concluded only that educators should "seek out the knowledge of linguists" and "declare Black education a national emergency" (Orr 1987: 215). Intriguingly titling her study *Twice As Less,* the author noted confusion and multiple paraphrases as children verbalized mathematical relationships. Beyond analyzing dialect structure and its lack of mathematical precision, however, Orr neglected to probe other connections between mathematical conceptualization and verbal expression. An Afrocentric educator might take a different approach, emphasizing first the accomplishments of African engineering (ancient Egypt, Zimbabwe), the prowess of African-American mathematicians (Benjamin Banneker's work with Pierre l'Enfant in the design of Washington, D.C.), the accomplishments of local scientists and teachers, and the mathematical relationships in everyday occurences, from skip rope to household budgets. Next, mathematical understandings expressed in vernacular paraphrases could be matched to standard forms of mathematical statement through dialect translation. This is the frequent practice in tutorial and group study sessions among foreign students, and even among standard-English speakers. Linguistic flexibility coupled with mathematical knowledge could allow additional minority group students to find their voice in technical subjects.

Beyond the academic agenda of applied linguistics, James Baldwin offered an op-ed opinion in the July 29, 1979, *New York Times* on the Ann Arbor decision regarding Black English vernacular speakers and public school teaching. "If Black English Isn't a Language, Then Tell Me, What Is?" challenged educators to recognize that deeper issues confront all groups who do not share the language of power:

> The brutal truth is that the bulk of White people in America never had any interest in educating Black people, except as this could serve White purposes. It is not the Black child's language that is in question, it is not his language that is despised: it is his experience. A child cannot be taught by anyone who despises him, and a child cannot afford to be fooled. A child cannot be taught by anyone whose demand essentially is that the child repudiate his experience, and all that gives him sustenance, and enter a limbo in which he will no longer be Black, and in which he knows he can never become White. Black people have lost too many children that way.

The consequences of these wider societal problems return us to the very real problems of implementation and application, the follow-up necessary once linguistic consciousness is raised. Teachers are not entirely to blame, since they are too often asked to change their attitudes and approaches after only brief exposure to sociolinguistics and social psychology. The ability to move beyond liberal cheerleading is lacking in much of professional development, and teachers need concrete ways to adjust the patterns of their own interaction and practice.

Democratizing Language Variety

A radical alternative to the teaching of Black dialect provides potential answers to the dilemma faced by educators of children from diverse linguistic and dialect backgrounds. This alternative derives from "whole-language" proponents in the United States (Goodman 1965), literacy movements based in the theories of Paulo Freire of Brazil (1970, 1971), and the pedagogical implications of the Freirean method elaborated by Emilia Ferreiro of Argentina (1971, 1977). Whole language emphasizes speaking, listening, reading, and writing as components of literacy that follow natural language development; it deemphasizes spelling and grammar and concentrates on authentic uses of language. Freire recognizes the cultural basis of all learning and the need for critical consciousness-raising to create a motivating personal connection to the quest for literacy.

Ferreiro, who spent most of her professional life on reading methods for Latin American children, presents a simple proposal that could be adopted at nearly no cost for both dialect speakers of English and speakers of other languages, such as Hispanics. It is simply this: have children read standard texts aloud and then translate what they read into their home dialect. The concept of dialect translation gives legitimacy to spoken varieties without artificially creating divisive dialect reading materials. The key to the method lies in the question, Which spoken language does the written language transcribe? (Ferreiro and Teberosky 1982: 259). The answer proposed by dialect translation respects the linguistic notion of language variety and presents an antiracist stance regarding vernaculars.

Language in its written form is basically a representation of deeper lexical and syntactic structures that can be rendered by various verbal forms. (The example of *photography, photographic,* and *photo* illustrates how phonetic rendering of stress and vowel allophones are surface phenomena of deeper psycholinguistic regularities.) Since speech never mirrors writing exactly (and does not need to), writing should not necessarily be understood as the phonetic transcription of speech. Although elementary stages of language-experience writing emphasize the transcription of speech, in finished writing editing enables the writer both to condense, and to elaborate upon, spoken communication. The argument by Ferreiro is that no single spoken dialect need be exclusively represented in writing, but that writing functions as a supraordinate variety, capable of encoding many pronunciations. In most languages, a wide variety of syntactic alternatives also may be accommodated within the conventions of grammaticality: "The written signs may correspond to phonic forms that do not coincide exactly with the actual sounds, but if the semantic similarities linking forms of the same lexeme are reflected in writing, then the writing system lends itself easily to dialect variations of pronunciation. Consequently, none of these dialect variations enjoys the status of correct pronunciation for learning to read" (Ferreiro and Teberosky 1982:260).

Thus we should allow children to learn to read the way they speak. This does not require a change in materials but rather in the way the literacy process is conceived. It demands that we agree that there are no bad dialects. It demands a change in the phonic teaching approach—with its emphasis on spelling, grammar, and decoding. In the same way, Spanish speakers may learn to read Spanish in their spoken dialect—but it is still Spanish. The next step is retranslation from the vernacular—now made legitimate—to the standard. The value of the standard derives not from elite prestige, but from wider access. Vernacular speakers of English may read in dialect forms and interpret dialect syntax from standard forms (as happens in paraphrase). In the process, recognition of standard form is achieved, again with the all-important acknowledgment of sociolinguistic appropriateness and vitality based in the pragmatic relativity of each variety. Ferreiro and Teberosky cite cases where "Black preschool children learn to read by themselves, and read, in Black English, texts written not in White English but simply in English" (1982: 261, quoting Smith 1973). In both the multidialectal and multilingual cases, nonthreatening speech-writing comparisons and cross-comparison of vernacular language and dialect varieties allow access to the standard and simultaneously clarify the position of the standard in the sociolinguistic compass.

Dialect variation should not be confused with pronunciation defects or disability. The misdiagnosis of a dialect speaker or non-English speaker as a person with communication disorders is all too frequent, and the high incidence of minority children in special education should be carefully examined. On the other hand, there are numerous instances of legitimate language disabilities and communication disorders not being assessed and treated, especially among non-English speakers, because no one in the school team knew how to evaluate in the native language, diagnose the problem, separate it from linguistic conventions in Spanish or English, and prescribe an intervention. Special education travesties present further examples of subtle linguistic racism without racists, which allows the machinery of the educational establishment to crush those with little access to the linguistic culture of power.

Barriers contain subordinated groups when these groups are silenced. Whether we consider African Americans and Latinos in the United States or the undereducated working class in developing nations, discrimination against subordinated people is facilitated by their inability to speak in the dominant variety, or to control literate standards. (Literacy was denied African Americans prior to Emancipation; contemporary reading scores show a sad continuation of the pattern.) Ferreiro and Teberosky (1982) assert that whether it is justifiable ideologically or not, linguistic accommodation—meaning mastery of the standard—must precede the eradication of discrimination and will require that the powerless learn another form of discourse, in literate form as well as in spoken. Freire (1970) goes further and links learning standard forms to conceptual development and liberation. Gay and Baber (1987) and Smitherman (1977), with a different approach, argue that expressive nonstandard communications are essential acts of assertion and self-description that can lead to self-esteem, identity development, and the communicative foundations for social change. Both views have validity: "Forms of speaking are learned, especially by children, in speaking contexts, in communicative situations. Let us teach people, if judged necessary, how to speak other dialects. But we must not demand this as a prerequisite to learning to read, because it would establish an invalid causal relationship" (Ferreiro and Teberosky 1982: 262).

The normative insistence on standard speech for access to reading is compounded in the United States by a longstanding two-category (white- black) racial ideology (Rodriguez 1989: 50). This thinking is indicative of a binary attitude in which the culture of power is considered a one, and all others are zero. With the surge in Asian and Latino populations, and the five-hundred-year reminder of Native American Indians, the terms of the dichotomy might more properly be white versus nonwhite. Nevertheless, this racial binary feeds a mindset that remains far too simplistic—we-they, good-bad, valuable-dispensible. Linguistic correlates of the dichotomy include standard versus nonstandard, and English versus non-English. The term *limited English* makes no reference to a speaker's prior linguistic resources and fuels the devaluation that reduces the language, culture, ability to think, and thus the humanity of vernacular and ethnolinguistic groups to zero. Not only does such a conceptual reduction condone a have versus have-not society, but it promotes the neglect of diverse cultural resources and contributions and closes avenues of access to them. The dichotomy pressures students either to try to change who they are or to negate themselves culturally, resulting in low self-esteem or self-rejection. This double bind pressures most nonwhite groups to revere and accept the dominant culture wholly and uncritically, only to enjoy partial access to its benefits. This is the classical pattern of cultural hegemony: fascination with the unattainable world of the oppressor and uncritical acceptance of pressures to assimilate. The negative views of self and of one's vernacular speech and home culture place both bilinguals and English dialect speakers in a dilemma regarding education and access to the wider society. First is the negative prestige of hating school and not succeeding; second is the contradiction of trying to excel in spite of oneself. Low self-esteem is counterproductive to acquiring new information; effective learning requires critical thinking, selective synthesis, and the active personal application of knowledge. Ferreiro's suggestion, as an alternative, retains the rootedness in cultural consciousness that Freire considers essential and at the same time provides flexible and natural linguistic experiences that lead to standard literacy.

Four solutions may be advanced to answer the ever-widening dichotomy that places both non-English and vernacular speakers in situations of linguistic inequality. These are: change speech, change attitudes, retain high standards, and allow diversity to flourish within the form and content of clear and creative linguistic expression.

There are two sides to speech modification. First, in the interest of access to the language of power, multicultural speakers need to learn standard varieties. This does not imply removal or suppression of vernacular home languages and local dialects. Rather, the example of dialect translation and the life experiences of successful role models who have developed bidialectalism and biliteracy should be guideposts. Second, all speakers have to excoriate racism from language. Words can be weapons, and slurs are assaults. Both verbal and nonverbal communication has to be sensitive to pervasive tendencies toward discriminatory discourse and must remove prejudice and hostility from speech, reference, and innuendo.

In terms of changing attitudes, it should be recognized that *everyone* speaks a dialect, and that each language variety has its own appropriateness and validity. Validity is more than standardization; it includes vitality. This helps us understand the attraction and endurance of vernacular forms. It is also necessary for teachers, employers, and supervisors to remove low expectations in interaction with non-English and vernacular English speakers, and to be sensitive to the erroneous association of standard expression with logic and cognitive skill. Teachers should remove rote activity from their teaching of the standard form and engage students in creative, accelerated learning where the development of standard expression is a by-product, not a prerequisite, for literate activity. Furthermore, pedagogy needs to revise its approach to standard and canonical works. Teaching based in biculturalism and bilingualism connects learning to family and promotes multicultural communication. Afro- and Latinocentric education may be seen as an early apprenticeship for global learning, which it also enriches. As a response to the dismissal of nonprestigious cultures, dialect differences and language minority communities should be seen in their role of affirming culture as self-worth and as survival, through traditions rich in verbal and emotional treasures. Once they are valued by formal educators, such reservoirs of culture become funds of knowledge in the service of education, rather than discarded markers in the increasing gulf between human cultures.

Next, acceptance of language variety does not require the absence of norms or standards. The opposite is true: successful persons from minority groups have had to be doubly competent to survive, let alone excel, in a discriminatory environment. The role-model writers, verbal artists, and teachers from multicultural groups attest to both the rigorous paths to excellence, and the humbling fulfillment when their achievement retains its connection to culture. An education that does not provide access to the widest cultural achievements does a disservice to all students. Majority-group monolinguals need also to understand the limits of their own socialization in the United States, with its isolationist tendencies, and, through multicultural contact and learning other languages, strive to overcome prejudgments and narrowness.

Finally, allowing diversity to flourish encapsulates the entire issue: it would

1. Recognize the valid contribution of speakers, whatever their speech;
2. Enable access to norms, literacy, standard communication, and the informational marketplace, without requiring the negation or eradication of varieties as the cost of admission;
3. Invigorate and enlighten the repertoire of all participants by infusing variety into the standard, promoting the notion of language expansion rather than purism;
4. Understand that literacy focuses on shared communication through the content of messages, not on accent or dialect phonology.

Since language is visible, ubiquitous, and both individual and societal, linguistic racism and discourse discrimination remain insurmountable barriers to completing the unfinished business of the civil rights agenda. Concerted effort and shared work to eradicate hostile, negligent, and suppressive sociolinguistic environments may constitute a primary instrument to close the gap between the principles of equal justice and educational opportunity and the fact of social inequality.

References

Allen, Irving L. 1983. *The Language of Ethnic Conflict: Social Organization and Lexical Culture.* New York: Columbia University Press.

———. 1990. *Unkind Words: Ethnic Labeling from Redskin to WASP.* New York: Bergin and Garvey.

Allport, G. W. 1954. *The Nature of Prejudice.* Cambridge, Mass.: Addison-Wesley.

Baird, Susan J. 1969. *Employment Interview Speech. A Social Dialect Study in Austin, Texas.* Ph.D. diss., University of Texas, Austin.

Brennan, E. M., E. B. Ryan, and W. E. Dawson. 1975. Scaling of Apparent Accentedness by Magnitude Estimation and Sensory Modality Matching. *Journal of Psycholinguistic Research* 4: 27–36.

Carranza, Miguel A. 1982. Attitudinal Research on Hispanic Language Varieties. In *Attitudes toward Language Variation,* ed. Ellen Bouchard Ryan and Howard Giles, 63–83.

Cole, Elsa K. 1991. Equality of Access and the Problem of Hate Speech. Paper presented at the 4th Annual Conference on Racial and Ethnic Relations in American Higher Education, San Antonio. Published by the University of Michigan Office of the General Counsel, Ann Arbor.

Crawford, James. 1992. *Hold Your Tongue: Bilingualism and the Politics of "English Only."* Reading, Mass.: Addison-Wesley.

Crystal, David. 1987. *The Cambridge Encyclopedia of Language.* New York: Cambridge University Press.

Delpit, Lisa. 1986. Skills and Other Dilemmas of a Progressive Black Educator. *Harvard Educational Review* 56:379–385.

———. 1988. The Silenced Dialogue: Power and Pedagogy in Educating Other People's Children. *Harvard Educational Review* 58:280–298.

Edwards, John R. 1982. Language Attitudes and Their Implications among English Speakers. In *Attitudes toward Language Variation,* ed. Ellen Bouchard Ryan and Howard Giles, 20–33.

Ferreiro, Emilia. 1971. *Les relations temporelles dans le langage de l'enfant.* Geneva: Droz.

———. 1977. *Problemas de la psicología educacional.* Buenos Aires: Producciones Editoriales IPSE.

Ferreiro, Emilia, and Ana Teberosky. 1982. *Literacy before Schooling.* Boston: Heineman.

Ferrell, C. S. 1992. Hate Crimes Ruling Puts Campuses on Guard. *Black Issues in Higher Education* 9 (10): 1, 50–51.

Flores, Juan, John Attinasi, and Pedro Pedraza. 1981. La Carreta Made a U-Turn: Puerto Rican Language and Culture in the United States. *Daedalus* 110:193–217.

Freire, Paulo. 1970. *Pedagogy of the Oppressed.* New York: Seabury.

———. 1971. *Education for Critical Consciousness.* New York: Seabury.

Gay, Geneva. 1987. Ethnic Identity Development and Black Expressiveness. In *Expressively Black,* ed. Geneva Gay and Willie Baber, 35–76.

Gay, Geneva, and Willie Baber, eds. 1987. *Expressively Black.* New York: Praeger.

Gere, Anne Ruggles, and Eugene Smith. 1979. *Attitudes, Language, and Change.* Urbana, Ill.: National Council of Teachers of English.

Giles, H., R. Y. Bourhis, and D. M. Taylor. 1977. Towards a Theory of Language in Ethnic Group Relations, In *Language, Ethnicity, and Intergroup Relations,* ed. Giles, 307–348. New York: Academic Press.

Glasberg, V. M. 1991. Offensive Expression, Free Speech, and Campus Civility. *Black Issues in Higher Education* 8 (14):21.

Goodman, K. 1965. Dialect Barriers to Reading Comprehension. *Elementary English* 42(8):639–643.

Goodwin, Marjorie Harness. 1990. *He-Said-She-Said: Talk as Social Organization among Black Children.* Bloomington: Indiana University Press.

Greenberg, Jeff, S. L. Kirkland, and Tom Pyszczynski. 1988. Some Theoretical Notions and Preliminary Research Concerning Derogatory Ethnic Labels. In *Discourse and Discrimination,* ed. Geneva Smitherman-Donaldson and Teun A. van Dijk, 46–72.

Greene, Marvin. 1981. Implications of the King Case. In *Black English and the Education of Black Children and Youth,* ed. Geneva Smitherman, 62–70.

Gwaltney, John Langston. 1980. *Drylongso: A Self Portrait of Black America.* New York: Random House.

Hamers, Josiane, and Michel Blanc. 1989. *Bilinguality and Bilingualism.* New York: Cambridge University Press.

Heath, Shirley Brice. 1983. *Ways with Words: Language, Life, and Work in Communities and Classrooms.* New York: Cambridge University Press.

Hecht, Michael, and Sidney Ribeau. 1988. Afro-American Identity Labels and Communication Effectiveness. In *Language and Ethnic Identity,* ed. William B. Gudykunst, 163–170. Philadelphia: Multilingual Matters.

Hess, G. A., Jr. 1991. *School Restructuring, Chicago Style.* Newbury Park, Calif.: Corwin.

Hess, G. A., Jr., and C. A. Warden. 1988. Who Benefits from Desegregation Now? *Journal of Negro Education* 57:536–551.

Hewitt, Roger. 1986. *White Talk Black Talk: Interracial Friendship and Communication amongst Adolescents.* New York: Cambridge University Press.

Hopper, R. 1977. Language Attitudes and the Job Interview. *Communication Monographs* 40:296–302.

Kalin, Rudolf. 1982. The Social Significance of Speech in Medical, Legal, and Occupational Settings. In *Attitudes toward Language Variation,* ed. Ellen Bouchard Ryan and Howard Giles, 148–163.

King, Joyce E. 1991. Dysconscious Racism: Ideology, Identity, and the Miseducation of Teachers. *Journal of Negro Education* 60:133–146.

King v. Ann Arbor Schools. 1979. Memorandum Opinion and Order in the case of *Martin Luther King Junior Elementary School v. Ann Arbor School District Board,* by Judge Charles W. Joiner, In *Black English and the Education of*

Black Children and Youth, ed. Geneva Smitherman, 356–358. Detroit: Wayne State University Press.

Kochman, Thomas, ed. 1972. *Rappin' and Stylin' Out.* Champaign: University of Illinois Press.

Labov, William. 1972a. *Language in the Inner City.* Philadelphia: University of Pennsylvania Press.

———. 1972b. *Sociolinguistic Patterns.* Philadelphia: University of Pennsylvania Press.

Massey, Grace C., Mona V. Scott, and Sanford Dornbusch, 1975. Racism without Racists: Institutional Racism in Urban Schools, *Black Scholar* 7 (November): 10–19.

Obudho, Constance E. 1976. *Black-White Racial Attitudes: An Annotated Bibliography.* Westport, Conn.: Greenwood.

Orr, Eleanor. 1987. *Twice As Less: Black English in the Performance of Black Students in Mathematics and Science.* New York: Norton.

Pérez, Bertha, and María Torres-Guzmán. 1992. *Learning in Two Worlds: An Integrated Spanish/English Approach to Biliteracy.* New York: Longman.

Piatt, Bill. 1990. *Only English? Law and Language Policy in the United States.* Albuquerque: University of New Mexico Press.

Rodriguez, Clara E. 1989. *Puerto Ricans: Born in the USA.* Boston: Unwin Hyman.

Ryan, Ellen Bouchard, and Howard Giles, eds. 1982. *Attitudes toward Language Variation: Social and Applied Contexts.* London: Arnold.

Ryan, Ellen B., Howard Giles, and Richard Sebastian. 1982. An Integrative Perspective for the Study of Attitudes toward Language Variation. *Attitudes toward Language Variation,* ed. Ryan and Giles, 1–19.

Simpkins, Gary, and Charlesetta Simpkins. 1981. Cross Cultural Approach to Curriculum Development. In *Black English and the Education of Black Children and Youth,* ed. Geneva Smitherman, 212–240.

Smith, F., ed. 1973. *Psycholinguistics and Reading.* New York: Holt, Rinehart and Winston. Quoted in Emilia Ferreiro, *Problemas de la psicología educacional,* 261.

Smitherman, Geneva. 1977. *Talkin and Testifyin: The Language of Black America.* Boston: Houghton Mifflin.

———. 1992. African Americans and "English Only." *Language Problems and Language Planning* 16:235–248.

———, ed. 1981. *Black English and the Education of Black Children and Youth.* Detroit: Center for Black Studies and Wayne State University Press.

Smitherman-Donaldson, Geneva, and Teun A. van Dijk, eds. 1988. *Discourse and Discrimination.* Detroit: Wayne State University Press.

Weir, R. 1966. Some Questions on the Child's Learning of Phonology. In *The Genesis of Language: A Psycholinguistic Approach,* ed. F. Smith and G. E. Miller. Cambridge, Mass.: MIT Press.

Woolard, Kathryn A. 1989. Sentences in the Language Prison: The Rhetorical

Structuring of an American Language Policy Debate. *American Ethnologist* 16:268–278.

Zentella, Ana Celia. 1988. English Only Laws Will Foster Divisiveness, Not Unity; They Are Anti-Hispanic, Anti-Elderly, And Anti-Female. *Chronicle of Higher Education,* November 23.

BRETT WILLIAMS

Babies and Banks: The "Reproductive Underclass" and the Raced, Gendered Masking of Debt

Specters of the black underclass and its bad behavior have loomed over poverty policy since the 1980s. The underclass is held to be left behind in dying cities, isolated from legitimate work and from appropriate role models. Sensationalized by television and print journalism, and probed by scholars in sociology and economics, the black underclass has assumed the proportions of a metaphorical urban cancer; a stagnant, festering swamp; a breeding ground teeming, maggotlike, with reproductive possibilities; and even a cannibal feeding on itself. *They* are poor while the rest of us are affluent; "dependent" while we are "stable." By virtue of not participating fully in patriarchal, heterosexual households, the underclass is portrayed as a grotesquely sex-segregated population composed of gun-wielding men on the one hand and unwed mothers on the other.[1] These gendered archetypes bolstered totalitarian proposals in the Reagan-Bush years—jail the men; force the women to work—and a widespread sense that poverty results from an attitude that urban African Americans inflict on themselves (see Lerman 1990; Mead 1986, 1989; Wilson 1987, 1989). These totalitarian policies threaten to become worse, intruding upon poor peoples' private decisions about birth control, marriage, and naming their children (see Reed 1991; Walsh 1991).

Social typologist Christopher Jencks (1991) tries to sort poor African Americans into (1) the jobless underclass (those who do not get their money from legitimate jobs); (2) the educational underclass (those lacking the skills to negotiate mainstream institutions); (3) the violent underclass (men who reject the "widely-accepted norm" that Americans should not be violent); and (4) the "reproductive underclass" (women flouting the equally widely accepted norm that people should not bear children until they are able to support them). Disregarding a long ethnographic tradition describing varied forms of household and family, Jencks finds these "underclass" women the witless victims of changing mainstream values about reproductive freedom which hold that women can live and rear children alone. (Jencks feels that in the 1960s, along with increased access to birth control, abortion, and jobs, norms changed. Women were expected to go to college before they bore children, to bear fewer children, and to wait until they were married, unless they could afford to support them alone. The poor embraced these changed values and took them too far.)

Underclass theorists talk incessantly of culture and values but rarely talk to poor people. Lemann (1991) writes of a strongly self-defeating culture with roots in the sharecrop system whose centerpiece is out-of-wedlock birth. Ellwood (1989), Mead (1989), and Sawhill (1988) likewise write of widely shared values and appeal to what Reed (1991) calls a cracker-barrel contractarianism holding that some "we" all agreed to uphold them. In such "explanatory" twists in underclass theory, poor women have adopted these values without the wherewithal to live them out (and white feminists are part of the problem as well). Black women's reproductive behaviors are thus "the transmission belt that drives the cycle of poverty" (Reed 1991). Once such women have babies and fail to support or enculturate them, the underclass grows metazoically, its evil progeny feeding on each other and themselves.

Even those who accept an adult woman's right to make her own reproductive and domestic decisions (and many do not) cling to teen pregnancy as the touchstone of pathology among the poor. While teenagers (if we asked them) might see their decision to become parents as a step toward maturity, they are infantilized as "babies having babies," or "children having children." In fact, for the last twenty years, fewer teenagers have elected to do so, and those who have borne children have borne fewer. Yet the phenomenon of teen parenthood has received accelerating attention, in nefarious contrast to drastic demographic changes among middle-class women who now wait until they are older and older to have fewer children. The "explosion" of teen pregnancy, which is in fact contracting, is magnified by this dramatic drop in the overall U.S. birth rate, and the shift upward in age of first live births for middle- and upper-class women. Some of the confusion stems from whether teen births are calculated relative to all teenagers or relative to all women. Fewer teenagers are having babies, but the birth rate for older women has plummeted (Ellwood and Crane 1990). Therefore, *proportionally* more babies are born to teenagers, although fewer teens are giving birth. Still, social scientists and poverty researchers ask, why can't she wait? They argue that Jim Crow defeatism, the heavy hand of sharecropper promiscuity, or a fantasy-driven capitulation to a boy's peer-driven line renders her unable to do so. They imply that if she honored the social contract and did wait, she would not be poor and would enjoy a rosy feminist future complete with college, husband, and job (Anderson 1989; Barnes 1987; Dash 1989; Lemann 1991).

Poverty researchers thus ignore the possibility that young childbearing might be biologically wise for poor women, or that multigenerational households and families are sensible ways to organize childcare and work. Many have denigrated the research of demographer Arline Geronimus (1991a, b), who demonstrates quantitatively: (1) that women who are poor do better to have their babies young, before the dire effects of poverty take a toll on their health; (2) that young mothers have usually had sufficient child care experience with younger kin so that they are prepared to see their babies as more than baby *dolls;* (3) that when one of two sisters has a baby as a teenager she does no worse educationally or economically than her sister who does not; and (4) that infants born to teen mothers do better than other poor children, both at birth and by educational measures later on. In explaining these numbers, Geronimus raises ethnographic questions: Are black women adapting sensibly to the constraints of poverty? Do they expect to raise their children in networks of supportive kin, and will they then be free themselves to care for both younger and older kin in their middle years? She suggests that poor African-American women may be organizing their lives rationally in a social time different from that of the middle class. However, she finds no ethnography in the last twenty years to answer these questions, and she has been pilloried for raising them both outside the academy and within.

The "reproductive underclass" and its icon, the teen mother, thus conflate social class with ideas about time within a class-appropriate life course. Her inability to defer gratification and her subsequent lifelong imputed dependency on the government make her responsible for her poverty, a reproductive threat to the rest of us, and the antithesis of the proper citizen worker who produces goods and services rather than babies and exists in a public rather than domestic relationship to the state. She thus normalizes the relatively recent ever-older and wearier middle-class mothers, as though it were somehow natural to bear children in the late twenties or beyond (Nelson 1984).

The nightmare of teen pregnancy has passed so easily into popular culture that it appears to represent common sense (Geronimus 1992). The rage that some whites and some middle-class blacks feel toward this "reproductive underclass" is unsettling. In collecting life histories of credit use by diverse Americans over the last three years, I was struck both by how varied and nonarchetypical teen mothers are, and by how certain many whites feel that they can describe the cycles of poverty that capture these young women. I have been struck especially by the enormous anger of some who feel victimized by the poverty of others, somewhat reminiscent of those rapists who claim to have felt disempowered and threatened by those they raped. Some assert them to be a drain of tax dollars; others, physically menacing; and still others, a threat to hard work and civic spirit, for they leech off the community but lack the resources (such as cars and telephones) to make appropriate contributions to social life. Why have these imaginary teenage mothers won so much academic attention, and why have academic underclass theories that so miss their experiential realities passed so richly into public culture?

Gilroy (1987) argues that ideas about imagined, socially constructed racial groups articulate political and economic relations, and that many Britons live in economic crisis and a morbid political culture with a heightened sense of race. This has also been true in the United States since the 1980s. The hot, loaded language for discussing the reproductive practices of poor African Americans does nothing to illuminate today's economic crisis. The emergence of underclass ideology during the 1980s has accompanied declining fertility and soaring household debt that is a far more appropriate indicator of this crisis. So let us shift from the overstudied to the underconceptualized in an effort to represent more accurately the levels of stress affecting both poor and "stable" U.S. households.

New electronic technology in the 1970s and deregulation in the 1980s offered retail bankers exciting opportunities to experiment with credit as a commodity, and they did experiment, wildly, at "penetrating the debt capacity" of varied groups of Americans. The Supreme Court's momentous yet unheralded *Marquette* decision in 1978 allowed banks to charge home-state interest rates in any other state. This crucial piece of deregulation undermined state legislatures' efforts to cap usury rates and made the penetration of citizens' debt capacities a Risklike game. The bank card became a valuable "interstate warhorse" in linking debtors in multifaceted connections over the long term to banks, which retail bankers call "relationship banking."

Bank credit cards fueled the consumer spending that refired the economy after the 1982 recession, and credit-card interest and fees served as banks' chief source of profit over the 1980s decade. This continues in the 1990s, as banks harvest high monthly interest from maxed-out consumers—what they call their "mature" accounts—and buy or sell prized credit-card portfolios to stay afloat as they reel from Third World and real-estate loans in default. They are complicit in the current entrenched recession, not only because citizens (better known as "consumers") have no more to spend, but also because lowering the prime and discount rates has no effect on credit card interest rates. As evidenced by their reaction to a proposed national interest cap, banks are determined to preserve the current rate spread (Berry 1991; Brenner 1989, 1990, 1991a, b, c; Crenshaw 1991b; Hightower 1991; Mandell 1990). When this spread became impossible to conceal, President Bush "suggested" a cap, the Senate passed one, the House considered one, and bankers threatened to revoke sixty million cards, arguing that only if they did so could they remain in business. They were successful, although their argument was disingenuous. Banks want poor credit risks as customers, as long as they don't charge off their accounts completely. The somewhat risky customer is the one who gathers perks and pays in full, and the truly risky customer is the high roller who is subsidized by ordinary people's interest.

The bank credit-card system is awash with inequality. By the early 1980s issuers had grown dissatisfied with their cardholder base of those who used credit for convenience or personal gain. They then worked hard to broaden that base to include more who would pay in installments. In the mid-1980s banks began to expand the uses of credit cards, proliferate new services, reach for the less affluent, and charge higher interest rates. For the last several years they have turned their attention to college students. All the while they have communicated in industry journals the results of large-scale research indicating who is more likely to delay paying in full (Canner and Cyrnak 1985, 1986; Pollin 1986, 1990; Scott 1987).

People of different means receive different cards and use them differently. Credit-card limits range from $200 to $25,000, and interest rates vary widely as well, with the gold card offering lower interest, the smaller value "secured" card the highest. Wealthier people take advantage of the interest-free grace period to generate more wealth or to travel extensively (when, as one man says, "My credit card was my home.") Many middle-class people use them for modest perks: to keep a record, pay for reimbursed travel in advance, buy big-ticket items on sale, get free insurance or theft protection, order concert tickets by telephone, accumulate airline miles and free rental car rates, or gain interest by paying large bills a month late while the money sits in an interest-bearing account. Those of more modest means use credit cards to maintain a falling standard of living; pay car repair, tuition, or medical bills; survive divorce; and in general combat the economic crisis we are all embroiled in. These users, who carry a balance, are called "revolvers" by the retail banking industry, which admits that "revolvers pay the float for non-revolvers." In other words, poorer people (along with merchants) help pay for the nearly free interest of the more affluent (Canner and Cyrnak 1985, 1986; Mandell 1990; Pollin 1986, 1990; Scott 1987; Wise 1990).

The growth of credit-card debt among college students is interesting and troubling. Banks offer a future-oriented marketing pitch aimed at building a good credit history and planning to get a mortgage, but they also may be establishing lifelong relations with students that begin with their acting somewhat in loco parentis. Many college students carry small debts and feel troubled by them. They can easily go over the edge if, for example, their financial aid is cut, a fairly common event during junior year at many universities. One student whose parents are convenience users, but who can only pay off a little interest each month, groaned to me: "I'm supporting my parents!"

In my exploration of the relationship between credit-card debt and household domestic cycles, I have found contradictions between what banks want and what people need. To a bank the most valued, "good" customer is one with a "mature" account. This means a maxed-out balance on which a customer draws nothing but regularly makes minimum payments of mostly interest for many years. Thus to be mature is to be bowed with debt, but slowly and faithfully paying it off. This life-cycle imagery both masks and reveals real life-cycle needs. The primary users of installment credit appear to be those between ages twenty-five and forty-four whose incomes are stagnant or falling. Many have relied on credit to shape an appropriately classed life course: to attend college, purchase durables and set up households, meet the needs of kin, and launch children. Credit cards have been particularly important following the death or divorce of a spouse, or during the transition from parental to new household. They have served like domestic partners to some who cannot live on one income. Thus, for the last ten years, many normative middle-class people have not been able to support the households they want when they want them, or to organize their lives, without loans and liens.

The stories I have gathered are rich with detail on these class differences. I have interviewed people who announce proudly that they never pay interest, and some who seem genuinely astonished at how things work for revolvers. I talked to a wealthy woman who was stunned and embarrassed to discover that her dead friend carried a Visa balance. I watched a couple use credit to adopt a baby, a single woman sink into debt to raise a troubled niece, and another woman borrow on cash advances to send three children to college. One young couple faces $18,000 in debt at age nineteen from trying to establish a household. On the other hand, a wealthy woman received her first card at eleven and got into trouble in junior high with bills sometimes reaching $1500 a month. When she married, her husband took over her credit card bills from her father; she now carries twenty-five cards and enjoys using them frequently.

How are Americans to understand this rapid change that confuses longstanding ideas about work, time, money, and property? Mass media offer a language of white narcissism: we live in a me-me-me society unable to defer gratification (denying statistics showing that we in fact consume less and less). This is often a language of drug abuse: we are credit-dependent, credit-card junkies, we should join Debtors Anonymous. There is also a gendered language that portrays white women sublimating sex for shopping, giddy housewives who want too much, divorcees whose husbands inherit their debt, "little secretaries" who want to act middle class. Some of the same language that marks black teen mothers recurs here in gendered discussions of self-esteem, immediate gratification, and dependency (Rock 1989).

People of color almost never appear in credit-card commercials, except as servers. This rule seems to hold true even on Black Entertainment Television advertisements for secured cards. Perhaps marketers find it risky to link minorities to debt. Ads change rapidly over time, with those of 1991 emphasizing maternal nurturance in the face of trouble and risk, parental responsibilities for children, and "One World One Card." Mastercard's effort to portray working-class people furnishing their homes was a huge failure, because "nobody wants to be the average Joe" (Ramirez 1990). (I have most noticed the power of media to reshape the message in my own work, which has been publicized by my university and picked up by television, magazines, and radio. In all but one case, my words have been twisted into a language of deferred gratification. The one exception was a radio talk show in Dallas, flooded by callers who wanted to tell their stories.)

I have been interested in how ordinary people try to negotiate their own understandings of all this, because commercials seem so out of touch with the realities of credit-card use. Credit cards have challenged and transformed much that we take for granted. One woman termed these transformed notions as "using money I haven't earned yet to pay for something that's already gone."

Some of the stories I have gathered echoed media drug/dependency themes. One man said of his wife's charging: "She used it to fill a void, it made her feel better, and I was a pleaser." Another woman reported, "Last year I had a charge-free Christmas. It was like coming away from drug abuse." Stereotypes about secretaries and divorce are countered by actual women's experiences. One secretary remembers first using a credit card to buy shoes at Sears when, following her divorce, she had to work outside the home. She continued to use credit for interview and work clothes, prescriptions and food at the drugstore, and to secure some class advantages for her children through summer camp, dinners out, concerts, real Christmases, and vacations.

Two other analogies are more illuminating than the drug metaphor. With industrial restructuring and falling wages, credit cards have functioned like both *welfare* and *domestic partners* for deflated middle-class households that cannot survive on one or even two incomes anymore. Some used credit cards to get a start; others, to maintain class advantages or ease transitions. It is too simple to argue that crack selling has been a poor person's credit card, but certainly the underground economy has served some of these same economic functions, along with the many other alternatives that the very poor can muster (Hopper, Susser, and Conover 1985; D. Jones 1989; Y. Jones 1988; Sullivan 1990; Valentine 1978; Williams 1989; Williams and Kornblum 1985). But credit cards have been deemed normal and normative, and other modes of cash access have not.

The ways people talk about credit-card debt reveal enormous ambivalence about issues of complicity, responsibility, and maturity. Those in the separate credit worlds know very little about each other and tend to personalize credit-card debt, especially their own. People who have not needed to carry debt often re-form their good luck as personal virtue. They imagine debt as resulting from an attitude. But those who carry debt and those who do not find it hard to believe that the debtor is not somehow complicit. All speak strangely of blame, as did the woman who had a short history of late payments and exclaimed upon hearing that Citibank was in trouble: "It's my fault!"

Many indebted people find it hard to sort out responsibility and blame and agonize over what they did that they should not have done, over being out of control and trying to regain it, by "paying down the balance." Many recount their credit careers, sometimes linking debt to youthful immaturity and positing benchmarks, when, as one woman said: "I just couldn't stand to live like that anymore." A schoolteacher married to a corporate lawyer and now engaged in a long-term project of stocking a very large house in which she lives in some affluence feels virtuous in what she sees as self-denial and lacks the faintest idea of what poorer people do with credit cards. Many pursue credit careers more similar to debt peonage, which they describe with such metaphors as "deep in the ditch" or "a sinking ship." Many, with presumably "mature accounts," are somewhere in between.

Some of those in debt feel grateful, sometimes because they can match credit, time, and the class-appropriate life course: "I wouldn't be able to go to college without my credit card." Sometimes they remember emergencies when "I wouldn't have made it without credit." This last comment came from a woman who after her divorce had to buy food at a drugstore which would accept her card, while grocery stores would not. Contrary to the anger that many Americans feel toward insurance companies, we persist in believing that credit cards are our friends for all seasons. They help us through hard times, allow us to stay on course, and underwrite periodic expenses such as holidays, rites of passage, summer camp, and furniture.

Class consciousness is missing from such formulations. One young woman, struggling with enormous debt, argues that poorer women have benefited from credit more than have wealthy women, who don't really need it. Often this gratitude changes with the harassment that accompanies late payment or default: people develop "get them back" schemes, and their own versions of relationship banking, as they line their bills up and decide which one to pay, often taking into account the personality and attitude of the telephone harasser. But most striking to me is the illusion of choice and complicity and the extraordinary depoliticization of bank credit cards, for they have helped to mask downward mobility and falling real wages, served as a social safety net for emergencies that government would otherwise provide for, and helped marginally middle-class people build appropriate, if illusory, middle-class lives.

Anthropology and history offer several ways to think about debt—as occurring from entering relations people never wanted; as intimately connected to work, place, and race (McMillen 1990; Sider 1989; Taussig 1987). Latin Americans do not call being in debt "mature" or "dependent," but rather being "*colgado,*" or hung. Even more provocative in terms of North America's history of work and race, a middle-aged black man told me: "The banks couldn't make money, so they decided to go back to the old sharecropping way." This interpretation has not helped him gain access to credit cards, but he certainly had a good point when he noted that "people work and work, but when they finish they still owe $2,300 to Mr. Bob Martin." The sharecropping analogy is especially poignant given the savage racism with which white planters argued "black wanderlust" forced them to apply the bonds of debt peonage. Today's banks find enormous profits from selling debtors on a secondary market much as landowners once sold sharecroppers they held in their debt (Davis, Gardner, and Gardner 1941; McMillen 1990). Nonetheless, this analogy has its limits, as debtors are as likely to be whites as people of color.

For many reasons, racism like sexism is hard to spot in the credit-card industry. The Equal Credit Opportunity Act of 1975 prohibited credit discrimination on the basis of gender, race, or national origin. This law and the Federal Reserve Board regulations that operationalized it technically ensure equal *access*, but not equal limits or rates. Large-scale survey research commissioned by the Federal Reserve Board focuses on households (called "families") and does not isolate race or gender except in the most superficial inquiries. Race and racism are not even indexed topics in the credit-card literature, and intensive research efforts have yielded no evidence that anyone has yet studied race as a factor in access to credit.

One problem concerns the many players and activities involved in bringing credit to people. Banks scrutinize both the economic "health" of a region and the property insurance rates prevailing in particular neighborhoods to make decisions about whether to market cards there, and what rates to offer. This initiative comes from the card sellers, as either out-of-state banks choose regions to target, or local banks select creditworthy customers from listings in the neighborhood where their branch is located. There are many banks at work, and many points at which racial discrimination may arise: in choosing neighborhoods for mailings, in deciding where to locate a branch, or in selecting whom to solicit within a neighborhood. When a card purchaser takes the initiative, we know nothing about how race affects the way they are treated, the amount of credit (if any) they are offered, or the widely varying terms of the cards they receive.

For example, Canner and Cyrnak (1985) offer the statistic that 45 percent of blacks and 43 percent of Hispanics "hardly ever pay in full" versus 25 percent of whites. We learn nothing from these data about how race intersects with anything else or whether or not these revolvers do pay on time. This research also confuses families with households, as well as the complexities of households that may include domestic partners and lots of kin and friends and wax and wane over time. In these surveys "families" are static, and only the attributes and activities of "the head" are calculated. This kind of research would benefit from the insights of bank employees, and we have attempted to interview some. I do know of one loan officer who claims to be able to identify the race of applicants "nine times out of ten." A former employee of Citibank reports that credit cards are much easier for both whites and blacks to get than any other type of loan.

The industry does not need to use overtly racist criteria for granting credit, for sophisticated software monitors and scores credit accounts according to many variables. These include whether or not a customer uses a card for a purchase or cash advance, the size of each purchase, the location and type of businesses patronized, the amount and timing of payments, and the amount of other debt. Computers can predict whether or not a person has excessive debt or is trying to conceal debt and can make decisions about the likely fate of a newly delinquent account; machines "decide" whether to increase credit lines, or authorize over-the-limit credit. Each of us carries a personal credit autobiography perhaps rendering overt class, gender, and racist judgments unprofitable and unnecessary.

But race is certainly a factor in the structure of access and denial underlying the variables that computers measure in our credit histories. Therefore it is imperative to look at other ways Americans get access to money. Welfare implies a kind of stasis, something for nothing; credit cards are often discussed using metaphors of fall—a sinking ship, deep in the ditch, burden you down. But other kinds of loans, not just commercial loans, imply an investment in some future, improved outcome. And here there is strong evidence of discriminatory practices.

For example, the 1991 Federal Reserve Board (FRB) study on mortgage and home equity loans documents much higher rejection rates for African and Latin Americans at all income levels, paralleling known discrimination by secondary lenders nationally and in Washington, D.C. Another national study by a bank marketing firm in 1992 found that black and white mortgage applicants were usually treated differently; blacks waited longer to see a loan officer and were often told their applications would take longer to process than were whites applying at the same bank (Munnell et al. 1992). The industry has critiqued the FRB study by arguing that it does not take into account applicants' wealth, debt loads, and "creditworthiness," implying, one gathers, that black and Latin customers at all income levels are less likely to pay back loans, that they have fewer assets, or that they have too much consumer debt already (Brannigan 1991; Crenshaw 1991c; Knight 1991; Lehman 1991; Mendel-Black and Richards 1991; Quint 1991).

These national mortgage studies have sinister implications: for many poor people, the house is the main source of equity, the only wealth to pass to the next generation. With race indisputably a factor in mortgage lending, let us consider the fuller context of lending practices and property relations in the poor urban neighborhoods where some teen mothers live. Several different practices recur in Washington and other cities. In black neighborhoods, property owners are disproportionately denied home equity loans. This loan discrimination sets the stage for urban renewal, gentrification, warehousing of emptied but liveable quarters, and convergent dislocations in poor black neighborhoods. Loan denials become a potential strategy to separate residents from their property, or to deny them the ability to maintain it. This hastens changes in the ownership of buildings and land. In some neighborhoods, finance companies join forces with sham home improvement companies to fill this redlining gap. They bilk long-term, fixed-income owners with high interest rates and shoddy work, thus setting them up to lose their homes. They then sell their loans to the banks who refused the lower-interest home equity loans in the first place. Banks eventually acquire the property and may dispose of it to developers or restart the cycle with new black homebuyers (Lapp 1991).

There is a renters' version of all this as well. Between 1982 and 1985 in Washington, speculators bought some two thousand small apartment buildings in the "isolated" and "underclass" neighborhoods of Trinidad, Capitol Heights, Anacostia, Deanwood, and North Capitol Hill. These speculators fraudulently appraised, dressed up, and resold the buildings to buyers with faked credentials who were insured by HUD loan guarantees. These new owners took advantage of rent-control exemptions for small units and raised rents, sometimes sevenfold. They evicted dozens of black tenants who could not pay the new rents, allowed the buildings to deteriorate further, and defaulted on their loans so that HUD acquired the property in now-decimated neighborhoods. HUD of course "reimbursed" the fraudulent buyers. These complicated schemes that devastated minority communities underlie a crisis in affordable housing more damaging to poor African Americans than at what age women decide to give birth. They are largely ignored by underclass theorists. One has to ask: Who is isolated? And who is growing cancerously? (Downey 1990).

These mortgage studies show that poor whites get mortgages more easily than do well-to-do minorities. In the District of Columbia, the rejection rate on all mortgages was 6.3 percent for whites, 8.7 percent for Asians, 8.9 percent for Hispanics, and 14.4 percent for blacks. This study also showed significant discrimination in home equity loans, an increasingly popular, tax-deductible debt bailout for the middle class. Linked to the prime rate, it offers lower interest rates and more flexible repayment schedules than bank credit cards. Creatively reused or abused for credit consolidation, cars, vacations, and large bills, home equity loans often do not serve even the discriminatory, regressive purpose for which Congress passed this tax reform. Finally, another recent study showed that Fannie Mae (Federal National Mortgage Association) and Freddie Mac (Federal Home Loan Mortgage Association) do not support housing loans to low-income people in anywhere near the proportions they are supposed to by law (Crenshaw 1991a; Harney 1991; Salmon 1991).

Thus, race is a crucial variable in loans linked to property because of the racially segregated settlement histories of cities—racial "steering" to and from selected communities, the failure of housing integration, the exodus of the middle class, and the gentrification of "changing" neighborhoods. With unsecured credit-card debt, racial discrimination then may occur mostly on the axis of class. Since the mid-1980s middle-class and working-poor African Americans appear to have had easier access to this form of unsecured debt than to debt secured by property. Like others, they have used credit cards to stretch wages, support children, and launch adult lives. Many have gotten into deep trouble, the deepest in my research being a young man who was solicited by creditors as soon as he got into college. In two years he owed $20,000, which will keep him indebted for a long time. Others, unemployed or underemployed, have had almost no access to bank credit until very recently. With much of the population all-too-well penetrated in the early 1990s, poor blacks in Washington began to receive numerous offers of secured and scam cards, dealings that usually begin with an expensive long-distance phone call to a 900 number.

Thus the racism of the current economic crisis is not as blatant as Jim Crow, but it is neither epiphenomenal nor simply additive to the inequality of class (McCarthy 1988). It multiplies the historic racism that has produced racially divided neighborhoods. It is entwined with gender in both structuring and masking our experiences and understandings of that crisis. The tangle begins with pompous pronouncements about how to time and organize adulthood. Credit cards have served as welfare and domestic partners in helping some to organize and time their lives, but rarely the poor who need this support the most. Women, especially black women, are termed unable to wait, and the economic problems of both white and black women are couched in the language of dependency.

Despite the many legal instruments that allow the rich to preserve and pass on great fortunes; and despite mortgage, child care, and educational subsidies for the middle class; many Americans appear to believe that poor black women defy cultural values and leech off the state. Underclass ideology is a pernicious distraction from the fact that poor urban African Americans cannot find jobs, that they attend abysmal schools, and that they have almost nowhere left to live. And credit cards lure and distract us from the real reasons households face economic crisis, which underclass theorists have ignored while industry professionals have communicated ravenously about how to hook credit users.

I have no doubt that there is racial inequality in access to credit, interest rates, fees, and the penalties people suffer for not paying. But I have suggested that the more serious discrimination occurs through redlining, government-insured scams that deprive both owners and renters of central city homes, and greater access for some blacks to credit cards than mortgages. But the poorest of African and Latin Americans have been totally excluded from the bank-credit banquet that for the last ten years has provided mock-welfare and plastic partners for others to stretch their stagnant incomes and organize and launch their lives.

Teen parents, and the poor generally, have found no such support, although they need it most. Like other mothers who combine child care with work and education, they might benefit from programs that support the ways they time and organize their lives. Yet welfare payments and food stamps have fallen dramatically over the last ten years, and increasingly recipients must find low-paying jobs, lose Medicaid and rent subsidies, and wind up worse off than on welfare.

The mythic figures inhabiting an inner-city, science-fiction wasteland belie the fact that we are all participating in the same economy, and that these seemingly unconnected phenomena are many faces of the same dollar bill. There is no Underclassland. The same borrowers who disinvested in cities, jobs, and workers spent their money on financial services, junk bonds, mergers, takeovers, and leveraged buyouts. The same developers who refused to maintain or build low-cost urban housing have gone bust on condominiums and overbuilt real estate in the suburbs. Buoyed by our money through the loan guarantees and reimbursements from FDIC and HUD that allow them to take high risks, they have left the banks to expand their funds off debtors and credit-card interest, and to niggle at small depositors with new fees to help make up for bad loans. *They* are the ones with the inability to defer gratification.

It appears that in the 1990s the loan industry will continue to push for a recapitalized Federal Deposit Insurance Corporation (FDIC) and further deregulation, so that banks can combine with industrial firms, exercise full securities power, and operate unhampered across state lines. The now-dead banking reform legislation of the 1980s proposed to roll back FDIC coverage of multiple and brokered accounts and to increase the power of examiners. But even this failed legislation did not increase the power of examiners *enough* to smash the deeply entrenched racism of the bank-loan-housing complex. Nor did it address the fact that the FDIC protects almost all depositors anyway under the doctrine of "too large to fail."

We do not need centralized, interstate megabanks taking ever-greater risks that result in squeezing capital from small depositors as retail banking compensates for wholesale disasters. We need a politically accountable Federal Reserve Board, smaller and geographically narrower banks, and guaranteed access to money for the communities banks serve. The underclass is more scammed, redlined, and battered than isolated; constructive investment in underclass neighborhoods may be more prudent than endless speculation on why women who live in them have their babies when they do.

The social contract that has been broken is also the law of the land. The Community Reinvestment Act of 1977 requires banks to reinvest in local enterprises and affordable housing in exchange for taxpayer backing for their speculative adventures. Credit cards give the nonpoor a small and expensive piece of the pie and encourage the rest of us to blame and distance ourselves from the poor. But the in-hock middle class, and strung-up poor, might cut up their credit cards and organize their domestic and reproductive lives as they find appropriate if we could agree and act on the real problem as not babies but banks.

Notes

I gratefully acknowledge the crucial research assistance and many good ideas of American University students Angela Guerra and Gina Pearson and also thank Abby Thomas, who first alerted me to the idea of the appropriately timed middle-class life course. I am also indebted to many fruitful discussions with Robert Manning, Adolph Reed, Micaela di Leonardo, Jeanette Sherbondy, and, especially, John Henry Pitt. I also thank the students in my American studies class who helped me think about many of these issues: Deborah Kerr, Dennis Powell, Pamela Fell, Jay Gestwicki, John Burdsall, Juliet Blair, Jennifer Grezlak, Michael Bayus, and Susan Phillips. In this paper I draw on ethnographic fieldwork in a gentrifying neighborhood in Washington, D.C., and on interviews over the last two years with varied Washingtonians concerning credit-card debt.

1. I review this literature on the underclass extensively elsewhere (Williams 1992). For particularly well placed criticism, see Reed (1988a, b, 1991). Collins (1989) makes the important point that in underclass theory social class becomes the dependent variable, with raced, gendered constructions of culture, family, and values the determinants of poverty. Maxwell (1991) notes the strategic placement of the underclass in space and time.

References

Anderson, Elijah. 1989. Sex Codes and Family Life among Poor Inner-City Youths. *Annals of the American Academy of Political and Social Sciences* 501:59–78.

Barnes, Annie S. 1987. *Single Parents in Black America.* Bristol, Ind.: Wyndham Hall.

Berry, John. 1991. Some Sa' Rate Cuts Are Just a Scratch. *Washington Post,* November 2.

Brannigan, Martha. 1991. Mortgage Requests by Blacks, Hispanics Denied by NCNB at Twice Rate of Whites. *Wall Street Journal*, September 13.

Brenner, Joel Glenn. 1989. Bargain Credit Card Rates Fade as Banks Raise Fees. *Washington Post*, December 15.

———. 1990. Where Consumer Credit Is Due. *Washington Post*, October 21.

———. 1991a. Bank Customers Are Picking Up the Check. *Washington Post*, June 3.

———. 1991b. Chevy Chase Stays on Path of Profitability. *Washington Post*, March 25.

———. 1991c. Region's Ailing Banks, Thrifts Await Recovery. *Washington Post*, October 21.

Brown, Jon. 1991. Risk, Regulation, and Responsibility: Reforming the Banks. *Multinational Monitor* 12(6):8–13.

Canner, Glenn, and Anthony Cyrnal. 1985. Recent Developments in Credit Card Holding and Use Patterns among U.S. Families. *Journal of Retail Banking* 7:9–18.

———. 1986. Determinants of Credit Card Usage Patterns. *Journal of Retail Banking* 8:9–18.

Collins, Patricia Hill. 1989. A Comparison of Two Works on Black Family Life. *Signs* 14:875–884.

Crenshaw, Albert. 1991a. Borrowing Surge Erodes Americans' Home Equity. *Washington Post*, May 28.

———. 1991b. Credit Card Rate Cap Now on Back Burner. *Washington Post*, November 19.

———. 1991c. Keeping Tabs on Card Holders. *Washington Post*, January 20.

Dash, Leon. 1989. *When Children Want Children*. New York: Morrow.

Davis, Allison, Burleigh Gardner, and Mary Gardner. 1991. *Deep South: A Social Anthropological Study of Caste and Class*. Chicago: University of Chicago Press.

Downey, Kirsten. 1990. The Real Price of Housing Fraud. *Washington Post*, September 2.

Ellwood, David T. 1989. *Poor Support*. New York: Basic.

Ellwood, David T., and Jonathan Crane. 1990. Family Change among Black Americans: What Do We Know? *Journal of Economic Perspectives* 4(4): 65–84.

Geronimus, Arline T. 1991a. *Maternal Youth or Family Background? Preliminary Findings on the Health Disadvantages of Infants with Teenage Mothers*. Ann Arbor: University of Michigan Population Studies Center, Research Reports.

———. 1991b. Teenage Childbearing and Social and Reproductive Disadvantage: The Evolution of Complex Questions and the Demise of Simple Answers. *Family Relations* 40:463–471.

———. 1992. Clashes of Common Sense: On the Previous Child-Care Experience of Teenage Mothers-To-Be. *Human Organization* 51:318–329.

Gilroy, Paul. 1987. "*There Ain't No Black in the Union Jack*": *The Cultural Politics of Race and Nation*. Chicago: University of Chicago Press.

Harney, Kenneth. 1991. Hill to Take Hard Look at Equity Loans. *Washington Post,* June 22.

Hightower, Jim. 1991. Busting the Banks. *Multinational Monitor* 12(6): 21–24.

Hopper, Kim, Ezra Susser, and Sarah Conover. 1985. Economies of Makeshift: Deindustrialization and Homelessness in New York City. *Urban Anthropology* 14(1–3): 183–236.

Jencks, Christopher. 1991. Is the American Underclass Growing? In *The Urban Underclass,* ed. Jencks and Paul Peterson, 28–100.

Jencks, Christopher, and Paul Peterson, eds. 1991. *The Urban Underclass.* Washington, D.C.: Brookings.

Jones, Delmos. 1989. The Almost Homeless. *Practicing Anthropology* 11:11–12.

Jones, Yvonne. 1988. Street Peddlers as Entrepreneurs: Economic Adaptations to an Urban Area. *Urban Anthropology* 17:143–170.

Knight, Jerry. 1991. Race Factor in Mortgage Lending Seen. *Washington Post,* October 22.

Lapp, David. 1991. Scamming the Poor. *Multinational Monitor* 12(6): 28–31.

Lehman, Jane. 1991. Fed Finds Wider Low-Income Loan Gap. *Washington Post,* November 2.

Lemann, Nicholas. 1991. *The Promised Land.* New York: Knopf.

Lerman, Robert. 1990. Value Issues in Poverty Policy and Poverty Research. Paper presented at the 12th Annual Conference of the Association for Public Policy Analysis and Management, San Francisco.

Mandell, Lewis. 1990. *The Credit Card Industry.* Boston: Twayne.

Maxwell, Andrew H. 1991. Some Further Reflections on the Concept of "The Underclass." Paper presented at the New York Academy of Sciences Conference, "Class and 'Underclass,' The Widening Gap between Rich and Poor," New York.

McCarthy, Cameron. 1988. Rethinking Liberal and Radical Perspectives on Racial Inequality in Schooling: Making the Case for Nonsynchrony. *Harvard Educational Review* 58:265–279.

McMillen, Neil. 1990. *Dark Journey.* Urbana: University of Illinois Press.

Mead, Lawrence. 1986. *Beyond Entitlement.* New York: Free Press.

———. 1989. The Logic of Workfare: The Underclass and Work Policy. *Annals of the American Academy of Political and Social Sciences* 501:156–169.

Mendel-Black, Daniel, and Evelyn Richards. 1991. Peering into Private Lives. *Washington Post,* January 20.

Munnell, Alicia, Lynn Browne, James McEneaney, and Geoffrey Tootell. 1992. *Mortgage Lending in Boston: Interpreting HMDA Data.* Federal Reserve Bank of Boston, Working Paper No. 92-7.

Nelson, Barbara. 1984. Women's Poverty and Women's Citizenship: Some Political Consequences of Economic Marginality. *Signs* 10:209–231.

Pollin, Robert. 1986. The Hidden Debt Crisis: U.S. Households Borrow More to Make Ends Meet. *Dollars and Sense,* October, 33–35.

———. 1990. *Deeper in Debt: The Changing Financial Conditions of U.S. Households.* Washington, D.C.: Economic Policy Institute.

Quint, Michael. 1991. Banks Raise Scrutiny of Cards. *New York Times,* May 27.
Ramirez, Anthony. 1990. Mastercard's Shift from Glamour. *New York Times,* April 9.
Reed, Adolph. 1988a. The Liberal Technocrat. *Nation* 246:167–170.
———. 1988b. Reed replies. *Nation* 248:662, 679.
———. 1991. The Underclass Myth. *Progressive* 55:18–20.
Rock, Andrea. 1989. Holiday Budget Busters and How to Avoid Them. *Family Circle,* December 19, 19–21.
Salmon, Jacqueline. 1991. Affordable Housing Eludes Poor Families. *Washington Post,* October 19.
Sawhill, Isabel. 1988. What About America's Underclass? *Challenge,* May/June, 27–36.
Scott, Charlotte. 1987. The Fairness Issue in Credit Card Pricing. *Journal of Retail Banking* 8(4): 5–17.
Sider, Gerald. 1989. *Class and Culture in Anthropology and History.* Cambridge: Cambridge University Press.
Sullivan, Mercer. 1990. *"Getting Paid": Youth Crime and Work in the Inner City.* Ithaca, N.Y.: Cornell University Press.
Taussig, Michael. 1987. *Shamanism, Colonialism, and the Wild Man.* Chicago: University of Chicago Press.
Valentine, Betty Lou. 1978. *Hustling and Other Hard Work.* New York: Free Press.
Walsh, Edward. 1991. Michigan's Welfare Cut A "Social Experiment." *Washington Post,* October 19.
Williams, Brett. 1992. Poverty among African Americans in the Urban United States. *Human Organization* 51:164–174.
Williams, Terry. 1989. *The Cocaine Kids.* Reading, Mass.: Addison-Wesley.
Williams, Terry, and William Kornblum. 1985. *Growing Up Poor.* Lexington, Mass.: Heath.
Wilson, William J. 1987. *The Truly Disadvantaged.* Chicago: University of Chicago Press.
———, ed. 1989. The Underclass: Issues, Perspectives, and Public Policy. *Annals of the American Academy of Political and Social Sciences* 501: 182–192.
Wise, Tim. 1990. Accounts Payable. *Nation* 250:845.

STEVEN GREGORY

Race, Rubbish, and Resistance: Empowering Difference in Community Politics

Research on race during the past decade stresses the instability and heterogeneity of racial categories and meanings (Dominguez 1987; Gates 1987; Goldberg 1990; Martinez-Alier 1989) and the complex ways in which ideologies of race, class, gender, and nation intersect in the construction of social identities and hierarchies (Anthias 1990; Balibar 1990; Hall 1980; hooks 1990; Sacks 1989; Stoler 1989; Williams 1989). We are gaining a better understanding not only of how racial ideologies are constructed, enacted, and rearticulated by those in power (Comaroff and Comaroff 1991; Hall et al. 1978; Omi and Winant 1986; Solomos 1988), but also of how nonelite and racialized groups selectively appropriate, contest, and transform racial meanings, forming oppositional identities and ideologies (Gilroy 1987; Sacks 1988; Silverblatt 1987; Sivanandan 1982) as well as local variations of racial ideologies in dominance (Rieder 1985; Russell 1991; Trouillot 1990).

In this essay, I examine how African-American women in Lefrak City, a black apartment complex in Queens County, New York, contested racialized images held by white activists in the surrounding area of the black housing complex and its residents, images that invested in local ideology and power relations, denied Lefrak City residents a positive role in political discourse and thereby set limits on their access to political power and resources.

My focus on the articulation of race in everyday practice speaks to a theoretical concern with how subordinated groups generate cultural meanings and symbols that sometimes stand in opposition to dominant ideologies and power relations (Certeau 1984; Williams 1977). This emphasis on recovering everyday sites and strategies of resistance has been pursued by researchers investigating oppositional forms of cultural production and consciousness among working-class youth (Hall and Jefferson 1976; Hebdidge 1979; Willis 1977), women (Abu-Lughod 1989; Ong 1990; Westwood 1985), peasants (Scott 1985), and colonized, or "subaltern," peoples (Comaroff 1985; Guha and Spivak 1988).

An ethnographic perspective on the processes through which racial ideologies are contested and rearticulated contributes to our understanding of race in significant and interrelated ways. First, such an approach shifts emphasis away from the study of race (and racism) as a coherent, discrete cluster of beliefs and attitudes held by individuals and social groups and toward the study of how racial meanings are implicated in discourses, institutional power arrangements, and social practices that may or may not be explicitly marked as "racial." Second, the study of the formation of racial ideologies "on the ground" makes it possible to consider how they are situationally enacted in constitutive yet shifting relation to class, gender, and other ideologies of difference. Last, given the heterogeneous composition of structures of power (Foucault 1990), a perspective that takes account of the multiple, often conflicting, intersections of power and ideology allows us to consider the various ways in which the contestation of racial meanings may disrupt, reconfigure, and even reaffirm class, gender, and other ideologies of power (cf. Abu-Lughod 1989).

The Construction of Lefrak City

Lefrak City is a high-rise apartment complex in Queens County, New York, providing residence to about twelve thousand (mainly) African-American tenants. Completed in 1964 by Samuel J. Lefrak, one of New York City's most powerful and political developers, Lefrak City was envisioned by its planners to be a self-contained "city within a city" for the middle class—a "magic world of total living" that would provide shopping, recreation, and other services and amenities within easy walking distance.

Until the early 1970s, Lefrak City was tenanted largely by white, middle-class persons, reflecting the racial, if not socioeconomic, composition of the surrounding, largely working-class community of Corona.[1] However, in 1972 the Justice Department filed a housing discrimination suit against the Lefrak organization, charging that it had discriminated against blacks in the renting of apartments owned by the company in Brooklyn and Queens. The discrimination suit was settled by a consent decree: the Justice Department agreed to drop the suit if the Lefrak organization would end discrimination in apartment rentals and give a month's free rent to fifty black families to assist them in moving into predominantly white buildings.

Although the suit was not directed specifically at Lefrak City, the Lefrak organization, by some accounts, relaxed tenant screening procedures and income criteria and began aggressively to recruit black tenants for the twenty-building complex. (One former tenant leader claimed that the Lefrak organization attempted to concentrate most of these new

African-American tenants within Lefrak City so as to comply with the terms of the settlement without affecting the racial composition of other Lefrak-owned properties in Brooklyn and Queens.) The black population of Lefrak City increased rapidly from 25 percent in 1972 to almost 80 percent in 1976. Many tenants and other area residents complained that the new arrivals were disruptive, threatening the community with crime, drugs, and "urban blight."

A white Lefrak City resident who witnessed the transformation while serving as a tenant leader remembered:[2]

> All of a sudden we just saw different people coming in. And I keep saying to you that it has nothing to do with the color. There were always black people here when I moved in. They were friendly people. They were very high-class people- rich people, some of them. And you would never think anything of seeing another black person move in- or another- or another- nothing to do with it. But when you saw these people coming in- in their *un*dershirts, and their hai::r- and their *sta*ggering. It really was the most *ho*rrible thing you ever saw. There were some good people too- but it was just such a drastic change. It was such a *shock*- it was the shock value. It was just unbelievable. And that's what *real*ly did it.

Not all white residents were prone to conserve the distinction, however tenuous, between race and social class. The rapid increase in black tenants, coinciding with a precipitous decline in building maintenance and security services, fueled perceptions that Lefrak City had become a "welfare haven"—a black ghetto enclave, menacing the surrounding white neighborhoods with poverty, crime, and drugs. "If you bleed in Lefrak, you bleed in Corona and Elmhurst," the *Long Island Press*, November 21 1975, reported in an article so titled, quoting a white activist at a community hearing and invoking the image of the spread of crime from Lefrak City to neighboring areas.

Despite the findings of a 1976 city-sponsored report that only 3 percent of Lefrak City tenants were receiving public assistance, blacks, crime, and "welfare" were conflated in the political discourse of white neighborhood activists.[3] These images and fears were buttressed, if not shaped, by two political conflicts that had been brewing in Corona and nearby Forest Hills since the mid-1960s, involving the construction of low-income, "scatter-site" housing for minorities. White civic groups in both communities had opposed the New York City Housing Department's integration plan, and in 1972 (the year of the Lefrak City suit), the controversy in Forest Hills was coming to a head and receiving nationwide media coverage.[4]

Mario Cuomo, appointed by Mayor Lindsay in 1972 to mediate the

Forest Hills dispute, described the attitudes he encountered while working with white activists in Forest Hills.

> I'm inclined to think that no matter what statistics and evidence we're able to marshal, this community's fear will not be totally dissipated. One story of a mugging at a project—whether or not true—will overcome in their minds any array of statistics. The syllogism is simple: Welfare and Blacks are generally responsible for a great deal of crime; there are Welfare and Blacks in projects; there will be a great deal of crime in and around the project. And then, too, there is a quick projection from the problem of crime—however real, fancied, or exaggerated—to all other middle-class complaints: taxes, education, etc. All of these may be legitimate, but this coupling of them with the crime problem results eventually in an indictment of the project for all the sins against the middle class. (1983:49)

This conflation of race, poverty, and social pathology was also encoded in media coverage of the Lefrak City "crisis." A 1976 *New York Times* article noted that the "principal issue within Lefrak City is not one of race but of standards of behavior," yet carried the headline, "Lefrak City Crucible of Racial Change" (February 1, 1976). Complaints of poor building maintenance, inadequate security, and "undesirable tenants" were often reported as problems of "racial balance" as in "Lefrak Moves to Correct Racial Makeup at Project" in the *Long Island Press,* March 31, 1976. In an effort to "stabilize" the complex and allay neighborhood fears, the Lefrak Organization pressured city officials for federal Section 8 rent subsidies, which local community leaders were assured would make it possible to rent vacant apartments to low-income, elderly *whites.* An infusion of elderly, white tenants was presented as a strategy for restoring the "racial balance," offsetting the threat symbolized by the "welfare mother" and her progeny.

A white member of the Community Board—a local citizens' board that advises municipal authorities on community issues—recalled the visit of a Lefrak official to win the board's support for the rent subsidies. His account provides a good example of the complex and shifting entanglements of race and class in white activist ideology:

> [The Lefrak official] came to the Community Board an- and he wanted *us* to fill his vacant apartments. So we got Section 8 approved. And he claimed- well in Section 8, that he would put 90 percent senior citizens in. You know, in order to ah. . . . stabilize the area. And also he claimed that the- the Section 8 would be used mostly for elderly *white* people- you know, because they were the ones being displaced and whatever. So we went along and he got the approval. And then of course it turned out that- you know, he gave all the Section 8 to the bi::g

> minority families and *not* to the senior citizens he promised to. And even the senior citizens he promised- the security was so *bad* that they- they were- that they would run for their *lives,* 'cause they couldn't survive with the kind of people he was letting in. But *again,* it was nothing to do with the *co*lor of the people. Because when I moved here we had people from the U.N.- we had black people, we had *In*dians, we had Chinese- we had a::ll kinds of people here. But they was- it was a different *class* of people.

The counterposed images of "big minority families" and "elderly [white] people" fused race, class, and age differences in a symbolic shorthand that encoded complex and conflicting ideologies and social forces. White opposition to black "welfare families" converged politically and symbolically with local resistance to the exercise of power by city government and "big business." On the one hand, white residents felt that their neighborhood was being victimized by city officials because of its political weakness as a "middle-class" community: low-income housing and other undesirable projects were "dumped" on Corona because, as one resident put it, "we were a soft touch." On the other hand, many residents attributed the decline of Lefrak City to the greed and opportunism of the Lefrak organization, which some held was resolving its lawsuit at their expense while failing to provide proper maintenance services.

For example, in response to the *New York Times* article, "Lefrak City Crucible of Racial Change," a reader wrote the paper's editor: "It was sad to read about what is happening at Lefrak City. Yet an unhappy thought keeps nagging at my mind. Those young hoodlums, the modern-day Visigoths who are ripping doors off their moorings may not be bringing any new techniques to that high-rise mausoleum. Perhaps they are merely continuing the ripoff policies of the management" (*New York Times,* March 21, 1976). Opposition to black "undesirables" in Lefrak City was thus entangled in white activist ideology with resistance to the power of big government and corporate greed.

This perception that the middle class is being squeezed "betwixt and between the impoverished and the affluent," as Rieder put it (1985:98), has been tied by Sidney Plotkin to the development of the "enclave consciousness," an ideological stance weaving together a diverse assortment of perceived threats to the local community. "Working- and middle-class urbanites understandably feel that their enclaves are squeezed between the economic depredations of the corporate and political elite and the random street attacks of drug users. For the enclave consciousness, the city is manipulated by greedy forces from above and beset by uncontrollable violence from below. It is an external arena of predatory interests, a conflict-ridden system aimed at controlling, exploiting, and destroying the enclave" (1990:228). Within the span of a few years, the "city within a city" for the middle class had been transformed, in the minds of many white activists, into a predatory beach-head within the enclave.

By the late 1970s, the worst of the Lefrak City crisis appeared to be over. Community activists, supported by local politicians, city officials, and the local press, succeeded in their effort to pressure the Lefrak organization to evict "undesirable" tenants and embark on an extensive renovation program. Strict tenant-screening procedures were enacted and minimum income criteria were reinstated in part to reduce the number of low-income families in Lefrak City. In "Troubled Lefrak City Turning The Corner," a March 11, 1984, New York Times article announcing the recovery, Samuel J. Lefrak praised his rehabilitated tenantry: "They're decent, hard-working, middle-class people who pay their rent and pay their full share of taxes. What's happened is the best kind of gentrification."

Despite such assertions, many community residents continued to view Lefrak City as a site of black crime, drugs, and poverty, symbolizing the vulnerability of the community to violence, decay, and the arbitrary exercise of elite power. These perceptions became institutionalized when the Community Board established a special committee during the 1970s to address problems emanating from Lefrak City. Unlike the board's other committees (e.g., Environment, Public Safety, and Youth Services), the purview of the newly formed Neighborhood Stabilization Committee was limited to Lefrak City and its environs. The formation of this committee gave institutional form to white activist ideology, which had constructed Lefrak City as a racialized symbol of urban decline. Prior to the formation of Concerned Community Adults, to which I now turn, African-American participation and influence in community politics had been restricted to, if not contained by, this committee.

Concerned Community Adults (CCA) was organized largely through the efforts of Edna Baskin, an African-American woman who moved to Lefrak City with her husband and two children in 1979. Raised in Buffalo, New York, Edna had been active in community politics and in a local Baptist church founded by her grandfather. Although she had worked as a medical lab technician, upon her arrival in Queens Baskin began working in her home as a sitter, or child-care provider, for women living in her section of Lefrak City. Ron Baskin, her husband, worked as a television newswriter.

Through her child-care work, Baskin developed a network of relationships with Lefrak City women. Each evening, when these women, whom Edna referred to as her "mothers," came to pick up their children, they would gather in small groups at her apartment to socialize and exchange information about community events and services. Only months after she arrived, Baskin's "mothers" and other neighbors elected her to be a Tenants Association representative.

The Lefrak City Tenants Association was organized during the 1970s "crisis" and was instrumental in pressuring the Lefrak organization to renovate the complex and tighten security. However, by the 1980s some tenants had come to feel that the association had "sold out" to management and become little more than a "social club." Moreover, although community leaders regarded the Tenants Association as the institutional voice of Lefrak City, its leadership played only a minor role in neighborhood affairs. The Tenants Association's lack of involvement in local politics, coupled with the perception held by some that it was working in tandem with Lefrak management, contributed to the political isolation of Lefrak City's African-American residents. During 1987, for example, no members of the Tenants Association attended meetings of Community Board 4, the most important local governing body in the community. However, two former presidents of the Tenants Association sat on the board: a white man and a black man, both of whom had fallen out with the Tenants Association leadership. Thus, personal animosities more than likely reinforced the perception that Lefrak City, as a "city within a city," constituted a separate political entity.

When the association's leaders did not support her suggestion to register voters during the 1984 election, Baskin organized her own voter registration drive, using the opportunity to inform tenants about other community issues. After the election, Baskin began attending meetings of the Community Board, bypassing the Tenants Association leadership. After each meeting, Baskin would meet with tenants in the lobby of her building to explain how the board's actions were affecting Lefrak tenants. Baskin stopped holding these meetings, however, when the Tenants Association's president objected, informing her that she was "rubbing against the grain." Such encounters with association leaders convinced Baskin of the need to develop an alternative base of political power within Lefrak City, one that would be more responsive to the needs of its tenants.

In 1986 Baskin was encouraged by the Community Board's district manager, a white woman, to join the Neighborhood Stabilization Committee. The district manager and the board's chairperson, also a white woman, had been involved in the appointment of people of color to the board. Under their leadership, Korean, Chinese, and Latino persons had been seated on the predominantly white American board, reflecting the changing demography of the community.[5]

However, despite the large African-American population in Lefrak

City, only one African American sat on the thirty-four-member Community Board in 1987. The district manager of the board often complained that the Tenants Association leadership—in particular, its male president—blocked her efforts to involve Lefrak City residents in Community Board affairs. Whatever the case, board leaders perceived Baskin and her social networks to be a potential resource for expanding relations between Lefrak City residents and the surrounding community.

Meetings of the Neighborhood Stabilization Committee generally focused on crime, drug sales, and other "quality-of-life" issues in the Lefrak City vicinity.[6] Agenda items targeted threats posed by Lefrak residents (primarily black youth) to the surrounding area, rather than problems faced by residents within the complex. Similarly, problem-solving strategies emphasized law enforcement, rather than attempts to rally Lefrak City residents around shared concerns. In short, the discourse and strategies deployed by the Stabilization Committee framed Lefrak City as a threat to be policed, rather than an ally to be engaged in neighborhood preservation.

A Stabilization Committee meeting that Baskin attended in February 1987 provides a good example of how Lefrak City and its residents were constructed through white activist discourse. The meeting focused on complaints that had been raised by area residents about the "Lefrak library," a public library located within the perimeter of the housing complex. The committee had invited the chief of investigation and security of the Queens Borough Public Library to address concerns that the library was being used as a "babysitting service" by Lefrak City parents. These "latchkey" kids, it was argued, were disruptive and were making it difficult for others to use the library appropriately.

Members of the committee wanted the library official to increase security at the library so that, as one woman put it, "the problem kids can be identified and removed—by force, if necessary." In response, the official suggested that the threat posed by the Lefrak City kids was being exaggerated, remarking cryptically, "The mind conceives and the eyes perceive. Lefrak isn't so bad." The district manager of the Community Board fumed. "Lefrak security *is* bad," she retorted. "These kids are ten going on forty; they have no respect for authority." She went on to argue that people in Corona were afraid to use the library and, for that reason, wanted a library of their own. The chair of the committee (and co-op board president of a building in the Lefrak City vicinity) agreed, adding that there were senior citizens who also were afraid to use the library. (During this period, meetings of the Neighborhood Stabilization Committee were held in the basement meeting room of its chair's co-op building. This choice of a meeting location not only privileged the attendance of co-op residents but also, to some extent, inscribed an economic distinction between Lefrak City renters and co-op apartment owners onto the activities of the committee.) When the official insisted that more security would not solve the problem, the district manager threatened to call his boss. Enraged, the library official and his assistants walked out.

The committee turned to its next agenda item: drug dealing on a major commercial strip bordering Lefrak City. The discussion of the drug problem followed a similar line of development: the activities of drug dealers were described in detail; a police officer reported on his department's efforts to arrest them; members of the committee demanded more police protection. As in the library discussion, Lefrak City was constructed as an object of surveillance and police work—an object that could be comprehended only negatively, as a shadow cast by a vague and indeterminate core.

Not surprisingly, Baskin and the two other African Americans attending the meeting remained silent during the discussions. As residents of Lefrak City, there was no discursive position for them to assume as subjects acting in the interest of the "enclave." It was *their* children who were being constructed as drug dealers, as disruptive, and as the objects of surveillance and law enforcement.[7]

Although race was never explicitly referred to, the problems of drugs, crime, and poverty invested in the "latchkey" kids and teenage drug dealers bore racial connotations that remained precariously close to the surface of discourse. When, for example, the police officer reported an incident involving two "white girls from Forest Hills" who were mugged after a drug buy in Lefrak City, the district manager quickly interjected, "We're not talking about race." Later, when the committee's chair described a mugger who was robbing people in her co-op building, she avoided explicit reference to his race: "He is about 35, has bushy hair and is Jamaican." Ethnicity served in this latter case both to signal and to deflect race within a discourse overdetermined by an ideology of black crime. Interestingly, when a white Lefrak City resident turned the discussion to security problems *within* the complex (teenagers hanging out in hallways), Baskin joined in, deflecting the racial implications of the topic with complaints about the negligence of "Spanish-speaking guards."[8]

Baskin joined the discussion because of a shift in its focus from the effects of Lefrak City to the conditions within Lefrak City—from threats to security to the problem *with* security. This discursive opening, however, was soon closed when the chair of the committee intervened, suggesting that "specific" problems within Lefrak City be discussed at another time "between the parties involved."

The discourse and activist strategy deployed at the February meeting constructed Lefrak City as a site of neighborhood disruption and decay—a threat to the quality of life of the surrounding area requiring constant surveillance and policing. Although the issues raised at the meeting were perceived to be problems by residents of Corona *and* Lefrak City, the manner in which they were discursively framed and strategically addressed hindered, if not precluded, the active participation of Lefrak residents as subjects in the process of "neighborhood stabilization."

Between Corona and Lefrak City there existed a political and symbolic boundary, constructed through decades of political conflict and discursive practice, delineating oppositions between notions of disorder and security, blackness and whiteness, and poverty and middle-class stability. Although race was seldom publicly affirmed in white activist discourse and ideology, it nevertheless served as a unifying category—a principle of articulation binding perceptions, sentiments, and concepts about danger, social pathology, and political agency, and importantly, materializing these heterogeneous meanings in space.[9]

Disrupting Racial Topographies

After attending a number of Stabilization Committee meetings, Baskin came to feel that the committee was not addressing the needs of Lefrak City residents and, in particular, those of its youth. Her participation on the committee waned as she began to form her own group, organizing her mothers for that purpose. In early summer of 1987, Baskin held the first meeting of Concerned Community Adults in her apartment, appointing five of her mothers to serve on the new organization's board of directors.

For CCA's first activity, Baskin and her board organized a Youth Forum to provide Lefrak City youth with the opportunity to "speak out" about their problems and needs. Baskin used her network of mothers to reach out to young people in the twenty-building complex and closely coordinated her activities with two women who directed Scout troops based in Lefrak City. To chair the forum, Baskin selected a young male college student whom she had recruited to CCA's board of directors.

The Youth Forum was attended by about fifty Lefrak City youth, about a dozen parents and Scout troop leaders, and three members of Community Board 4 (a Korean woman, the board's chair, and a white man). Flanked by Baskin and two CCA board members, the youthful chair of the forum described CCA's purpose and then invited the teenagers to speak about their needs and aspirations. A few adults stood and made statements concerning the need for more tutoring and recreation programs while the teenagers remained silent.

For some thirty minutes the discussion dragged on, alternating between parents' appeals for more programs and the chair's inspired lectures on career planning, positive thinking, and "the new world of computers." After a Scout leader asked about the possibility of getting funding for bus trips, a young man sitting in the back of the room stood to speak. He was the first teenager to do so that night.

> Um . . . all this time people been talkin' about, "let's go on this trip and let's
> → go on that trip." Why get away from the community? We should concentrate
> → on having more fun *in* the community. They run us out- you know, like from
> the park or whatever. I- I mean they say it's late at night- but *think* about it. I
> recall last week Thursday, they ran us out the park 2:30 in the afternoon. You
> → see, now there was only five of us. I mean sittin' on a *bench*- said we couldn't
> → sit on the bench. They run us out of Lefrak altogether. I don't understand
> that. Now you talkin' about, "Oh, let's go out, do this trip here, and have fun
> here." Why can't we have fun where we live?

The audience erupted in wild applause. Baskin, who had not yet spoken, stood, nodding her head and motioning with her hand to the back of the room. The audience quieted down.

> The young man who just made that comment- thank you very much. I did not
> *re*::alize that there was a problem with Lefrak Security . . . runnin' the youth
> → *out.* See, that's another reason for us getting together- so that we, the *o*ther
> → adults here who *don't* know what's going on, can be made aware.

In fact, Baskin *did* know that there was this problem with Lefrak Security, and she often complained about the harassment her teenage son received from the guards, as well as from the police. Her intervention was directed to "the *other* adults" present—in particular, to the members of the Community Board who, unlike adults living in Lefrak City, had not yet heard this side of the story.

The discussion, now animated and dominated by the teenagers, moved to the topic of the security services. A young man in his late twenties linked the harassment by Lefrak Security to the representation of teenagers as drug dealers. His comment is interesting because it marks the reduction of [black] "teenager" to drug dealer but then expands the category to include a broader "us"—an adult, employed us.

> They done blamed these young people as all drug pushers. That's what they
> → doin'. And they wanna clear us *all* out. Every teenager is bad in their eyes.

And the guys- you be comin' home from work and go to the park- and they push us out 'cause they suspect you to be a drug pusher.

This eruption of frustration and criticism over how they, as black teenagers, were stereotyped and harassed by Lefrak City's security services challenged a central theme in white activist ideology and practice. By inverting the familiar relation between black teenagers and security, so central to the ideology of black crime, the testimony (and Baskin's marking of its significance) raised the possibility that black teenagers, often the victims of police actions, could play a positive role in neighborhood life. This novel prospect was given further support, ironically, when the forum's chair, intent on being a source of useful information, suggested that the teenagers voice their grievances about Lefrak Security at the next meeting of the Neighborhood Stabilization Committee.

The Youth Forum, which ended with the planning of a youth and adult "march against crack," established CCA as a grass-roots force in the eyes of both Lefrak City residents and representatives of the Community Board from the "surrounding community." The importance of the event can perhaps be judged by the reaction of the Lefrak City Tenants Association: a few days after the forum, the president of the Tenants Association approached Baskin and asked her to place her organization under his "umbrella." When Baskin refused, the association's president told her that CCA would never get off the ground without his support. The forum, however, had legitimized CCA and encouraged the leadership of the Community Board to deal directly with Baskin on youth issues, without the mediation of the Tenants Association.

A few weeks after the Youth Forum, Concerned Community Adults became involved in a neighborhood "clean-up" competition that further increased the organization's visibility and influence in the neighborhood. Community boards throughout Queens were invited by the office of the Queens borough president to organize teams of youth to clean sidewalks and educate merchants about sanitation codes. The winning team would go to Disneyland.

Again mobilizing her network of women, Baskin organized a team of twelve youth, for many of whom she had babysat at one time or another. Because no other organization in the community had been able to organize a group, CCA's clean-up team—consisting entirely of black youth from Lefrak City—became the official representative of Community Board 4. Baskin also gained the support of the area's Korean merchants through a Korean who had attended the Youth Forum as a representative of the Community Board and the Mid-Queens Korean Association, an association of Korean businesspersons. Because relations between

Korean merchants and African Americans in New York City had often been strained, this linkage was important, politically and symbolically.

The clean-up team's activities received considerable attention from community leaders and the press. Community Board members visited the clean-up team at work in the field. Merchants donated refreshments, free haircuts, and school supplies and posed with team members during picture-taking sessions. The Korean owner of a local grocery store offered to hire two clean-up team members when business picked up. Lefrak management informed Baskin that Samuel J. Lefrak himself had noticed that the neighborhood looked cleaner. Viewed within the context of Lefrak City's history as a political issue and object of discourse, the clean-up campaign was extremely significant.

The image of black Lefrak City youth removing rubbish from the streets surrounding the complex undermined the construction of Lefrak City as a site of danger, decay, and dirt—images linked symbolically with pollution and disorder (Douglas 1966), as well as with "blackness" (Gilman 1985; Jordon 1977; Kovel 1984). (Prior to the construction of Lefrak City, the Lefrak site was used as a garbage dump and called "Corona dumps" by residents. Both earlier uses of the site might have reinforced the symbolic logic at work in more recent times.) The potency of garbage as a polysemous symbol of disorder and threat to community was intensified during the summer of 1987 by a highly publicized political controversy surrounding the disposition of a "garbage barge." A seagoing barge containing over three thousand tons of New York area garbage had been turned away by officials in Louisiana, where it was to be dumped. After wandering around the Gulf of Mexico for a few days, the barge returned to New York City, where it triggered a crisis of sorts. City officials refused to allow the barge to dock until it could be tested for environmentally hazardous materials. A state supreme court judge in Queens ordered the barge to be placed under twenty-four-hour surveillance while city officials and politicians debated the origin and content of the garbage and *New York Newsday,* May 21, 1987, reported a "Holiday in Harbor for Barge Crew."

"It's nothing but 100 percent, all-American garbage," a New York State inspector assured the public under the *Newsday* headline "Whatever Evil Lurks in Trash, Made in USA, Experts Say," on May 19, responding to fears raised by some politicians that it might contain "vermin"-carrying diseases from Mexico or Belize. When the town of Islip, Long Island, agreed to accept the garbage for its landfill, the borough president of Queens refused to allow it to be transported across her borough until more testing was done. The town supervisor of Islip accused the Queens official of using the garbage as an issue to mask her "image problems," alluding to a political corruption scandal that had rocked Queens the year before, *Newsday* reported on May 20 in "No Repentance from Leaders over Trashing." "I heard her say Islip's garbage will never travel the streets of Queens," he noted. "And she presides over the corruption capital of the universe."

The meanings associated with garbage, manipulated by politicians to symbolize corruption and violations of turf, resonated with local symbolic deployments of such notions as "vermin" and "garbage" to signify the threat posed by Lefrak City. A Community Board member, for example, once reported to the board, after a Lefrak City "tour" sponsored by the Stabilization Committee, that the inspection team had encountered the "smell of rats"—a claim that was recorded in the board's minutes. Baskin herself was well aware of the potency of the "garbage barge" as a mass-mediated symbol framing the activities of her clean-up crew.[10]

SG: Do you think the fact that it was a clean-up campaign- as opposed to something else- had something to do with its . . . //success?

EB: Of course.
Because . . . all during the summer, you know, the garbage barge sitting out there . . . O.K?, only emphasized the problem that the whole country is having with *ga*::rbage. You under*stand*? And that *our chi::l*dren could *see* that this is really a problem. See, we have to make our children aware that there's a problem to*day.* So that when *they* become adults, *they* have some- some knowledge to draw on . . . as to how to *deal* with problems like this. You have to *lea::rn* this. This is nothing that somebody- that you could read in a book and do. It's something that you have to get out here and do.

Although CCA's team did not win the boroughwide competition, Baskin was able to strengthen support for her organization among politicians and Community Board members, and also to extend that support to local merchants, significantly, to representatives of a major new immigrant community in Queens. The Mid-Queens Korean Association invited Baskin, the clean-up team, and CCA board members to attend a dinner at a Korean restaurant to "honor" the young people.

Although Korean–African-American relations in New York City were not the explicit focus of the event, the topic surfaced repeatedly, suggesting that issues of race and ethnic relations were being negotiated through activities surrounding the clean-up competition. During a brief speech, Baskin remarked that relations between Korean merchants and African Americans in Lefrak City had been good during the summer. "The most important thing for our group," she continued, "is our children. When we brought our children to you, you helped." The Korean Community Board member who had attended the Youth Forum responded: "Our body is just a rented car. Sometimes you are driven by a back seat driver, but the real driver is colorless." The dinner was reported in the *Korean Times,* a Korean-language newspaper.

The clean-up competition, like the Youth Forum, undermined ideological themes that had been articulated in activist discourse since the desegregation of Lefrak City in 1972. African-American youth involvement in activities that not only addressed the need for black youth empowerment but also disrupted the way black teenagers and Lefrak City had been constructed in ideology and practice created possibilities for the formation of new political subjects and alignments that cut across race and ethnic lines.

Empowering Difference

By summer's end, the activities of Concerned Community Adults had attracted the attention of local politicians. An awards dinner held to honor clean-up team members was attended by the area's state assemblywoman and a representative of the local city council, both of whom began exploring ways to provide CCA with funding to support a tutorial program that Baskin had begun in the Lefrak library. CCA awarded certificates to merchants, Community Board supporters, and clean-up team members. The district manager of the board described the activities of the Lefrak group (and her certificate) at the Community Board's next meeting and redoubled her efforts to have Baskin seated on the board. Already active on the board's Youth Services Committee, Baskin was appointed cochair of its Daycare Committee.

Perhaps the most telling translation of the summer's organizing work into political power, however, involved CCA's participation in the election of the local Area Policy Board. The Area Policy Board (APB) is a community-based, popularly elected body that defines local funding priorities and makes recommendations to the city concerning the allocation of Community Development Block Grant funds. APB members serve as volunteers and, at least in theory, are "representatives of the poor," insofar as their candidacy is contingent upon residence in designated "poverty areas."

Procedurally, candidates must submit petitions to the NYC Community Development Agency to appear on the ballot. Once members are elected, the APB holds public hearings to define social service needs within the community and then meets to review proposals for funding from local agencies. Although the APB is only empowered to make funding recommendations, their decisions are generally supported by the city. For this reason, the Area Policy Board wields considerable power over the control of local resources.

After concluding that Lefrak City needed better access to community development funds for youth and other social service programs, Baskin and her board decided to field candidates for the APB election. To that end, Baskin invited a representative from the city to speak to residents in her building about the Area Policy Board and the election process. After the orientation, Baskin encouraged a number of Lefrak City residents to begin the process of collecting signature petitions.

Most of these persons were members of social networks activated during CCA's summer organizing activities. For example, six of the eight candidates who qualified for the election were women: three were among Baskin's child-care mothers (one was a clean-up team leader), two served as volunteer tutors in CCA's Lefrak library program, and the sixth was a senior citizen activist in Lefrak City. Of the two male candidates, one was the husband of a "mother" on CCA's board of directors, and the second was a retired civil servant who lived in Baskin's building. Since the retired man would serve on a citywide advisory board, Baskin and her board selected a "man of experience," familiar with the workings of government bureaucracies.

Baskin's increasing visibility as a grass-roots leader in Lefrak City was demonstrated when the area's state assemblywoman contacted her to request that she include the assemblywoman's candidates on "CCA's slate." Although voter turnout was light in Lefrak City, three of Baskin's candidates were elected to the Area Policy Board—two women and a "husband."

Shortly after the APB election, Baskin's group was incorporated. Status as a not-for-profit corporation would enable CCA to receive public funds and corporate donations. Baskin and her board, however, were wary of applying for public funds: it was felt that such funding might compromise CCA's ability to act independently. "Public-sector funding is a trap," her husband, Ron, argued at a CCA board meeting in September. "If you want to take money from the city, you have to hire people who are acceptable to the very same people who failed us already." (Concerned Community Adults did not apply for APB funding because its board of directors felt that to do so would have presented a conflict of interest.)

Ron and his brother, Duane (who shared residence with the Baskins), often disagreed with Edna about strategy. After a dispute over accepting donations from Lefrak management, the two brothers contended that

Baskin had "stacked the board" with her "mothers" to offset their voting power. When a subsequent meeting led to the reversal of the earlier decision to accept the Lefrak donation, Baskin remarked that she had lost the vote because her "people didn't show up," referring to two women board members.

Ron and Duane (a Wall Street paralegal) often appealed to "professional," workplace-based expertise when structuring arguments in opposition to Edna and her "mothers." For example, at an August board meeting Baskin's husband and brother-in-law criticized her for not calculating the dollar value of donations made by merchants during the clean-up competition. Her husband argued that such a calculation would be necessary if, at some date in the future, CCA were subjected to an audit by the tax authorities. And although Baskin tended to discount the significance of gender relations when explaining the internal dynamics of the organization, she frequently emphasized the role that gender played in her dealings with outside agencies.

For example, when CCA held meetings with officials of government agencies and private corporations, Baskin often encouraged her husband or brother-in-law to serve as the group's representative because, as she put it, "men get more respect—they take you more seriously." Prior to a meeting with Lefrak management, which was to be conducted by her husband, Baskin explained: "This is a white man's world. It's much easier to deal with corporate America if you are a black male—women act as back up." She went on to say that it was also important for black men to be seen in leadership positions, "as positive role models for our youth." This dual purpose stood behind her decision to appoint a young black male to chair the Youth Forum and her insistence that her teenage son (very much against his wishes) participate in the clean-up competition.

Baskin's tactical appropriation of patriarchal ideology to present the strongest face to institutional power *and* to disrupt negative images of black masculinity illustrates not only the complex manner in which race and gender ideologies cross-cut in the construction of political subjects, but also how, to quote Abu-Lughod, "intersecting and often conflicting structures of power work together," sometimes positioning women in the equivocal situation of both resisting and supporting existing power relations (1989:42).

The distinction drawn by Baskin between the public face of masculine political authority and women's roles as organizers, or "back up," resonates with Karen Sacks's description of women union activists at Duke University. Sacks found that some women activists at Duke expressed the view that "women are organizers; men are leaders." The activists "suggested that women created the organization, made people feel part of it, and did the routine work upon which most things depended, whereas men made public pronouncements and confronted and negotiated with management" (1988:78–79).

Contrasting the movement's "spokes*men*" with what she called its "centerwomen," Sacks observed that the centerwomen played key leadership roles in constructing social networks at the workplace and transforming them into a social force. Centerwomen politicized notions about work, adulthood, and responsibility, first learned in a family context, by bringing them to bear in the workplace in the form of an oppositional working-class culture. "Centerwomen created and sustained social networks and mobilized them around a militant work culture. That culture validated their view of their work and its worth through consensus language based on 'familistic values'—namely, a notion of adulthood and responsibility conceptualized in family terms and contexts. These values capture concretely the unity or continuity between family and work that feminist scholarship is seeking. To recognize this structure of leadership, and to expand the term leadership to encompass it is to make the invisible visible" (1988:93).

The concept of the centerwoman, and the attention it directs to the mobilization and politicization of everyday social ties and networks, proves helpful in understanding how gendered relations and forms of resistance inscribe the political terrain upon which racial meanings are contested and rearticulated. Just as Baskin used a gendered ideology of leadership to negotiate institutional power *and* contest racial stereotypes, so too did she appropriate a rhetoric of "family" and "family values" to signal political strength and unity.

When asked why, given his marginal involvement, she had paid special tribute to the husband of one her mothers at the clean-up competition's closing ceremony, Baskin replied:

> I wanted people to see that there were families involved. Not just my family, but other families like [this] family where we had mother, daughter, father, smaller daughter- you know. That was our whole point- was to show that we had *fam*ily involvement, which of course makes you a stronger group- when the families can see what you doin'. And of course this would encourage other families to become involved with us.

Like women organizers at Duke University, Baskin often explained her strategy, her political relations, or, more generally, her political philosophy in terms of a conception of women's political power and collectivity rooted in "familistic" values and—in her case—tied to household and church.

SG: Now that your organization is established, would you consider getting involved in politics? I mean, let's say, running for political office?

EB: I always want to be just where I'm at right now- right in my own home, working to organize an extended group.//But see-

SG: a what?

EB: An ex*ten*ded group. Just like the Area Policy Board- that's an extension of what our committee [CCA] is. We're just extending ourselves outward- you know. Because that's the problem. We have nothing. And a long time ago, of course, coming from this good church background, . . . I learned that . . . women are the key. And as a woman, *you* set the tone in your household- *I* set the tone. I set the rhythm in here. You know what I'm sayin'? And so do other women in their households. *You* set the tone. You set the *rhy*thm . . . you know. You determine how we gonna make this work, and how we gonna make this flow. You know when you want your husband to do something and he's not agreeable, you just work around him- find another *way*- you know. Find *ano*ther way to deal. And it's the same thing here.

SG: How would a "political role" be different from this- from what you called before, grass roots?

EB: Because you're dealing- as a politician you're dealing with . . . *o*ther people's ideas and how . . . you have to implement these ideas- versus me in this setting. We're dealing with our ideas and *we* determine how *we* wanna do it- collectively as a group, without any . . . input from outside. Whereas when you're a politician, you have other influences . . . that are paramount to what you're doing.

The "household" serves here as a *political* model not only for grassroots collectivism and autonomy, but also for creating, negotiating, and contesting power relations. This is not an ideology of "family," akin to familiar discussions that reduce the political, economic, and social condition of African Americans to a "crisis" of the black family.[11] Rather, Baskin's deployment of "family" and "household" speaks to a broader conception of political mobilization, accountability, and women's power that, although enacted in the household, is not contained by domestic ideology. The distinction between domestic and public, discredited in feminist scholarship but virile in discussions of black poverty and the "underclass," collapses as both are politicized.[12]

In this essay, I have examined how racial meanings and identities are constructed, negotiated, and transformed through the politics of everyday life. In white activist discourse Lefrak City was constituted as a site of black crime, poverty, and drugs—a racialized threat to the area's quality-of-life and a focus of law enforcement and neighborhood "stabilization" strategies. Edna Baskin and the organizers of Concerned Community Adults contested the significance of race within this discourse, disrupting its representational logic and repositioning African-American identities within local networks of power. Such community events and activities as the Youth Forum and clean-up competition thus not only provided important services for Lefrak City youth but also performed key symbolic functions, challenging and rearticulating the matrices of meaning within which political identities, alignments, and spaces are constructed and racialized (cf. Escobar 1992; Melucci 1989).

However, as Karen Sacks and others have pointed out, race, class, and gender identities are not analytically separable (1989; see also Hicks 1981; Rutherford 1990). Ignoring the complex ways in which ideologies of difference intersect within specific spatiotemporal contexts risks obscuring the heterogeneous composition of power and the equally complex, often contradictory contours of resistance (Abu-Lughod 1989; Sawicki 1991).

Gender ideologies and relations framed the development of Concerned Community Adults, inflecting the goals and strategies of its organizers and the political spaces within which they operated. In challenging the criminalization of black youth, Baskin and her "mothers" were contesting a racial ideology "structured in gendered terms" (Stoler 1989) that located black poverty and crime within the moral economy of the African-American family—in the fantasy world of the "welfare mother." Baskin's rhetorical appropriation of "family" and "household" mapped out the terrain where this gendered ideology of race would be contested and oppositional practices generated and, as she put it, "extended outward" to engage white male power. It was here, across this ideological divide between domestic and public, that Baskin deployed black masculinity, displacing the stereotype of the vanishing black male and at the same time affirming essentialist constructions of masculine authority.

Just as gender inscribed the landscape upon which racial meanings were negotiated, so too did class relations and ideologies. For in contesting the racialized construction of Lefrak City, Concerned Community Adults distanced, or recovered, the identity of its residents from constructions of the black poor. Within the context of neighborhood activism, this recovery did not call into question the political and economic conditions that produce black poverty or class-based perceptions that define the presence and interests of the poor as antithetical to community stability.[13] As Baskin once put it, when describing problems she encountered organizing tenants in a poor section of Lefrak City, "Racial integration can work, but economic integration will never work."

Rather, CCA's rearticulation of racial meanings yielded a more inclusive and, to some extent, deracialized conception of the working- and middle-class enclave.

By demonstrating that Lefrak City residents were an important force in addressing neighborhood safety, cleanliness, and other issues privileged in quality-of-life politics, Baskin and her co-workers succeeded in increasing the political power of African-Americans in Corona. But this empowerment process was itself shaped, if not constrained, by the political topography of local governing institutions that, like the Community Board, tend to recognize, legitimate, and respond to constructions of the political that resonate with middle-class definitions of community needs and interests (see Gregory 1992).

It would be simplistic, however, to reduce Concerned Community Adults to a middle-class movement, politically and socially isolated from lower-income groups on the one hand, and incorporated unproblematically into multi-ethnic, class-based alliances on the other. As Chantal Mouffe has noted, "Class position is only one of the terrains where antagonisms exist and on which collectivities in struggle can organize themselves" (Laclau and Mouffe 1982:108). In Corona, as elsewhere, these terrains and the identities constructed within them overlap and cross-cut in shifting, context-bound configurations of power and meaning, yielding heterogeneous political subjectivities, ideologies, and practices.

Notes

I would like to thank George Bond and Leith Mullings for their comments. I would also like to thank the reviewers of *Cultural Anthropology* for their excellent suggestions. Funding for this research was provided by the National Research Council and the National Science Foundation (BNS 8719051).

1. In 1970, 69.8 percent of Lefrak City's 11,501 tenants were non-Spanish-speaking whites, 14 percent Latin American, 7.7 percent Asian, and 8.6 percent black. Neighborhoods surrounding the complex shared a similar demographic profile. Corona Heights, for example, a once predominantly Italian neighborhood immediately adjacent to Lefrak City, was 81.5 percent non-Spanish-speaking white in 1970 and 1.2 percent black. Cuomo (1983) suggests that white Lefrak City residents during the 1960s had more in common with middle-class white residents in Forest Hills farther to the south than they did with their largely working-class Italian neighbors in Corona. Although Lefrak City is located within Corona, residents of Lefrak City have traditionally referred to their neighborhood as Rego Park, perhaps reflecting a perception of class differences. Throughout this essay, I will use Corona to refer to the neighborhood surrounding Lefrak City, a distinction that, at various times, has taken on race, class, and ethnic significance.

2. My transcript conventions are as follows:

italics	speaker's emphasis in amplitude or pitch
: :	lengthened syllables
-	glottal-stop, self-editing marker
→	points of interest to discussion
. . .	long pause
[ ]	text I have added for clarification
//	point at which utterance is overlapped by that transcribed below it

Punctuation reflects the speaker's intonation or pace rather than the rules of grammar.

3. See Hall et al. 1978 for an analysis of the development of an ideology of black crime in Britain during the 1970s and Rieder 1985 for a discussion of how blacks, welfare, and "mugging" were conflated in the activist ideology of whites in Canarsie, Brooklyn. See also Lawrence 1982 for a discussion of the roles that "inadequate family," "criminal youth," and "cultures of deprivation" play in the "common-sense" images of black people in Britain.

4. "Scatter site" housing was a federal housing initiative designed to inte grate the black poor into white middle-class neighborhoods by requiring cities to devote a portion of their federal housing funds to the construction of low-income housing projects in white communities. In 1966, the New York City Housing Authority designated sites for low-income housing in both Corona and neighboring Forest Hills. For a discussion of both controversies, see Cuomo 1983:3–23. Cuomo suggests that the Forest Hills housing controversy was an important factor in inducing the Nixon Administration to abandon the scatter-site housing concept in 1973 (149).

5. Between 1970 and 1990 the racial and ethnic composition of Corona changed dramatically. The white non-Spanish-speaking population of Corona Heights decreased from 81.5 percent in 1970 to 29.9 percent in 1990. The Latin American and Asian populations increased, respectively, from 15.7 percent and 1.6 percent in 1970 to 56.3 percent and 10.7 percent in 1990. Interestingly, during this same period the black population of Corona Heights increased only negligibly, from 1.2 percent to 2.3 percent.

6. "Quality-of-life" is a phrase used by community residents to describe a range of issues that center on the quality of municipal services and infrastructure, such as police protection, sanitation, roads, schools, and so on. As a mode of activism, quality-of-life politics emphasizes the accountability of municipal government and business interests to the local community, often expressed as an opposition between the neighborhood and "outsiders." Although not associated exclusively with the middle class, local activists often associate quality-of-life issues with "middle-class values" and life-style, and with perceived middle-class interests, such as property values. For this reason, "quality-of-life" often serves in activist speech as a euphemism for "middle-class" and, sometimes, white perceptions and interests.

7. See Labov 1990 for a similar discussion of how ideological elements, not explicitly racial in character, can operate through discourse to exclude the involvement of racialized groups.

8. See the Community Board member's narrative transcribed earlier in this essay for a similar use of ethnicity to mask race. In his case, the invocation of the U.N. serves both to undermine a racial distinction ("it was nothing to do with the color of the people") and to signal class differences ("it was a different class of people"). Nevertheless, what is really being constructed is the distinction between "big minority families" and "elderly white people."

9. Foucault's discussion of silence proves useful here by directing attention to how race is not spoken about: "There is no binary division to be made between what one says and what one does not say; we must try to determine the different ways of not saying such things, how those who can and those who cannot speak of them are distributed, which type of discourse is authorized, or which form of discretion is required in either case. There is not one but many silences, and they are an integral part of the strategies that underlie and permeate discourse" (1990:27).

10. In fact, Claire Shulman, the borough president of Queens, had mentioned the garbage barge and the political crisis it instigated at the "kick-off" ceremony for the clean-up competition held at Borough Hall. Edna and her clean-up team attended the ceremony. Garbage has been used as a metaphor for race, crime, and poverty. For example, a white resident of a housing complex in Brooklyn, responding to a 1987 court order requiring its owner to end discrimination against blacks, declared: "We're being dumped on. We worked so hard to keep this place the way it is [i.e., predominantly white]. Why bring in the garbage?" *New York Newsday* reported May 7, 1987, under the headline "Starrett City Wins Stay of Bias Ruling."

11. See Collins 1989, Williams 1992, and Zinn 1989 for recent critiques of this continuing tendency in the literature on black poverty.

12. Much of the literature on black poverty and the "underclass" separates a public domain of politics from a domestic sphere of family by locating the determinants of black poverty in African-American domestic relations. Those are seen to exist in either a "breakdown" in relations between black fathers and mothers with children (the "crisis of the black family" or the "vanishing black male"), or a failure to transmit normative family values and resources across class lines (the "exodus" of the black middle class). This separating of the "domestic" from the "public" results in the depoliticization of race, class, and gender oppression, on the one hand, and the masking of resistance, on the other.

13. I am not suggesting that the local community would necessarily be the place to conduct wider struggles for economic justice. Rather, I am emphasizing the importance of the local community as an arena where political consciousness is formed and ideologies articulated that are brought to bear on broader societal issues (e.g., tax policies, welfare reform, and so on) through electoral and other forms of political practice. Rieder (1985), for example, points to the key role that local political struggles played in shaping the opinions and voting patterns of Canarsie residents on issues of regional and national significance. Indeed, Fisher and Kling argue that one of the main dilemmas of activism in America "hinges on the difference between the systemic class origins of the problems working

people face in their neighborhoods and the tendency of neighborhood activists to identify solutions with local political strategies" (cited in Plotkin 1990).

References

Abu-Lughod, Lila. 1989. The Romance of Resistance: Tracing Transformations of Power through Bedouin Women. *American Ethnologist* 17(1):41–55.

Anthias, Floya. 1990. Race and Class Revisited—Conceptualizing Race and Racisms. *Sociological Review* 38(1):19–42.

Balibar, Etienne. 1990. Paradoxes of Universality. In *Anatomy of Racism*, ed. Theo Goldberg, 283–294. Minneapolis: University of Minnesota Press.

Certeau, Michel de. 1984. *The Practice of Everyday Life.* Berkeley and Los Angeles: University of California Press.

Collins, Patricia Hill. 1989. A Comparison of Two Works on Black Family Life. *Signs* 14:875–884.

Comaroff, Jean. 1985. *Body of Power, Spirit of Resistance: The Culture and History of a South African People.* Chicago: University of Chicago Press.

Comaroff, Jean, and John Comaroff. 1991. *Of Revelation and Revolution: Christianity, Colonialism, and Consciousness in South Africa.* Vol. 1. Chicago: University of Chicago Press.

Cuomo, Mario. 1983. *Forest Hills Diary.* New York: Vintage.

Dominguez, Virginia R. 1987. *White by Definition.* New Brunswick: Rutgers University Press.

Douglas, Mary. 1966. *Purity and Danger.* London: Routledge and Kegan Paul.

Escobar, Arturo. 1992. Imagining a Post-Development Era? Critical Thought, Development, and Social Movements. *Social Text* 31/32:20–56.

Foucault, Michel. 1990. *The History of Sexuality.* Vol. 1. New York: Vintage.

Gates, Henry Louis, Jr., ed. 1987. *Race, Writing, and Difference.* Chicago: University of Chicago Press.

Gilman, Sander L. 1985. *Difference and Pathology.* Ithaca, N.Y.: Cornell University Press.

Gilroy, Paul. 1987. "*There Ain't No Black in the Union Jack.*" London: Hutchinson.

Goldberg, Theo, ed. 1990. *Anatomy of Racism.* Minneapolis: University of Minnesota Press.

Gregory, Steven. 1992. The Changing Significance of Race and Class in an African American Community. *American Ethnologist* 19:255–274.

Guha, Ranajit, and Gayatri Spivak, eds. 1988. *Selected Subaltern Studies.* Delhi: Oxford University Press.

Hall, Stuart. 1980. Race, Articulation, and Societies Structured in Dominance. In *Sociological Theories: Race and Colonialism,* 305–345. Paris: UNESCO.

Hall, Stuart, and Tony Jefferson. 1976. *Resistance through Rituals: Youth Subcultures in Post-War Britain.* London: HarperCollins.

Hall, Stuart, Chas Critcher, Tony Jefferson, John Clarke, and Brian Roberts. 1978. *Policing the Crisis.* New York: Holmes and Meier.

Hebdidge, Dick. 1979. *Subculture: The Meaning of Style*. New York: Routledge.
Hicks, Emily. 1981. Cultural Marxism: Non-Synchrony and Feminist Practice. In *Women and Revolution*, ed. Lydia Sargent, 219–237. Boston: South End.
hooks, bell. 1990. *Yearning: Race, Gender, and Cultural Politics*. Boston: South End.
Jordon, Winthrop D. 1977. *White over Black: American Attitudes toward the Negro, 1550–1812*. New York: Norton.
Kovel, Joel. 1984. *White Racism*. New York: Columbia University Press.
Labov, Theresa. 1990. Ideological Themes in Reports of Interracial Conflict. In *Conflict Talk: Sociolinguistic Investigations of Arguments in Conversations*, ed. A. Grimshaw, 139–159. Cambridge: Cambridge University Press.
Laclau, Ernesto, and Chantal Mouffe. 1982. Recasting Marxism: Hegemony and New Political Movements: Interview with Ernesto Laclau and Chantal Mouffe. *Socialist Review* 12(6): 91–113.
Lawrence, Errol. 1982. Just Plain Common Sense: The "Roots" of Racism. In *The Empire Strikes Back*, 47–94. London: Hutchinson, in association with the Centre for Contemporary Cultural Studies, University of Birmingham.
Martinez-Alier, Verena. 1989. *Marriage, Class, and Colour in Nineteenth-Century Cuba*. Ann Arbor: University of Michigan Press.
Melucci, Alberto. 1989. *Nomads of the Present*. Philadelphia: Temple University Press.
Miles, Robert. 1989. *Racism*. New York: Routledge.
Omi, Michael, and Howard Winant. 1986. *Racial Formation in the United States*. New York: Routledge and Kegan Paul.
Ong, Aihwa. 1990. State versus Islam: Malay Families, Women's Bodies, and the Body Politic in Malaysia. *American Ethnologist* 17:258–291.
Plotkin, Sidney. 1990. Enclave Consciousness and Neighborhood Activism. In *Dilemmas of Activism*, ed. Joseph M. Kling and Prudence S. Posner, 219–239. Philadelphia: Temple University Press.
Rieder, Jonathan. 1985. *Canarsie: The Jews and Italians of Brooklyn against Liberalism*. Cambridge, Mass.: Harvard University Press.
Russell, John. 1991. Race and Reflexivity: The Black Other in Contemporary Japanese Mass Culture. *Cultural Anthropology* 6:3–25.
Rutherford, Jonathan, ed. 1990. *Identity: Community, Culture, Difference*. London: Lawrence and Wishart.
Sacks, Karen. 1988. Gender and Grassroots Leadership. In *Women and the Politics of Empowerment*, ed. Sandra Morgen and Ann Bookman, 77–94. Philadelphia: Temple University Press.
———. 1989. Toward a Unified Theory of Class, Race, and Gender. *American Ethnologist* 16:534–550.
Sawicki, Jana. 1991. *Disciplining Foucault: Feminism, Power, and the Body*. New York: Routledge.
Scott, James C. 1985. *Weapons of the Weak*. New Haven, Conn.: Yale University Press.

Silverblatt, Irene. 1987. *The Moon, Sun, and Witches*. Princeton: Princeton University Press.

Sivanandan, A. 1982. From Resistance to Rebellion: Asian and Afro-Caribbean Struggle in Britain. *Race and Class* 23(2–3): 111–132.

Solomos, John. 1988. *Black Youth, Racism, and the State*. Cambridge: Cambridge University Press.

Stoler, Ann L. 1989. Making Empire Respectable: The Politics of Race and Sexual Morality in Twentieth-Century Colonial Cultures. *American Ethnologist* 16:634–661.

Trouillot, Michel-Rolph. 1990. *Haiti: State against Nation*. New York: Monthly Review Press.

Westwood, Sallie. 1985. *All Day, Every Day: Factory and Family in the Making of Women's Lives*. Urbana: University of Illinois Press.

Williams, Brackette F. 1989. A Class Act: Anthropology and the Race to Nation access Ethnic Terrain. *Annual Review of Anthropology* 18:401–444.

Williams, Brett. 1992. Poverty among African Americans in the Urban United States. *Human Organization* 51:164–174.

Williams, Raymond. 1977. *Marxism and Literature*. Oxford: Oxford University Press.

Willis, Paul. 1977. *Learning to Labor: How Working Class Kids Get Working Class Jobs*. New York: Columbia University Press.

Zinn, Maxine Baca. 1989. Family, Race, and Poverty in the Eighties. *Signs* 14:856–874.

Index

Printed in the United States
44229LVS00004B/64-129

9 780813 521091